Humanitarianism, War, and Politics

NEW MILLENNIUM BOOKS
IN INTERNATIONAL STUDIES

SERIES EDITORS

Eric Selbin, Southwestern University
Vicki Golich, Metropolitan State University of Denver

FOUNDING EDITOR

Deborah J. Gerner, University of Kansas

NEW MILLENNIUM BOOKS issue out of the unique position of the global system at the beginning of a new millennium in which our understandings about war, peace, terrorism, identity, sovereignty, security, and sustainability—whether economic, environmental, or ethical—are likely to be challenged. In the new millennium of international relations, new theories, new actors, and new policies and processes are all bound to be engaged. Books in the series are of three types: compact core texts, supplementary texts, and readers.

EDITORIAL BOARD

Humanitarianism, War, and Politics

SOLFERINO TO SYRIA AND BEYOND

Peter J. Hoffman and Thomas G. Weiss

Foreword by Jan Egeland

ROWMAN & LITTLEFIELD
Lanham • Boulder • New York • London

Executive Editor: Traci Crowell
Assistant Editor: Mary Malley
Senior Marketing Manager: Deborah Hudson
Cover Images: Willis John Abbot; AP Photos/ SIPPL Sipa USA

Published by Rowman & Littlefield
A wholly owned subsidiary of The Rowman & Littlefield Publishing Group, Inc.
4501 Forbes Boulevard, Suite 200, Lanham, Maryland 20706
www.rowman.com

Unit A, Whitacre Mews, 26-34 Stannary Street, London SE11 4AB,
United Kingdom

Maps courtesy of the United Nations

British Library Cataloguing in Publication Information Available

Library of Congress Cataloging-in-Publication Data
Names: Hoffman, Peter J. (Peter Joshua), 1969– author. | Weiss, Thomas G.
  (Thomas George), 1946– author.
Title: Humanitarianism, war, and politics : Solferino to Syria and beyond /
  Peter J. Hoffman and Thomas G. Weiss ; foreword by Jan Egeland.
Description: Lanham : Rowman & Littlefield, [2017] | Series: New millennium
  books in international studies | Includes bibliographical references and
  index.
Identifiers: LCCN 2017009205 (print) | LCCN 2017023699 (ebook) | ISBN
  9781442266148 (electronic) | ISBN 9781442266124 (cloth : alk. paper) |
  ISBN 9781442266131 (pbk. : alk. paper)
Subjects: LCSH: Humanitarianism—Political aspects. | Humanitarian
  assistance. | War relief. | War and society.
Classification: LCC HV553 (ebook) | LCC HV553 .H657 2017 (print) | DDC
  363.34/98—dc23
LC record available at https://lccn.loc.gov/2017009205

Printed in the United States of America

Contents

Tables, Boxes, and Maps

Tables

Boxes

Maps

Abbreviations

AA	Alcoholics Anonymous
ALNAP	Active Learning Network for Accountability and Performance in Humanitarian Action
AMIS	African Union Mission in Sudan
AMISOM	African Union Mission in Somalia
AQIM	Al Qaeda in Mesopotamia
ARA	American Relief Administration
ART	antiretroviral therapy
AU	African Union
CAR	Central African Republic
CARE	Cooperative for Assistance and Relief Everywhere
CIA	Central Intelligence Agency (United States)
CPA	Coalition Provisional Authority (Iraq)
CRB	Commission for the Relief of Belgium
CRS	Catholic Relief Services
DAC	Development Assistance Committee
Daesh	al-Dawla al-Islamiya al-Iraq al-Sham (also known as Islamic State, ISIS)
DHA	Department of Humanitarian Affairs
DRC	Democratic Republic of the Congo
ECB	Emergency Capacity Building Project
ECHO	European Commission's Department of Humanitarian Aid and Civil Protection

ENMOD	UN Convention on the Prohibition of Military or Any Other Hostile Use of Environmental Modification Techniques
ERC	Emergency Relief Coordinator
EU	European Union
FCA	Forgotten Crisis Assessment (ECHO)
GAO	Government Accounting Office (United States)
GCC	Gulf Cooperation Council
GHD	Good Humanitarian Donorship
GNP	gross national product
GOARN	Global Outbreak and Alert Response Network
GWOT	Global War on Terrorism
HDI	Human Development Index
HIV/AIDS	human immunodeficiency virus/acquired immune deficiency syndrome
HPG	Humanitarian Policy Group
HRC	Human Rights Council (United Nations)
HRI	Humanitarian Response Index
IASC	Inter-Agency Standing Committee
ICC	International Criminal Court
ICISS	International Commission on Intervention and State Sovereignty
ICJ	International Court of Justice
ICRC	International Committee of the Red Cross
ICTR	International Criminal Tribunal for Rwanda
ICTY	International Criminal Tribunal for the former Yugoslavia
ICU	Islamic Courts Union (Somalia)
IDP	internally displaced person
IFRC	International Federation of the Red Cross and Red Crescent Societies
IGO	intergovernmental organization
IHL	international humanitarian law
ILC	International Law Commission
IMT	International Military Tribunal (at Nuremberg)
IMTFE	International Military Tribunal for the Far East
IOM	International Organization for Migration
IPCC	Intergovernmental Panel on Climate Change
IR	International Relations
IRC	International Rescue Committee
IRO	International Refugee Organization
JEM	Justice and Equality Movement (Darfur, Sudan)

KFOR	Kosovo Force (NATO)
KLA	Kosovo Liberation Army
LRA	Lord's Resistance Army (Uganda)
LWR	Lutheran World Relief
MDG	Millennium Development Goal
MONUSCO	Mission de l'Organisation des Nations-Unies pour la Stabilisation en Republique Démocratique du Congo
MSF	Médecins sans Frontières (Doctors without Borders)
NATO	North Atlantic Treaty Organization
NCP	National Congress Party (Sudan)
NGO	nongovernmental organization
OCHA	Office for the Coordination of Humanitarian Affairs
OfFP	Oil-for-Food Programme
OHCHR	Office of the High Commissioner for Human Rights
OIC	Organisation of Islamic Cooperation
OLS	Operation Lifeline Sudan
ONUC	United Nations Operation in the Congo
OPCW	Organization for the Prohibition of Chemical Weapons
OSCE	Organization for Security and Cooperation in Europe
Oxfam	Oxford Committee for Famine Relief
PCIJ	Permanent Court of International Justice
PDD-25	Presidential Decision Directive 25
PDPA	People's Democratic Party of Afghanistan
PMSC	private military and security company
PSC	private security contractor
POW	prisoner of war
PRS	protracted refugee situations
PRT	Provincial Reconstruction Team
P5	permanent five (UN Security Council)
RHA	revolution in humanitarian affairs
RMA	revolution in military affairs
RPF	Rwandan Patriotic Front
R2P	responsibility to protect
R2EP	responsibility to environmentally protect
RWP	responsibility while protecting
SDG	Sustainable Development Goal
SGBV	sexual and gender-based violence
SLM/A	Sudanese Liberation Movement/Army
SPLM	Sudan People's Liberation Movement
TNC	transnational corporations

TRIPS	Trade-Related Aspects of Intellectual Property Rights
UIC	Islamic Courts Union (Somalia)
UK	United Kingdom
UN	United Nations
UNAMA	United Nations Assistance Mission in Afghanistan
UNAMI	United Nations Assistance Mission for Iraq
UNAMID	United Nations/African Union Mission in Darfur
UNDP	United Nations Development Programme
UNEF	United Nations Emergency Force
UNEP	United Nations Environment Programme
UNHCR	(Office of the) United Nations High Commissioner for Refugees
UNSIFA	United Nations Interim Security Force for Abeyi
UNICEF	United Nations Children's Fund
UNIFIL	United Nations Interim Force in Lebanon
UNITAF	United Task Force (Somalia)
UNMIK	United Nations Interim Administration Mission in Kosovo
UNMIS	United Nations Mission in Sudan
UNMISS	United Nations Mission in South Sudan
UNOSOM	United Nations Operation in Somalia
UNPROFOR	United Nations Protection Force (in the Former Yugoslavia)
UNRRA	United Nations Relief and Rehabilitation Administration
UNRWA	United Nations Relief and Works Agency
UNTSO	United Nations Truce Supervision Organization
US	United States
USC	United Somali Congress
USSR	Union of Soviet Socialist Republics
VHF	viral hemorrhagic fever
WFP	World Food Programme
WHO	World Health Organization
WMD	weapons of mass destruction
WTO	World Trade Organization
WWI	World War I
WWII	World War II

Foreword

Rwandan refugees displaced due to the genocide set up camps outside Goma, Zaire, in 1994 following a cholera epidemic. (UN photo/John Isaac)

There has never ever been a generation with more available information about the suffering of fellow human beings elsewhere on the planet than this one. And there has never been a generation with greater resources, more sophisticated technology, or better methods or organizations at hand that can prevent and end human suffering. It is perhaps therefore increasingly difficult to accept the tragic juxtaposition between the indomitable humanitarian spirit yearning to aid and protect the vulnerable, and the cruel realities foisted by malicious predators, hypocritical governments, and a numbed public.

I have had a front-row seat for too many of these horrors in my four decades of humanitarianism—beginning as an eighteen-year-old volunteer in Colombia and later in Amnesty International, the Red Cross, as United Nations under-secretary-general for humanitarian affairs and emergency relief coordinator, to my current position as secretary-general of the Norwegian Refugee Council. Not a day passes without the sense of outrage and impotence realizing what we are unable to do to aid and protect the civilians in the Aleppos and Eastern Congos of our time. But an even stronger conviction from frontline humanitarian work is that we succeed more often than we fail, that we can effectively cry out against the injustice of denying rights to those in emergencies and to rally those who stand with us. Bloodstained battlefields and desolate famines compel us to speak truth to power. Silence is, ultimately, complicity. Those of us who can act have a duty to do so.

Having clambered through work in the field and strategized briefings to the Security Council, I have also seen the complexity of the humanitarian story. Whether it is Gaza, Fallujah, or Bangui, or whether it is wars, blockades, or tsunamis, humanitarian crises refract the political. There are not just a metaphorical billion lives and fundamental humanitarian principles at stake, but also a million political, economic, and strategic interests at play. To make sense of the political mess that precipitates and compounds humanitarian tragedies, I have an intellectual affinity and compassion kinship with the authors of this volume. Tom Weiss, a longstanding friend whose work I have followed for years, is older than I, and Peter Hoffman, a more recent acquaintance, is a generation younger. But we share a common commitment to understand what distinguishes, what ails, and what uplifts humanitarianism. Furthermore, we all believe that with light comes heat; that a candid look at the phenomenon will provoke controversy and criticism. But thoughtful reflection and debate is necessary to remedy some of the malaise and maladies that currently infect the international humanitarian system.

To that end, *Humanitarianism, War, and Politics: Solferino to Syria and Beyond* is comprehensive in scope and hard-hitting in analysis. It provides a clear and insightful guide for those who wish to understand the last quarter-century of efforts to come to the rescue of individuals caught in the crosshairs of violence and war. It also speaks directly to the fears of humanitarians themselves regarding the shrinking of humanitarian space and an altered perception of the enterprise as noble and worthwhile. As I wrote in *A Billion Lives*, "the age of innocence has gone." I recall my briefings on humanitarian priorities in mid-August 2003 as I was taking up my UN job and news broke that the UN headquarters in Baghdad had been bombed and one of my predecessors, Sergio de Mello, among other colleagues, had been killed.

It has been a routinely wrenching task simply trying to digest, let alone tame, all the moving parts in the international humanitarian system as we seek to galvanize support for moving forward with an agenda of realizing humanitarian rights in a post-9/11 era of terrorism and counterterrorism. As a flood of worry poured into an ocean of uncertainty, there was no guide to navigate the shoals in these unchartered waters. We now have one. Hoffman and Weiss parse the conventional wisdom and its power with a critical perspective that does not shy away from ascribing dysfunction. Their book identifies the traditional challenges of access but argues that this picture must be supplemented with a structural critique of means and ends. As I write, mounting casualties in, and record displacement from, an array of swelling and spiraling disasters feed the already grim mood within the humanitarian sector. Consequently, humanitarians are driven to reimagine and reinvent what we do and how we do it—the 2016 World Humanitarian Summit was illustrative of the demand for renewal accompanied by the harsh reality of inertia.

Hoffman and Weiss do a masterful job of situating this moment by analyzing unfolding changes in bedrock principles that produce the shifting sands of politics seen in ideas, actions, and results. The reader is taken on a journey from the dawn of modern humanitarianism to its contemporary configurations, stitching together a complex quilt that clearly traces the past to the present and considers what the future may hold. Along the way we are thoughtfully and thoroughly introduced to a wide range of conceptual tools that help illuminate historical developments. Ultimately, the book provides a panoramic prism through which we can see political colors, on the one hand, and the shape of humanitarianism, on the other. At the same time, it equips us to make our own judgments. *Humanitarianism, War, and Politics* is absolutely essential reading for both academics and humanitarian practitioners.

Jan Egeland

Preface

The "Killing Fields" memorial near Phnom Penh, Cambodia, attests to mass atrocities of the Khmer Rouge. (UN photo/John Isaac)

The perennial existential quandary of the ethic of care in war and emergencies is whether it is only able to offer a neutral, impartial, and independent "bed for the night," or whether such aid can also ensure rights and dignity. The mass atrocities of the 1990s and their repercussions prompted pursuing the latter agenda as humanitarians looked to more politicized ends and more militarized means. However, although the September 11 terrorist attacks and the Global War on Terrorism (GWOT) temporarily derailed this trajectory by casting a shadow over humanitarianism as security issues became paramount, new humanitarian instruments nonetheless developed. In December 2001, the "responsibility to protect" (R2P) doctrine spelled out a framework to justify the use of force for human protection purposes. On another front and almost simultaneously, accountability for war crimes was legally grounded with the birth of the International Criminal Court (ICC) in July 2002.

Over the past fifteen years these grand, noble plans have gone awry. R2P was initially drowned out by doctrines of counterterrorism and counter-proliferation; and concerns over a revival of Western imperialism as well as the chaotic aftermath of the Libyan case have soured prospects for future applications. The ICC has spent around $1.75 billion and produced a total of three convictions; and with all those who have faced adjudication coming from Africa, the critique of it as a "white man's court" has resonated far more loudly than any claim that justice has been served. Attacks against aid workers also evidenced significant blowback on relief operations. Furthermore, humanitarianism has become a niche in global markets with aid agencies competing for funds and waging turf wars while the private sector signs profitable contracts to provide support services, including private military and security companies (PMSCs).

Since our earlier treatment of humanitarianism in this series, *Sword & Salve*, was published in 2006 and began to feel outdated, we decided to revisit our analysis and digest a decade of new cases, data, and insights in order to justify reusing that book's subtitle, *Confronting New Wars and Humanitarian Crises*. However, once we started, we realized that we had a different book in mind. What remained on target was, first, interpreting humanitarianism as a political phenomenon deeply connected to security, and second, how sensitive we were to drivers of change. Motivating *Sword & Salve* were transformations after the Cold War that were revealed in the connection between the "new humanitarianisms" and the "new wars." At the time of writing, the vitality and viability of humanitarianism seemed in doubt as wounds were still open and nerves remained raw from a succession of crippling traumas: 9/11; the death of humanitarian champion, the special representative of the secretary-general to Iraq Sergio Vieira de Mello; and revelations regarding the torture and legal oblivion of detainees at Guantánamo Bay.

Ten years later, different political winds are blowing and reshaping the humanitarian landscape. The mood remains somber and anxious as overarching contextual features are informed by mass atrocities in Syria, including the use of chemical weapons, and the refugee crisis in Europe and elsewhere. The past decade has also changed our understanding of humanitarianism—its modalities, metrics, and meaning—and pushed us to rethink our framing and analysis. This volume is thus not *Sword & Salve 2.0*. Indeed, the three nouns in the title—*Humanitarianism, War,* and *Politics*—capture the central elements of the story and more visibly acknowledge the relentless influence of power. But our hope is not only to survey the topography but also to illuminate the tectonic shifts that account for its present as well as former and future contours.

Historically, humanitarianism has more boldly aimed to move beyond ensuring the "bare life" of "victims" to delivering the "good life" to "stakeholders"; but operationalizing this objective has exacerbated an ongoing identity crisis and produced in many instances, and in many organizations, a debilitating and schizophrenic humanitarianism. The most recent incarnation is a system that does not rescue populations in Syria or provide a haven in Europe. And even when allowing temporary refuge in camps, the system re-victimizes the displaced by robbing them of dignity. In such settings, humanitarianism is reduced to cynical population management dressed up as charity.

Today's panoply of crises is overwhelming, for politicians and policy makers in Europe and beyond, but they also represent a major challenge for people like us and readers. As analysts, we bring research and insights to bear on these crises to describe, calculate, and evaluate the triangulation of humanitarianism, war, and politics. Our aim is to provide knowledge about humanitarianism, including the practical lessons learned, and also the means of knowledge production and policy assessments.

We would like to thank colleagues who have routinely inspired rigor and diligence, warmly encouraged our critical reflections, and patiently endured our occasional flummoxed frustrations. Susan McEachern of Rowman & Littlefield, our editor, has given us the requisite gentle nudging and supporting latitude for us to produce a book that adheres to our vision. Nancy Okada of the Ralph Bunche Institute has been an avid champion of our intellectual and normative cause. Peter is also grateful to the Studley Faculty Research Fund for underwriting some of the research.

This book is dedicated to our respective children (Sam Onat, and Hannah, and Rebeccah), and in Tom's case, grandchildren too (Amara, Kieran, and Grace). In the darkest hours, our offspring remind us of how fortunate we are. They have inspired us to better understand and bear witness to the human spirit. Their love and support sustained us while we chronicled the trials and tribulations of humanitarianism. Our drive to decode, analyze, and criticize is fed by the fervent desire to start a conversation on humanitarianism that better responds to the crisis-riddled world that our children will inherit.

Peter J. Hoffman and Thomas G. Weiss
New York, May 2017

Introduction
Humanitarian Cosmology and Mythology

Red Cross recruitment poster showing a Red Cross nurse dragging a wounded soldier from the battlefield (published between 1914 and 1918).

<table>
</table>

In This Chapter
• What Is Humanitarianism?
• Social Science and the Study of Humanitarianism
• The Argument
• About the Book

Humanitarianism is not simply a perfunctory logistical or legal exercise of providing assistance in emergencies; it is also a profoundly political activity. That is, who we save, for what purpose, and how we save them says a great deal about who we are, what humanitarianism is, and what power it has. Given that this process frequently plays out in the context of armed conflicts, humanitarianism's true nature can be found in paraphrasing Carl von Clausewitz's classic axiom: "Humanitarianism is the continuation of war and politics by other means." To that extent, humanitarianism is a peculiar area of world order that effectively allocates four public goods to distressed populations in emergencies: rights, relief, rescue, and refuge.

Over the past three decades each of these has witnessed momentous changes that influence the quality of humanitarianism and speak to an international sacrificial order that determines who lives and who dies per the configuration of power in international affairs. As such, there are four Rs in the international calculator:

Rights: Referring to protections guaranteed by international agreements, humanitarian rights have expanded greatly over the past 150 years from covering the sick, wounded, or captured combatants to civilians as well as special categories of victims; rights also have grown to address those not only who have crossed borders because of conflict (refugees) but also who have been uprooted within them (internally displaced persons, IDPs). However, the main innovation in this dimension of humanitarianism is primarily seen in the realization of courts and tribunals, most notably the ICC as of 2002, which strengthens respect for rights found under international humanitarian law by adjudicating those suspected of committing war crimes and making those found guilty accountable.

Relief: The numbers of those requiring aid has been soaring. For example, in 2005 the UN Office for the Coordination of Humanitarian Assistance (OCHA) provided for about 40 million; just over a decade later, in 2016 it was aiming to sustain nearly 93 million. Although humanitarian space—the physical area where assistance is provided in crises—is under siege due to armed belligerents attacking aid workers, the size of the resource flows has grown tremendously and quickly: in 1989 humanitarian relief totaled around $800 million, by 1999 it was $4.5 billion, by the end of 2001, $10 billion, and in 2015 it reached $28 billion.[1]

Rescue: After little was done to protect vulnerable populations during the 1990s, in 2001 the new R2P normative framework articulated criteria for using military force to halt mass atrocities by states against populations within their borders. Initially contention over R2P concentrated primarily on whether militarized humanitarianism was legitimate, but in recent years the premise has become widely accepted while the parameters of debate have shifted to focus on how to operationalize it. R2P mandated missions in Libya and Côte d'Ivoire in 2011 were notable instances.

Refuge: The size and nature of refugee flows has changed since 2001, when there were nearly 16 million refugees, 25 million IDPs, and 1.1 million asylum seekers. In 2015, the numbers exceeded 21 million refugees, more than 40 million IDPs, and more than 2 million asylum seekers. The granting of asylum has been in retreat for years; and given xenophobic fears about the burdens, if not dangers, of accepting refugees, the odds for accepting more displaced populations are dismal, with greater limits on their movements likely. And the dire perceptions in Europe stemming from a flow of Middle East refugees, which has at least generated funding and publicity, as well as in the United States where the concern regards Central American populations in particular, can obscure the fact that the overwhelming majority of migrants and displaced people continues to live in developing countries that lack the resources to host them—and the numbers of displaced in such host countries are large as a percentage of their own populations.

General humanitarian principles about tending to victims have not changed much, but what has changed is greater calls within the humanitarian sector to expand its work. This is not merely a call for more money but also is fundamentally more ambitious. Reconfigured humanitarianism seeks more than saving a handful of lives in the world's worst emergencies to survive at the fickle whims of the powerful. It also aims to make humanitarianism transformative in bringing not only sustenance but also dignity and freedom.

There is an allocation of resources in the humanitarian system, a set of "humanitarian classes," with three different hierarchies: recipients, delivering agents, and donors. The "recipient" classes represent a hierarchy of who receives which resources, such as funding, protection, and justice. Power is found in the dubbing of "victims" and "perpetrators" and those who come to their aid or provide rescue. The class of "delivering agents" plays a role in enacting strategies of supplying humanitarian goods and determining who is saved or not. Hierarchies within this class revolve around organizational size and feature contestation over defining humanitarianism while being the agents for the "donor" class.

The challenge of ending or even flattening this international sacrificial order (the contemporary configuration of humanitarian classes) whereby some die due to uneven, often inadequate, access to humanitarian resources, requires a greater understanding of "humanitarian cosmology" and "humanitarian mythology." We examine the origins and beliefs of humanitarianism, and their relationships to war and politics. Our use of "humanitarian cosmology" aims to understand the birth and evolution of the international humanitarian system as defining and refining class relations. But there is a sociopolitical normative character that exists beyond the material moorings of the system and impacts class relations. Thus, the material conditions must be supplemented with the cultural dimension, the "humanitarian mythology" that legitimates and normalizes.

What Is Humanitarianism?

The term "humanitarianism" has been broadly applied to assistance given to remedy the suffering of others. Two aspects are noteworthy. First, "humanity" is a comprehensive and inclusive category. Traditionally outsiders were branded as "others" or "strangers" and often treated as subhuman. Second, the idea of finding "humanity" in special contexts is usually implicit in this sort of behavior; that is, it connotes a condition of extreme need and actors under duress.

The notion of humanitarianism may be timeless and certainly existed long before the term itself crystalized. For example, thirteenth-century philosopher St. Thomas Aquinas (1225–1274) included *"misericordia"* on his list of virtues, to bond through a sensitivity to the misery of others and render mercy.[2] However, it was not until the early nineteenth century that the term "humanitarianism" came into use to convey schemas to improve the welfare of all people. Initially it referred to a movement that celebrated Christ's humanity (not divinity) and posited a religion of man that was to connect the suffering of others to one's own life. By the late 1800s the label was applied to a wide variety of activities and social movements, both domestic and international: missionaries used the word to describe their work to bring civilization and Christianity to colonies; temperance activists invoked the term; labor protections and calls for welfare also used this packaging; prison and penal reform termed their efforts thusly; abolitionists referenced it; and the early animal welfare movement cited it.

The "H" word retains great resonance, but one searches in vain for a definition. Like Justice Stewart Potter's determination of obscenity, the general instinct is to suggest that though humanitarianism is not clear-cut, we nevertheless know it when we see it. Provided an opportunity in the *Nicaragua v. United States* case, the International Court of Justice (ICJ) waffled. It stated that humanitarian action is what the International Committee of the Red Cross (ICRC) does—deferring responsibility for determining and allowing for change. The 1819 edition of the *Oxford English*

Dictionary's first citation relies on tautologies: humanitarian is "having regard to the interests of humanity or mankind at large; relating to, or advocating, or practising humanity or human action." In common discourse, humanitarianism (noun) consists of actions to improve well-being or welfare; a humanitarian (noun) is a person who actively promotes such improvements; humanitarian (adjective) usually means charitable.

Natural disasters, such as Nepal's 2015 earthquake, as well as those exacerbated by human influence and unintended effects, such as the 2011 tsunami and Fukushima nuclear meltdown, tend to present straightforward emergency needs; and so, assistance is roundly encouraged and welcomed while access is not problematic. Help during wars is far more fraught. Governments fighting wars—especially civil ones—may look unfavorably on outside help as signaling their own weakness or callousness. Moreover, aid and protection are factors in winning a war; belligerents as well as governments may manipulate assistance and population flows as part of a war-fighting strategy. In other words, obstructing the distribution of relief is a means for strangling the opposition.

However, whether it takes the form of subtle acknowledgements or a direct transfer of resources, aid influences existing power arrangements. Politics is concerned with power, and specifically asks the question of who gets what, when, how, and why. In the context of humanitarianism, we inquire into who gets what type of assistance, when, how, and why. To this end, one scholarly tradition that resonates with this approach is found in the work of Michel Foucault, who emphasized what he called "biopower."[3] He specifically used this to denote the state's control over populations through the power over the production/reproduction of life and to more broadly consider "biopolitics." In the realm of humanitarian affairs, the state no longer has a monopoly on biopower, but rather the humanitarian sector contests the limitations of leaving it to the state and its organs to tackle the suffering of people in need—indeed, humanitarianism as a principle turns to moral and medical values, and opposes protecting the sovereignty of states to make decisions about the tending to the afflicted and maintaining lives.

Aside from the politics of a struggle over who possesses biopower—whether it is states, militaries, armed nonstate actors, local populations, or humanitarian agencies—there are also politics engendered by the act of giving assistance. While some may conjure an image of a fulfilled or renewed sort of social contract that reflects concerns with justice, there is often something else at work here. The concept of "moral economy" may be useful.[4] Originally this idea was conceived to express an economy not predicated purely on profits but rather one intended to build social relations. But for our purposes, the allocation of resources per the humanitarian logic of responding to suffering fosters a different sort of moral economy—one in which providers of aid have a distinctive social role and standing, one that may be perceived as noble but may also be fundamentally paternalistic or conducive to making recipients dependent.

Humanitarianism thus creates power, and the allocation of power moves the idea and its manifestations to the domain of politics. Who gets saved under today's world order? Who decides? What are the implications of the emergence of the power to save? Is this justice or a reconfigured hegemony?

Social Science and the Study of Humanitarianism

The analysis of the politics of humanitarianism proffered here draws on social scientific theories and methods. Can principles and practices inspired by the virtuous impulse to address suffering be studied in an objective and orderly fashion?

Science requires systematic, empirical inquiry. We characterize features and take measurements to deduce connections between variables. After a description of what is to be studied, we explore relations to provide explanations. The social sciences are somewhat different from the natural sciences not only in their focus—the former looks at the social world, the latter the physical universe—but also in the types of analyses. The natural sciences are often able to isolate or manipulate what is to be studied such that other influences do not factor into analysis. For instance, in chemistry an element can be removed from a compound in a controlled experiment. In the social sciences, we are usually unable to control our units of analysis so readily and therefore do not experiment. There are also certain legal and professional restrictions as well as moral issues raised by performing tests on human subjects.

Our social science approach to humanitarianism must confront core methodological challenges: there are few, if any, clear units of analysis that are uniformly recognized and agreed upon. Measuring and evaluating compassion and the treatment of suffering may defy the sort of mathematic calculations that are commonly employed in scientific work. As the poet Muriel Rukeyser has written, "The universe is made of stories, not atoms."[5] However, that is not to suggest that scientific rigor has no place in studying humanitarian politics, or that evidence is irrelevant. First, we ascribe to the philosophy of transparent and systematic methods. Second, we accept the reality of inconvenient truths—as Aldous Huxley has remarked, "Facts do not cease to exist because they are ignored."[6]

In pursuing social science, we must not only try to generate explanations for social behaviors and outcomes but also explain our qualifiers and lexicon in defining and measuring behaviors and outcomes. Box I.1 enumerates the most essential terms encountered in the text, and box I.2

BOX I.1
Basic Humanitarian Terminology

- **Humanitarian ideology and culture:** This is the collection of norms associated with a moral concern with the suffering of "others." Within this corpus of beliefs exist two bedrock ideas, the condition of "humanity" expressed and felt by recipients/beneficiaries/victims (the beliefs of individuals claiming rights to assistance), and the condition of "humaneness" expressed and felt by providers/donors (the belief in a solidarity or fellowship in the act of compassion).
- **The humanitarian movement:** An aggregation of the different social movements that have embraced humanitarian culture. This may include individuals as well as more clearly identified civil society elements.
- **International humanitarian law (IHL):** This body of jurisprudence is to govern the conduct of actors in emergencies, notably war, and thereby define the "rights" of people. It is interchangeable with the expression "the laws of war." Its cornerstone is the Geneva Conventions and Additional Protocols, but it has come to include other treaties giving protections to vulnerable populations in emergencies, such as refugees.
- **Humanitarian organizations:** The formal agencies and bureaucracies that have been established to achieve humanitarian ends (i.e., are embedded in humanitarian culture). Often they are not-for-profit nongovernmental organizations (NGOs) to underscore their credentials, but governmental and intergovernmental versions exist as well.
- **Humanitarian action:** Operations to distribute such aid as food, water, medicine, and shelter as well as those to afford legal and physical protection.
- **Humanitarian space:** The physical area that is available to aid and protection agencies to pursue their mandates without interference or danger from authorities or belligerents. Areas where relief is distributed, such as hospitals or refugee camps, are the clearest examples.
- **Humanitarian intervention:** The use of military force to protect populations in danger—to "rescue" people without the consent of host authorities. "Non-forcible" intervention also includes the imposition of sanctions and international judicial pursuit, once again without consent. The most recent reframing of this concept is the "responsibility to protect."
- **International humanitarian system:** The network of humanitarian organizations and IHL that span rights, relief, and rescue.
- **Humanitarianization:** The process whereby an emergency becomes officially recognized as a "humanitarian" issue, which spurs aid and protection actors to engage.
- **Humanitarian narrative:** The dominant image of the sector emphasizing the central respect for human life.
- **Complex humanitarian emergency:** "Complex" has been added to indicate that the multiplicity of causes and actors in a crisis as well as its duration influence international responses. Complexity also suggests that the situation is determined more by large political factors than the relief capabilities of agencies.

BOX I.2
Actors in the International Humanitarian System

Our look at humanitarianism necessarily involves analyzing the behavior of key actors. Who are they?

- **Nongovernmental organizations:** Formal, independent, nonprofit institutions that do not operate at the direct behest of states. Examples include Save the Children, the International Rescue Committee (IRC), Mercy Corps, Oxfam, Catholic Relief Services (CRS), World Vision, and Médecins sans Frontières (MSF, or Doctors without Borders).
- **Intergovernmental organizations (IGOs):** These are formal institutions that are the product of interstate cooperation and whose member states pay a substantial portion of the bills, although resources can be supplemented by voluntary contributions. Examples include several humanitarian agencies within the United Nations system, such as the Office of the UN High Commissioner for Refugees (UNHCR) and the Office for the Coordination of Humanitarian Affairs (OCHA).
- **The International Committee of the Red Cross:** This unique entity is both an IGO and NGO. Legally, it is the guardian of IHL, thus embedding its formal legal standing. Although governments primarily finance the ICRC, it fundamentally determines its own agenda. It is also a member, along with national society affiliates and the International Federation of the Red Cross and Red Crescent, of the broader International Red Cross and Red Crescent Movement—the ICRC is the lead agency in the movement and has a role in recognizing new members.
- **States:** National governments play a variety of roles with respect to humanitarianism. They may be donors to humanitarian agencies, providing critical financial resources. Their militaries or bilateral aid agencies may engage in the delivery of emergency assistance or protection. They may host humanitarian crises and control territory and thus be essential in gaining access to vulnerable populations.
- **Local interlocutors:** In places where states are not able to provide access, important local actors may be vital. For example, warlords and their militia forces may in essence be gatekeepers. Local civil society and merchants may provide the first line of humanitarian defense and help coordinate outside resources.
- **Transnational corporations (TNCs):** The private sector may undertake activities that facilitate relief operations. For instance, international business may deliver aid or subsidize them. Aside from supplies and logistics, there are also firms that provide security.

- **Media:** Print and electronic, local and international media are sources of information and publicity, essential for decision making, advocacy, and resource mobilization. The advent of round-the-clock media coverage and the development of social media have also expanded the range of those who contribute to the dissemination of information and its influence.
- **"Victims":** Often overlooked are the affected populations who are important in the administration of aid; they have capacities of their own that are usually ignored. Their routine treatment as passive, inconsequential objects, not valuable subjects, is part of their victimization and the reason why quotation marks appear here—they do not, however, elsewhere because there is no better term.

identifies the key actors. Moreover, our inquiries must acknowledge the social constructs and power inherent in this undertaking. We must recognize the power of measurement; it is no coincidence that a tool for measuring is called a "ruler." We must be vigilant in grounding our examination empirically, in drawing clear connections in relating variables, and in evaluating outcomes. In short, we will apply scientific principles in seeking to determine how humanitarianism and its governance is measured and assessed, and how this knowledge structures beliefs, behaviors, organizations, and outcomes in the process of tending to afflicted populations in emergencies as well as shapes the very study of these actors and occurrences.

The Argument

Our main concern is to explain the "why?" for humanitarianism's troubles: Why is it frequently under attack from external parties, be they armed belligerents targeting aid workers or donors dropping the budgetary axe? Why within the sector is there often deep despair and despondence by humanitarians over their limits in addition to ubiquitous appropriation and exploitation of the term? To get to the heart of these questions, we must understand humanitarianism as a phenomenon that can be seen in ethics and relationships born out of emergencies, and which require special analytical lenses. Our argument is that two distinct crises face humanitarianism that have resulted in dysfunction whereby aid agencies and their personnel may no longer be "humanitarian" in the sense of practicing the ethic that they preach. The first crisis comes from the nature of organizations and reflects their cosmology, in which turf wars plague donors and aid manipulation undermines operations. The second crisis is one of identity that stems from mythology, a struggle to define the core principles that constitute "humanitarianism." The confluence of these two crises explains how humanitarian dynamics drive humanitarian organizations to become more organizations than humanitarian, and how aid workers become disheartened and overwhelmed by their work. In this book, we portray the emergence of these crises from the establishment of humanitarianism through the various changes it has undergone in order bring to the fore how the lens itself has been obscured and thus threatens to redefine "humanitarianism."

The central questions are not merely technical issues of how to save people but rather are deeply political. In particular, they ask why, and to what effect, and even more critically, how do we know and why is that. To that end, this book on humanitarianism, war, and politics has two conjoined agendas: the practical concerns associated with the structural problems of making humanitarian work viable, and analytical insights into those structural problems.

There are two basic drivers in our work, what might be called "the existential" and "the empirical." The former refers to an identity crisis redolent among humanitarians. While there are boundaries of the peculiar area of social and moral life called "humanitarianism"—compassion crossing borders coupled with a transcendental significance for the individual and perhaps also world order—where lines are drawn about who is and who is not saved, and why, are in fact fluid and even nebulous. In short, humanitarianism is contested; the confusion and confrontation in principle overflows into contestation in practice.

Moreover, humanitarianism is more complex and controversial than conventional wisdom suggests. It involves more than simply the moral imperative to respond to disasters because it entails power and reflects political dynamics. Thus, in analyzing the phenomenon, we begin and end our inquiry by exploring what humanitarianism is and what power underpins it.

The other driver appreciates the empirical and underscores that whether it is out of inspiration to address the suffering of "others" or frustration with how such efforts have gone astray, a demand exists for a greater supply of knowledge about humanitarianism. The premise of our social science is that the world can be improved through knowledge. Early social science had an idealistic and perhaps naïve quality that was shaken by the experiences of two world wars in the first half of the twentieth century, which triggered a sharp turn toward objectivity and what has come to be called "behavioralism." The focus on reason and sharper scientific protocols led to a narrower set of tools and findings, which were more rigorous but also more disengaged as they endeavored to boil the human or social content out of analysis. After the Cold War, social science became broader in what it investigated, and also opened itself more thoroughly to other approaches beyond the rationalist behavior-centered ones. In this context, new scholarship on humanitarianism has arisen. Beyond quantifiable data, there also are qualitative assessments. In fact, in recent years there is something verging on a new subfield, "critical humanitarian studies." Here the agenda has unfolded to investigate what are the metrics of compassion, what power underlies and is evidenced by humanitarianism, and whose knowledge matters.

The moment is propitious for bringing together the existential and the empirical. We reside in a world in flux; new conflicts and crises have created new conditions under which humanitarianism operates, under which it thrives or withers. What was once true for yesterday's humanitarianism may not hold for today's or tomorrow's. Therefore, while we take the contemporary pulse, we also explore its roots and its ambitions, to understand not only that humanitarianism is a form of politics but also how the range, nature, and impacts of this politics are evolving. There remains some continuity with the dream—that humanity will care for those in harm's way. At the same time, change is afoot in the means, ends, and meaning of humanitarian action.

In short, our aim is to analyze and explain the what, why, and how of what could be labeled "revolutions in humanitarian affairs." The term "revolution" has perhaps been typecast inaccurately by events such as "the French Revolution," with the dramatic seizing of the Bastille as a readily recognizable turning point. "Revolution" in our depiction of the itinerary of humanitarianism is analogous to "the Industrial Revolution." Technological advances in fields such as chemistry and metallurgy had existed for quite some time, but it was the social organization that ignited and ultimately realized an intense, wide-ranging, and long-term remaking of the world at ideological, material, and sociopolitical levels. Thomas Kuhn's analysis of the sociology of science and change is similarly instructive. He notes that the social support for, or widespread popularity of, a scientific idea is critical to the dissemination of breakthroughs.[7] Only when norms are embraced and espoused by experts does the content of those ideas become meaningfully established as innovative. A final parallel can be found in the "revolution in military affairs" (RMA) put forward by scholars of military science to characterize technological and organizational alterations that have an impact on the mechanics of war.

In a similar vein, a "revolution in humanitarian affairs" represents a change in ideas that fundamentally alters the behavior of organizations and outcomes. This angle's advantage is that it acknowledges an absence of certainty that a change necessarily becomes embedded—some actors are advocates of a complete revolution, others may resist, and others may vacillate. Our approach accounts for both revolutionaries and counter-revolutionaries in major developments, and this model avoids overly deterministic or teleological approaches to understanding changes, but it instead concentrates on identifying contingency in and tripwires for transformation, and denoting the consequences of dramatic metamorphoses. We analyze the net effect of changes in practices and organizations that articulate the meaning of humanitarianism—the revolutions that have occurred and current politics that are influencing what humanitarianism will become.

About the Book

This volume is conceived to provide an interpretive toolkit along with seminal historical cases in order to analyze the contemporary problems and prospects for robust humanitarianism. Our method is essentially qualitative because there is no single calculation for assessing it, and indeed that reflects the reality that we are analyzing. The deeper examinations of specific vignettes of the humanitarianism-war-politics configurations speak to the evolving role of humanitarianism in world order—Solferino to start, but certainly Auschwitz, Biafra, Phnom Penh, Mogadishu, Goma, Srebrenica, Benghazi, Kabul, Aleppo, Bangui, and Mosul are also pivotal and poignant. They are episodes in the making of the contemporary revolution in humanitarian affairs. The chapters are sequenced historically to promote coherent presentations that build toward more thematic and analytical treatments, but individual chapters can also be read in isolation—however, readers should note that any overlap in thematic chapters cuts across time periods to give attention to the evolution of a certain norm, discourse, practice, behavior, or outcome. No single book can exhaustively catalogue and effectively speak to every aspect of humanitarianism—and we do not aspire for this one to be everything to everyone. Instead, we offer a targeted survey that spotlights humanitarianism (where it came from, what it means at a specific moment, who enacts it, and how and with what implications) and then addresses its shifting coverage (how it has changed) and depth (what it has come to mean and how it has an impact on politics).

Chapter 1, "Humanitarian Culture, Traditions, and Theories: Concepts and Tools," provides theoretical foundations. It begins by zeroing in on the core contestation in humanitarianism, essentially its boundaries: What constitutes humanitarianism? It then proceeds to enumerate elements of international relations (IR) theory that inform interpretations of relief organizations and other humanitarian phenomena. This précis outlines various worldviews to explain the phenomenon, spanning both conventional approaches and critical theory. In particular, we present a framework of "critical humanitarianism," which is centered on a concern for humanity and the construction of knowledge; it analyzes the gaps between principles and practices in the quality of the consequent social relationship between providers and recipients. Additionally, in comprehensively laying out conceptual treatments of humanitarianism, the chapter also reviews just war theory. It concludes by locating humanitarianism—its meaning and impact—within today's world order.

Chapter 2, "Humanitarian Genesis and Gravity: Solferino to Biafra and African Famines," examines the origins of international humanitarian law and humanitarian organizations. Starting in the late nineteenth century, normative, technological, and organizational innovations enabled the establishment of the international humanitarian system. World War I (WWI) and World War II (WWII) contributed to another round of change, continuing to embed law and expand relief operations. During the Cold War, humanitarianism again evolved as it responded to the problems associated with decolonization and proxy wars of the superpowers. The perennial challenges of access and manipulation challenged and divided humanitarian culture, to wit a fracture between the neutral, impartial, and consent-based ICRC and the witness-bearing *sans frontières* movement, which framed the "identity crisis" in the 1990s.

Chapter 3, "New Wars and New Humanitarianisms of the 1990s: Northern Iraq, Somalia, Rwanda, and the Balkans," dissects formative cases in the evolution of humanitarian culture and organizations that began at the outset of the post–Cold War period. It spotlights how changes in the nature of humanitarian crises—mass atrocity–laden wars—heightened calls for reform or redesign of operating principles. These episodes of the 1990s showcased new ethical and political challenges that would spark new innovations and generate new lessons.

Chapter 4, "Humanitarianism and Security: The Responsibility to Protect," analyzes the normative development and operational performance of this seminal shift in responding to situations in which states or armed belligerents commit mass human rights violations against their own populations. After delving into the history of humanitarian intervention, the chapter picks up with a reflection on the lessons of the 1990s about how to legitimately as well as legally use force for purposes of human protection. The chapter then parses the 2001 report of the International Commission on Intervention and State Sovereignty (ICISS) and traces its influence before concluding with an examination of the contemporary politics of R2P.

Chapter 5, "Humanitarianism Adjudicated: The International Criminal Court," considers legal means of pursuing the humanitarian agenda and provides an in-depth treatment of war crimes. First, it looks at the emergence of international judicial thought about mass atrocity crimes, including some early instances of action. Second, the chapter breaks down the development and the debates surrounding the foremost contemporary illustration, the ICC.

Chapter 6, "Humanitarianism in the Post-9/11 World: Afghanistan, Iraq, Libya, and Syria," assesses what are arguably the four most controversial and yet defining cases of humanitarianism since the terrorist attacks of September 11, 2001. This interpretation of the past turbulent decade and a half assembles a range of themes and relates them to its reshaping in the wake of the so-called GWOT, once again bringing to the fore the central debate about what and who is a humanitarian, and revealing its operational significance.

Chapter 7, "Humanitarianism Forgotten and Forsaken: Darfur, South Sudan, Uganda, and Neglected Victims," takes up other humanitarian crises that persist outside of the spotlight created by GWOT, the Arab Spring, and the interests of the great powers. This chapter problematizes how disasters figuratively disappear, thereby adding to the victimization of afflicted populations, and it illustrates this dynamic in specific country cases and thematically in a class of victims, those who experience sexual or gender-based violence (SGBV).

Chapter 8, "Humanitarian Limbo: Displaced Populations, Prolonged Sufferings, Contested Camps," considers dysfunctional outcomes of the international humanitarian system in addressing the uncomfortable politics of managing forcibly displaced populations. It also discusses the current surge of refugees from the Middle East and North Africa into Europe, including the vexing politics of "refugee-terrorists."

Chapter 9, "The Humanitarian-Industrial Complex: Media and Markets," examines two interrelated themes that have become more conspicuous since the 1990s. First, the role of the media in humanitarian crises both in depicting emergencies and portraying the performance by responders. The power to cast an issue as within the domain of humanitarianism and construct humanitarian narratives, or "humanitarianization," is central to developing a receptive audience that will donate funds. Second, marketization pressures from inside and outside the system compel agencies to vie for niches, and motivate private-sector service providers to consider entering the market.

Chapter 10, "Humanitarianism Unbound: Public Health Disasters and Environmental Emergencies," analyzes other major issues that have come to fit under the broad umbrella of humanitarianism in conflict-prone or post-conflict states, the problems of infectious diseases and environmental catastrophes. While these concerns are usually considered outliers for humanitarians because they are mostly situated under the "development" rubric, the connections to principles found in IHL and the operations and capacities of relief organizations make them natural and growing functional niches in the humanitarian sector. After noting that these issues are at on the frontier of humanitarianism, it examines how they fit into humanitarian work and specifically take up recent and emerging challenges, such as Ebola and climate refugees.

Chapter 11 consists of our conclusions, "The Study and Practice of Humanitarianism: Making Sense and Finding Meaning in Saving People." It pulls together the various strands of humanitarianism, war, and politics to interpret scholarly findings and the situations confronted by practitioners. It begins with a snapshot of the sector, surveying where aid goes, who provides it, the limits of what is provided, and variations among agencies, including contrasts between intergovernmental organizations and nongovernmental organizations as well as those based in the North versus in the Global South. The chapter considers the issue of change, specifically speaking to the "revolution in humanitarian affairs," highlighting shifts in ethics and principles, space and security, economics and markets, and perceptions and relationships. It ends with a reflection for aid workers on what practical lessons have been learned or spurned, and thoughts about what could be done to reinvigorate humanitarianism.

This chapter has outlined the road ahead to analyze humanitarianism; this bumpy, winding itinerary involves exploring the connections to war and politics as well as teasing out its materiality and normativity. Thus, we conclude this initial foray with a truism: the humanitarian cosmos and myth are mutually reinforcing. To know what the phenomenon entails, we must grasp this duality: ideas about humanitarianism are essential to its reality—it is what we believe it to be. But that belief is rooted in experience, which in turn tempers our beliefs.

Our candid analysis and criticism express our sincere concern for people, both those in need and those who provide for them. We admire the intrepid dedication of humanitarians, and we hope to enhance their efforts with our reflection on their history and culture, their capacities and their challenges, their values and value. Humanitarianism, to a greater extent than many other phenomena subject to politics, is also buoyed by faith in and hope for humanity.

1

Humanitarian Culture, Traditions, and Theories

Concepts and Tools

Internally displaced persons return to their home village of Sehjanna, Sudan, after living seven years in an IDP camp in Aramba. The voluntary repatriation program is organized by the Office of the United Nations High Commissioner for Refugees (UNHCR) and the Sudanese Humanitarian Aid Commission (July 14, 2011). (UN photo/Albert González Farran)

In This Chapter

- Humanitarian Values and Visions
- Humanitarian Organizations and IR Theory
- Humanitarian Organizations and Critical Theory
- Just War
- Early Thinkers and IHL
- Debates about Just War
- Conclusion: The Meaning and Place of Humanitarianism

This chapter contains the foundations for the subsequent analyses and cases of humanitarianism, war, and politics. It begins by shining a spotlight on the core contestation in this arena, namely what constitutes humanitarianism. Next the chapter outlines a variety of worldviews derived from international relations and critical theory that make the phenomenon of humanitarianism intelligible—and these diagnostic tools subsequently inform prescriptions. The last section examines the principles of just war. The central lines of inquiry are a problematization of humanitarianism that involves the nature and role of values, organizations, and power.

Humanitarian Values and Visions

The major fault line in humanitarianism runs through the scope of action, the demarcation of its borders. Although the net was once cast quite broadly, contestation remains over how it should presently be defined. In the late eighteenth and early nineteenth centuries, humanitarian movements, sociopolitical projects to salve the suffering of strangers, took up issues of slavery, welfare, alcohol consumption, prison reform, forced and voluntary migration, and war-induced suffering. In the early twentieth century, other aspects were included such as preserving cultural heritage and scientific knowledge. However, humanitarianism has come to focus primarily on addressing the tribulations specifically associated with wars or large-scale natural disasters. Craig Calhoun gets to the heart of how humanitarianism evolved by underlining the importance of an "emergency imaginary," or the perception of crises as extraordinary events that undermine global order.[1] While humanitarianism generally speaks to the improvement of the human condition, there is something special about extreme, often seen as sudden, emergencies that inflict misery, dehumanize people, and shock consciences. Some "emergencies" have become routine and verge on perpetual, and evidence of political fatigue has appeared;

but in its initial crystallization as an internationally recognized practice, humanitarianism was born out of the ethics and urgency of emergencies.

There is an ongoing debate about the modalities of response, whether the international humanitarian system should concentrate on mitigating suffering through relief aid, or whether it should be integrated into a larger project of building a better world order. An advocate for the first approach, David Rieff, argues that only a narrow definition of humanitarian action can be successful in patching up in the wake of crises.[2] The "hazards of charity" appear when a larger agenda jeopardizes the unique contribution of humanitarian work and reeks of controlling, power-based relations that ultimately undermine the value of humanitarianism. This view is rooted in critiques about imperialism, such as Walter Benjamin's observation that "every document of civilization is also a document of barbarism."[3] For example, food aid can undercut local producers and produce dependency—the goal to provide sustenance appears "civilized" but making a society reliant on imports is "barbaric."

Michael Ignatieff, on the other hand, contends that humanitarianism is part of a "revolution of moral concern" to build a better world order in which there will be less suffering.[4] There is a choice between doing nothing and accepting that disasters will take a human toll, or responding robustly and accepting that such responses invariably invoke questions of power and domination—he refers to his preference for the latter as the "lesser evil." Others from this tradition include John Stuart Mill, who contended that "despotism is a legitimate mode of government in dealing with barbarians, providing the end be their improvement."[5] From this perspective, the potentially corrupting influence of food aid is counterbalanced by sustaining a population whose production can be nurtured into eventual self-sufficiency—what may seem "barbaric" at the outset can produce positive outcomes in the long term.

In sum, there are contrasting visions of humanitarianism. One is a minimal interpretation based on a deontological ethic of charity, and the other is a maximal version descended from a consequentialist framework of progress.

Humanitarian Organizations and IR Theory

Our aim is to shed light on humanitarianism as not only a theory or value, but as a concrete phenomenon; we analyze illustrations connected to organizations to explain actors and impacts. As a preliminary note to an examination of humanitarian organizations, a brief word is in order about situating them within IR theory. Although we draw on an eclectic array of social science approaches and tools, the perspectives in this discussion represent different ideal types of "worldviews"—this term denotes the range of traditions and perspectives that are paradigmatic of interpretations of world order as a whole (i.e., explaining how international affairs and politics work). Often they are delineated as "theories" in the sense that they organize (and in some instances, parse) variables to generate explanations of norms, discourse, practices, behavior, and outcomes, as well as enrich our understanding of sociopolitical phenomena.

Theoretical schools are primarily heuristic devices, which may not capture and explain every aspect of a phenomenon but provide insights for understanding characteristics and illuminating disconnects emanating from contrasting interpretations. To that end, it is necessary to be cognizant of seven major schools of thought in analyzing humanitarianism—realism, liberalism, constructivism, Marxism, feminism, post-colonialism, and critical humanitarianism. Each school posits what humanitarianism is, why humanitarians do what they do, and what role both play in world order.

We begin with the conventional approaches, realism and liberalism. The former contends that international politics is fundamentally in a state of anarchy. In this framing, states are the only meaningful units, and each pursues its own national interests through the acquisition of power. Indeed, the central concern of realism is the distribution of power, and therefore it approaches humanitarianism in terms of how it may influence power allocations.[6] Given the obsession with competition, realism has an instrumental attitude toward humanitarianism, its ideology, and its operational agencies. Furthermore, realists measure the impact of humanitarian work with respect to "relative" versus "absolute gains." A relative gain is one in which the more powerful state gains more out of an interaction than a less powerful state; an absolute gain benefits both parties. And if a state can achieve a "relative gain," it will support humanitarianism.[7] To realists, humanitarianism is fundamentally a tool of great powers; its primary effect is to preserve existing arrangements, which favors the powerful at the expense of the weaker while labeling it an ethical practice.

Liberalism highlights cooperation and emphasizes the impact of interdependence. It argues that the pursuit of collective goods amounts to an "absolute gain" for all states. This critique of realists' pursuit of "relative gains" highlights that gains can be hard to measure (e.g., a pandemic or climate change where all parties will eventually be harmed if coordinated action is not taken soon, though some may "gain" more than others at the start), but also that over time, states may be willing to gain less on one transaction given that interdependence creates other opportunities in which they may gain more in the future.[8] Moreover, liberalism also has a wider view of international affairs than realism; although states remain the most important actors in international affairs, others—such as IGOs, NGOs, and TNCs—may also have significant roles. Putting these pieces together, liberalism sees that there are certain collective goals that no state can achieve acting on its own, and therefore all states gain in forming international organizations to tackle such matters.[9] The pressure to achieve collective ends in the context of interdependence influences the behaviors of states and consequent political outcomes. To liberals, international organizations, or more narrowly centered on the issues that concern us, humanitarian agencies, can make a difference. Despite their limited power relative to states, international organizations can set or shape agendas that facilitate cooperation.

Humanitarian Organizations and Critical Theory

Beyond these two common worldviews are others of a more recent vintage; their origins, if not their actual analyses, can be grouped under the rubric of "critical theory." Realism and liberalism accept the dominant role of states and political power as essentially expressed through material means—military or economic power. The critical theory lineage, by contrast, poses alternative ways of looking at the world. What makes theory "critical"?[10] It groups several worldviews that share two elementary characteristics: a commitment to changing the world, not merely describing or studying it, and a view of power as stemming from normative sources, that ideas can be transformative, including the power inherent in the application of analytical frameworks. In other words, critical theory appreciates not only that ideas have power, but, going deeper, recognizes that interpretive analyses contain agendas—sometimes obvious, sometimes hidden. Coined "critical theory" in the 1930s by German social scientists from the Frankfurt School, this approach to social phenomena has sprouted many offshoots that apply different influences on knowledge and discourse, and ultimately behavior and outcomes. With respect to humanitarianism, five schools from the critical tradition can offer insights into the workings of agencies and the understandings of aid workers: constructivism, Marxism, feminism, post-colonialism, and critical humanitarianism.

Constructivism arose in the late 1980s and early 1990s as a variant of post-modernism; it ascribes considerable power to the role of values, identity, and "intersubjective understandings" in constructing international politics. Although it is not a "theory" in the sense of providing a parsimonious model with explanations and predictions as do realism (which posits that a balance of power will invariably result from the self-help behavior of states) and liberalism (which foresees growing interdependence as inevitable in fostering peace), it is more of an "approach." Constructivism nevertheless highlights the inadequacies of these ostensibly more rigorous theories in deciphering power. The constructivist logic emphasizes that ideas or "norms" are powerful because they shape our comprehension of the world, link a set of ethics to our identities, and define what counts (or vital interests), which, in turn, affects behavior and outcomes. Aid agencies are the embodiment of an idea that humanity is one and that no one should suffer, which along with its organizational apparatuses can take on lives of their own. Thus, constructivism presents international organizations as having authority and autonomy—they are not purely part of or to service power, but are self-governing and able to establish norms and take independent action. Martha Finnemore and Kathryn Sikkink emphasize the influence that comes from being a "norm entrepreneur," who draws on what is considered legitimate to craft, disseminate, and instill new meanings.[11] For instance, if an agency dubs a forcibly displaced person who has crossed a border a "refugee," this label elicits specific obligations for states under IHL; or if humanitarians call an act of violence "genocide," this label demands a specific response. A constructivist would argue that the independent ability to classify is power.

To look deeper into constructivism, from where does the normative power of humanitarian organizations come? For actors in political systems of any kind, the main currency is authority—who determines what. The classic perspective comes from Max Weber, who recognized the rise of bureaucracies as a form of rationalized authority.[12] For humanitarian agencies there are three relevant sources of authority.[13] The first is the delegated variety that comes from states acknowledging or delegating authority to an international organization. The second is the moral authority resulting from a distilled collective agenda, one that resonates with ethical concerns. The third is expert authority, the product of access to recognized specialized knowledge. In this framework, authority becomes power. There may be specific power or a range of activities designated by states, but organizations may also establish productive power; that is, the ability to determine for themselves the activities in which they may engage.

A second aspect from the constructivist agenda is why humanitarian organizations with authority and power matter. Whether they do or do not, or whether they have an impact or not, is crucial. However, in studying organizations and how they evolve, there are problematic behaviors that may undermine goals. Several kinds of pathologies are notable.[14] The first is the irrationality of rationalization, when rules become ends in themselves. The second pathology is bureaucratic universalism, when technical knowledge becomes the standard template and other perspectives are dismissed. The third is the normalization of deviance, when agencies make exceptional activities commonplace, sometimes called "mission creep." The fourth is insulation, when departments or functions are compartmentalized and there is no feedback between branches. And the fifth pathology is cultural contestation, when there are debilitating disputes over values within organizations.

If organizations have authority and power, the content of their organizational culture is critical to understanding discourses, behaviors, and outcomes from the system. If the international humanitarian system indeed has power—constituting an "empire of humanity" as Michael Barnett contends[15]—then we must consider what propels and constrains it, and also what the consequences are.

Marxism dates to the nineteenth century and bears certain similarities to realism in that it sees the importance of material power (in this case capital), but it is focused not on states but on economic classes and the domination of the means of production. Additionally, given that relations of production can be changed through revolution and thereby transform sociopolitical life, it does not seek to operate within the existing material confines of international affairs, but rather to change them by disseminating new norms (a new consciousness that shakes workers out of their stupor of servitude and organize as a class). Marxism propounds that humanitarianism and the organizations that claim this ideology do not fundamentally address issues of inequality and, in fact, contribute to social control because humanitarianism eases the pressures of crises that stem from misappropriated capital accumulation.[16] Moreover, Marxists often claim that capitalism inspired and engendered a strange type of humanitarianism because the dislocations wrought by capitalism created conditions for the emergence of a humanitarianism as a secular means to stifle demands for changing economic systems, which produced the wealth that funded charitable organizations.[17] Critics such as Slavoj Žižek point to this disturbing, devious, and paradoxical dynamic.[18] Lastly, Marxism also views humanitarianism as creating opportunities for capitalist exploitation—what Naomi Klein has termed "disaster capitalism."[19] In short, Marxism contends that humanitarianism is comforting rhetoric and a meager material crutch that enables capitalism to flourish.

Feminism originates from similar principles that inform constructivism. It too presents a critique that there is only one type of rationality, but it then goes further to specify that such a narrow mindset is born from a "gendered" premise. Feminism contends that portrayals of international politics extol, reify, and embed the role of men and masculine values and overlook women and femininity; the result is a gender-based hierarchy, or patriarchy, which marginalizes those who do not fall into line with its values.[20] With respect to issues of war, women have been defined almost entirely as victims—as Jean Bethke Elshtain has pointed out, men are portrayed as "just warriors" and women as "beautiful souls" in need of protection.[21] Indeed, Helen Kinsella has argued that IHL mirrors this gendered notion in its definitions of combatant and noncombatant (or civilian).[22]

In addition, feminism maintains that despite the premise of protecting the vulnerable, the actual conduct of humanitarianism marginalizes women (and groups cast as minorities) because they focus on the emergency and the provision of aid to the exclusion of other needs. This perspective is myopic because different vulnerable groups are affected in different ways and magnitudes; hence, responses that do not acknowledge this reality often reinforce the dynamics of inequality.[23] Even when aid organizations identify gender issues and offer specialized programming, it is piecemeal and does not address underlying structural problems. Jennifer Hyndman and Malathi de Alwis observe, "Gender is treated as a portable tool of analysis and empowerment that can be carried around in the back pockets of both international humanitarian and development staff."[24] For instance, the result may be greater assistance to women, but it does not substantively increase the role of women in making policies. Feminist framings of humanitarianism have articulated the problem in terms of "gender" because the impact falls on men and women—for example, the targeting of men and boys for massacre in the ethnic cleansing campaign in Srebrenica.[25] Finally, feminism has examined the dominant narratives of humanitarian intervention to indicate that such operations are rooted in honoring the intervenor.[26] Thus, feminism views humanitarianism as fundamentally catering to gendered power, to validating and either reinforcing or restoring inequalities derived from socially constructed divisions.

Post-colonialism emerged after the accelerating decolonization of the 1950s–1970s and addressed the structural impediments that prevented the Third World, later called the Global South, from achieving development, prosperity, peace, democracy, and human rights. In this view, Western influences are central to understanding sociopolitical realities, including humanitarianism. This interpretation is underscored by the experiences of colonialism, which were suffused with humanitarian rhetoric. Self-righteous moralizing paired with grotesque levels of exploitation is illustrated by Rudyard Kipling's pronouncement of a "white man's burden" to civilize the non-West, or Cecil Rhodes's belief that colonialism is "philanthropy plus five percent." Post-colonialism, therefore, highlights how Western values and concerns structure the international humanitarian system, pushing an ideology that justifies and legitimates the underlying interests that foist inequalities based on a cultural divide with the West.

Critical humanitarianism has not been recognized as a distinct and formal school of thought and thus is not as clearly defined as previous theories and approaches—indeed, the phrase itself is our invention. As it infuses most pages in this book, we parse it at some length here. Our view emanates from sensibilities found throughout critical theory to identify and challenge power (especially that which is knowledge based, normative, and justice centered) and incorporates the self into the equation. As Michel Foucault has argued, "The real political task in a society such as ours is to criticize the working of institutions which appear to be both neutral and independent: to criticize them in such a manner that the political violence which has always exercised itself obscurely through them will be unmasked, so that one can fight them."[27] Critical humanitarianism is attuned to the exegeses of the exigencies of emergencies, particularly a rationalization of extreme measures in crises. In other words, the power of humanitarianism springs from its fit with the "state of exception"—Carl Schmitt's expression for a sovereign's license to alter politics[28]—both being empowered by it and, in turn, empowering it. Humanitarianism's role in world order is manifest in saving or abandoning populations. It can be understood as a form of what Foucault called "biopower," which signifies "that ancient right to take life or let live [that] was replaced by a power to foster life or disallow it to the point of death."[29] In this way, aid agencies exercise power at two levels: first and directly, to save those who need assistance; but second and more abstractly, to determine the standard for who should receive assistance and, thus, humanitarianism's meaning.[30] The act of saving aids but also establishes the norms of rights, relief, rescue, and refuge.

Critical humanitarianism is focused on the politics of ideas, identities, relationships, and knowledge related to the provision and protection of human welfare in emergencies; three characteristics are especially pertinent. First, it presents an analytical lens for identifying the divergences between the idea and perception of humanitarianism that builds its identity and reputation as a legitimate set of practices, on the one hand, and the state of the sector that constitutes its organizational and material underpinnings, on the other hand. The political and technical aspects of humanitarianism thus become clear. For example, Barbara Harrell-Bond asks the paramount question, "Can humanitarian work with refugees be humane?"[31] To expand on her analysis and borrow from other schools of thought, critical humanitarianism models a class system between the providers and recipients, and thus it is sensitive to issues of paternalism.[32] Humanitarianism in its purest form moderates the relationship between these classes based on an ethic of care by the former that is recognized by the latter—though other values may influence the providers.[33] However, instances that depart from this dynamic still may be "humanitarian" because the provider represents a larger structure beyond a specific recipient. For example, how should one interpret the logic that aid be withheld because it results in long-term dependency?

Critical humanitarianism points to the paradoxical and tragic notion that shielding the humanitarian mantle in this case has greater value to some than saving individuals.

Second, critical humanitarianism draws on concepts of "reflexivity" to uncover the image and responsibilities hidden under the humanitarian mantle to expose the interactions between normative and material dimensions. Humanitarianism's politics and operations are structured by views about its role—where humanitarianism is unpopular, agencies are attacked; where it is welcomed, agencies tend to perform better. In this way, humanitarian actors are reflexive—that is, they work to realize their values. And the sector too is reflexive in that its own behaviors, for better or worse, significantly define its viability and influence. Critical humanitarianism incorporates the concept of "ontological security" first coined by psychiatrist R. D. Laing. It reveals how individuals realize themselves through routine behavior, "a sense of his presence in the world as a real, alive, whole, and in a temporal sense, a continuous person."[34] Sociologist Anthony Giddens elaborates on "the confidence that most human beings have in the continuity of their self-identity and in the constancy of the surrounding social and material environments of action."[35] To a humanitarian agency or aid worker, identity must be proven (and re-proven) to themselves and to recipients for several reasons: to reassure everyone, to solidify the relationship to recipients, and to build confidence among donors and interlocutors. Critical humanitarianism examines how the pursuit of their roles and responsibilities influences behaviors and operations. The absence of agreement about genuine humanitarianism contributes to ontological insecurity.

Third, critical humanitarianism analyzes the politics of knowledge, or what might be called "epistemic power," by determining what type is produced, who produces it, how, and to what effect. Expertise and metrics are essential, and critical humanitarianism seeks to avoid reducing individuals to objects (statistics on a ledger, generic consumers of resources); also it is concerned with the power resulting from knowledge. The legitimacy of agencies and their personnel is predicated on technical (e.g., medical or logistical) proficiency. Their possession of specialized knowledge can itself tilt the subsequent production and use of knowledge. Bruno Latour's analysis of "imperial science" is instructive.[36] The act of knowing has led to "centers of calculation" based in the North, while those in the Global South must use those conceptual framings to communicate in the international arena. Much as the post-colonial concept of "orientalism" sees a structure of knowledge that subordinates Eastern civilization to the West,[37] there is an intellectual division of labor in the humanitarian field: agencies in the North construct knowledge of humanitarianism and crises, while counterparts in the Global South are objects of analysis, and even those with capacities to provide relief are often forced to work through the Western intellectual structure. Thus, humanitarianism is based on Western knowledge of what constitutes a crisis and how it is measured. A final criticism is that humanitarian knowledge can also be used as a form of surveillance. When an agency conducts assessments and uses them to raise resources, that same information can be applied to manage and repress populations. For example, an agency employs data about refugees to direct assistance, but a state or military may use that same data to position forces to contain and control people.

Increasingly a body of critical humanitarian thought emanates from radical critics, anthropologists, and aid workers. Views by scholars such as Giorgio Agamben and Didier Fassin are emblematic. Agamben contrasts *"zoe"* ("populations" who may become victims of humanitarian crises) with *"bios"* (who are "citizens of the world," including aid workers) to draw attention to unequal lives (those who can be sacrificed versus those who are sacred), and stresses that humanitarianism is picking up after war, not tackling its causes.[38] Fassin denominates the "politics of life," contending that all human lives are precious but profoundly unequal in how they are valued by international society.[39] He and others have noted a strange contradiction in risking lives (of aid workers) in order to carry out the practice of saving lives (of victims). Furthermore, he brings attention to a substantial inequality in the value of expatriate versus local aid workers. The former are routinely celebrated, better compensated, and often given greater tools to protect themselves in operating in dangerous environs; the latter are mostly overlooked and treated far less generously in terms of remuneration and protection. Fassin spotlights the dichotomy between victims whose stories are narrated by others, and those who narrate. In a critical theory tradition, despite the noble aims of humanitarians, their work should not be held out as exceptional if they display crass utilitarianism in which people are treated as objects (who are manipulated by others) rather than as subjects (who have value, agency, and humanity). Moreover, this viewpoint also suggests that in meeting the needs of recipients, the needs of providers may also be met. Thus, critical humanitarianism sheds light on the corrupt and corrupting influence of agencies that prioritize their own organizational interests and factor into maintaining a world order predicated on sacrifice for some but rewards for others.

Table 1.1 distills of the major features of the seven worldviews. Keep them in mind as the analysis unfolds.

Table 1.1. International Relations Theory and Humanitarianism

Issues	Realism (power)	Liberalism (order)	Constructivism (ideas)	Marxism (capital + class)	Feminism (gender)	Post-Colonialism (culture)	Critical Humanitarianism (humanity)
Organizing Principle of World Order	Anarchy	Interdependence	Identities, intersubjective understandings	Historical materialism → class systems	Patriarchy	Westernization	Human lives as precious (equal value of lives—equality in "politics of life")
Purpose of Humanitarianism	States: relative gains	Absolute gains, collective goods, shadow of the future	No prediction, content is social construction	Social control	Address violence (including domestic), exploitation, marginalization	Protect Western interests, propagate Western values	Save lives
Limits of Humanitarianism	Trust, lack of agreement on concept	Often few resources, limited power	No prediction	Does not address inequality (end class domination)	Emergency narrative obscures and trivializes inequality	Reiterates Western dominance	Lives risked to save lives, expatriates vs. nationals, narrators vs. narrated
Impacts of Humanitarianism	Tool of great powers → preserve power arrangements	Facilitate cooperation → power in agenda setting	Constructor of social world → norm entrepreneurs as autonomous agents	Facilitate and buffer capitalism and accumulation	Reiterates gender inequalities	Legitimates Western domination	Organizational interests achieved, maintain inequality of sacred vs. sacrificed

Just War

Humanitarian thought injects a specific morality into sociopolitical inter-actions surrounding emergencies, including armed conflicts. Throughout these pages, one configuration historically has provided core values about the causes of and conduct in warfare. Just war has been instrumental in establishing institutions and organizations and thus is worth a prefatory discussion. There is a bizarre and perhaps unexpected relationship among those who fight in war, especially modern wars. Although individuals rarely, if ever, know one another, they become enemies. The result is often two sets of strangers seeking to eliminate the other for reasons beyond their immediate interests or prior experiences. Indeed, some warriors or conscripts may have limited knowledge or sympathy for the fundamen-tal grievance that animates an armed conflict. In a weird symmetry, hu-manitarianism celebrates addressing the suffering of strangers while war emphasizes inflicting harm on strangers.

Aside from this sociological component to war, there is also a legal dimension. Large-scale armed conflict between states frequently has a specific niche in international relations—according to Quincy Wright, war is a "legal condition, which equally permits two or more groups to carry on a conflict by legal force."[40] Despite the aphorism put forth by Cicero, *"inter arma enim silent leges"* ("in time of war, the law is silent"),[41] "war" is legally sanctioned if it respects the template agreed by states and thus has a standing under international law. Underscoring this logic is a set of be-liefs (norms) about war, and specifically about what justifications can be used to go to war (recourse or *jus ad bellum*) and in how it can legitimately be fought (conduct or *jus in bello*). Together they constitute "international humanitarian law," also known as "the laws of war."

War is usually regarded and portrayed as being a chaotic activity where anything goes. Some subscribe to a notion of "absolute war," which holds that in the dangerous world of international politics, behaviors that may be morally repugnant are still legitimate—in fact, realism's perspective. This approach has a considerable history. Thucydides described the Pelo-ponnesian War (431–404 BCE) to illuminate debates about the recourse to war. Athens, the large imperial power of its time, was subjugating other city-states. In 428 BCE, Mytilene rebelled against Athens's domination and broke its treaty to ally with Athens. Within the Athenian assembly, the debate was how to respond: One side argued that all Mytilenes should be killed or enslaved because they were refusing to submit to Athens. An-other side contended that punishing them (a doctrine later called "collec-tive guilt") would not produce security or ensure that other treaties would be respected. This latter view eventually carried the day, and they spared the Mytilenes. However, in 416 BCE a similar situation arose when Athens sent emissaries to Melos to demand that they join the Athenian alliance or be destroyed. Despite the Melians' invocation of morality, neutrality, and precedent, Athens dismissed their claims and candidly explained that "the strong do as they will, the weak do as they must."[42] Thus, realism's worldview fuels a struggle for power, which leaves no room for mercy or justice. In terms of recourse to war, the pursuit of power is legitimate; in terms of conduct, any methods that achieve goals are acceptable.

By contrast, Michael Walzer and others subscribe to a different ethical tradition and believe that war should and can be moral.[43] The price of war is steep; both military and civilian casualties are likely. Moreover, informed democracies that value justice should consider both recourse and conduct in authorizing a use of force. In short, the victims of war are not only those killed or wounded on the battlefield but also those in whose name war is waged. Walzer and others do not oppose all wars, but they want states to decide with respect to moral criteria. Some have criticized him and his ideological compatriots for implying that the state should continue to have authority over these decisions—for instance, why does this power not reside within more cosmopolitan political entities such as the United Nations?

Either liberalism or constructivism may underpin "moral war," which stands in opposition to the "absolute war" framing espoused by realism. Liberalism is like realism in that states are the principal but not the only actors in international affairs; entities such as NGOs and IGOs also may have significance. However, liberalism differs considerably from realism in that its recognition of anarchy is complemented by interdependence that may alter state behavior. For liberals, there are collective goods that require cooperation because no one state can achieve them alone. In the humanitarian realm, a good illustration is the treatment of captured soldiers. A realist state might kill prisoners because providing for their welfare may be a drain on resources. But liberals suggest that there is a common goal for all militaries, even those fighting one another, and that is the preservation of soldiers' lives after they have been defeated. Once the war is over and the conflict resolved, soldiers can return home; the guarantee of protections provides an incentive for soldiers to obey the order to fight. Constructivists do not focus on the practical implications of humanitarianism; they are more concerned with its birth and power to bind. The constructivist agenda highlights that a social norm of humanitarianism was created and stands against realist notions and practice. Constructivism's "intersubjective understandings" about war can transcend and supersede inclinations toward pure power calculations.

The proponents of Marxism, post-colonialism, and critical humanitarianism have negative views about just war and humanitarianism. Marxism states that it is a ruse of capitalism to maintain the economic status quo; post-colonialism denounces its invocation as another form of cultural imperialism; critical humanitarianism argues that the privilege of protection is filtered through organizational interests that skew the allocation of resources yet paint a picture of saving the day.

We should be mindful of how opposing sides view justice in war and utilize a post-colonial lens to understand divergent forms of just war. Although Al Qaeda and other terrorists as well as Islamic-inspired rebel forces are routinely branded as outlaws, they often acknowledge legal principles and argue that their conduct reflects a "moral" code. Within Islam there is a distinction between *dar al-Islam* (the world of Islam) and *dar al-Harb* (the outside world). In the first instance war is rule governed and determined by a central authority, which includes such restraints as only attacking combatants but sparing civilians. In the second, more extreme measures may be taken, especially in defense of Islam. Al Qaeda's extremist form deviates from traditional Islam in that the Islamic domain exists where there is a Muslim majority or in lands that they once populated. In addition to expanding the scope of territory, it also classifies any who support states that may oppose Islam as "aggressors." As such, any and all means are acceptable. Yet, Al Qaeda's interpretations have been criticized, especially in targeting civilians. Although some say such debates have not fundamentally changed the practices of terrorists, others note that in 2006 the Taliban issued a "Book of Rules" that includes avoiding civilian casualties.[44]

In fact, there are some commonalities between Islamic and Western just war traditions. Both believe that interactions between states should be based on order and peace. The use of force should be tied to legitimate authorities and for the protection of the common good. And violence should only be directed at military targets, not civilians. Both sides have demonstrated a selective application of their own principles.

Early Thinkers and IHL

Just war has been proposed by a wide variety of authors from a wide variety of religious and cultural traditions, which have informed the formal establishment of IHL and humanitarian organizations. For the sake of brevity, we touch on philosophers from the Christian tradition that took up the issue beginning in antiquity, up through the medieval period, and on into the modern age.[45] However, it should be noted that the Christian version of just war comes with some important assumptions: the doctrine was in a framework of *Res publica Christiana* (a public community of Christendom), which was at least initially based on *auctoritas spiritualis* (spiritual authority). In essence the doctrine was formulated for Christians who fought other Christians; it often distinguished "wars" (between Christian kingdoms) and "feuds" (battles with Arabs, Turks, Jews, or those who did not acknowledge the authority of the Church).

Key early thinkers expounded on just war. St. Thomas Aquinas (1225–1274) built on the work of St. Augustine (354–430). In *Summa Theologiae: On War*, Aquinas looked at what are the justifiable reasons for going to war. Three conditions must be present: a proper sovereign authority must authorize war, it must right wrongs, and it must be of pure intent (that is, it must serve a public good as defined by the sovereign, not private interests). Conduct was not an issue for Aquinas.

Henry V (1387–1422, ascended the throne in 1413) was not a philosopher, but his monarchical decrees during the Hundred Years' War (1337–1453) were seminal in shaping our thinking about morality in war. During the battle of Agincourt (August 1415), depicted in Shakespeare's *Henry V*, British troops faced a crucial moral dilemma:[46] what to do with the large number of captured French soldiers. The British forces massacred many while offering several rationalizations. The first was "military necessity," because of the need to prevent any French soldier from returning to fight. Several chroniclers of this episode point out that new French forces were entering the battle; had they liberated the captured soldiers, then the British would certainly have been outnumbered. The second justification was "retribution" against French soldiers for having attacked British forces and noncombatants. During the battle of Agincourt, French troops discovered that British armed forces were miles ahead of their supply camp, which also contained treasure and plunder. The French attacked the camp and killed some of those managing the baggage of the British soldiers. The third was less of a stretch, the vengeful "slaughter" of unarmed, defeated soldiers.

Following this experience, Henry V became more explicit about demanding better conduct from his soldiers, which he drafted into his *Ordinances of War* (1419). Accordingly, Henry V should be recognized as facilitating two innovations: First, in differentiating between acts committed by soldiers in their official capacity who were subject to "command responsibility" (*respondere superior*) and private acts of soldiers subject to "individual responsibility" (*respondere non sovereign*). Second, prohibiting pillage and other violations of defeated parties.

Francisco de Vitoria (1485–1546) was a Spanish Dominican priest who wrote in the early sixteenth century a response to Spain's efforts to defeat the indigenous in the Americas that asked: Can Christians engage in war? Who can declare war? What causes motivate a just war? What measures can justifiably be used in war? In discussing the recourse to war, Vitoria contributed additional elements to the just war tradition. Only one side may be just; wars to stop threats are permissible. In regard to conduct, he is considered one of the earliest proponents of "proportionality," or using only the amount of force required to defeat the opponent and not inflict unnecessary suffering—including distinguishing between combatants and civilians. Which value is more important, military necessity or sparing innocents? Where is the line drawn between them? As the example of the battle of Agincourt and subsequent British behavior demonstrates, settling for the temporary neutralization of threats may have longer-term military implications.

Alberico Gentili (1552–1608) was an Italian jurist who argued that war could be just on both sides; usually both sides claim it. Furthermore, he also believed that quarter—or that surrendered or defeated parties are not killed—should be granted. He critiqued Henry V by saying that "I cannot praise the English who, in that famous battle in which they overthrew the power of France, having taken more prisoners than the number of their victorious army and fearing danger from them by night, set aside those of high rank and slew the rest. 'A hateful and inhuman deed,' says the historian, and the battle was not so bloody as the victory."

Finally, we mention Hugo Grotius (1583–1645), who is usually considered the "father of international law" because his 1625 book *De Jure Bellis ac Pacis* (*On the Laws of War and Peace*) is the first lengthy treatment of formal international rules established by states.[47] Grotius believed that individual rights arise from natural law but wanted to see them officially acknowledged by states; in that sense, he contributed to the secularization of just war. He argued that monarchs were to be accountable for their soldiers' actions (the doctrine of "command responsibility"): "Kings and public officials are liable for neglect if they do not employ the remedies which they can and ought to employ for the prevention of robbery and piracy." And, he opposed punishing entire populations for the acts of their armed forces (the doctrine of "collective responsibility"): "nature does not sanction retaliation except against those who have done wrong. It is not sufficient that by a sort of fiction the enemy may be conceived as forming a single body." Lastly, Grotius also advocated that the use of force should be "proportional."

Debates about Just War

The central debate is often couched as one between realism and just war but is substantially more complicated. Our previous brief discussion could be captured from the following quick survey of the central debates:

Jus ad Bellum—the recourse to war, or when is it just to go to war. Answers to five sets of questions permit a judgment about how just such a decision is to wage war:

- Is attacking another state inherently criminal? Are there justifiable reasons for attacking a state that has not attacked?
- What is the threshold of violence/casualties carried out before a state should engage in war? How big a massacre is required before a response is justified?
- When war is justified, who should fight it? Are some states more qualified to conduct just war than others?
- Aside from having a right to engage in just war, is there a duty? More justification in acting, is there an obligation?
- Can war solve human rights problems?

Jus in Bello—the conduct in war, or how to fight a just war. Answers to four sets of questions help make a judgment about the quality of behavior during war:

- What level of force is permitted?
- What restraints should there be on methods of war? Which weapon systems and tactics are permissible?
- Who is a legitimate target of war? Who should have immunity?
- How should captured forces be treated? Should those who have not abided by the laws of war be treated differently from those who do?

Several observations can help make sense of just war theory. The first concerns the changing focus of the theory itself. Whereas *jus ad bellum* was a common preoccupation in the ancient and medieval world, *jus in bello* has received more attention in modern history and especially in the contemporary period. More recent innovations that have yet to attain the same acceptance are *jus post bellum* (justice after war), which seeks to hold those who have violated the laws of war accountable, and *jus ex bellum* (justice to end wars), which evaluates methods to terminate armed hostilities.[48]

A second comment relates to the forms of *jus ad bellum*. Two reasons for war have come to be considered "just." A response to aggression (self-defense), particularly by the state that is being attacked, is legitimate. And attacking to punish those who violate international rules (wars of law enforcement) is also seen as permissible. Indeed, both are codified as acceptable in Chapter VII of the UN Charter.

The third observation relates to the increasing secularization in moving from customary to harder (or codified) forms of law. From ancient times to the nineteenth century, humanitarian norms emerged out of *Res publica Christiana*, underpinned by *auctoritas spiritualis*, which was consolidated into *jus gentium* (the law of nations). This is often termed a move from natural law (morally based) to positivist law (based on states).

The fourth remark regards the actors that facilitate humanitarian rule making. "Heralds" were predecessors of modern humanitarians, experts in the customs of war (which were embedded as part of chivalry) who carried messages between sides and arranged truces. Their role was to bring a form of order that reflected moral rules. They also dressed distinctly to mark their status as noncombatants.

A final observation concerns the acceptance of IHL itself, which reflects the impact on the specific behavior of specific armed belligerents in specific wars. Each type of armed actor weighs the advantages and disadvantages of subscribing to the laws of war. The advantages are limits to destruction beyond necessary objectives, protections for victims of war, spared neutral parties, reciprocation in treatment of captured soldiers, legitimacy for recognized use of force, more disciplined military, and improved chances for postwar reconciliation. The disadvantages of the laws of war are that they are still subject to interpretation, have limited practical impact as militaries may ignore them, are an acknowledgement of international humanitarian rights used as a propaganda tool, and sanitize war in way that may increase the willingness to use force. As is clear in later chapters, IHL imposes obligations on states, but many armed actors in contemporary conflicts are not states—from militias to warlords, from terrorists to private military contractors. They do not necessarily consider themselves bound by this body of law.

Conclusion: The Meaning and Place of Humanitarianism

A single chapter is hardly an adequate basis for definitive conclusions about the meaning and place of humanitarianism in the contemporary world. The purpose here was to emphasize not only a wide spectrum of interpretations of humanitarianism but also the different values within them. Debates over humanitarianism—what it means, what it can accomplish, what its effects are—in fact are debates about what agendas and ideologies have power. Conventional IR theory has basically dismissed humanitarianism as largely an outcome to serve power and provide cosmetic comfort to gloss over its harsh realities. Critical theory has a variety of approaches that shatter that premise, with constructivism taking up independent organizations as challenges, Marxism emphasizing class relations, feminism elucidating the position of women and other marginalized actors, and post-colonialism trumpeting the domineering influence of the West. Critical humanitarianism offers another critique by centering on the relationship between aid provider and recipients—it puts people first.

Humanitarianism was born as a moral impulse, but its political implications require interpretive frameworks and conceptual tools that go
beyond a mere scrutiny of ethics. The diagnostic tools in this chapter can
help guide the review of history and the contemporary period, as well as
help situate why various worldviews matter in determining the meaning
and significance of humanitarianism. The next chapter locates it in the
context of other Enlightenment-inspired social movements and political
projects to improve human welfare.

2

Humanitarian Genesis
and Gravity

Solferino to Biafra and African Famines

Zouave ambulance crew demonstrating removal of wounded soldiers from the field (circa 1860–1865).

In This Chapter

- The Crystallization of Modern Humanitarianism
- The Birth of IHL and the ICRC
- Two World Wars and Humanitarian Aftermaths
- New Actors and Tools Early in the Cold War
- New Humanitarian Wrinkles Later in the Cold War
- Conclusion: The International Humanitarian System in Historical Perspective

---

Having laid the foundations with a discussion of major schools of thought used to interpret humanitarianism, we turn to the genesis of the phenomenon as an organized practice in the late nineteenth century and trace its expansive evolution through the Cold War. Specifically, we examine how behaviors and outcomes in the humanitarian universe correspond to the gravitational pull exerted by war and politics.

The main questions are: What is the origin of humanitarianism? Why and how did humanitarian ethics take organizational form? What is humanitarianism's meaning as reflected in the mission statements and work of aid agencies? How has humanitarianism evolved from its institutional foundations in the nineteenth century through the end of the Cold War in the late 1980s? How can we explain the founding and unfolding of organized humanitarianism?

The Crystallization of Modern Humanitarianism

Although Western societies were the first to establish formal humanitarian organizations, the values that inform the practice of humanitarianism are global, as can be gleaned from the summary of traditions in box 2.1. Many and various traditions since time immemorial have conceived and nourished humanitarian thought, including some version of the "Good Samaritan" (a person who gives to those in distress) as a valued role in society and often along with the sentiment of *inter arma caritas*, or charity in war. However, the establishment of organizations that became the cornerstone of the contemporary international humanitarian system are a product of Enlightenment beliefs in the eighteenth and nineteenth centuries. Indeed, the vocabulary of "humanitarianism" grew directly from them. For example, Emmerich de Vattel (1714–1767), a Swiss lawyer, claimed that nations were bound by *"offices d'humanité"* (humanitarian obligations): "If a nation is visited with famine, all those who have provisions enough to spare should come to its assistance. . . . Help in such an extremity is so much in accord with the dictates of humanity that no civilized

BOX 2.1
Religious Traditions of Humanitarianism

No culture has a monopoly on concern for the welfare of others. In fact, many different religions and cultures have articulated and held some form of humanitarian belief:[*]

- Christianity: The value of compassion includes a duty to strangers. Moreover, according to Matthew 25:10, Jesus said, "what you do to the least among you, you do to me," thereby emphasizing that the underprivileged are especially worthy of care.[†] Furthermore, Evangelical Christians (out of Protestantism) believe that doing good deeds fosters heaven on earth.
- Islam: One of the pillars of Islam is "*zakat*," volunteering public service, which builds solidarity in a community.[‡]
- Arab: Although not all Arabs are Muslim and not all Muslims are Arab, there is considerable overlap between Arab and Islamic traditions. In Arab culture, the key concept is "*insānīya*," or charitable work.[§] The term became popular in the 1960s but originates in the *Quran*, 23:51 and 23:52, which uses "*Al-wehda al-insānīya*" to reference humanity as a single race.
- Judaism: Central to Jewish identity is the idea of "*tzadakah*," or fixing the world.[¶]
- Confucian: Here the concept is couched as "*rendao zhuyi*," which is described in the *Book of Rites* (part of the Five Classics), written before 300 BCE.[**] *Rendao*, the characteristics of humanity, are comprised of benevolence (*ren*), righteousness (*yi*), propriety (*li*), and knowledge (*zhi*). Further, the "Mandate of Heaven" charged leadership with responsibility in alleviating suffering.
- Buddhism: This tradition connects to Confucian thought in many ways, but it offers its own vocabulary depicting humanitarian values, such as "*shan*" (charity, benevolence) and "*shanju*" (good deeds).
- Hinduism: This tradition also embraces a humanitarian ethic as seen in the classic collection of Hindu texts known as the *Upanishads* (likely from the second-to-seventh-century BCE period) which states, "wisdom means a life of selfless sacrifice," because we must "realize that all life is one."[††]
- Bahai: This faith from nineteenth-century Persia sees and seeks a unity of religions and humanity.

---

[*]Elizabeth Ferris, "Faith and Humanitarianism: It's Complicated." *Journal of Refugee Studies* 24, no. 3 (2011): 606–25.

[†]Also see Norman Fiering, "Irresistible Compassion: An Aspect of Eighteenth Century Sympathy and Humanitarianism," *Journal of the History of Ideas* 37, no. 3 (1976): 195–218.

[‡]Wael Hallaq, *Sharī'a: Theory, Practice, Transformations* (Cambridge: Cambridge University Press, 2009), 230–34.

[§]Jasmine Moussa, *Ancient Origins, Modern Actors: Defining Arabic Meanings of Humanitarianism*, HPG Working Paper (London: Humanitarian Policy Group, Overseas Development Institute, 2014).

[¶]Susan R. Holman, "Orthodox Humanitarianisms: Patristic Foundations," *Review of Faith & International Affairs* 14, no. 1 (2016): 26–33.

[**]Confucius, et. al., *The Book of Rites*, Dai Sheng, ed., James Legge, trans. (Beijing: Intercultural Press, 2013).

[††]*The Upanishads*, Juan Mascaró, trans. (London: Penguin, 1965). Also, see Ephraim Isaac, "Humanitarianism across Religions and Cultures," in *Humanitarianism Across Borders: Sustaining Civilians in Times of War*, ed. Thomas G. Weiss and Larry Minear (Boulder, Colo.: Lynne Rienner, 1993), 13–22.

nation could together fail to respond," and "mutual assistance and duties which men owe one another as social beings who must help each other for their self-preservation and happiness and in order to live according to their nature."[1] Another illustration is that of French philosopher Jean-Jacques Rousseau (1712–1778) who posited in *The Social Contract* (1762) that soldiers who were no longer active instruments of the state (captured, wounded, or sick) reverted to the status of individuals with human rights of protection.[2] In this same period, a major natural disaster, the 1755 earthquake, leveled Lisbon (at the time Europe's fourth-largest city) and galvanized the first pan-European relief operation. Voltaire (1694–1778), a career pessimist, was so inspired by the response that he wrote *Poème sur le désastre de Lisbonne,* a moving depiction of hope about the future. In short, this era gave birth to the term "humanitarian."[3]

The appellation first appeared in France in the late 1760s (*humanisme*) and referred to a feeling of love for humanity. It quickly spread across the continent—indeed, the normative artifice spread long before the organizational architecture. In religious circles, the model of benevolent behavior gained prominence and fueled another generation of missionary activity beginning in the late eighteenth century.[4] Hannah Arendt claimed that Europe at that time had a "passion for compassion," so much so that the dangers of a politics of pity threatened to incite interventions that would alter power relations.[5]

"Humanitarianism" thus had entered the language and taken on the connotation of a religion—that is, concern for all humankind was the center of focus.[6] Early Socialist writers such as Auguste Comte (1798–1857) commented on this movement; he referred to a "humanitarian religion" to better social conditions and thereby enable emotional and intellectual development that builds cooperation and altruism. This mode of thinking inspired the establishment of the Humanitarian League in the 1890s "to enforce the principles that it is iniquitous to inflict avoidable suffering on any sentient being," and "to protect not only against the cruelties inflicted by men on men, in the name of law, authority, and conventional usage but also, in accordance with the same sentiment of humanity against the wanton ill-treatment of the lower animals."[7]

However, at the time humanitarianism was still cast rather broadly and included goals ranging from improving conditions of labor, the poor, children, and animals. The term was invoked by those who opposed slavery and alcohol as well as advocates for prison reform and better sanitation.[8] These efforts were dedicated to addressing suffering or bettering humanity on some level, but the appropriate means and the end goals were debated. In fact, part of the humanitarian lineage stems from the practice of colonialism whereby the terrible effects were mildly moderated by the provision of assistance but were also conjoined with a righteous proselytizing. Nineteenth-century colonialism and its "White Man's Burden" or *"mission civilisatrice"* continually expanded in imperial domains. Some actors who identified their efforts as "humanitarian" spoke of the need to ensure that peoples deemed less worthy did not reproduce with those viewed as superior—in short, eugenics served humanitarian aims. As we see later, anyone familiar with the sins of colonialism can be forgiven for not automatically approving an activity simply because it is preceded by the "H" adjective.

Humanitarianism was born out of a sentiment that humankind would only advance through a reconceptualization of social relations. Aside from the message of unity, this set of beliefs also underpinned a modern sensibility of agency. Not only was compassion a reflection of a shared understanding that fundamentally all human beings were one common people, but they were connected and possessed an obligation and ability to act because there was no higher power or authority to address suffering, let alone halt mass atrocities. In the language of sociologist Max Weber, a modern "ethic of responsibility" emerged that trumped a traditional and religious "ethic of ultimate ends."[9] For example, in writing on the 1755 earthquake, Rousseau contended that some victims died of poor construction (i.e., negligence), and that the community had the duty to minimize such consequences; his argument preceded modern notions of responsibility on two levels, in causing disasters and in responding to them. The movement from a purely charity-based approach (giving because it is good) to responsibility (giving because we are somehow complicit) was a core normative development that nourished the establishment of humanitarian organizations.

The Birth of IHL and the ICRC

The legal basis of the humanitarian sector and its early operational agencies emerged in the nineteenth century, a period of progress in the sciences and international order. Innovations in medicine made treating a greater number and types of injuries possible and therefore enabled the realization of a relief-based international humanitarian system. For instance, Florence Nightingale (1820–1910), an early figure in the humanitarian movement who had witnessed the consequences of armed conflict in a hospital nursing soldiers who had fought in the Crimean War (1854–1856), was among the first to recognize the precarious sanitary conditions in medical facilities. Her campaign to create cleaner hospitals and protocols for stemming the spread of diseases and infections saved many lives.

Turning toward legal frameworks that regulate the conduct of war and thereby define the place and rights of humanitarian actors, among the earliest documents that have informed modern sensibilities appeared during the US Civil War (1861–1865). At the request of Abraham Lincoln, Francis Lieber compiled his *Instructions for the Government of Armies of the United States in the Field, General Order No. 100*. It prescribed that violence should be "directed toward the enemy's forces and is not used to cause purposeless, unnecessary human misery and physical destruction."[10] The Lieber Code was the first legal embedding of the distinction between civilians (or noncombatants) and combatants. These guidelines became a model for other major national militaries (the Netherlands, France, Serbia, Spain, Portugal, and Italy) over the next few decades. Nevertheless, critics philosophically opposed any such agreements. Prussia's military commander, General von Moltke, later denounced the 1880 Declaration of St. Petersburg, which codified rules of war, in the following way: "The greatest kindness in war is to bring it to a speedy conclusion."[11] From the outset of organized humanitarianism, a central critique has regarded it as a numbing distraction to addressing the political problems driving armed conflicts.

Aside from legal instruments and formal codes of military conduct that coalesced in the late nineteenth and early twentieth centuries,[12] the watershed episode of humanitarian action—the delivery of relief assistance to victims of war—followed the Battle of Solferino (June 24, 1859), a bloody skirmish fought between France and the Austro-Hungarian Empire over Italian independence. Jean-Henri Dunant (1828–1910) was a Swiss businessman who, after witnessing the grisly scene of soldiers abandoned where they had been wounded with no medical care available, had an epiphany.[13] His impulse to save lives and transcend political identities was recorded in his 1862 *Memory of Solferino*:

> The moral sense of the importance of human life; the human desire to lighten a little the torments of these poor wretches, or restore their shattered courage; the furious and relentless activity which a man summons up at such moments: all these combine to create a kind of energy which gives on a positive craving to relieve as many as one can. . . .
>
> Seeing that I made no distinction between nationalities, following my example, showing the same kindness to all these men whose origins were so different, and all of whom were foreigners to them. "*Tutti Fratelli*" [all are brothers], they repeated feelingly.[14]

Consequently, he formed a medical corps neither bound by national interests nor guided by religious ties. In February 1863, the Geneva Society of Public Utility created a permanent subcommittee of Dunant and four other humanitarians—Gustave Moynier, a financier; Theodore Maunoir and Louis Appia, doctors; and Guilliame Henri Dufour, a general—which was renamed the International Committee for Aid to

Wounded in Situations of War. The committee brought together states to sign an agreement in 1864, the Convention for Better Conditions for Wounded Soldiers. Twelve states signed (France was the first to ratify), and four others soon agreed to join (the United States signed in 1868) this first "Geneva Convention."

However, not all humanitarians approved. Florence Nightingale, who had been an inspiration in the creation of an organization to aid wounded soldiers, was a fervent critic. For one thing, she did not believe that she and others would be able to function in war zones because politics would overwhelm the endeavor.[15] Moreover, she contended that "such a society would take upon itself duties which ought to be performed by the government of each country and so would relieve them of responsibilities which really belong to them and which only they can properly discharge and being relieved of which would make war more easy."[16] General Dufour worried similarly but reasoned that improvements in conditions were preferable to none.

The agreement featured many of the principles of just conduct (*jus in bello*), but it also established the basis for a new organization to bring aid to wounded and captured soldiers. The committee's first major operation was during the Franco-Prussian War (1870–1871), the earliest instance in which both sides had Red Cross Societies. By 1875 the organization's ubiquitous emblem of an inversely colored Swiss flag (which has a white cross on a red background) led to the "Red Cross" being added to its name. During the Russo-Turkish War (1877–1878), a Muslim Turkish aid society formed an equivalent organization albeit with a more Islamic-friendly name and symbol, "Red Crescent." This conflict was also the first case of the Red Cross providing relief to noncombatants (though it was not legally mandated to do so). The "Red Cross and Red Crescent" movement also took root in the United States when Clara Barton (1821–1912), a nurse during the US Civil War, established an affiliate in 1881. The ambition of the organization also grew in this formative period, and in 1884, at the Third International Red Cross Conference, the ICRC decided to conduct humanitarian relief work during peacetime as well as wars.

The organizational structure of the movement calls for the development of national Red Cross and Red Crescent societies to focus on wounded nationals.[17] In addition to national societies in France or Sweden, there also was a role for coordinating bodies of many of these national societies: the International Committee of the Red Cross (ICRC)—which is the main one—and the International Federation of the Red Cross and Red Crescent Societies (IFRC) (which is a looser yet wider confederation of agencies).

In 1965, Jean Pictet defined the ICRC's seven defining principles: humanity (the priority of human welfare); neutrality (do not takes sides in conflict); impartiality (treat victims equally); independence (operate separate from the military or governments); voluntary service (workers donate labor); unity (work together to achieve goals); and universality (willingness to work wherever there is need).[18] The first four are the core. Humanity is uncontested whereas the other three desiderata are more debatable—and they certainly are debated. Neutrality demands that organizations refrain from taking part in hostilities or any action that either benefits or disadvantages belligerents. Impartiality requires that assistance be based on need and not discriminate based on nationality, race, religion, gender, or political affiliation. Independence necessitates that assistance not be connected to any party with a stake in a war's outcome.

These principles reflect decades of practical experience. Although many observers now treat them as beyond question—sacrosanct absolutes and the essence of humanitarian culture—they began as pragmatic judgments about what worked best in interstate conflicts and natural disasters. If aid agencies are perceived by combatants as beholden to donors or allied with the opposing side or with vested interests in the outcome, their access may be limited and they may even become targets of attacks. If these principles are religiously respected, so the argument goes, both aid workers and recipients benefit.

The ICRC's functions are to provide victims with direct relief (food, blankets, medical services, shelter) in emergencies. The ICRC also monitors the treatment of detained prisoners of war (POWs) as well as political prisoners. Lastly, the ICRC prepares drafts of conventions, which if states legally commit to them, become IHL. Then the ICRC plays a role disseminating them and monitoring compliance. Over the years since the first 1864 Geneva Convention, states have agreed to others in 1906, 1929, and 1949, with additional protocols added in 1977 and 2005.

Although the ICRC is the architect of IHL, it is not the sole wellspring. The Hague produces conventions concentrating on rules for soldiers. The First Hague Conference in 1899 had twenty-six states pass conventions and declarations on the need to settle disputes peacefully and on the customs of land and maritime warfare, including restrictions on certain weapon systems such as asphyxiating gases. Other Hague Conventions were passed in 1906, 1907, and 1909.

Two World Wars and Humanitarian Aftermaths

The first armed conflicts confronted by the international humanitarian system in the late nineteenth century had serious casualties and fatalities, but World War I (WWI, 1914–1918) and World War II (WWII, 1939–1945) were of a far greater magnitude because they were waged by more powerful and better equipped states. With increasingly lethal firepower and growing militaries, the results were previously unimaginable levels of violence that included mass atrocities, burgeoning displacement, and overwhelming numbers needing assistance. The aftermaths of these conflicts also demonstrated divisions over post-conflict humanitarian issues, such as the adjudication of war crimes and resettlement of refugees.

In WWI, 8 million soldiers and 8.3 million civilians perished, and between 7.7 million and 9.5 million were displaced.[19] During this conflict the ICRC expanded from its initial purpose of relief and added aid to detainees to its purview. The organization's work in WWI raised its profile—in 1917 the ICRC received the Nobel Peace Prize—and its performance heightened the legitimacy of its norms.

Besides the world wars, other humanitarian disasters erupted. From 1915 to 1917 the Ottoman Empire committed genocide against Armenians (the *Aghet*), with between 800,000 and 1.5 million deaths.[20] In Ukraine in the early 1930s, the Soviet government intentionally starved millions to control the population (the *Holodomor*).[21] These crises challenged humanitarians because they exhibited many of the worst aspects of armed conflicts but were not technically wars and therefore did not fall under the jurisdiction of war-relieving agencies. WWI's destructiveness also crippled food production in Western and Central Europe with farmers unable to tend to crops during hostilities or to transport production with a greatly damaged infrastructure. Under the leadership of Herbert Hoover, the Commission for the Relief of Belgium (CRB) was formed and assisted French and Belgian populations. Although it mostly ignored Germans, Hoover made the case to both Germany and Britain that aid was neutral and independent, thus contributing to deepening the norm of how humanitarianism should operate. Later the CRB became the American Relief Administration (ARA), delivering aid in Ukraine during the later phases of the Russian Revolution. Indeed, many new sorts of specialized humanitarian organizations responded. In 1919, Dorothy Buxton and Eglantyne Jebb founded Save the Children to address the plight of children caught up in war, not just those of allies but also of Germany. In this period, there was even a flurry of activity on children's issues—the September 1923 "Declaration of Geneva" on child rights and in 1924 the League of Nations established the Child Welfare Committee.

In addition to agencies offering emergency assistance, others concentrated on such refugee services as relocation and legal status. Following WWI, one major problem was that many forcibly displaced populations were in new countries following the breakup of several empires. The League of Nations authorized Fritdjof Nansen as high commissioner for Russian refugees (1920–1923) to help with resettlement. His vision for creating new documentation for travel—called "Nansen passports"—facilitated the movement and resettlement of many refugees after the collapse of the Russian, Austro-Hungarian, and Ottoman empires. Nansen would accept the newly created post of high commissioner for refugees;

shortly thereafter he was recognized for his accomplishments with the 1922 Nobel Peace Prize. In Central Europe in 1933, refugee Albert Einstein founded the International Rescue Committee to give assistance to those fleeing the rise of fascism. Between the wars, additional international agreements banned or regulated specific weapons systems, and supposedly outlawed war itself.[22]

WWII—with approximately 23 million soldiers and 57 million civilians killed (including the 6 million Jewish and other minorities in the Holocaust), and between 40 million and 55 million uprooted[23]—showed not only that new laws and agencies did not stop the horrors of war, but also that the international humanitarian system could be manipulated. The ICRC's behavior in WWII has been subject to much debate: First, it was silent on Italy's invasion of Ethiopia in 1935, and many of its members supported fascist parties (against Bolshevism). Second, as the war expanded with growing evidence of Nazi atrocities, the ICRC continued to maintain a principle of neutrality toward the Third Reich and remained silent so as to maintain some access to Allied POWs. As a 1948 booklet explained:

> Protest? The International Committee did protest—to the responsible authorities. . . . A whole department of the Committee's work was to make one long series of protests: countless improvements in the [concentration] camps, for example, were due to steps of this kind. . . . Every man to his job, every man to his vocation. That of the Red Cross is to nurse the wounded where it can with the means at its disposal. For the Committee to protest publicly would have been not only to outstep its functions, but also to lose thereby all chance of pursuing them, by creating an immediate breach with the government concerned.[24]

The ICRC held firm to its practice of neutrality, arguing that political denunciations would only jeopardize their access and the aid pipeline, and that any public pronouncement would not in any way change Nazi behavior. Others lamented that there had been an "Aryanization" of German and Polish Red Cross societies; and after the invasion of France, Germany had co-opted much of the Red Cross movement. Furthermore, many have contended that by not speaking out, the ICRC essentially provided legitimacy for the Third Reich.

There were also new humanitarian organizations established in this period. For example, following the model of the ARA after WWI, the Cooperative for American Remittance to Europe (which later became the Cooperative for Assistance and Relief Everywhere, or CARE) was founded in the 1940s. Religious-based agencies were also set up, such as Catholic Relief Services (CRS) and Lutheran World Relief (LWR). Another notable organization arose as a consequence of a famine in Greece after Germany had conquered the country. The British government hoped that a blockade of Greece would impel Germany to withdraw, but others in

Britain were concerned about the severity of the famine—from November 1941 to February 1942, between 100,000 to 250,000 died in Athens from hunger (more than would die in the firebombing of Dresden). Quakers established the Oxford Committee for Famine Relief (it later adopted the name Oxfam), which sent aid to all parties because they believed that all victims deserved assistance.

The United Nations Relief and Rehabilitation Administration (UNRRA) was the first UN agency that operated between 1943 and 1947. The mandate focused on aid to civilian nationals and displaced people in countries liberated by the Allies; like its predecessor, it mostly ignored Germany and instead furthered the political agendas of the Allies. The commitment to defeating fascism was displayed not only with Allied military muscle but also evident in humanitarian operations as well as in other initiatives in other fields ranging from education to trade, from agriculture to aviation.[25] UNRRA's quintessentially liberal work was a realist necessity, not optional window dressing. It remains the world's largest and most integrated post-conflict aid and reconstruction body, whose budget was based on contributions of 1 percent of member states' gross domestic products during and immediately following the war; it supported activities from China to Belarus, which ranged from self-managing refugee camps to replacing industrial machinery. Nonetheless, UNRRA's pioneering multilateral efforts are all but invisible in scholarship,[26] eclipsed by the bilateral Marshall Plan.

Finally, WWII reopened debates about adjudication of crimes and punishment for those who violated the laws of war. As we see later, earlier precedents were modest with only brief references to compensation and jurisdiction in national penal legislation. However, the intensity of WWII and the scope of atrocities sparked the creation of international war crimes tribunals. Although the Soviet Union called for extensive executions (Stalin had proposed shooting 50,000 to 100,000 German officers), others, most vocally the British, pleaded for trials. The latter carried the day, as US prosecutor Robert Jackson (Supreme Court justice and former attorney general and solicitor general) argued in his opening statement: "That four great nations, flushed with victory and stung with injury, stay the hand of vengeance and voluntarily submit their captive enemies to the judgment of the law is one of the most significant tributes that Power has ever paid to Reason."[27] In August 1945, the London Agreement for the Prosecution and Punishment of the Major Criminals of the European Axis defined three offenses: crimes against the peace (planning aggression or atrocities); war crimes (murder, ill treatment, slave labor, deportation, plunder, and unnecessary levels of violence); and crimes against humanity (extermination or persecution based on political, racial, or religious grounds).

The International Military Tribunal at Nuremberg (IMT, 1945–1946) had universal jurisdiction—regardless of where the crime was committed, the offender could be held accountable—and was grounded in individual responsibility. On October 1, 1946, twenty-two defendants received verdicts: twelve death penalties by hanging; seven ten-years-to-life sentences; and three acquittals. Similarly, Japanese wartime atrocities were judged by the International Military Tribunal for the Far East (IMTFE, 1946–1948). Of the twenty-eight defendants, two died during the trial, one was found mentally incompetent, and twenty-five were found guilty (seven executed, eighteen sent to prison).

These trials and their outcomes have been criticized on numerous grounds, which figure in chapter 5.

New Actors and Tools Early in the Cold War

After WWII and the Nuremberg and Tokyo tribunals, new actors and tools appeared with ramifications for humanitarians. Soon after the defeat of the Axis powers, rivalries among the Allies morphed into the Cold War between the West under US leadership and the East bloc anchored by the Union of Soviet Socialist Republics (USSR). Tensions were particularly high over the partition of Germany. On June 24, 1948, the USSR blockaded Berlin in an attempt to starve the residents of the city's Western sectors and compel the Allies to withdraw. However, the Allies were determined to maintain the viability of West Berlin although it was geographically inside of East Germany and under occupation. US, UK, and French air forces commenced a massive airlift on June 25. This military-led relief operation, which had the benefit of fielding logistic capabilities far beyond those of humanitarian agencies, lasted until May 12, 1949, when the Soviet Union relented and allowed supplies to flow via the previously agreed land corridors. This experience was militarized humanitarian action—with the personnel and equipment of national militaries involved in the delivery of aid—which contrasted starkly with the neutrality and independence principles under which the ICRC had operated. Indeed, this earlier Allied occupation of Germany and Japan set the historical precedents for what later would be called "military humanitarianism."[28]

Other notable humanitarian operations during the Cold War were fielded by the United Nations. Although the primary focus of these undertakings was to preserve and maintain international peace and security, they also influenced humanitarian conditions. In fact, the regulations for going to war, including self-defense provisions, found in the UN Charter (Articles 42, 43, and 51) embodied just war principles. The world organization also invented peacekeeping, which had important effects on humanitarianism worldwide in terms of security and access.[29]

Moreover, other agencies within the UN system had specific humanitarian mandates. Key entities include the Office of the UN High Commissioner for Refugees (UNHCR, established in 1951 after having been preceded by UNRRA and the interim International Refugee Organization, IRO); UNICEF, also founded in 1951 when the "E" was dropped from its original name of the UN International Children's Emergency Fund); and the World Food Programme (WFP, founded in 1961), which focused on food aid and logistics.[30]

Several significant treaties arose from WWII's ashes. The UN Convention on the Prevention and Punishment of the Crime of Genocide was signed on December 9, 1948. It stated that it was a crime whether committed in time of war or peace and that not only was the act of genocide itself punishable but also conspiracies, incitements, and complicit behavior. The Genocide Convention set a legal standard; those who commit the act are to face justice, which is to be pursued by states party to the convention. On December 10, 1948, the Universal Declaration on Human Rights pushed forward the broader agenda of human rights with implications for humanitarian conditions as we see later. Moreover, from late April to mid-August 1949, international humanitarian law experts and national delegates negotiated another round of the crucial Geneva Conventions (see box 2.2) with the intention of elaborating on and offering greater clarity to the laws of war.[31]

BOX 2.2
The 1949 Geneva Conventions

The four components of the 1949 Geneva Conventions are the most frequently cited provisions of IHL:

I. Wounded and sick on land: Reiterated previous restrictions on attacking injured soldiers but included additional ones that granted greater protections for medical personnel captured by enemy forces.

II. Wounded and sick at sea: Attempts to strengthen protections for hospital ships, particularly against submarine warfare.

III. Prisoners of War: Replaces previous, inadequate regulations. It addresses situations of detainees and POWs that arose during WWII, such as granting POW status to "partisans" (i.e., irregular forces that nonetheless obeyed laws of war) and gives other protections to POWs.

IV. Civilians: The pioneering component of these conventions consists of the first agreement devoted exclusively to the protection of civilians caught in wars. It also establishes responsibilities for occupying powers regarding food supplies, public health, forced labor, and penal sanctions.

At present, 196 states have signed and ratified the Geneva Conventions—that is, three more are state parties than are UN members. The Geneva Conventions apply to both international and civil wars, but the specific provisions do not officially apply to armed nonstate belligerents. The Geneva Conventions and Additional Protocols criminalize certain egregious forms of violence and mistreatment. They also define "humanitarian" in a particular way—all four conventions refer to an "impartial" element of humanitarian action and call for no discrimination in treating victims.

New Humanitarian Wrinkles Later in the Cold War

The post-WWII international humanitarian system was shaped by how the war was fought in Europe and East Asia and thus geared primarily to the challenges of interstate conflict and transnational atrocities. In many ways, the Korean War (1950–1953) fits this template. However, a swelling number of conflicts were civil wars and often did not correspond to the type of crises for which the system had been engineered. To address these distinctly different challenges, new wrinkles were added.

It is worth reflecting about the UNHCR because the refugee regime during and immediately after WWII was looked upon as ineffective for two reasons. First, it clashed with UNRRA policy on repatriating the displaced. Second, the USSR withdrew from the IRO in protest because of what it saw as American domination—the USSR wanted its refugees returned, but the West wanted to allow them to remain where they had fled. Negotiations for a new organization nonetheless proceeded and by 1951 a compromise was reached whereby those displaced in Europe would receive relief aid and legal services to facilitate resettlement in the country that was hosting them or a third country, or return them to their country of origin. However, refugees could not be forced to return to their countries of origin against their will—the 1951 convention embedded the principle of *non-refoulement*. The politics of forced returns were one challenge; in addition, the underlying conception of the problem as short term and geographically limited was off target because displaced populations outside of Europe faced similar needs. The result was an expanded refugee regime with the 1967 Protocol Relating to the Status of Refugees that made UNHCR's jurisdiction universal and without time limits. More about the development and performance of the regime is in chapter 8.

Whereas the Battle of Solferino planted the seeds for the International Red Cross and Red Crescent family of organizations, perhaps the most crucial point of departure for a new breed of humanitarianism was the Nigerian Civil War (1967–1970)—such internal armed conflicts with obstinate central governments unwilling to allow humanitarian access foreshadowed the "new wars" of the 1990s and their dire humanitarian challenges. When the Ibo ethnic minority attempted to carve out a new country, Biafra, and seceded, the central government attacked and exercised the prerogative of sovereignty to refuse humanitarian agencies access, consequently inducing a famine. UN organizations are supposed to respect sovereignty, especially UNHCR and steered clear of the conflict. Other agencies, such as Oxfam and CRS, saw an opportunity to move beyond neutrality and support the oppressed of Biafra. Within the Red Cross, a debate raged about whether respecting neutrality and operating only with governmental consent needlessly imperiled victims. The French Red Cross decided to deploy fifty doctors despite the absence of a formal request from the Nigerian government. One of them, Bernard Kouchner, would become instrumental in forming Médecins sans Frontières (Doctors without Borders),[32] a movement that viewed neither borders nor sovereignty as sacrosanct. Thus, within the humanitarian sector a rift emerged about the centrality of neutrality, impartiality, and consent.

Within a short period, MSF received considerable attention for its efforts, and this spotlight revealed tensions within humanitarianism, which resurfaced for the 700,000 or so "boat people," refugees who fled Vietnam after the Saigon regime collapsed in 1975. Kouchner would have a falling out with other members of the MSF leadership over his plan to send hospital ships, and he would leave the organization—they diverged over what humanitarianism called for in this situation—and founded Médecins du Monde. The crisis would worsen with the overthrow of the Khmer Rouge government in Cambodia and a puppet government under Vietnam's tutelage. By this point, other agencies were also struggling with the crisis; the ICRC, UNICEF, and UNHCR would eventually initiate large cross-border operations in Thailand, but they were filtered through or controlled by the genocidal Khmer Rouge.

MSF emerged from the Red Cross movement, but its principles are distinct.[33] It argues for what it terms "non-ideological ideology," which is grounded on the French "Rights of Man."[34] The MSF movement finds kinship with the 1968 generation and Third World solidarity, leading Paul Berman to refer to MSF as "a sort of medical wing to the world guerrilla movement."[35] Whereas traditional ICRC humanitarianism is contingent on the international politics that prescribe operational principles of neutrality, impartiality, and consent, MSF is premised on the more radical political stance that is not bound by state consent and instead explicitly takes sides—on behalf of victims. Moreover, MSF presents its work as adhering to an "ethics of refusal," which is to resist the moral failing of accepting that wars and world order inevitably must produce victims. Its work is not only the delivery of relief but also a form of disruption or agitation to rouse others to challenge the conventions of world politics.

To that end, MSF emphasizes advocating the rights of access to victims (agencies must be unfettered in giving aid to those who need it); monitoring the impact of aid (agencies must examine the consequences of aid given); and protecting aid workers (belligerents must respect the staff of agencies).[36] Should these criteria not be met, MSF may withdraw and not provide aid. Furthermore, MSF violates traditional humanitarian practices by defying respect for national borders (MSF operates on the basis of need without consent or respect for sovereignty—it espouses an organizational model of "without borders"); and bearing and sharing witness (*témoignage*—MSF does not remain silent during crises but is outspoken in naming war criminals and violators of human rights). MSF resembles the ICRC organizationally in that both have national affiliate branches.

In response to shifts to the humanitarian landscape encountered in numerous civil wars, the Geneva Conventions were also expanded during the late Cold War. By the end of the 1970s, Third World countries (particularly those unallied with either the United States or the USSR) sought new rules to govern decolonization and national liberation movements—they bristled at being bounded by the 1949 Conventions in whose formulation they had not participated. In 1977, the Additional Protocols to the 1949 Geneva Conventions were signed (see box 2.3).

In addition to confronting recalcitrant governments, humanitarians also encountered in the Africa of the 1980s the return of a nefarious tactic of war: food as a weapon.[37] Human-created famines have been used to weaken the resistance of populations to domination by occupying pow-

---

BOX 2.3
Additional Protocols to the 1949 Geneva Conventions (1977)

- Protocol I was on international armed conflicts: It broadens the application of the laws of war to "fighting against colonial domination and alien occupation and against racist regimes." It also emphasized that only "lawful belligerents," those having distinctive emblems and carrying arms openly, receive the protections of POWs. Other armed actors, notably mercenaries, were prohibited and not entitled to POW status. Three states have signed and 174 states are parties to Protocol I.
- Protocol II was on internal armed conflicts: Some viewed this as violating state sovereignty, although its restrictions were far less than in Protocol I. Furthermore, the standard for internal armed conflicts was high, sustained levels of violence, not riots or sporadic violence, thus disqualifying some struggles from its jurisdiction. Three states have signed and 168 states are parties to Protocol II.

ers. Examples range from the Belgian Congo and Rhodesia–South Africa campaigns in the late nineteenth century, German scorched-earth policies during WWI in what has become Rwanda, British famine regulations in Sudan in the 1920s, and Britain's redirection of food production in Bengal (pre-partition India) in the early 1940s. Contemporary wars indicate that colonial powers did not have a monopoly on this form of atrocity.

Prototypical of the way famine was orchestrated in the 1980s is Ethiopia, where three provinces (Wollo, Tigray, and Eritrea) had continually rebelled against the central government. In addition to military attacks that sought to either kill or displace opponents, when agricultural resources in the area were threatened by droughts and crop failures (1983–1985), the Ethiopian government masked its counterinsurgency program as humanitarian relief. The relocation of populations was made under the pretense that they were being moved to more fertile and water-rich areas, but such transfers were intended to weaken guerrilla movements. MSF went public with its criticism of relocations—Rony Brauman, its president, complained that "humanitarianism can serve a murderous political project, and that the interests of victims is not necessarily at the end of humanitarian action."[38] Subsequently, MSF was expelled. Although Ethiopia ended the practice, this case highlights that violence other than wars can be equally problematic for agencies, and humanitarian organizations have minimal to no power when it comes to stopping states from carrying out human rights violations.

Conclusion: The International Humanitarian System in Historical Perspective

A review of the establishment and evolution of humanitarian agencies shows a dramatic evolution from the early consensus about neutral emergency medical assistance to wounded soldiers. Contrasting interpretations and alternative practices bred a variation of humanitarianism that nurtures other functional tasks such as the protection of civilians, refugee law, economic development, and human rights protection. This period of humanitarianism raises several sets of questions.

First, what is the relationship between ideas and action? At what point do normative concerns become translated into law and organizational structures for relief operations? How do traumatic events shape and reshape humanitarian arrangements? Which events are seminal and why? One aspect worth highlighting is the importance of the shift away from exclusively religion-centered humanitarianism. The rise of secular thought along with scientific sensibilities invoked a rationality that sought to devise bureaucracies to carry out humanitarianism. The ethics of compassion and conscience-shocking crises clearly played a part, but it is worth recognizing how different ethics based on responsibility and rationalities became embedded in organizations. While many relief agencies continue to be inspired by religion, most no longer exclude those who do not share their faith, nor do they proselytize during aid operations.

Second, what are the ethics of humanitarian action? Whereas humanitarians generally agree about providing aid—though specifically to whom and how is often disputed—the debate continues over the conditions under which aid is delivered. The case of the ICRC during WWII and its reaffirmation of neutrality versus MSF's critique typify the normative and political dilemmas that routinely haunt the sector. Such controversies also arise with respect to militarized refugee camps (as detailed in subsequent chapters), where those who have been victimized use aid to continue war. How should agencies respond? What principles are prioritized and why? Historically, the international humanitarian system began as the product of a compromise among states, but even early it was not wedded to working only with states. From 1863 to 1869, only 39 percent of Red Cross operations were in response to international conflicts, and 55 percent helped nonstate actors.[39] This reality continued into the twentieth century—for example, the ICRC's work with resistance groups during WWII—but neutrality and impartiality continued to suit states and therefore predominated official humanitarian ethics.

Third, what are the implications of different organizations with different interpretations of humanitarianism? The ICRC, MSF, and others are ethically grounded but are still organizations—bureaucracies with differing views of operational principles and staff who require paychecks and benefits. What are the relations among different humanitarian agencies? The prospect of one agency giving aid while another does not shows incoherence, but it also may mean that the latter's message of protest is lost.

Fourth, does the international humanitarian system matter? Some see it as making no difference in saving lives or changing belligerent behavior (the realist interpretation). Others contend that it does so but only in a piecemeal fashion—only some receive aid, and it is too limited (the Marxist or post-colonialist view). Another view holds that it is meaningful in saving lives and a powerful symbolic gesture of cosmopolitanism (the liberal and constructivist take). Another perspective contends that humanitarianism matters more to donors and aid workers than to the people whom it is intended to serve because assistance without addressing larger structural problems is impotent, normalizes emergencies, and reinforces forms of domination (the critical humanitarian view).

The emergence of humanitarian thought entails hoping for a better world, and the birth of the international humanitarian system is often traced to such idealism. But organizational manifestations and operations require a deeper understanding of the political milieu in which the system operates. Humanitarian action is not separate from the world that it is trying to tame. Indeed, it seizes a role for itself in collaborating to heal the world. It is fitting to consider the place and function of the ICRC, which

> occupies an official position within international law, and operates under a more formal mandate: "to provide humanitarian help for people affected by conflict and armed violence and to promote the laws that protect victims of war." The association with war is telling, since it demarcates a clear boundary for action and places humanitarianism within a state of exception. If a state of war suspends laws and norms, then the ICRC operates beyond ordinary conditions, reintroducing humanity into inhumane settings. To the extent that it ventures beyond such exceptional moments it does so through the promotion of laws that might affect them, preemptively responding to future ruptures. The Red Cross humanitarian legacy is clearly delimited, and stands strictly apart from political struggles.[40]

Thus, humanitarianism raises questions about how organizations become independent and self-defining as well as convey power. History (including the Enlightenment's principles and imperialism's practices) have nurtured a political context in which ongoing humanitarian programming occurs. The affirmation of the principles and practices of rights, relief, rescue, and refuge becomes a path to express humanitarianism. However, in reflecting on who actually benefits, the contours of a world order predicated on different degrees of the sacred and the sacrificed comes into focus.

Therefore, despite the promises and pleas about being apolitical, an accurate humanitarian story of its founding and developments through the end of the Cold War is not just one of morals, nor is it to be understood purely with respect to emergencies. Rather, fundamentally it depicts the struggle inherent in the political.

3

New Wars and New Humanitarianisms in the 1990s

Northern Iraq, Somalia, Rwanda, and the Balkans

Soldiers of the British battalion monitor the movement of Bosnian Muslims at a United Nations checkpoint in Stari Vitez, Bosnia and Herzegovina (May 1994). (UN photo/John Isaac)

The history of humanitarianism, war, and politics in the previous chapter indicated an embedding of norms in law and organizations in the nineteenth and twentieth centuries; here we build and systematically explore the nuts and bolts of humanitarianism on the ground in the most pivotal cases of the 1990s. The international humanitarian system was born of war and developed responses to the problems of emergency care, refugees, and famine that were aligned with the prerogatives of the great powers concerned about large-scale interstate armed conflicts or destabilizing population flows. Despite the substantial normative and material investment in humanitarian architecture over the 125 years that followed the original Geneva Convention in 1864, contestation emerged over the precise modalities of actions—notably the contrasts between the ICRC and MSF. The Cold War's end called for revisiting this debate and transforming humanitarianism. New factors and types of crises called for alternative solutions that would unlock new potential and aspirations in the sector.

We begin with a brief overview of the landscape as the Berlin Wall came tumbling down before examining the almost manic pace of humanitarianism in the early 1990s embodied by the operations in Iraq during and following the 1991 Persian Gulf War. Then we turn to the stark setbacks in Somalia in 1992–1993 following an ambitious US-led operation. We then examine the 1994 Rwanda genocide and its aftermath, in many ways a watershed—the spectacular failure on multiple fronts questioned the rudiments of humanitarianism and led to much soul-searching. These two African cases linger as disasters, respectively in Somalia itself and in the wider Great Lakes region. The chapter concludes with two other crises in the Balkans (the former Yugoslavia) that are a microcosm of the evolution in humanitarian norms over the course of the decade, and particularly spotlight "new humanitarianisms." The first, in Bosnia-Herzegovina, began shortly after Somalia and continued at roughly the same time as Rwanda, and the experiences cemented feelings of frustration with classic approaches and pointed to the need for agencies and states to rethink humanitarian principles and practices. This reconceptualization manifests itself most concretely at the end of the 1990s in Kosovo. There are other cases that we do not include because of limitations of space—in particular, Haiti and East Timor—but they would not change the pattern found in other formative cases. We conclude by considering how actions in the decade that followed the end of the Cold War often departed from the traditional template and thus have been branded the "new humanitarianisms."

The Humanitarian Landscape at the Cold War's End

To a great extent the Cold War deadlocked international politics and froze meaningful initiatives for humanitarianism—any issue or action that potentially challenged either the Western or Eastern bloc was immediately rebuffed or undermined. However, this situation began to change as the decline of the Soviet Union became apparent in the mid-1980s. With the USSR's economy collapsing and its military defeat in Afghanistan revealing diminished power, the Soviet leadership started to look for ways to engage the West and defuse costly tensions. By 1989 the Warsaw Pact of Communist states, which had been formed and led by Moscow, was crumbling; Poland and Hungary announced that they would hold competitive elections; and the fall of the Berlin Wall set the scene for the reunification of Germany. In December 1991, Mikhail Gorbachev, who had come to power in 1985 to save the Soviet system by reforming it, resigned, and the USSR disbanded—some would say "imploded."

The demise of the Soviet Union and Cold War rivalries brought a new level of cooperation to international affairs. The great powers had much to gain in Security Council cooperation; the United States had support for building order, and the declining powers maintained relevance. In this new era of political agreements, the United Nations, and particularly its Security Council (the preeminent global organ charged with maintaining international peace and security), were re-energized. Initially founded to counter the notion of a chaotic and inherently unstable balance of power that had given birth to two world wars, the UN proffered a system based on collective security (i.e., that an attack on one state was an attack on all). Despite some obvious weaknesses in stopping several conflicts (such as the Vietnam War), the United Nations nonetheless was effective at preventing a full-blown nuclear war between the United States and the USSR, and it invented peacekeeping to keep a lid on armed conflicts when the superpowers agreed.

However, after the Cold War the meaning of collective security was reconceived by the great powers, which had permanent seats on the Security Council. They found common interest in bringing peace and stability to areas that had formerly been battlegrounds for their respective proxy forces: Central America, Southern Africa, Southwest Asia, and Southeast Asia. The significance of moving beyond the Cold War and attempting to clean up its political detritus in the Third World was momentous for humanitarian action; historically, the end of wars presented an opportunity to renegotiate the parameters of humanitarianism, and this dynamic has often helped advance the agendas and abilities of agencies and others identifying as part of the humanitarian movement.

Evidence of a changed humanitarianism was the December 1988 General Assembly resolution 43/131, which called for states to facilitate work by IGOs and NGOs in providing humanitarian assistance (i.e., grant them access). In a bit of exaggeration, it was billed as the "right to intervene" for humanitarian agencies, which was advocated by humanitarians such as Bernard Kouchner (at the time the equivalent of the French secretary of state for humanitarian action) but opposed by ICRC's Frédéric Maurice, who feared that this more politically zealous orientation was "the aberrations and canker of humanitarianism."[1]

The wars that broke out at the Cold War's end routinely had different characteristics from the international armed conflicts that had framed the origins of the humanitarian system. Termed the "new wars," they were usually civil wars populated by nonstate actors, which were driven by motives disconnected to great power rivalries, such as the pursuit of economic resources (greed) or identity politics (grievance).[2] These armed conflicts were also higher profile as compared to those in the Third World during Cold War as advances in technologies disseminated information more widely and to bigger audiences than ever before (the "CNN" or "BBC" effect). Moreover, these "new wars" predominately had civilian victims, comprising nearly 90 percent of battlefield casualties—during WWI, the ratio had been roughly 1 to 1, with slightly more soldiers dying than civilians; though these figures are contested, the general premise of substantially increased civilian casualties holds true.[3] The conflicts in northern Iraq, Somalia, Rwanda, Bosnia, and Kosovo departed from conventional lines, corresponded to this "new wars" pattern, and challenged traditional principles. Each raised issues of neutrality versus taking sides, impartiality versus preferences, sovereign consent versus universal jurisdiction, and independence versus working with militaries in achieving humanitarian ends. The humanitarian sector was poised for change, and the crises of the 1990s prompted a new operational philosophy that sought to operate with a more explicit political agenda of securing space to deliver aid—the "new humanitarianism."[4]

Northern Iraq: Coercing Access and Confronting Sanctions

In 1990, the first major international crisis of the post–Cold War period, replete with a significant humanitarian disaster, took place in Iraq (see map 3.1).[5] It is worth noting that before this turning point, the country

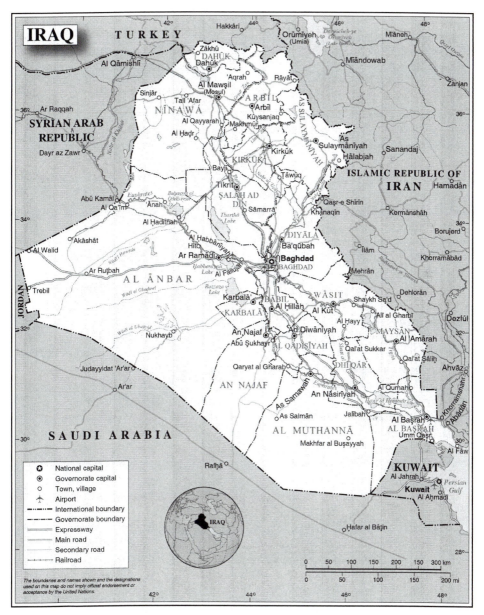

IRAQ

TURKEY

Hakkâri

Orūmïyeh
(Umia)

Mīāneh

Zākhū
DAHŪK
Dahūk

Mïāndowab

Al Qāmishlī

'Aqrah   Rāyāt

Zanjan

Al Mawşil
(Mosul)

Sinjār

Tall 'Afar

Ar Raqqah

NĪNAWÁ

ARBĪL

Arbīl

Kūysanjaq

SYRIAN ARAB
REPUBLIC

Al Qayyarah   Makhmūr

As SULAYMĀNĪYAH

Al Ḥaḑr

As
Sulaymānīyah   Sanandaj

Dayr az Zawr

KIRKŪK

Kirkūk

Hālabjah

Bayjī

Tāwūq

ISLAMIC REPUBLIC OF
IRAN   Hamādān

Tikrīt

Abū Kamāl
Al Qa'im   Ānah

SALĀH AD
DĪN   Sāmarra'

Qaşr-e Shīrīn

Khānaqīn

Kermānshāh

Al Ḥadīthah

DIYĀLĀ

Borujerd

Akāshāt

Al Walid

Al Habbānīyah
Hīt

Ar Ramādī

Ba'qūbah

Īlām

Khorramābād

Baghdad
BAGHDAD

Al Fallūjah

AL ĀNBAR

Mehrān

Trebil

Al Hillāh   WĀSIT

Dehlorān

Karbalā   BĀBIL

Shaykh Sa'd

KARBALĀ   Al Kūt

Dezfūl

Nukhayb

An Najaf

Al Hayy

'Alī al Gharbī

MAYSĀN

Ad Dīwānīyah

Judayyidat 'Ar'ar

Abū Şukhayr
AL QĀDISĪYAH

Qal'at Sukkar

Qal'at Şāliḥ

Al Amārah

Ahvāz

Ar'ar

Qaryat al Gharab

DHĪ QĀR

Al Qurnah

As Samāwah

AN NAJAF

An Nāşirīyah

Al Başrah

As Salmān

Jalībah

AL BAŞRAH
Umm Qaşr

SAUDI ARABIA

AL MUTHANNĀ

Makhfar al Buşayyah

Al Fāw

Rafḥā

KUWAIT

Al Jahrah

Persian
Gulf

Kuwait

Al Aḥmadī

IRAQ

Ḥafar al Bāţin

Legend:

- ✪ National capital
- ◉ Governorate capital
- ○ Town, village
- ✈ Airport
- International boundary
- Governorate boundary
- Expressway
- Main road
- Secondary road
- Railroad

The boundaries and names shown and the designations
used on this map do not imply official endorsement or
acceptance by the United Nations.

0   50   100   150   200   150   300 km

0   50   100   150   200 mi

Map 3.1

had already been the site of innovations in humanitarian work. During the war between Iraq and Iran from 1980 to 1988, the ICRC had conducted cross-border operations without the consent of the Iraqi government, and the ICRC also played an important role in facilitating the return of Iraqi POWs from Iranian prisons.

On August 2, 1990, Saddam Hussein's troops invaded Kuwait. This immediately set off a wave of displacement as 850,000 people from other countries fled along with some 300,000 Palestinians who were in Kuwait at the time of the attack. The Security Council immediately condemned Iraq's aggression in resolution 660—it was the first consensus statement on an act of aggression since the start of the Korean War in 1950, and set up the first arguably genuine collective security decisions in UN history. On August 6, the Security Council passed resolution 661 calling for economic sanctions against Iraq (only the third time the UN had done so). In September, the Security Council passed several more resolutions (666, 667, 670, 674) strengthening the sanctions as well as calling for Iraq to abide by IHL in its treatment of civilians in occupied areas, in some instances specifying obligations under the Fourth Geneva Convention. This appeal was followed in December when the ICRC, which struggled to get access inside Kuwait, sent out to what was then all 164 parties to the Geneva Conventions the "Memorandum on the Applicability of International Humanitarian Law." In addition to summarizing responsibilities regarding noncombatants and respect for Red Cross activities, it specified the prohibition on chemical and bacteriological weapons and other weapons of mass destruction (WMD). However, the ICRC was unprepared to pursue legal arguments that might have provoked a refusal of access.

On November 29, 1990, Security Council resolution 678 called for states to use "all necessary means" to extricate Iraq from Kuwait. By early 1991 a coalition of states launched a war, beginning with air strikes on January 17 and then with a brief land war from February 24 to 28. Its impact on Iraq was overwhelming: 60,000 to 120,000 soldiers and around 3,500 civilians killed, and $100–200 billion in damage.

This armed conflict raised a host of humanitarian concerns, particularly with regard to just war. The conduct of Iraqi forces was horrendous. First, the crime of aggression was never prosecuted. Second, according to IHL, Iraq had obligations to civilians in Kuwait that were entirely disregarded. The ICRC was basically silent about its own lack of access to victims until Iraq was ousted; clearly, they feared that public condemnations would circumscribe their efforts. Third, Iraq indiscriminately resorted to violence both in its use and abandonment of landmines in Kuwait and in launching Scud missiles against civilians in Saudi Arabia and Israel. Fourth, Iraq caused significant environmental damage in setting more than 600 Kuwaiti oil wells ablaze—a violation of the 1977 UN Convention on the

Prohibition of Military or Any Other Hostile Use of Environment Modification Techniques. The coalition forces, led by the United States, also were criticized. First, the question of proportionality in the use of force was prompted by the destruction of a sizable amount of Iraq's infrastructure[6] and later by the "highway of death," along which US airpower killed fleeing, often unarmed, Iraqi soldiers. Second, the coalition also violated Geneva Convention III in showing Iraqi POWs on television. Ultimately, IHL was ignored because Saddam and other Iraqi offenders were not captured, and there were no investigations of the West and its allies.

While Iraq was pushed from Kuwait, the focus shifted to Iraq itself where parts of society that had long been repressed by Saddam Hussein—Kurds in the north and Shiites in the south—rose up in an attempt to topple the dictator. In response, the regime unleashed its military forces to reassert control. However, the Security Council sought to stem Hussein's ability to repress by limiting the space in which he could use his air force: "no-fly zones." Furthermore, Security Council resolution 687 of April 3 laid down conditions for a cease-fire that were consequences of attacking and occupying Kuwait, which included inspections to monitor disarmament and a fund for humanitarian assistance to Iraqi civilians under the sanctions regime.

Moreover, and truly a landmark in humanitarianism, the Security Council also demanded that humanitarian relief be allowed in resolution 688 of April 5, which argued that Saddam's aggression against Kurds and Shiites constituted a violation of "international peace and security." Technically, the violence was within Iraq's territory and thus would have conventionally been dubbed a domestic matter and beyond the purview of the Security Council. But the council insisted on a right to humanitarian access and threatened force should it be blocked. Indeed, Secretary-General Javier Pérez de Cuéllar described this example as "the collective obligation of States to bring relief and redress in human rights emergencies."[7]

In northern Iraq Hussein's counterinsurgency campaign had led to massive displacement for Kurdish populations (roughly 2 million people or about half of Kurds in northern Iraq). The coalition's "Operation Deny Flight" established a no-fly zone above the 36th parallel. In regard to providing humanitarian assistance, in March 1991 they also organized "Operation Provide Comfort"—22,000 coalition troops engaged in the delivery of aid and escorting refugees back to safe areas in the north. The combined communication and logistical capacities of Western militaries enabled deliveries to begin only seven days after the resolution was passed. In April, the UN negotiated a memorandum of understanding (MOU) with Iraq for access and security. Northern Iraq in 1991 would be the first instance in which UNHCR brought food to the displaced rather than await them on the other side of the border. The humanitarian impact was immediate: an increase in repatriation rates and a decrease in mortality rates.

In the south, many Shiites attempted to flee; 700,000 went to Iran, and 30,000 took refuge in Kuwait and Saudi Arabia. However, Hussein's forces trapped approximately 850,000. The US-led allies were slower to react to the situation in the south. The no-fly zone below the 32nd parallel, "Operation Southern Watch," did not take effect until August 1992. Furthermore, there was no substantial aid operation for Shiites within southern Iraq.

An additional set of decisions had good humanitarian intentions, but this road led to humanitarian hell. As discussed, in the run-up to the Persian Gulf War, the Security Council authorized sanctions against Iraq in resolution 661; afterward, in the conditions stipulated for a cease-fire, it demanded that Iraq establish a fund for humanitarian assistance in resolution 687. The continuation of sanctions following the war had undercut Iraq's ability to purchase food. In a country where 60 percent of the population lived hand-to-mouth, the consequences of sanctions were severe: from 1991 to 1998, 270,000 children died of malnutrition, 75 percent of which would have been preventable had sanctions not limited food deliveries and supplies. The ICRC played a prominent role in depicting the extent of the impact on Iraqi civilians; Cornelio Sommaruga, ICRC president, met with US, UK, French, and UN diplomats to share documentation and advocate for easing restrictions. A UNICEF study similarly found that 90,000 children were dying yearly due to sanctions.

With this gruesome toll as backdrop, pressure mounted for the UN to end or modify the sanctions against Iraq. It was proposed that Iraq be allowed to sell some oil on the international market to generate funds and yet have these transactions monitored and limited. In May 1996, the Oil-for-Food Programme (OfFP) began under the watchful eye of the "661 Committee"—named after the Security Council resolution that initially imposed sanctions.

This program became controversial because the proceeds of oil sales were manipulated and diverted to funding the Hussein regime.[8] However, in evaluating OfFP, several aspects should be kept in mind. First, in regard to accomplishing humanitarian goals from 1996 to 2001, the average daily caloric intake for Iraqis increased from 1,200 to 2,200. Second, while the program was enormous—$64 billion from 1996–2003—the total amount that was stolen was a rather small percentage.[9] A US Government Accounting Office (GAO) report found that 93 percent of funds went where they were intended; another study conducted by a commission led by former head of the US Federal Reserve Bank Paul Volcker indicated that the rate was 98 percent. Third, the major recipients of Iraqi oil under this program were US allies (Turkey and Jordan) as well as an ally of

France and Russia (Syria). Thus, while the program is often lambasted as a case of extreme corruption, it also served the interests of great powers who had a stake in seeing that their allies received energy supplies.

Sanctions regimes in general are among the most bizarre versions of humanitarianism—cutting off assistance to civilians to protest a political decision by their government. The logic of civilian pain for political gain is a doubtful proposition in many contexts,[10] but the OfFP was particularly odd in adding the condition that acceptable aid could be delivered if the government paid for it. This procedure gave the government responsible for the wrong for which it was being punished by sanctions an opportunity to improve its image and quell dissent by strategically distributing aid. In addition, it forced national resources that belonged to the afflicted local population but were under the control of the violating government to be expended to pay for relief. This convoluted humanitarianism punished the victims and presented their society with the bill.

Somalia: Conflict, Crisis, and Syndrome

Accompanying the crisis in northern Iraq was another brewing in Somalia (see map 3.2). Despite some similarities—large-scale violence and displacement that, coupled with famine, was killing tens of thousands— these disasters had marked differences in the nature of their conflicts and the type and level of responses by Western governments. Nevertheless, the threads that connect them illustrate how post–Cold War humanitarianism was shaping up.

Whereas many civil wars are rooted in culture or race, Somalia's is different: a single ethnic group shares a common religion, history, and language. The primary cleavage in Somalia reflects clan affiliations, sometimes even sub-clan divisions. However, this basis for identity construction was not a major factor in driving Somali politics until the late twentieth century.

For much of Somalia's history, it had endured colonial occupation. In the late 1800s, Britain, Italy, France, Ethiopia, and Kenya carved up the country. For European powers, Somalia's proximity to important shipping lanes and other colonies made a port along its coasts a strategic necessity. Regional African powers saw the potential to expand their influence and bolster their security. However, in 1899 Somalis revolted against British and Ethiopian forces. This led to a nearly twenty-year insurgency featuring Muslim guerrillas against foreign imperialists. In the 1930s, fascist Italy was active in building its colonial reach in East Africa, and in 1935 attacked Ethiopia; as part of its imperial rivalry with other European powers, it conquered what had become British Somaliland. During WWII,

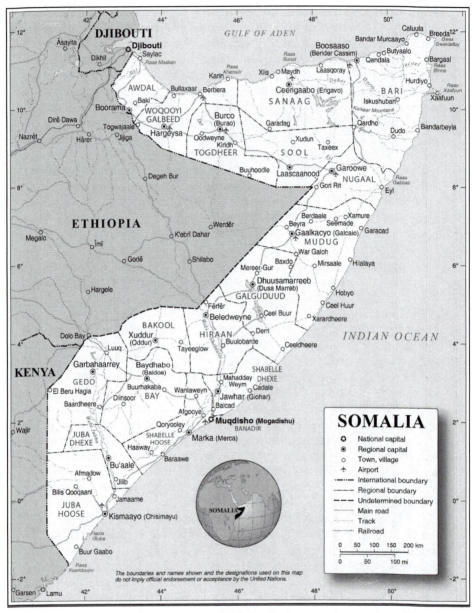

Map 3.2

Britain would expel Italy and regain its colony. Following ten years of administration under UN trusteeship, in July 1960 Italian Somaliland and British Somaliland united and became independent.

The first three decades of Somali independence witnessed a coup that brought General Mohamed Siad Barre to power and drew Somalia into a proxy war between the United States and the Soviet Union. In 1977–1978 Somalia sought a "Greater Somalia" and fought a war against Ethiopia for control of the Ogaden Desert but was trounced by a better equipped, trained, and organized Ethiopian army. During the conflict, the Barre regime manipulated and undermined humanitarianism not only by using refugee camps to recruit fighters but also, as Ken Menkhaus has observed, by "position[ing] themselves as intermediaries in the flow of resources to refugees, diverting much of the relief in what became a lucrative racket." However, he notes that the West nevertheless supported the government: "the option of openly criticising the government's egregious violations of humanitarian principles, or of calling for the suspension of aid to the refugee camps on the grounds that it was being misused, was not on the table. Somalia during the Cold War was too valuable an ally of the West."[11] This defeat led to a coup attempt in 1978 and initiated an insurgency that would unravel Somalia. This process was likely hastened by Somalia's loss of Soviet patronage and foreign assistance—formerly a crucial ally, the USSR had sided with Ethiopia in the war over the Ogaden region.

After the Soviets abandoned Somalia, it effectively switched sides during the 1980s and became a US ally. With American support, aid from international organizations began to flow. By 1987, international assistance accounted for 57 percent of Somalia's gross national product (GNP) and about half of the government's budget. There were negative, albeit unintended, consequences. First, although the amount of food coming into the country had grown substantially, domestic production fell greatly: by 1980–1984, about 85 percent of food consumed in Somalia was imported. Second, clans competed for access to and control of this new resource. Food was no longer merely a means of sustenance; it became the focal point of armed struggle.

In January 1991, Mohamed Siad Barre was overthrown and fled to Garbahaarreey, a town in the southwest. Mohamed Farah Aidid (sometimes spelled Aideed) who was leader of the United Somali Congress (USC) and head of the Hawiye clan (the most powerful at that time) unseated him, secured Mogadishu, and then pursued Barre. But within the USC there was a disagreement about who should assume the presidency; while Aidid chased Barre, Ali Mahdi was elected interim president. This split the USC and soon other clans were also jockeying for power in a variety of areas of the country. With no functioning government and some fifteen clans or factions fighting, civil war quickly engulfed the country. Some parts of Somalia attempted to form their own state as illustrated by the May 1991 declaration by the clans in northern parts of Somalia that had been British Somaliland. During 1991 the civil war grew in intensity, so much so that in March both the WFP and UNICEF withdrew their staff; although agencies such as the ICRC, World Vision, and MSF remained, food supplies dwindled.

From November 1991 to March 1992, fighting escalated; Aidid pressed against his former allies in the USC; and fewer food imports worsened the famine.[12] In this period 30,000 to 50,000 civilians died from combat and 200,000 to 300,000 starved. Fighting and famine also displaced about 1.5 million people (out of a total population of around 7.5 million). In mid-April 1992, with hunger climbing ever higher, the Security Council planned a peacekeeping force with a humanitarian assistance component, but it was minuscule and ineffective. At the end of August, Security Council resolution 775 authorized the deployment of peacekeepers to protect aid deliveries (the first UN Operation in Somalia, UNOSOM I).[13] Although initially the clans consented to the presence of a small peacekeeping force to address bandits, UN Secretary-General Boutros Boutros-Ghali pushed for a larger one without consulting either the UN representative in Somalia or the warring parties. In this period the ICRC was feeding some 1.2 million people daily.

The crisis in Somalia informed action by the international humanitarian system. In December 1991, the UN General Assembly underlined its affirmation of sovereignty but also empowered humanitarian agencies in resolution 46/182: "The sovereignty, territorial integrity and national unity of states must be fully respected in accordance with the Charter of the United Nations. In this context, humanitarian assistance should be provided with the consent of the affected country and in principle on the basis of an appeal by the affected country." Despite the fact that operations should be consent-based, this legally grounded the right of agencies to access victims, which generated the concept of "humanitarian space"—a safe area in which to provide relief. The 1991 articulation of humanitarian space expanded strategies and modalities because the concept does not explicitly appear in international humanitarian law. It does, however, build on the 1949 Geneva Conventions, which contain the possibilities of "hospitals and safe zones and localities" of a permanent nature in areas far from the fighting, and Additional Protocol I's reference to demilitarized zones for civilians. Yet, these both require consent from host governments; only the UN through a Chapter VII Security Council resolution can ignore the request for consent.

Additionally, resolution 46/182 created the position of Under-Secretary-General and Emergency Relief Coordinator (ERC) and the Department of Humanitarian Affairs (DHA) to promote coordination within the UN system. The ERC leads a body called the Inter-Agency Standing Committee (IASC), created as the primary mechanism for inter-agency coordination among relevant UN and non-UN organizations, a role affirmed in General Assembly resolution 48/57. In 1998, the DHA would be reorganized into the Office for the Coordination of Humanitarian Affairs (OCHA), currently the UN system's main humanitarian coordinating mechanism.

In August 1992, "Operation Provide Relief" was ramping up deliveries as the US military took over the airlift work from the ICRC and the WFP. But access remained problematic when UNOSOM forces arrived in September. Five aid workers from CARE died when their convoy was attacked after the organization refused to pay a militia for protection. This added urgency to pleas for armed protection of aid workers, but many other humanitarians objected. Indeed, some derisively began to refer to their mission as "Operation Shoot to Feed." Nevertheless, since violence intensified in 1991, agencies had been hiring the militias themselves—in many instances, formerly the perpetrators of violence—to safeguard their personnel. James Orbinski, former director of MSF's mission in Rwanda during the genocide, commented, "Some of the old humanitarian rules of neutrality and independence seemed to be falling apart, and it wasn't clear what the new rules would be. For the first time ever, the Red Cross, MSF, and other aid agencies were paying armed guards from various clans to protect aid workers and food supplies."[14]

By October 1992, the clans were openly defying UNOSOM I's soldiers and clashing over control of the country and the humanitarian assistance being imported. After seeing some aid go to his opponents, in the later part of October, Aidid evicted the UN humanitarian coordinator, and again Somalia was without security or food. In December, US president George H. W. Bush pushed for a US-led humanitarian intervention, and the Security Council concurred in authorizing resolution 794: "to use all necessary means to establish a secure environment for humanitarian relief operations in Somalia as soon as possible." Thus, "Operation Restore Hope" and the Unified Task Force (UNITAF) was created and brought 36,000 troops in to ensure security. This operation saved 10,000–25,000 Somalis but was short lived (from December 1992 to May 1993). On May 3, 1993, the Security Council authorized a second mission (UNOSOM II), this time to facilitate access as well as disarm warlords who opposed the relief operation.[15]

With Aidid persistently refusing to provide access and to disarm, on June 6, Security Council resolution 837 ordered his arrest. The result was a bungled military operation that ended in two downed US helicopters and a battle to rescue US Rangers in them. The episode, which has since been called "Blackhawk Down" (from the name of the aircraft shot down), produced eighteen US fatalities. Given these losses,

Washington quickly lost its appetite for intervening anywhere—labeled the "Somalia syndrome" because it resembled the reluctance to commit troops to faraway wars of unclear importance for national interests after the Vietnam War.

In May 1994, US president Bill Clinton signed Presidential Decision Directive 25 (PDD-25), which set extensive criteria for US involvement in multilateral operations. After PDD-25, Washington was only to support operations viewed as feasible or essential to vital interests. In many ways PDD-25 signaled a turning point in US attitudes toward humanitarian intervention. Other countries were similarly repulsed by the experience, and this sentiment eventually manifested at the United Nations; UNOSOM II pulled out in March 1995. Even more significantly, PDD-25 was signed while mass murderers ran amok in Rwanda. Perhaps just as telling, UN organizations, NGOs, and donors developed the 1995 Code of Conduct for International Rehabilitation and Development Assistance in Somalia, which emphasized security measures to promote the delivery of aid and protect their personnel, not local populations.[16]

Somalia remains in disarray. The country is essentially divided into the self-declared republic of Somaliland, an autonomous area in the northeast (Puntland), and the south-central section where the federal government of Somalia is located. A large and growing Muslim movement emerged around 2002, the Islamic Courts Union (ICU), and by 2006 had gained control of most of the country. Many Somalis supported the ICU as having the potential to bring order as compared to the endless clan wars. However, the growth of the ICU and its victory against the government in November of that year raised concerns for the United States and GWOT. In December, Ethiopian troops (backed by Washington) pushed the ICU out of Mogadishu—in the process, it destroyed about one-third of the city and caused 700,000 to flee. During 2007, while Ethiopia conducted a brutal campaign against clans supporting the ICU, the African Union (AU) attempted to organize a peacekeeping force; but few countries were willing to provide soldiers.

A decade and a half after the 1990s crisis, UNHCR's country representation declared that Somalia still was the "most pressing humanitarian emergency in the world today—even worse than Darfur." One million had been uprooted, the rate of malnutrition was 15 percent, and access was so poor that UNHCR could not operate. The fight against Ethiopia had inspired the rise of an Islamist insurgency, al-Shabab. During 2008, conditions did not improve, and aid workers struggled to reach 3.5 million in need; aside from the war, limited rainfall had rendered a poor harvest.

After facing several military losses, Ethiopia withdrew from Somalia by mid-January 2009. The African Union Mission in Somalia (AMISOM) had limited impact in stopping the ICU from governing, including instituting

Sharia law. The 2007–2010 war killed just over 20,000 and displaced 1.7 million (out of a population that had decreased to about 9 million). Furthermore, international assistance declined because in February al-Shabab ousted the WFP. Partially a means to control aid so that food only went to supporters, it built their support among local farmers who complained that food aid was undermining local prices and production. In the short term the humanitarian crisis worsened because 40 percent of the population (roughly 3.5 million) relied on UN assistance, including 20 percent of children, who were malnourished. However, by late 2010 there was a modest boost in food supplies and the number of people in need fell to about 2 million.

In 2011, a massive drought and famine took hold throughout the Horn of Africa; by summer, nearly 11.3 million in the region survived on aid, of whom 3.7 million were in Somalia. The famine was concentrated in districts controlled by al-Shabab, where six of every 10,000 died daily, and 50 percent of children were malnourished. Finally, the UN was permitted to resume shipments in July for the first time since early 2010; in August AMISOM evicted al-Shabab from Mogadishu, and UNHCR delivered food for the first time since 2006. Nevertheless, 4 million Somalis suffered from food shortages and the country had the world's highest child mortality rate: 180 per 1,000 live births. This was worsened by MSF's withdrawal in August 2013 after a twenty-two-year history operating in the country.

Later that fall, outside powers increased efforts to eradicate al-Shabab. In October Kenya intervened; in November Ethiopia sent troops; in February 2012 the UN Security Council authorized more AMISOM forces (up to almost 18,000 troops, of which approximately 15,000 are deployed). Al-Shabab ousted many foreign aid agencies as "imperialist influence." The ICRC suspended operations, leaving 4 million in need and 250,000 facing famine (defined as the risk of dying in the following four months). In late September, although Kenyan soldiers expelled rebels from their last stronghold in Kismayo, al-Shabab vowed to establish an Islamic state through a guerrilla campaign that escalated in 2013, including a June attack on the UN's Mogadishu compound.

Armed conflict and the dire humanitarian crisis in Somalia remain despite improving security conditions in Mogadishu and elsewhere as well as declining numbers afflicted by the crisis. Nonetheless by the end of 2016, around 5 million or almost 40 percent of the population required international assistance, of whom more than 1.1 million were IDPs while roughly the same number remained refugees in the region.[17]

Two final notes speak to the definition of a "permanent crisis" after a quarter-century. First, improvements in food deliveries and the consolidation of order under a government have increased, but the threat of pirate attacks in the Gulf of Aden and al-Shabab expropriations at ports continue to challenge the nearly 90 percent of aid arriving by sea.[18] Second, refugees continue to flee, destabilizing to the region. Across the border in Kenya, Dadaab has become the world's largest refugee camp, at one point sheltering some 500,000 (becoming Kenya's third-largest city), although it has since declined to about 300,000.

Rwanda: Genocide, Global Response, and Ghosts

The major divide in Rwandan politics has centered on rivalries between two groups, Tutsis and Hutus. (A small third group is the Twa, distinguished by their smaller size and a distinctive form of the common language.) Although Tutsis and Hutus speak Kinyarwanda, there are significant differences between them. Historically, Tutsis were pastoralists (raised cattle), while Hutus were cultivators (farmers); some suggest that the division really reflects one of economic class with the Tutsis the wealthy and the Hutus the poor. Hutus have always been a considerably more numerous population than Tutsis.

The area that became Rwanda (see map 3.3) was originally colonized by Germany in the 1890s, but after WWI Belgium became the governing colonial power. Both German and later Belgian imperialism favored the Tutsi minority. The European powers may have felt they would be more likely to maintain their influence in the region by supporting a minority that would have to rely on them for control, but they also subscribed to what has been called the "Hamitic hypothesis" that considers Tutsi a Caucasoid race and superior to Hutus.[19] The latter, however, viewed themselves as superior because they are part of the indigenous "Bantu" populations of the region while Tutsis are "Nilotic" invaders. Whatever the merits or origins of these perceptions, given that there were no significant instances of systematic violence between Hutu and Tutsi during the colonial period, it seems likely that these ethnic identities were either constructed or hardened after independence.

In the late 1950s and early 1960s, as pressures for decolonization swept across Africa, Belgium realized that it would have to grant Rwanda independence. However, Belgium still sought to exert influence; fearing that Tutsis were embracing nationalism, they gave their support to the Hutus. On July 1, 1962, Rwanda became a republic under Hutu leadership. During 1959–1963, some 200,000 Tutsis fled to neighboring countries— Uganda, Zaire, and Burundi—especially after a burst of ethnic violence in 1963 killed 20,000 Tutsis. At the same time, in next-door Burundi, Tutsis held onto their privileged position and repressed Hutus. In the 1970s, Hutus cemented their political power, particularly after the coup that installed General Habyarimana as leader. He continued to limit Tutsis

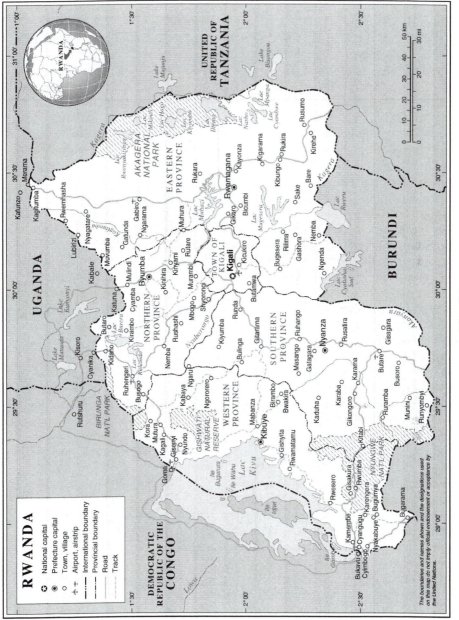

Map 3.3

participating in politics and also sponsored Hutus in Burundi against its Tutsi-led government.

In the late 1980s and 1990s, Tutsis returned to Rwanda, which would initiate the tensions that sparked the 1994 genocide. In Uganda, Tutsi refugees who had fled Rwanda in the 1960s assisted a guerrilla faction led by Yoweri Museveni, who was successful in overthrowing the government under Tito Okello. In exchange for Tutsi help in the war in Uganda, the new government permitted Tutsis to use Uganda as a base for organizing against Rwanda's Hutu government. In 1988, Tutsis in Uganda formed the Rwandan Patriotic Front (RPF); they sought to return to Rwanda and establish a new government that would share power between Hutus and Tutsis. Within Rwanda pressure was also building as the economy was crumbling. Dependent on taxing coffee exports for 60–80 percent of revenues in the 1980s, the government faced a crisis when the price of coffee plummeted in 1983. Moreover, a growing population resulting from high birth rates and returning refugees created a competition for land and resources. In the early 1990s, with coffee prices low and the economy shrinking (by about 30 percent from 1990 to 1993), the main lifeline for Rwanda became international development aid, nearly a quarter of the country's GNP. By the mid-1990s, economic strain and demographic stress in the context of mounting ethnic-based pressures made for a volatile mix.[20]

On October 1, 1990, the RPF invaded Rwanda with a force of some 6,000 Tutsis backed by 3,000 Ugandan soldiers. The Rwandan government and the RPF fought several battles over the next three years. The Security Council, seeking to contain the violence and prevent war from breaking out between Rwanda and Uganda, in June 1993 passed resolution 846 and sent peacekeepers to monitor the border and essentially stop supplies from flowing to the RPF. Peace negotiations began that summer, and on August 4 produced the Arusha Peace Accords, which called for power-sharing arrangements, a cease-fire, demobilization and demilitarization, and the repatriation of Tutsis. With an agreement in place and the consent of the Rwandan government, the Security Council sent peacekeepers. By contrast, the UN was unwilling to send peacekeepers to neighboring Burundi which was torn apart by civil war (100,000 killed in 1993 alone) because there was no peace to keep.

However, what was agreed at Arusha and what was happening on the ground were different. First, the Rwandan government was recruiting Hutus and arming militias. Second, the returning Tutsis were joining the RPF. Meanwhile, the UN was unable to stop the movement of people, supplies, and arms. On January 11, 1994, UN force commander Roméo Dallaire sent a fax to UN headquarters outlining intelligence that he had gathered about ethnic violence being planned by Hutu extremists. UN headquarters ordered Dallaire not to get involved, though it was clear violence was at hand, and that external powers not only did not care but also were abetting Hutu militancy. Jean Bradol was working at MSF and recalled "the 'extremely shocking' nature of the French military presence in Rwanda: 'I saw French soldiers perform identity checks at the exits from Kigali, side by side with the Rwandan army of Habyarimana. I saw them patrol Kigali airport and ensure its interior security using arms. . . . The impression was one of a real intermingling of Rwandan forces and French troops, while the regime was radicalising in a genocidal direction.'"[21]

On April 6, a plane carrying the presidents of Rwanda and Burundi (both Hutus) was shot down. In response to this event the Rwandan military and Hutu militias targeted Tutsis and moderate Hutus and set modern records for rapid suffering. Over the next hundred days, out of a population of 7.5 million people, some 800,000 would be killed, 2 million would become internally displaced, and 2 million would flee to Zaire, Tanzania, or Burundi—a genocide; or, "*itsenbabwoku*" in Kinyarwanda. The Hutu government would eventually be toppled by the RPF and fled the capital in May; the surging Tutsi army would take control of most of the country by the middle of July. The genocide ended as extremist Hutus relocated to refugee camps on the Zaire side of the border.

The international humanitarian system responded in a variety of ways to the genocide, with emergency relief and advocacy for military intervention,[22] including MSF, which had traditionally declined to call for military force but now argued differently: "You don't treat a genocide with doctors; you don't respond to a humanitarian crisis with a stethoscope."[23] UN forces, which were providing aid and assisting with the implementation of the Arusha Accords, were caught in the middle of this surge. Ten Belgian peacekeepers were killed and dismembered in early April, and wishing to avoid more casualties for peacekeeping forces and recognizing the limited effect the UN could have on the situation, Security Council resolution 912 reduced the number of UN troops on the ground from 2,500 to 270.

Approximately fifteen weeks after the genocide, the French government decided that if the UN would not send additional soldiers to Rwanda to aid refugees, they would. France proposed "Opération Turquoise"—2,500 French soldiers to provide security for southwest Rwanda and to distribute relief to displaced populations. The Security Council approved the operation on June 22 in resolution 929. By July 4 the safe haven was established, thereby permitting over one million to exit the battle zone in Rwanda and cross safely into Zaire by the end of July. The operation wrapped up on August 21. However, Opération Turquoise was not well received by the RPF. They contended that the operation was providing aid to Hutus as longtime French allies; moreover, many who received assistance and safe passage had been perpetrators of the genocide.

The refugee camps built in what was then Zaire immediately became contentious as the *génocidaires* resumed control over the Hutu populations that had fled—with war criminals and civilians alike in their midst. Should agencies provide assistance and risk supporting militants? UN High Commissioner for Refugees Sadako Ogata argued, "there were also innocent refugees in the camps; more than half were women and children. Should we have said: you are related to murderers, so you are guilty, too? . . . My staff had to continue feeding criminals as the price for feeding hundreds of thousands of innocent women and children."[24] This situation flummoxed humanitarians. Many UN agencies and NGOs opted to withdraw when they felt not only that they could not help but that they were abetting actions by perpetrators. In October 1994, CARE Canada withdrew after receiving death threats. In December 1994, MSF would do likewise, and so would IRC in early 1995.

The United States also organized a short humanitarian mission— "Operation Support Hope." Similar to French efforts, the United States distributed aid to Hutu refugees, but its efforts were not as focused on southwest Rwanda but on the capital, Kigali, and the growing refugee camps in Goma (across the border in Zaire). However, it, too, was brief, lasting only from July 23 to August 27.

After mass violence and the attempted genocide ("attempt" because although the intention was to exterminate all Tutsis, the effort fell short), what could be done about preventing a recurrence of genocidal violence? Three solutions were proposed: adjudicate war criminals (law), build a stable and peaceful society (politics), and pursue and destroy perpetrators of violence (force). While only one of these falls within the domain of humanitarianism, discussing all helps to contextualize the role of humanitarianism.

The first, adjudicating war criminals of the genocide, proceeded along three fronts; international, national, and local. At the international level, the November 8, 1994 Security Council resolution 955 authorized the International Criminal Tribunal for the Prosecution of Persons Responsible for Genocide and Other Serious Violations of International Humanitarian Law Committed in the Territory of Rwanda and Rwandan Citizens Responsible for Genocide and Other Such Violations Committed in the Territory of Neighboring States Between 1 January 1994 and 31 December 1994 (usually abbreviated as ICTR). This court initiated its first trial in 1996 and rendered its first verdict in 1998 when Jean-Paul Akayesu was convicted of the crime of genocide; it was also the first time that an international court viewed rape as an act of genocide. In the subsequent two decades, the ICTR has indicted ninety-three, sentenced sixty-two, acquitted fourteen, and referred thirteen to other jurisdictions.

In addition to a seemingly small number of cases, the ICTR has been criticized on several grounds. First, it was rather costly; by the time it closed at the end of 2015, it had spent nearly $2 billion.[25] Second, its punishments are considered limited because the detention facilities offered a more comfortable existence than most Rwandans have at home, and there is no death penalty. Third, the ICTR reaffirms the morality of the great powers rather than Rwandan ethics. Fourth, the ICTR does not tackle crimes committed by the RPF, only those of Hutu *génocidaires*.

Domestic justice stems from the September 1, 1996 Organic Law on the Organization of Prosecution for Offenses Constituting Genocide or Crimes against Humanity since October 1, 1992. This classifies four categories of criminals: leaders and notorious murderers operating with excessive malice; perpetrators or accomplices to homicide; accomplices without intent to kill; and offenders against property. This legal mechanism has detained many alleged offenders (well over 100,000); even holding annual trials for a thousand would still require over a century for adjudication. Besides being slow, the domestic justice system suffers from corruption.

A local mechanism began in February 2001 with the Organic Law for the Creation of Gacaca Jurisdictions.[26] It operates at the province, district, sector, and cell level. Each trial begins with listing every victim of every criminal act and debates the evidence. It was created to incorporate local participation and to ease the burden on the formal legal system. However, it too has been criticized: *gacacas* have been used to falsely incriminate some, there is no legal representation, local influence may tilt outcomes, and few women have been elected judges.

The second set of possible preventive measures revolves around politics. Post-genocide Rwanda under Tutsi leadership has not become a free and democratic society, although it has become a "model" of sorts for rapid economic development and stability after a traumatic war. Shortly after the RPF defeated extremist Hutus and formed a new government, disturbing signs that the RPF sought to monopolize political power appeared. Tutsi-led forces carried out violence against Hutus; between April and September 1994, some 20,000–35,000 Hutus were killed, and in 1995 camps for displaced Hutus were attacked. From 1994 to 2000, there were extensive claims of corruption and tyranny that led to numerous resignations of top officials from the RPF; many of these individuals subsequently fled the country for fear of retaliation. In fact, the 2001 elections were seen as fixed to favor Tutsi candidates. Similarly, in 2003, Paul Kagame, head of the RPF, was elected president with 95 percent of the vote while arrests, intimidation, and "disappearances" of opponents were frequent. Kagame remains in power to this day. Overall, there has been a growing "Tutsiza-tion" of Rwanda under the RPF, which has marginalized Hutus.

More encouraging developments also hold the potential for positive change. There is a growing bi-ethnic opposition movement that signals the possibility of power sharing or moving beyond a rigid Hutu-Tutsi divide. The number of women in politically important roles has grown dramati-cally, which some argue may usher in greater reconciliation and peaceful behavior. And Rwanda has one of Africa's fastest growing economies.

The third solution revolves around force. Fearing that the RPF would exact revenge for the genocide from all Hutus, many fled across the bor-der to Zaire. For several years, many Hutu militants used the refugee camps to organize armed resistance against the RPF and even conducted some raids in Rwanda. The camps essentially became a safe haven for the extremist Hutu regime to continue to control Hutu populations—they had shepherded Hutus into Zaire so as to maintain the appearance that they represented a large population and could draw humanitarian aid. To root out these genocidal elements, Rwanda supported a guerrilla group in Zaire to overthrow the host government. This situation led to the conflict that has come to be known as the "First World War of the Congo," which lasted from November 1996 to May 1997. The guerrilla group ousted longtime authoritarian Mobutu Sese Seko and installed Laurent Kabila, who renamed the country the Democratic Republic of the Congo (DRC). However, Kabila did not remain allied with the Tutsi-led government in Rwanda, and Hutu forces continued to fight from DRC bases.

This fight also contributed to the so-called Second World War of the Congo, which lasted from August 1998 to July 2003. During this period Rwanda not only sponsored Tutsi forces (*"Banyamlenge"*) but also plun-dered precious metals and timber from the DRC. One UN estimate placed the value at around $320 million.[27] The UN brokered a peace in 2003, but the war between Hutus and Tutsis persisted albeit at a lesser level. Space does not permit spelling out yet another case of humanitarianism vexed and distorted, but since 1998 there may have been 6 million deaths.[28] Ad-ditionally, as of 2016, millions remain displaced (1.5 million in 2015 alone) and at least 7.4 million require assistance.[29] While those numbers are contested, it is worth noting that the UN maintains its largest peacekeep-ing operation with around 22,000 MONUSCO (Mission de l'Organisation des Nations Unies pour la Stabilisation en République Démocratique du Congo) personnel, costing about $1.3 billion a year. In short, the Hutu-Tutsi fight has been displaced from Rwanda itself and is now primarily fought in the eastern part of the DRC. We return to parts of the DRC story in several chapters, however, because it not only indicates an intractable crisis but also illustrates the intractability of the war itself, the clash over natural resources, the possible counterproductive nature of aid, and danger of camps in addition to widespread sexual violence.

Bosnia-Herzegovina and Kosovo:
Well-Fed Dead and "Humanitarian War"

For much of the twentieth century, Yugoslavia was a unified multiethnic state of Serbians, Croatians, Slovenians, Macedonians, Montenegrins, Albanians, Bosniaks, Kosovars, and others (see map 3.4). During WWII, the country was divided among three factions: a Croatian group allied with Nazi occupiers (Ustache); Serbians supporting the monarchy (Chetniks); and a Communist movement comprising many nationalities (Partisans). This last faction, under the leadership of Josip Tito, drove out the German army and reconstituted a stable state that experienced negligible levels of ethnic violence. With Tito's death in 1980, the Yugoslav system began to unravel. Economic problems, especially soaring inflation, in the 1980s were accompanied by ethnic nationalism caused by the crumbling of Soviet Union and other Eastern European Communist states. The result was Yugoslavia's disintegration in the early 1990s. On June 25, 1991, the country effectively broke into Serbia (which retained the title of Federal Republic of Yugoslavia), Croatia, and Slovenia. Other republics within Yugoslavia would also eventually break off: Macedonia (September 8, 1991), Bosnia-Herzegovina (April 6, 1992), and Montenegro (June 3, 2006).

In terms of humanitarianism, the two armed conflicts of most direct relevance are Bosnia-Herzegovina and Kosovo. We begin in 1991–1992, when the center of the conflict in Yugoslavia was between Croatia and Serbia. Serbs within Croatia were particularly concerned with the rise of Croatian nationalism, having experienced intense persecution during WWII at the hands of Ustache forces. In October 1990, fearing that Croatia would soon break away, Croat Serbs declared a Serb Autonomous Region in Krajina. By the end of 1991 some 10,000–15,000 had been killed, and 250,000 Serbs and 100,000 Croats displaced. The Security Council authorized a peacekeeping mission, the UN Protection Force for the Former Yugoslavia (UNPROFOR), which was to guarantee a cease-fire until a peace agreement could be worked out and which had the support of both Serb and Croat parties.[30]

While the fighting between Croatia and Serbia captured international attention, violence was mounting farther south in Bosnia where Serbs and Croats as well as Muslims (Bosniaks) were warring over control of territory; these ethnic populations had intermingled for centuries in Bosnia, which was the most diverse and mixed of what became the

THE FORMER YUGOSLAVIA

- International boundary
- Republic boundary
- Autonomous province boundary
- ⊙ National capital
- ⊚ Administrative capital
- Railroad
- Principal road
- Secondary road

Map 3.4

former Yugoslav republics. Despite this history of integration, it would become the birthplace of the ugly term "ethnic cleansing," a diplomatic euphemism for the forcible eradication of racial or national groups that fell below the threshold of "genocide."

The capital of Bosnia, Sarajevo, was a prominent battlefield in the war. In April 1992, Serbian forces blockaded the city, which lasted until early 1996, after the war's end. The "siege of Sarajevo" is illustrative of the interlocking of humanitarianism with the war and the prevailing politics of the period. Peter Andreas has written:

> For the nationalist Serb besiegers, the siege kept the city bottled up and useful as a political lever and as a distraction from more severe atrocities elsewhere. For the inner circle of Sarajevo's political leadership, the siege helped them maintain power, consolidate their party's political position, marginalize opponents and generate and sustain international sympathy and support. For the UN and its western sponsors, the siege provided a remarkably viable working environment to showcase aid provision in the Bosnian war, avoid more direct military entanglement and contain the flood of refugees. For foreign journalists, the siege offered a front row seat in a high drama spectacle and the most accessible war zone in Bosnia. Finally, for well-placed black market entrepreneurs on all sides, the siege conditions assured a captive market with highly inflated profits.[31]

The Bosnian War (1992–1995) exhibited the difficulties of deciding how best to operationalize the humanitarian impulse. Trying to deliver aid and avoid manipulation was tricky, but even when successful, recipients were still at risk. This dynamic engendered the tragic irony of the "well-fed dead," populations receiving assistance without protection—or fed today to avoid starvation but die tomorrow due to violence. The Security Council expanded the mandate of UNPROFOR to include helping to ensure UNHCR's assistance in Bosnia. The UNHCR was designated the "lead agency," although its aid went not to refugees but to those who had not crossed borders. In fact, UNHCR was fundamentally redirected to address the Balkans, consuming roughly half of the agency's budget during this time for what were victims falling outside of their mandate. Furthermore, Security Council resolution 758 of June 8, 1992, authorized UNPROFOR to secure and take control of the Sarajevo airport. However, Serb militants were blocking aid delivery, and therefore in August the Security Council decided to authorize force to bring in relief assistance without the government's consent (resolutions 770 and 771), and in September to guard aid convoys (resolution 776). Despite the growth and elaboration of mandates, there were inadequate economic and military resources to conduct the wider missions.

In 1993, the UN pushed both peace and humanitarian assistance in Bosnia. Member states negotiated the Vance-Owen plan to divide Bosnia into semiautonomous ethnic enclaves. However, this negotiation ratified that Serbs controlled 70 percent of the territory, Croats another 20 percent, and Bosnians only a sliver. As to humanitarian aid, in February, Serb militias blocked aid deliveries to eastern Bosnia, and Bosnians reacted to the absence of a political solution or effective protection by banning aid in order to pressure the UN for action. Ogata objected to Bosnian leadership immiserating its own population to make a political point, but she abided by local wishes and suspended operations; she later admitted that "no decision that I took in my ten years as high commissioner [of refugees] caused so much havoc."[32] However, UN Secretary-General Boutros Boutros-Ghali overruled her by arguing that the withdrawal of UNHCR would cause the collapse of all international efforts. He ordered UNPROFOR to protect UNHCR, although resources were inadequate to protect vulnerable populations. On April 16, 1993, Security Council resolution 819 called on UNPROFOR to establish "safe areas," which was expanded in May (resolution 824) to include Sarajevo, Gorazde, Zepa, Tuzla, and Bihac. Aside from UNHCR's working with UNPROFOR, other humanitarian agencies worked with military forces, although the ICRC maintained its distance and independence.[33]

The creation of "safe areas" was regarded as an innovation to maintain vulnerable populations where they were, as opposed to waiting until after they had fled. However, while they may have solved the immediate problem of civilian protection, safe areas contributed to a long-term political problem. Ogata explained the acute dilemma of evacuations: "If you take these people you are an accomplice to ethnic cleansing. If you don't you are an accomplice to murder."[34] Nevertheless, many Bosnians flocked to these areas in search of aid and protection. Thus, UNPROFOR's and UNHCR's collaboration normalized the complicity of aid agencies in fostering violence and amounted to militarizing and politicizing humanitarianism.

This already distressed and unstable situation became ever more volatile over the next two years and worsened in 1995. In May, the aircraft of the West's collective security organization, NATO, responded to a Serbian siege of Sarajevo by attacking an arms depot in Pale. Serbs countered by capturing 300 UN soldiers. In addition to holding peacekeepers hostage, Serbian militants chained them to Serb antiaircraft weapons to deter NATO from counterattacking. The situation continued to worsen and led to what some might consider the signature moment of the crisis: the massacre at Srebrenica (July 11–22, 1995). Dutch peacekeepers had been assigned to guard the town but withdrew after incurring one fatality and left the Bosnians unprotected. Serbs then carried out an ethnic cleansing that included the execution of 7,000–8,000 men and boys. This slaughter shamed and embarrassed NATO to intervene—there had been no such mass atrocity in Europe since WWII.

NATO eventually acted at the end of August and September by bombing Bosnian Serb militias. Croatia reconquered territory and a peace agreement resulted. While this led to the abatement of Serb violence against Bosnians, it also created an opportunity for Croatia. Seeing Serbia busy fighting NATO in Bosnia, Croatia carried out its own ethnic cleansing against Serbs in reclaiming the Krajina and other parts of western Bosnia. In November 1995, the Dayton Agreement was signed. It froze the borders such as they were, established a new federal constitution, organized a new police force, created a war crimes tribunal (discussed below), required free and fair elections in each country, and promised repatriation of the displaced. The Dayton Agreements were also predicated on and protected by the deployment of 60,000 NATO peacekeepers—a force larger and better equipped than UNPROFOR. In addition to NATO forces, there were peacekeepers from other countries, including Russia, which facilitated implementation. International forces remained in Bosnia until December 2004.

We now move to the end of the decade in Kosovo to determine whether the earlier humanitarian crises of the 1990s led to learning lessons. The Bosnian crisis and the UN debacle in failing to protect civilians in places such as Srebrenica was not the last human-made disaster to unfold in the former Yugoslavia. Kosovo, a southern part of Yugoslavia, was populated primarily by ethnic Albanians ("Albanian Kosovars") who sought independence; but this territory was deemed "Serbian" because its national identity was tied to the location of significant historical events in what had been part of the Serbian heartland. On June 28, 1389, near the town of Polje ("the field of blackbirds"), Serbs lost the Battle of Kosovo, which initiated dominance of Serbia by the Ottoman Empire. On the 600th anniversary of the battle, Serbia's president, Slobodan Milošević, gave an inflammatory speech promising local Serbs that they would never again experience conquest at the hands of Muslims. However, for most of the 1990s Kosovo remained quiet as compared to Bosnia and elsewhere in the former Yugoslavia. The Dayton Agreement was designed to bring peace to Bosnia. Part of accomplishing that was not to further antagonize Serbia and therefore the deal intentionally ignored Kosovo—where ethnic violence in the mid-1990s had not reached dramatic proportions.

In early 1998, local Serb militias in Kosovo backed by the Yugoslav (Serbian) army skirmished with a new guerrilla group, the Kosovo Liberation Army (KLA), which sought to secede from Yugoslavia. But this remained rather small-scale relative to Bosnia; by the end of 1998, some 9,000–12,000 Albanians had been killed, along with some 3,000 Serbs. That set off a refugee flow from Kosovo, mostly to Albania but also to other parts of Europe, and the prospect of another destabilizing mass displacement spurred UN action. In September 1998, Security Council resolution 1199 recognized that the "deterioration of the situation in Kosovo constitutes a threat to peace and security in the region," thereby signaling that a use of force could be required to address the human rights abuses and the humanitarian crisis.[35]

When talks in February 1999 in Rambouillet, France, failed to produce a peace agreement, the potential for the crisis to evolve as in Bosnia—replete with waves of ethnic cleansing and inadequately guarded safe areas—challenged the international community of states to respond. Within the Security Council, no agreement could be reached about whether to use force—whereas the United States and other Western powers wanted to, Russia and China actively defended the principle of sovereignty and characterized such an approach as a violation of the UN Charter.[36] In addition to the fear of establishing a precedent for such operations, Russia's opposition was adamant because of historic ties to Serbia; both countries were Eastern Orthodox. With no consensus in the Security Council, the West turned to NATO to use force to halt Serbian atrocities. On March 24, NATO began bombing Serbian targets in Kosovo and Serbia.

This military action was another turning point in humanitarian thinking about appropriate responses to mass atrocities because many humanitarians embraced force as a means of human protection and looked to a security organization outside of the UN when the Security Council was deadlocked. In this view, the invocation of "humanitarian war" provided the legitimacy—indeed, an international commission of independent experts declared that although the operation was "illegal" in violating the sovereignty of Serbia without a Security Council decision, it was nonetheless "legitimate" because of its humanitarian motivation.[37] Russia's claim to the international legal high ground was weakened when it failed to garner a council resolution criticizing NATO's bombing and demanding its halt. The wide margin (12–3) of defeat could be interpreted as burnishing NATO's claim to legitimacy, even if it did not make the intervention "legal" because it contravened the UN Charter. Secretary-General Annan drew considerable fire for his speech at the opening of the General Assembly in September 1999, when he tempered his misgivings about the absences of Security Council approval with the sentiment that he could not condone idleness in the face of Serb atrocities and suffering.[38]

Others spat out the phrase "humanitarian war," ruefully or ironically, to critique what they deemed an oxymoron. Indeed, some preferred the expression "humanitarian bombing" to denote that NATO embarked exclusively on a high-altitude campaign to coerce Serbia into complying rather than a ground campaign with civilian protection that would have entailed risks to Western troops. Some observers within the humanitarian system and elsewhere commented that the situation in Kosovo suited NATO, which was looking for relevance after its Cold War–era mission seemed to collapse along with the USSR. However, there were also new actors staking a claim to the humanitarian mantle with this posture. In a speech on April 20, 1999, UK prime minister Tony Blair stated, "I can make to you all the arguments about how important it is strategically for NATO that we are engaged, but we have embarked on it for a simple humanitarian reason and cause and we are not going to allow Milošević to get away with this policy of ethnic cleansing . . ."[39]

Seventy-eight days after bombing began, with Serbia in retreat and ruins, negotiation began; on June 3, Milošević capitulated and a deal was reached to end hostilities. Serbian armed forces would withdraw from Kosovo, the UN and NATO would deploy soldiers to ensure peace, the KLA would demilitarize, and refugees and the displaced would return. In fact, a huge number of returnees had previously fled to Albania. Initially, the intervention accelerated suffering as 1.8 million Kosovar Albanians fled. However, almost immediately they began returning home. The agreement included the deployment of an international civilian and security presence with substantial NATO participation, the establishment of an interim administration, safe return of all displaced persons, demilitarization of the KLA, and a self-governing Kosovo.

On June 10, 1999, Security Council resolution 1244 called for the establishment of the UN Interim Administration Mission in Kosovo (UNMIK). This body would coordinate the work of international organizations—the UN, Organization for Security and Co-operation in Europe (OSCE), and EU—in administering the territory, bringing in humanitarian relief, and rebuilding and reconstructing infrastructure and housing. In addition to the vast investments in peacebuilding, NATO provided the Kosovo Force (KFOR) to keep the peace in a fashion that was distinctly different from the UN's traditional "peacekeeping" troops because NATO's were warfighters. At its height, KFOR troops numbered almost 50,000 and came from thirty-nine different NATO and non-NATO countries. The stabilization and transition process was an essential contribution to providing the space to move beyond the war. UNMIK and the military support made Kosovo essentially self-governing.

Indeed, it is no exaggeration that the mission was path-breaking in making massive post-conflict peacebuilding a logical follow-on to humanitarian intervention. The scope could hardly have been more ambitious. The undertaking of comprehensive civil administration included health, education, energy and public utilities, postal services and telecommunications, judicial and legal activities, public finance, trade, science, agriculture, environment, and democratization. Simultaneously, over 800,000 people had to be repatriated; 120,000 houses rebuilt; schools reestablished; food, medicine, and other humanitarian assistance provided; electrical power, sanitation, and clean water restored; land mines cleared; and security ensured.

Kosovo unilaterally declared its independence from Serbia on February 17, 2008. International reaction was mixed, and UN member states continued to be divided on the international recognition of Kosovo. However, since 2008 over half of them—108 out of 193—have recognized it. States near Serbia and in the West support full, legal independence for Kosovo, whereas Russia, China, and others sensitive to issues of sovereignty oppose it. Thus, recognition comes from twenty-three out of twenty-eight of the EU's current members and twenty-four of twenty-eight NATO members, along with thirty-four of fifty-seven members of the Organisation of Islamic Cooperation (OIC). Serbia does not recognize Kosovo but has begun to normalize relations with the government of Kosovo.

Whether one supports or opposes Kosovo's independence or the NATO operation that brought about the present situation, this case, too, is unusual. Perhaps as a reaction to Bosnia—not wanting to repeat the failure of the "well-fed dead"—the West mounted a humanitarian intervention to halt massacres. Moreover, Western powers protected Muslim populations against Christian oppressors, which confutes the powerful critique that humanitarian interventions are solely the product of cultural and political ties between victims and the intervening power.

As in Rwanda, the humanitarian agenda pursued trials for war crimes in the Balkans. The post-WWII tribunals in Nuremberg and Tokyo had been ad hoc, designed only to address those acts committed by Nazi Germany and Imperial Japan. On May 25, 1993, Security Council resolution 827 called for the establishment of a "tribunal for the sole purpose of prosecuting persons responsible for serious violations of international humanitarian law committed in the territory of the former Yugoslavia"— or the International Criminal Tribunal for the former Yugoslavia (ICTY). Like military force and economic sanctions, the work of the ICTY also is a form of "intervention" that did not require consent from the sovereign state of Serbia because the Security Council invoked UN Charter Chapter VII. Like the ICTR, the ICTY was an important building block for the ICC, as discussed in chapter 5.

Trials began in the mid-1990s with the first verdict issued in 1996 when Serbian leader Dražen Erdemović was convicted of war crimes. Slobodan Milošević, one of the prime instigators of ethnic violence, was also indicted in the 1990s, but he went into hiding. Although he was eventually surrendered by the Yugoslav government and transferred to The Hague to stand trial, he died before its completion. Other notable figures such as

Radovan Karadžić have also been extradited. Yet because he lived openly in Belgrade for many years, albeit under a false name, there clearly remains sympathy for resistance to prosecuting those who committed war crimes on behalf of Serbia.

As of 2016, the ICTY has indicted a total of 161 people for violating international humanitarian law: 154 of the cases have been concluded, with 83 sentenced, 13 referred to domestic jurisdictions, 37 indictments withdrawn (including 16 who have died), 19 acquitted, and two are to face retrials. There are seven cases presently ongoing. The ICTY's early budget was rather modest but grew to about $250 million a year; by 2016 it had spent cumulatively about $2.5 billion. With its work winding down, that figure has dropped to about $170 million for the next two years.[40]

The Meaning of the 1990s for Humanitarians

In standing back from the specifics of northern Iraq, Somalia, Rwanda, Bosnia, and Kosovo, the new ways of war and the erratic politics of protection profoundly influenced the militarization and politicization of humanitarianism in the 1990s. The security, political, and organizational changes in the sector produced dramatic changes in humanitarian culture.

Helping in war zones was never easy, but it has proved especially daunting in the post–Cold War era.[41] David Rieff and others demonstrate a misplaced nostalgia in lamenting today's "humanitarianism in crisis,"[42] because such pensive introspection is not a "mid-life" version, especially because the ICRC was established over a century and a half ago.[43] Whatever the vintage and Steven Pinker notwithstanding,[44] humanitarians are not necessarily on the side of the angels—their motivations and mastery, their principles and products continue to be passionately debated.[45]

The "new wars" presented a set of characteristics that departed from the conventional variety that humanitarianism had been devised to address, and traditional humanitarian practices were not suited to address many of the challenges that they produced. The danger to civilians, including aid workers, is perhaps most striking. Increasingly, aid personnel are targeted intentionally because some belligerents view such attacks as a lever for repelling outsiders from being on the ground in conflicts, or alternatively by criminals who prey on the economic resources of agencies. Traditionally, for example, the ICRC's emblem afforded protection; but by the 1990s, such identifiers made them targets.[46] Despite rules prohibiting violence against aid workers, rebukes by humanitarian agencies, and Security Council resolutions calling for their protection, as well as the 1994 *Convention on the Safety of United Nations and Associated Personnel*, attacks persisted throughout the decade and beyond.

The uncertain political terrains of armed nonstate actors and perverse political economies along with mass human rights violations and attacks on aid personnel were confusing and debilitating. The "classic" operational principles of humanitarianism best exemplified and embodied by the ICRC—neutrality, impartiality, independence, and consent—were manipulated by belligerents, which in turn undermined the ability to provide assistance. In response, agencies rethought and refined their practices in the "new humanitarianisms."

The main modalities of humanitarianism each experienced a renaissance in the 1990s. In IHL, accountability was furthered with the establishment of numerous war crime tribunals and other transitional justice mechanisms. With regard to humanitarian action, it became ever more sizable and significant, and in many instances relief operations incorporated militarized means to achieve politicized ends. In short, humanitarian intervention became far more common.

To appreciate the transformation of the 1990s, we should consider the change in classic humanitarianism, which strongly embraced traditional operational principles and engaged separately from military forces while supporting the interests of states. For example, giving aid to wounded soldiers and facilitating prisoner exchanges benefited states and their militaries. In this formulation, politics were officially off-limits—humanitarianism was ostensibly designed to operate outside the political agendas of states, but in fact subscribed to operational spaces that suited the interests of states. Nevertheless, there are some well-known exceptions during which agencies worked hand in hand with states, such as the Berlin Airlift, the 1948–1949 mission to supply the city after the Soviet Union's blockade, but for the most part, independence was maintained. Reflecting the separation of humanitarianism from other agendas, the UN Security Council, whose primary jurisdiction is matters of international peace and security, customarily made no mention of humanitarian conditions or actors—from the beginning of the Security Council's deliberations in 1945 until the Six-Day War in 1967, no resolution mentioned humanitarianism. And it only referenced the ICRC starting in 1978, when there was consensus among the great powers that humanitarian access was required in Lebanon.[47] In short, in its earlier life classic humanitarianism was not militarized.

Cracks in the classic edifice of humanitarianism first appeared during and after WWII. The ICRC's wartime experience with respect to the Holocaust left many searching for a new modality. Similarly, civil wars and those resulting from decolonization also moved humanitarians to rethink the relevance of traditional operational principles. But these tensions were contained until they erupted and took on substantial proportions pointing toward a wholesale retooling of the endeavor in the 1990s, which produced a more outspoken, and in some cases militarized, humanitarianism.

At the heart of "new humanitarianisms" are the intertwined challenges of access and atrocities. Agencies needed to deliver not only aid but also protection while ensuring that it was not manipulated. But to do so, the means were viewed as provocative or intrusive by belligerents, interlocutors, and sometimes local populations. The customary *modus operandi* of neutrality, impartiality, independence, and consent was hamstrung in many situations. If the state was unwilling to receive assistance on its territory, agencies would have to look elsewhere to gain access and create humanitarian space by dealing directly with local political and military actors—be they government officials or armed nonstate actors. Some agencies experimented with alternative tactics and sought to co-opt obstinate actors by essentially engaging in trade-offs by losing some aid to get other aid through—what in other contexts would be called "bribery" or at least "taxation." For example, in 1994–1995, UNHCR accepted such aid manipulations in the refugee camps in Zaire. Beyond the usual fare of neutrality or the more recent political economic bargaining, still other agencies confronted those who impeded operations by withdrawing altogether from a theater, such as WFP and UNICEF from Somalia in March 1991.

There was, however, another route to open humanitarian space, the use of military force. Trade-offs also characterized this option. On the one hand, it can be problematic for agencies to use or work with militarized actors to deliver relief because force itself causes casualties and undermines the principles of independence and neutrality. On the other hand, without applying the leverage from the armed forces, access to victims would be limited by the whims of those local armed belligerents with superior firepower. Meanwhile, both the General Assembly and the Security Council supported the notion of creating "humanitarian space," and they defined areas of protection where agencies could distribute aid. Different versions surfaced in Iraq ("safe havens"), Bosnia-Herzegovina ("safe areas"), and Rwanda ("secure humanitarian areas"). When force was actually deployed to guarantee space, access was generally but not always attained; armed escorts often proved effective at least for a time.[48] This shift in operational thinking was cemented in the 2000 analysis of the post-decade reflection found in the Brahimi report on UN peace operations, whose paragraph 50 states: "The Security Council has since established, in its resolution 1296 (2000), that the targeting of civilians in armed conflict and the denial of humanitarian access to civilian populations afflicted by war may themselves constitute threats to international peace and security and thus be triggers for Security Council action."[49]

Aside from the obvious implications in overriding sovereignty with military force to create humanitarian space, another critique was that such space did not go far enough in addressing the longer-term problem of ethnic cleansing or genocide—that atrocities were a part of a larger political process, and tending only to the immediate bloody aftermaths of an emergency was far too modest. The relevance of this criticism was graphically demonstrated in Bosnia, because when international intervention arrived "it did so in the form of armed escorts for humanitarian relief convoys . . . [and] while the policy protecting aid convoys saved hundreds of thousands who would otherwise have perished during the harsh Balkan winters of 1992-4, helping the needy in this way is not the same as rescuing them from danger."[50] The creation of space can save populations today but does not speak to tomorrow.

Moreover, the UN forces tasked with creating space were inadequately mandated and resourced to tackle the root causes of violence. As a force commander observed, "If someone wants to fight a war here on moral or political grounds, fine, great, but count us [the UN] out. Hitting one tank is peacekeeping. Hitting infrastructure command control, logistics, that is war, and I'm not going to fight a war with painted tanks."[51] Thus, many humanitarians moved from protecting humanitarian space to endorsing humanitarian intervention. In Bosnia, agencies started to give in to the impulse to consider the possible value of military force, for example UN-HCR, while others, such as the ICRC, resisted. However, in Kosovo, many more agencies called for and worked with force to achieve their goals; for example, Oxfam, which had formerly opposed the practice, endorsed it.

In addition to the political changes that produced the "new humanitarianisms," there were also organizational ones—the sector became bigger in absolute and relative terms, and more self-conscious of the economic conditions that had an impact on the field and headquarters. Although humanitarian aid had always played a role significant in previous armed conflicts, in the "new wars" the size of aid flows changed the place and view of humanitarianism. As a veteran aid worker observed, "When it occupied the margins of conflict—as, for example, in refugee camps outside conflict areas—humanitarian action was an activity of generally minor consequence to belligerents. Aid agencies were accepted or tolerated as beneficial, or at least non-threatening. Now humanitarian action is very often at the center of conflicts and of international concern."[52]

This reasoning emerged against a backdrop of changes within the humanitarian sector during a period of enormous growth with bigger and bigger disasters with more and more victims. In 1989 humanitarians spent about $800 million, which grew by the end of the century to almost $6 billion. This more than sevenfold increase had a crucial influence on a wide range of agencies. In the 1990s, NGOs effectively broke the ICRC's and

UN's monopoly on humanitarian action.[53] Up until then the ICRC coordinated network of national societies and several relevant UN organizations mandated to humanitarian tasks—specifically the UNHCR, UNICEF, and the WFP were the UN's "Big 3." But new funding allowed NGOs and other UN bodies to play a larger role. In fact, NGOs surged—in 1995 in Bosnia and Herzegovina there were more than 250 organizations, in Kosovo in 1999 there were at least 180.[54]

The role of conflict resources in the "new wars" of the 1990s generated much debate among scholars about whether violence was motivated by "greed" or "grievance" or both. Within the humanitarian sector, one economic resource was of particular concern: relief aid itself.[55] The concern was that aid sustained those who sustain war, whether they engaged in predatory practices in causing the need for aid or in manipulating the use of aid. Some agencies ascribed to a philosophy of "do no harm," making a similar oath to that taken by medical doctors: to not act in any way to worsen the condition of patients in the course of treatment, humanitarian operations should cease where they result in fueling conflicts.[56]

The growth of the sector also influenced performance. Among humanitarian agencies there were several mechanisms for promoting coordination. The first can be essentially complementary, which means that agencies work together because their programming meshes well—for example, one works on sanitation, another on children's issues and therefore collaborates on a water project at an orphanage. There is also coordination that centralizes or attempts to provide more top-down direction in the atomized world of humanitarian organizations. The best illustration is the UN's OCHA, which on paper can exert influence but whose lack of budgetary authority makes it less than authoritative. There is also coordination that integrates humanitarian agencies into the actions of states and militaries, which compromises humanitarian principles whether the forces are occupiers or not. Coordination may run along each or all of these dimensions, and so the results often are contested. The 1990s showcase a divergence of perceptions among humanitarians about the types of activities in which they should or should not engage—everything from short-term emergency relief to long-term reconstruction and nation-building, with and without human rights provisions.

The pursuit of a wide range of goals and, consequently, of different tactics by humanitarian organizations has had an appreciable impact on the coherence of the entire system. Different tactical engagements, or a sort of "shopping around" by agencies for local actors that would enable access, have led to a strange mixture of military-humanitarian bedfellows. Belligerents have often interpreted any form of joint action between humanitarians and soldiers as taking sides, thus making aid workers targets for violence—"blowback" from helping in war zones. Beyond competing philosophies that imperil staff as well as principles, institutional competition for funding has also endangered humanitarian work broadly speaking. The marketplace for donors to choose among humanitarian agencies has promoted rivalries that ultimately undermine shared objectives. The proliferation of agencies and atomization of the international humanitarian system produces a twofold collective dysfunction: Agencies have material incentives (resources) and normative imperatives (ideas) driving behaviors to defect from common principles and goals. And the engagement by some agencies in behavior that draws attacks from belligerents has security implications for all organizations because belligerents usually do not differentiate among competing logos. Much more about the "business" that is humanitarianism is found in chapter 9.

Conclusion: New Humanitarianisms in Historical Perspective

The "new humanitarianisms" emerged from self-reflection throughout the 1990s, and the dots can be connected between thinking in one crisis and the next. In Somalia, the "Blackhawk Down" incident was the first of many traumas and suggested that working closely with military forces can also make aid workers targets; when states become casualty adverse, the result can be precipitous military withdrawals that leave populations vulnerable and make humanitarian action untenable. In Rwanda, the genocide and militarized refugee camps showed the dangers of responding with "too little, too late" along with the hazards of aid manipulation in the context of continuing insecurity. Bosnia dramatized the issue of the "well-fed dead," or just how little emergency delivery means without effective protection. In Kosovo, international law was trampled in the rush to stop Serbia from ethnic cleansing—many considered NATO's precipitous bombing without Security Council authorization as "too much, too soon," even though the operation sought to use overwhelming force to halt atrocities, deliver aid, and build a new political governance system after hostilities ceased. As Kofi Annan stated in his Nobel lecture, "Today, no walls can separate humanitarian or human rights crises in one part of the world from national security crises in the other."[57] In other words, humanitarianism had become a part of problematizing security, and in turn security had become part of solving the problems of humanitarianism. The traumas of the first part of the decade partially paved the path for other tactics by the end of the decade.

"New humanitarianisms" could also be interpreted as part of a lengthier historical context as an outgrowth of long-term and ongoing shifts in humanitarian culture that has moved from deferentially providing sustenance to any in war to being more politically sensitive. The movement to conflate humanitarian action and intervention had been building at least since the atrocities of the 1970s. As MSF's founder and later French foreign minister Bernard Kouchner summarized, "The logic of humanitarian action has led directly from the actions of the French doctors in Biafra to the U.N. administration in Kosovo."[58]

The politicization of humanitarianism in the last decade of the twentieth century hinged on an acknowledgement of changed circumstances alongside a willingness to reconceive humanitarianism as something more robust and deeper reaching. For many the impediment to departing from neutrality, impartiality, independence, and consent was imposed. For example, in reflecting on work in the camps in Kosovo at the end of the decade, Toby Porter observed:

> There were neither security concerns nor difficulties negotiating access to the refugee populations with parties to the conflict. There were no donors insisting on strategies to minimize incorporation of aid into the dynamics of the conflict. On the contrary, working in the camps actually required agencies to set aside impartiality. That they were prepared to do so with such dispatch creates the strong suspicion that the value of humanitarian principles for many agencies is a means more than an end.[59]

The reflection within the system was existential—given the contexts of the "new wars," the political machinations of manipulating parties and skewed economic structures, what had humanitarianism become and why? In the 1980s and 1990s, the development of revolutionary technologies, particularly with regard to information, communication, and transport, promised to solve many problems of relief work. But they also raised the prospect that humanitarianism had become type-cast as a functional and not a fundamentally power-altering endeavor. Indeed, drawing on his Rwandan experience, James Orbinski, remarked, "In retrospect, the response of MSF was technically near perfect, but politically uninformed."[60] The technical is not the political, and Pyrrhic victories fueled the quest for a better humanitarianism.

While some agencies basically retained their usual interpretations—for example, the ICRC continued to espouse neutrality as paramount—soul-searching took others in different directions with many "new humanitarians" becoming more explicit about their political sympathies and inclinations to use force. Oxfam, for instance, had already moved away from the traditional humanitarian canon in its 1995 handbook: "Oxfam is not neutral, in that it is on the side of poor and disadvantaged people in their search for social justice and equitable development." In 1999, MSF similarly maintained that it had moved away from the ICRC's "silent neutrality" because MSF sought to prioritize "interests of victims ahead of sovereignty considerations."[61] In this version of humanitarianism, impartiality is achieved in that an agency does not discriminate in aid work and does not take sides with warring parties, but it sides with the victims.

In short, identity issues altered the cultural values toward characterizing humanitarianism as political, but a politics invested in protecting vulnerable populations and undertaking more extensive operations to tackle root causes.[62] Consequently, a cultural-ethical divide appeared between classicists (those upholding neutrality, impartiality, independence, and consent) and solidarists (those taking sides with victims),[63] as well as those espousing more extreme views such as militarized humanitarians (working with militaries to deliver aid) and "humanitarian hawks" (cooperating with militaries to stop mass human rights abuses and change political conditions that cause humanitarian crises). Explanations for the emergence of a wider spectrum of humanitarianisms can be found in various schools of thought: realists, Marxists, and post-colonialists tended to make the same point: great powers (which in this period were essentially Western and capitalist) used the opportunity of post–Cold War consensus to harness humanitarianism for their own ends. More aggressive aid operations were only at the behest of the West. Liberals interpreted the shift in agencies to solidarism and an openness to forceful means as recognizing humanitarianism's role in cementing multilateral approaches and in rightfully building a more just world order. Constructivists called attention to the power and autonomy of humanitarian organizations as well as to the salience of ideas and norms. Critical humanitarians viewed the changes that followed the Cold War in terms of trade-offs; more aid and protection saved lives but in so doing amplified the potential for abuse and distortion.

With "new humanitarianisms" repudiating or at least questioning the value of traditional principles, by the end of the 1990s the paramount concern for humanitarianism, and perhaps world order, was the limits of state sovereignty. The cases of northern Iraq, Somalia, Rwanda, Bosnia, and Kosovo became touchstones for humanitarians, in particular, who asked: under what conditions should intervention to halt mass atrocities be permitted? It is to this breakthrough norm that we now turn.

4

Humanitarianism and Security

The Responsibility to Protect

In the southern town of Nyala, Sudan, tens of thousands of people lined both sides of the road leading to the Kalma camp to greet Secretary-General Kofi Annan, as he arrived in the region to get a firsthand impression of the humanitarian situation there (May 28, 2005). (UN photo/Evan Schneider)

In This Chapter

- Background
- The International Commission on Intervention and State Sovereignty
- Contemporary Politics and R2P
- The Enduring Debate
- Conclusion: Explaining and Evaluating R2P

This chapter investigates the responsibility to protect, the major innovation during the post–Cold War era in the ideas and institutions of humanitarian intervention—defined as the use of force to protect vulnerable populations, thereby eliminating one of the root causes of a humanitarian crisis. Routinely humanitarians, along with the public and diplomats, queried, if not lamented: What can be done when sovereign states commit mass atrocities against populations within their borders? The result was the emergence of R2P, which in turn has raised other ethical, political, and operational issues: Military force is intrinsically political, but can specific uses be recognized as genuinely serving humanitarian purposes? What are the criteria for deploying force for human protection purposes? What has been R2P's impact? What is its future?

Background

A review of the history of genocide and ethnic cleansing is horrifying on two levels. The first regards how such atrocities end. Empirically, most seem to have ended only when the perpetrators decide that their objectives have been achieved.[1] Examples include the German campaign against the Herero in southwest Africa (1904–1905), the Armenian genocide by Ottoman forces (1915–1918), and Italy's obliteration of Ethiopians (1937–1939). However, in some noteworthy instances perpetrators have been defeated militarily, such as the Nazi regime that ravaged minorities throughout Europe (1941–1945), which raised the prospect that military interventions can, in fact, have dramatic humanitarian benefits. The second consists of the politics of applying the adjective "humanitarian" to acts of intervention—in many cases its application has been manipulated or dismissed while lives are in the balance.

The birth of the international system is usually pegged to the rise of states starting with the 1648 Peace of Westphalia. This treaty marked the end of the Thirty Years' War (1618–1648), an armed conflict centered on religion; if fought today, it would be characterized as both civil and transnational given that states and nonstate actors throughout north-central Europe coerced or cleansed minority populations. Many actors invoked a right or duty to protect those who shared their faith. The Peace of Westphalia settled the dispute such that political leaders would make decisions about the religion of populations under their authority as well as accept minority rights, and that this arrangement would be mutually respected—thus constituting sovereign authorities. It could be argued that the establishment of states was and remains a solution to protection, and that it was facilitated by a series of largely humanitarian interventions.[2] However, as mass human rights violations have recurred, the sanctity of sovereignty has continued to be challenged by the practice of humanitarian intervention, both practically and normatively.

Since the late eighteenth century, states often have referred to legal authority or international law for using force to stop atrocities and changed underlying political conditions. An early instance is the Treaty of Kucuk Kaynarca, which in the wake of the Russo-Turkish War of 1768–1774 gave Russia the right to protect Christian minorities in the Ottoman Empire. This treaty subsequently led to interventions in Romania, Bulgaria, Greece, the Balkans, and Georgia. In the nineteenth century, the establishment of the Concert of Europe as a vehicle for security and human rights governance legitimated stopping massacres of Greeks by Turks in the 1820s, France's intervention in Syria in the early 1860s to protect Christian minorities, a protection force for Christian populations on Crete from 1866 to 1868, and Russia's war against the Ottoman Empire from 1877 to 1878 that resulted in independence for Bulgaria. Indeed, there was a social movement during this period that embraced the concept of humanitarian intervention and advocates dubbed themselves "atrocitarians."

In some instances, this humanitarian ideology was co-opted by disastrous imperialist projects, such as the Congo Free State, which was allocated to Belgium in the 1884–1885 Berlin Conference with the purpose of modernization. The rhetoric of humanitarian intervention was used to justify the unjustifiable, King Leopold II's genocidal and profitable methods in the name of ending of slavery. In 1898, the United States also drew on this perspective to vindicate its so-called liberation of Cuba, which purportedly prevented atrocities by Spain. Similar language was cited by the combined forces of Britain, Austro-Hungary, Russia, and other European powers that intervened in Macedonia from 1903 to 1908.

However, in the twentieth century, the use of force for humanitarian purposes had become much more controversial and contested due to cases where any humanitarian aspect was primarily a veil for other interests and dwarfed by them. This is typified by the oratory employed by Imperial Japan in Manchuria (1931), fascist Italy in Ethiopia (1935–1936), and Nazi Germany in Czechoslovakia (1939) in the lead-up to WWII. Accordingly, following the defeat of these aggressive powers, the UN Charter made explicit restrictions on the use of force, especially with respect to violating state sovereignty (Article 2, particularly paragraphs 1, 4, and 7).

Furthermore, after decolonization new member states reiterated the commitment of the international organizations to restrictions on intervention in statements such as the 1970 UN Declaration on Principles of International Law Concerning Friendly Relations:

> No state or group of states has the right to intervene, directly or indirectly, for any reason whatever, in the internal or external affairs of any other state. Consequently, armed intervention and all other forms of interference or attempted threats against the personality of the state or against its political, economic and cultural elements, are in violation of international law.

These international agreements firmly grounded the notion of state sovereignty, giving states absolute authority within their territory—a model we characterize as "sovereignty as control." With past as prelude, it is easier to understand why former colonies could be excused for not forgiving the sins of colonial powers and looking askance upon any "humanitarian" packaging of intervention.

But this was not the end of "humanitarian intervention." During the Cold War the great powers continued to invoke it to justify their actions, although such undertakings had more to do with security and prestige than addressing humanitarian conditions: the Soviet Union invaded Hungary (1956) and Czechoslovakia (1968); the United States carried out its own versions in the Dominican Republic (1965) and Grenada (1983); Belgium intervened in the Congo (1960) and later Stanleyville (part of what is now the DRC, 1964); and France interceded in Shaba (now in the southeastern DRC, 1978) and central Africa (1979). Developing countries also took up this practice.[3] First, India intervened in East Pakistan in December 1971 to liberate what would become Bangladesh after perhaps as many as 3 million had been killed and 10 million fled; India argued that Pakistan had committed "refugee aggression" by creating displacement. Second, Vietnam overthrew the genocidal Khmer Rouge regime in December 1978 to end the "killing fields" that had resulted in the deaths of between 1.7 and 2.5 million people, or a quarter of its population of 8 million. Third, Tanzania deposed the dictator Idi Amin from Uganda between October 1978 and April 1979 after he targeted ethnic minorities, killing approximately 500,000. Yet, far from settling the issue or forging acceptance of a norm of humanitarian intervention, they furthered controversy.

After the Cold War, international politics entered a new, albeit abbreviated, period of stability as tensions between the superpowers receded, which generated hope among humanitarians that a new commitment to addressing crises would emerge. Initially the United Nations sought to balance the demand for access and an acknowledgement of sovereignty in the December 1988 General Assembly resolution 43/131. However, some began to speak of what French legal scholar Mario Bettati termed *"le droit d'ingérence,"* or "the right to interfere."[4] The debate over humanitarian intervention and civilian protection more broadly was revisited and gained greater attention as numerous crises unfolded in the 1990s—including the ones previously discussed as well as others that were not (including Haiti, East Timor, Liberia, and Sierra Leone). Indeed, in the post–Cold War political atmosphere, the meaning of sovereignty and security was shifting. In his 1992 *An Agenda for Peace*, Secretary-General Boutros Boutros-Ghali argued, "The time of absolute and exclusive sovereignty, however, has passed; its theory was never matched by reality. It is the task of leaders of States today to understand this and to find a balance between the needs of good internal governance and the requirements of an ever more interdependent world."[5] Rwanda's horrors led to UNDP's 1994 *Human Development Report*, which critiqued, "The concept of security has for too long been interpreted narrowly: as security of territory from external aggression, or as protection of national interests in foreign policy or as global security from the threat of nuclear holocaust. It has been related more to nation state than to people."[6] Furthermore, the outcome of the 1999 war in Kosovo, where NATO ultimately used force to stop mass human rights violations despite its ignoring the international legal provisions of the UN Charter regime, galvanized political will to confront the issue.

As the decade was ending, UN Secretary-General Kofi Annan challenged members of the world organization to reconceptualize sovereignty in a way that respected the role of states and at the same time protected human rights, or "two sovereignties," by which he meant "developing an international norm in favor of intervention to protect civilians from wholesale slaughter."[7] The September 1999 Security Council resolution 1265 sustained this position by stating a "willingness" to consider "appropriate measures" in response "to situations of armed conflict where civilians are being targeted or where humanitarian assistance to civilians is being deliberately obstructed"; states are to ratify key human rights treaties and work toward ending the "culture of impunity" by prosecuting those responsible for genocide, crimes against humanity, and "serious violations of international humanitarian law." In addition, the resolution noted that the council would explore how peacekeeping mandates might be reframed to afford better protection to endangered civilians.

This framework's dual responsibility—internal and external—drew substantially upon the pioneering work of Francis Deng and Roberta Cohen at the Brookings Institution, the concept of "sovereignty as responsibility."[8] This essential building block emphasized the need—indeed, the duty—for the international community of states, embodied by the United

Nations and mandated since its creation to deliver "freedom from fear," to do everything possible to prevent mass atrocities. In particular, Deng's and Cohen's analyses and advocacy confronted head-on the paradox of sovereignty in the face of massive abuse by a state: the protection of IDPs depended on the cooperation of the state authorities that caused the forced displacement of their citizens in the first place. Ironically even citizens who remained within their own countries had fewer protections than refugees, who in crossing a border could call upon IHL, IGOs, and NGOs for help, but IDPs could not. The scene was set for a normative breakthrough building on the responsible exercise of sovereignty.

The International Commission on Intervention and State Sovereignty

In September 2000, the Canadian government lobbied the General Assembly and then created an autonomous group to analyze the state of the debate on humanitarian intervention and to develop a normative framework to address the problem of large-scale violence by states against populations within their own borders. The result was the establishment of the International Commission on Intervention and State Sovereignty.[9] This panel of twelve experts from around the world—six were from the West, six were from the Rest—was charged with beginning a global dialogue and promoting a new international consensus on the issue.[10]

After numerous consultations and diplomacy with governments, IGOs, NGOs, civil society representatives, and scholars, ICISS settled on a reformulation of sovereignty that underscored that states have authority in protecting people within their jurisdiction, but when they are unable or unwilling, the UN Security Council possesses the authority to address the situation. ICISS essentially argued for reconceiving the issue to focus on the rights of victims of atrocities rather than on those of states (both those that instigated the problem with violence or those responding through intervention). The commissioners explicitly drew upon Deng and Cohen's "sovereignty as responsibility" and also situated it with respect to three responsibilities of the international community of states:

- The responsibility to prevent: Long before any humanitarian crisis breaks out, it should be engaged in promoting human rights, development, and peace to avert conflicts from arising or from turning into episodes of mass violence.
- The responsibility to react: If a compelling crisis occurs, it should take measures to stop violence and the circumstances that feed it.
- The responsibility to rebuild: After military force is used, it should provide assistance for recovery, reconstruction, and reconciliation.

The responsibility to react was ICISS's main justification. Military interventions with substantial humanitarian justifications—against the wishes of a government or without genuine consent—have over the last quarter-century made humanitarianism possible in areas previously out of bounds. Cases appear elsewhere, but here we emphasize the extent to which determining whether, when, where, and why to intervene to protect civilians caught in the crosshairs of war and violence increasingly is guided by R2P. With the possible exception of Raphael Lemkin's advocacy for the 1948 Genocide Convention, no idea has moved faster or farther in the international normative arena. Friends and foes alike point to the commission's central conceptual contribution and value added: reframing sovereignty as contingent rather than absolute.[11] Unlike many other commissions, this one was demand- and not supply-driven; its recommendations have had a concrete public policy impact rather than, in one of the chair's view, "consigned directly to bookshelves or hard drives and forever thereafter unread and unremembered."[12]

The ICISS coined "R2P" to move beyond the pitched battles of "humanitarian intervention" and sought to switch the optic toward "an evaluation of the issues from the point of view of those seeking or needing support, rather than those who may be considering intervention."[13] As such, the commission shifted the Security Council's moral frame of reference from state to individual security.[14] More than 150 heads of state and government at the September 2005 World Summit took a giant step in that direction with an intergovernmental agreement on the occasion of the UN's sixtieth anniversary; the decision to have R2P apply to genocide, war crimes, ethnic cleansing, and crimes against humanity was a turning point but not quite "an international Magna Carta"—Anne-Marie Slaughter's hyperbole.[15]

Beginning with the international response in northern Iraq in 1991, the invocation of the phrase "humanitarian intervention" led to circular tirades about the agency, timing, legitimacy, means, circumstances, consistency, and advisability of using military force to protect vulnerable populations. As we have seen, two crises were seared in diplomatic imaginations—doing "too little, too late" in Rwanda's 1994 genocide and purportedly "too much, too soon" in Kosovo.

R2P's main tactical advantage is that state sovereignty is conditional; it entails duties, not simply rights; and it permits a conversation about the limits of state power even with the most ardent defenders of sovereign inviolability. After centuries of largely looking the other way, sovereignty no longer provides a license for mass atrocities in the eyes of legitimate members of the international community of states. Every state has a responsibility to protect its own citizens from widespread killings and other gross violations of their rights. If any state, however, is manifestly unable or unwilling to exercise that responsibility, or is actually the perpetrator of mass atrocities, its sovereignty is abrogated. Meanwhile the responsibility to protect civilians in distress devolves to other states, ideally acting through the UN Security Council.

Syria as well as South Sudan, to name but two cases of ongoing mass atrocities, demonstrate that a robust R2P response is not automatic, and that even universal norms are subject to geopolitics. Moreover, it remains unusual for countries to come to the rescue militarily with the risks of quagmire, and so wagering on collective spinelessness is a better bet than on collective security. And even in the event of an R2P military action, there are limits to what force can achieve—it may halt atrocities, but it cannot rehabilitate the societies that birthed them. We should also keep in mind that the bar is quite high. R2P does not aim to stop the garden variety of abuse and repression but war crimes, crimes against humanity, genocide, and ethnic cleansing. But at least the conventional interpretations of privileges for sovereigns have made room for responsibilities in the direst situations.

Critics lambaste "humanitarian intervention" or "humanitarian war" or "humanitarian bombing" as an oxymoron,[16] and David Rieff as a former advocate for military intervention has declared *resquiescat in pace* for R2P.[17] Critics are uncomfortable with military priority-setting and the absence of meaningful follow-up. In terms of the argument here, the essential takeaway is that if consent is an essential building block for traditional humanitarianism, R2P represents a normative departure, a coercive form of humanitarianism.

Although this reformulation of sovereignty and responsibilities was and remains original and radical, in many ways the broad goals and underlying responsibilities of R2P were easy to define. Moreover, support for the normative entrepreneurship was found among many UN member states that were seeking guidance after the controversies of the 1990s. That is, and to return to the earlier contention, the work of the ICISS was responding to demand unlike the work of other eminent commissions (e.g., disarmament and development or sustainable development or human security) whose ideas may have been forward-looking but beyond the feeble imaginations of government representatives.

The substantive challenge for the ICISS lay thus in crafting principles for military intervention—what specifically must be done in organizing and fielding armed responses to humanitarian crises. St. Thomas Aquinas, and the contemporary moral voices of Michael Walzer and Bryan Hehir,[18] would undoubtedly be pleased with "the precautionary principles" underlying the responsibility to protect. The debate in the 1990s can actually be seen as moving beyond "whether to intervene" to "how."[19] Concepts from the just war tradition animate much of the discussion about appropriateness, and ICISS's modified just war doctrine is clear when perusing box 4.1.

BOX 4.1
ICISS Criteria for R2P

1. "Just cause threshold": No intervention unless large-scale killings or ethnic cleansing have occurred.
2. "Right intention": The main purpose of intervention must be to halt or avert suffering.
3. "Last resort": Other options must be explored before resorting to intervention.
4. "Proportional means": The scale and duration of intervention must not exceed what is necessary to meet humanitarian goals.
5. "Reasonable prospects": The intervention must have a good chance of success or it should not be undertaken.
6. "Right authority": To be legitimate, intervention must be authorized by the UN Security Council. This criterion includes a plea to the Security Council's P5 not to use their vetoes for decisions about humanitarian operations that do not directly interfere with protection of their own national security.

What was supposed to be the final consultation of the commission in late August 2001 to finalize their report ended up being a penultimate session because as the report was in production, the 9/11 attacks occurred. Another brief consultation followed, but nothing substantive was changed; the commissioners agreed that all military intervention, including a response to terrorism—which it distinguished from purely humanitarian motives—had to follow the precautionary principles. The final report was presented to Secretary-General Annan early in December. Having been harshly grilled by the Global South for his suggestions that individual sovereignty can trump state sovereignty, his reception of the R2P reframing was memorable: "I wish I had thought of that."[20]

Contemporary Politics and R2P

As a part of the team of researchers working for the ICISS in 2001, we can attest to the almost giddy sensation experienced in thinking that the issue of humanitarian intervention was going to be given new and widely respected life by being embedded as a recognized norm. We also vividly recall the additional sadness felt as the World Trade Center towers fell on 9/11 in thinking that the efforts of the ICISS were for naught as terrorism would quickly upstage prospects for an international consensus on civilian protection. After years of reflection, we had second thoughts about the heady 1990s and the shock of the 9/11 attacks: "In retrospect, we were on the wrong page—politically and historically."[21] The world, plagued by other more pressing tensions, was not yet ready for R2P.

Nevertheless the R2P idea is alive and occupies what is now the middle ground in the growing attention to the protection of civilians in war.[22] The UN's 2004 High-level Panel on Threats, Challenges and Change endorsed "the emerging norm,"[23] which Kofi Annan also approved in his 2005 report, *In Larger Freedom*.[24] As noted, at the 2005 World Summit, R2P was only one of a few issues about which member states agreed.[25] A 2007 International Court of Justice ruling cemented the norm, stating that states "must employ all means which are reasonably available to them" to prevent genocide.[26]

While such recognition of R2P is welcome, the contrast with terrorism was stark: there was no agreement about even a definition of the latter, but it was nonetheless the subject of eleven paragraphs rather than two (R2P was essentially in paragraphs 138 and 139). Furthermore, R2P was effectively narrowed by cutting references to the responsibility to rebuild and avoiding explicit language about moving toward an obligation to intervene—that is, a Security Council blessing became indispensable. The text notes that the international community of states is "prepared to take collective action . . . on a case-by-case basis," which means that R2P is not in principle applied in every instance but only in select ones. Assessing the 2005 revisions of R2P, the former ICISS research director Thomas G. Weiss christened this change "R2P lite."[27] Yet support came from countries that had previously not backed R2P, such as Brazil, India, Nigeria, and South Africa. However, several adamant critics persisted: Venezuela, Cuba, Nicaragua, and Sudan.

Nevertheless, we should note that the following year the Security Council again reiterated an embrace of R2P's commitment to stop four types of mass atrocities. Within the UN as an organization, there have also been steps taken to reaffirm the place of R2P: in December 2007, the Security Council approved the creation of an Assistant Secretary-General position whose title is "Special Advisor on the Responsibility to Protect," and since 2001 there has been a Special Advisor to the Secretary-General on the Prevention of Genocide. In 2009 the secretary-general released a report, "Implementing the Responsibility to Protect," and the General Assembly continues to hold annual interactive dialogues each year on the issue. This demonstrates that R2P remains on the agenda and has not been forgotten and continues its normative journey from an emerging to an internalized norm,[28] which Ramesh Thakur and Thomas G. Weiss called "the most dramatic normative development of our time."[29] UN Secretary-General Ban Ki-moon in a September 2011 statement perhaps best encapsulates how far we have come: "It's a sign of progress that our debates are now about how, not whether, to implement the responsibility to protect. No government questions the principle."[30]

Moreover, there has also been normative development with regard to planning and follow-up of R2P authorizations. In 2011, Brazil introduced the idea of "responsibility while protecting" (RWP), which the UN General Assembly has supported—"the international community, as it exercises its responsibility to protect, must demonstrate a high level of responsibility while protecting." The RWP notion calls for forging a consensus on an operation before the Security Council authorizes it. It also requires the Security Council to monitor and review R2P actions. These elaborations of "responsibility" in humanitarian thought illustrate how pressures from actors aside from the moral impulse expressed by intervening powers are having an impact. R2P may have been born at the insistence of the great (and middle) powers of the West, but it is also being reshaped by the Global South.[31]

Overall, in the last few years, some criticism has remained, but R2P has nonetheless continued to become more deeply engrained in the international normative landscape. Thakur and Weiss have commented, "Norm displacement has taken place from the entrenched norm of non-intervention to the new norm of the responsibility to protect."[32] In the wake of the R2P operations in Libya and Côte d'Ivoire in 2011, a spokesman for the French mission to the UN summarized: "There is a new trend in the Security Council in which the responsibility to protect principle is gaining a new hold."[33] Further, recalling Rwanda, Bosnia, and other recent crises, "There is a desire to intervene before war crimes or ethnic cleansing can take place." This is also evidenced by the number of states that reference R2P in their remarks at the start of opening sessions of the General Assembly during the last few years. Additionally, a coalition, the S-5 (or "Small Five": Costa Rica, Jordan, Lichtenstein, Singapore, and Sweden) continue to lobby behind the scenes in the General Assembly—joined more recently by France and Mexico—for a resolution that requests veto-wielding members to refrain "from using a veto to block council action aimed at preventing or ending genocide, war crimes, and crimes against humanity." In sum, R2P occupies a niche as a recognized norm in international politics despite the pall cast by persistent contestation over the term and practice.

The Enduring Debate

The routine debates over R2P, therefore, ask whether the act of intervention—politically fraught and militarily perilous—is permissible on the one hand, and achievable on the other hand. At its root, R2P reiterates just war principles. Hugo Grotius during the Thirty Years' War was the first to explicitly articulate this idea—in fact, some proponents of this concept refer to themselves as "neo-Grotians"—which is fitting as historian Martin Gilbert comments:

> Since the Peace of Westphalia in 1648, non-interference in the internal policies of even the most repressive governments was the golden rule of international diplomacy. The Canadian-sponsored concept of "responsibility to protect" proposed the most significant adjustment to national sovereignty in 360 years. It declared that for a country's sovereignty to be respected, it must demonstrate responsibility to its own citizens.[34]

While some view this concept as intrinsically threatening to sovereignty, such advocates as Michael Ignatieff—an ICISS commissioner—argue that R2P itself does not threaten but rather reinforces sovereignty because it places the onus on the state and only seeks redress when the state fails in this seminal responsibility. Furthermore, proponents contend that it is fundamentally only those who perpetrate mass human rights abuses who express worries about sovereignty; meanwhile, the actual victims of atrocities support intervention as revealed in one of the few studies of their views.[35] Lastly, supporters of ICISS also note that part of the political challenge of realizing R2P lies in grounding the principle globally. Thus, it cannot merely reflect Western values and power—in other words, it is crucial to embed the norm as power spreads from the West to the Rest.

The Security Council is the centerpiece for R2P actions because it renders decisions as to its legitimacy in specific cases, and it can call for the resources necessary to operationalize it. In this way, the council is a lever of humanitarian power not just for a specific mission but also for normalizing the practice. The Security Council has made references to R2P on numerous occasions: It began with an April 2006 resolution 1674 on the protection of civilians in armed conflict, which expressly "reaffirms the provisions of paragraphs 138 and 139" of the September 2005 World Summit outcome. The August 2006 resolution 1706 on Darfur repeats the same language with specific reference to that conflict. The first meaningful operational references to R2P came against Libya in 2011: resolution 1970 had unanimous support for a substantial package of Chapter VII efforts (arms embargo, asset freeze, travel bans, and reference of the situation to the International Criminal Court); no state voted against resolution 1973, which authorized "all necessary measures" to enforce a no-fly zone and protect civilians. Subsequently in July 2011, in approving a new peacekeeping mission in South Sudan, R2P once again figured in resolution 1996. Between the 2005 World Summit decision and the end of 2016, the council had referred to R2P on some fifty occasions. In addition, in 2011 the Human Rights Council referred to R2P for the first time in resolution S-15/1, which led to the General Assembly's resolution 65/60 that suspended Libyan membership in the council. At that moment, there also were forty-nine member states and the EU actively participating in the "Friends of R2P," along with two New York–based advocacy groups (the Global Centre on the Responsibility to Protect and the International Coalition for the Responsibility to Protect).

The R2P norm has moved quickly, but the concept is still young as the first special adviser on R2P, Edward C. Luck, notes: "like most infants, R2P will need to walk before it can run."[36] Nonetheless, many victims will suffer and die if R2P's adolescence is postponed. The process begun by ICISS continues to be a cause for civil society and supportive governments that push skeptical countries and the UN bureaucracy to take seriously Ban's earlier rhetorical call to translate "words into deeds."[37]

Initially, many observers feared that further debate would lead to diluting the September 2005 commitment. Fears about normative backpedaling seemed concrete enough; for instance, on the eve of the 2005 debate, *The Economist* described opponents who were "busily sharpening their knives."[38] The Nicaraguan president of the General Assembly, Father Miguel d'Escoto Brockmann, unsheathed his Marxist dagger and suggested "a more accurate name for R2P would be . . . redecorated colonialism."[39]

R2P naysayers have surely been disappointed by the discernible shift from antipathy to wider public and state acceptance, and in some cases even embrace, of the norm.[40] Indeed, a 2016 public survey of views about contemporary armed conflicts commissioned by the ICRC found the following: "The majority of people would still like to see more political intervention from the international community in the future in order to help stop violations of the laws of war. This is particularly true among people living in countries affected by armed conflicts."[41] And the uneasy criticism with the so-called Trojan Horse for Imperialism that is supposed to be R2P surfaced at higher decibel levels around Libya, as we discuss later.

For some time, Mohammed Ayoob has insisted that the record of the use of force in international affairs has been invariably shrouded in humanitarian aspirations, but they are intrinsically about great powers dominating weaker powers and instituting governance structures that benefit those who intervene.[42] "The 'new interventionism' is a replaying an old record. It is an updated variant of traditional practices that were impeded in a bipolar world system that allowed some space for nonalignment—a concept that effectively vanishes when one of the two poles disappears," Noam Chomsky argues. "The Soviet Union and to some extent China, set limits on the actions of the Western powers in their traditional domains, not only by virtue of the military deterrent, but also because of their occasional willingness, however opportunistic, to lend support to targets of Western subversion and aggression."[43]

In short, colonial history clearly colors perceptions of contemporary discourse. As Ramesh Thakur remarks, developing countries "are neither amused nor mindful at being lectured on universal human values by those who failed to practice the same during European colonialism and now urge them to cooperate in promoting 'global' human rights norms."[44] And more recently he wrote: "the inconsistent practice, double standards, and the sporadic nature of Western powers' interest in protecting human rights shows that noble principles are often convenient cloaks for hegemonic interests."[45] Mahmood Mamdani echoes this sentiment but goes further in arguing that R2P perpetuates a system that allows those in the West to assert their freedoms and privileges (including critiquing non-Western societies as unfree) while subjecting others in the name of giving them security and guaranteeing their rights. R2P thus creates "sovereign states whose citizens have political rights, and de facto trusteeship territories whose populations are seen as wards in need of external protection."[46]

While many of the usual suspects in the Global South—from Sudan to Zimbabwe, from Burma to Venezuela—remain ardent foes of R2P, other developing countries have become more supportive.[47] The academics, activists, and state representatives who oppose R2P often complain about different aspects; box 4.2 contains the ten main critiques of the norm. "Sovereignty is like one of those lead-weighted dolls you can never get to lie down," writes Gareth Evans. "One might have thought that multiple changes in the global and regional landscape had worked in the modern age to limit the salience of the concept."[48] That international military force for human protection remains a policy option represents significant new middle ground in international relations, along with the limits already placed on economic, legal, and political freedom of action by interdependence, international law, and pressure to solve trans-boundary problems.

In short, the long-standing controversies about humanitarian intervention endure regardless of whether it is packaged as R2P. The fraught nature of R2P is evidenced by more than 1,100 pages of *The Oxford Handbook of the Responsibility to Protect* published in 2016.[49] The contentions remain front and center in discussions of R2P in foreign and defense ministries as well as UN forums. In addition, other issues concern R2P's operationalization. For instance, are more "Syrias" inevitable if, as the 2005 World Summit document asserts, the Security Council is the only source of legitimate authorization? How should military capacity (namely rapid response forces) be organized to implement R2P? What military doctrine and rules of engagement should be followed? How can accountability be ensured in cases in which interveners violate human rights? How can gender elements be incorporated into R2P? What role do victimized populations play in realizing R2P? How does R2P relate to IHL and the ICC?

BOX 4.2
Criticisms of R2P

1. "Impulse" vs. "imperative": Some argue about the extent to which R2P should be mandatory in situations of mass human rights violations. Is there a "humanitarian impulse" (those who want to may respond) or a "humanitarian imperative" (all must actively engage)? The vagueness of the threshold makes it either too subject to selectivity or an overwhelming endless commitment.
2. The narrowing of the R2P package of responsibilities: Some contend that "prevention" and "follow-up" have become marginal components of R2P and aim simply to ease acceptance of the "intervention" module. That is, R2P is fundamentally about using force and its other aspects are political window dressing designed purely to obscure that intervention is the most likely product of its normative elements.
3. R2P criteria of right intention are problematic: Motives are impossible to measure and if a clear and exclusive humanitarian goal is the purpose, the operation will never be realized because states are unlikely to expend treasure and resources solely or even mainly for this reason.
4. R2P sanitizes war: The operational principles of R2P create a myth that the use of force is tightly regulated and that humanitarian intervention is somehow distinct from the ugly reality of war.
5. R2P is not a deterrent: The premise that atrocities will elicit a use of force against perpetrators has seemingly not made states less inclined to engage in mass human rights violations.
6. R2P creates a "moral hazard": The prospect of external intervention in response to genocidal violence may establish a disturbing incentive structure whereby rebel groups engage in resistance or reject negotiated settlements, which continues or escalates violence (i.e., the opposition engages in provocation that ultimately results in greater harm to civilians by retaliatory governments); the larger and more sinister the atrocity, the greater likelihood for outside parties to come to the rescue.*
7. R2P does not address dangerous situations beyond obvious atrocities: Some maintain that R2P does not go far enough in defining

(continued)

---

*Alan J. Kuperman, "Mitigating the Moral Hazard of Humanitarian Intervention: Lessons from Economics," *Global Governance* 14, no. 2 (2008): 219–40.

BOX 4.2
Continued

situations that warrant the use of force and should include responding to the overthrow of democracy or environmental disasters or the destruction of cultural heritage. Although coups and invasions may trigger humanitarian crises that cross the designated threshold of R2P, there may also be other human rights violations or dangers that are essentially bloodless; some mechanism should be put in place to address these problems.

8. R2P addresses symptoms rather than structural problems: Force can protect populations and perhaps remove or eliminate abusive regimes, but it does not solve underlying political problems and build a sustainable peace.

9. R2P focuses on intervention but ignores the dominance of great powers in fostering an environment conducive to atrocities: Similar to the argument about structural influences, R2P often overlooks the influence of hegemonic states in sustaining or propelling preconditions for mass human rights violations, such as repressive conceptions of statehood or oppressive neoliberal economic systems.*

10. R2P is a new version of imperialism: Warmed-up colonialism is undoubtedly the most prevalent and visible criticism. This line of criticism contends that the power to rescue is nonetheless power and an imposition usually enacted by a great power or regional power exerting and glorifying its influence.

---

*David Chandler, "The Responsibility to Protect? Imposing the 'Liberal Peace,'" *International Peacekeeping* 11, no. 1 (2004): 59–81.

Conclusion: Explaining and Evaluating R2P

R2P has come a long way, including the politics surrounding it. Although specific decisions about when and where to invoke R2P remain controversial, fewer and fewer commentators suggest that it is entirely flawed as a premise for organizing global responses to mass atrocities. Instead, the debate now centers on achieving R2P's aims, including creating responsible paths for exiting once large-scale violence has been averted or ended. Gareth Evans is certainly correct to calculate the period since the release of the ICISS report in December 2001 as "a blink of the eye in the history of ideas."[50] R2P has moved from the passionate prose of an international commission's report toward being a mainstay of international public policy debate. Luck reminds us that the lifespan of successful norms is "measured in centuries, not decades,"[51] but R2P already seems firmly embedded in the values of international society and occasionally in policies and tactics for a particular crisis. And it certainly has the potential to evolve further in customary international law and to contribute to ongoing conversations about the qualifications of states as legitimate, rather than rogue, sovereigns.

That said, military force is not a panacea, and its use is not a cause for celebration. Armed force was largely absent from the international R2P agenda until the action in Libya in 2011, a reality that substantiates the judgment by Gary Bass in his history of efforts to halt mass atrocities: "We are all atrocitarians now—but so far only in words, and not yet in deeds."[52] Ramesh Thakur, an ICISS commissioner whose earlier comments suggest his openness to the concerns of post-colonialists, took the occasion of the commission's fifteenth anniversary to examine the academic and policy literatures and cautioned:

> The failure to guarantee reliable UN protection of at-risk victims of atrocities ensures a continuing interest in unilateral humanitarian intervention which will remain attractive to many people and countries as an alternative moral framework for trying to respond effectively and in time. But this can only be at the cost of immediate global controversy and long-term damage to the principle of an international order governed by the rule of law.[53]

Embodying the state of the art of humanitarian intervention, R2P reflects the perennial humanitarian zeitgeist of addressing atrocities that came to a head in the 1990s. The worries and fears about burgeoning massacres have powered a revolutionary new framework for delivering rights, justice, and security. However, after the fiercely contested case of Libya in 2011 and the seemingly impossible one of Syria, it is unclear whether the tragedies that first sparked R2P can sustain it.

Theory offers some interpretive answers to R2P's significance. Realism sees it as an expression of pure power politics that downplays R2P's normative appeal; realists also note that great powers have not enhanced their security in deploying the tool. Given that R2P has unfolded as a norm-based project, it appears to be better explained by liberal thought and constructivist processes. Little evidence has surfaced to support the Marxist worry that R2P is another means of sustaining capitalism. The absence of clarity of the impact of R2P on gender suggests that feminism's agenda for investigation remains largely untested. Critical humanitarianism perhaps best illuminates the trade-offs inherent in R2P: rescue is invaluable to those it saves, but its selective use can be problematic for those who might be sacrificed so that others might be saved. In essence, to keep this dream alive, who will have to die? We return with partial answers in chapter 6, but first we examine another striking institutional development, the ICC.

5

Humanitarianism Adjudicated

The International Criminal Court

Logo of the International Criminal Court

This chapter focuses on the legal adjudication and international judicial pursuit of violators of humanitarian principles underlying the laws of war. In interpreting humanitarianism as a social relationship, the necessary starting point is providing justice—for example, in the case of relief, a transfer of life-saving succor; in this instance, recognition of injustice and, where appropriate, punishment or reparations. Courts, tribunals, and truth and reconciliation commissions are an extension of humanitarianism itself because international judicial organizations and processes judge the application of humanitarian standards and advance justice. Although we discussed this modality of humanitarianism earlier with reference to history and specific catastrophes, here we concentrate on and provide the backdrop for the foremost international institution for addressing the problem of war crimes, the International Criminal Court. The key questions underpinning this chapter are: Why and how did the ICC emerge? What has been its performance, and how can it be evaluated? What does the state of the ICC suggest about the nature of humanitarianism?

Jus Post Bellum and War Crimes

Our analysis of the pursuit of justice focuses on legal norms and organizational procedures, although at the outset it should be noted that other options have also rendered "justice," itself a highly contested idea. Among the alternatives are executions, show trials, castration, deportation to a neutral country, and ignoring violent behavior to make peace.

In addition to the discussion of *jus ad bellum* and *jus in bello* in chapter 1, we locate the central tenets of international war crimes law as descending from just war but in the form of a relatively new concern with *jus post bellum*.[1] In addition to IHL's coverage of decisions to go to war and conduct in war, *jus post bellum* involves just conduct in the aftermath of war that consists of three elementary principles. First, the judgments of law are grounded in agreed rules and not subject to the political whims of the powerful. Second, laws transcend state borders and apply uniformly everywhere (universal jurisdiction). Third, trials incorporate fundamental liberties to ensure fairness in the proceedings (due process), which includes the right to representation (to have a lawyer or advocate assist with defense and speak on behalf of defendants), the right to present evidence (to offer documentation of facts and behaviors), and the right to cross-examine witnesses (to question those providing testimony).

International Justice for War Crimes Prior to 1998

Other attempts to address war crimes occurred long before the ICC was established in 1998 and began its work in 2002.[2] In the nineteenth and early twentieth centuries,[3] trials were conceived and debated but not effectively carried out. For instance, after the Napoleonic Wars in 1815, France held a few treason trials to prosecute Bonapartists who supported the return of Emperor Napoleon from exile on the island of Elba. However, the burst of international law in the early 1900s made little or no mention of adjudicating war criminals—for example, the Fourth Hague Convention of 1907 contained no penalties for violating codes of land warfare.

In 1918, following WWI, provisions of the Treaty of Versailles pledged judicial action. Article 227 stated that "the Allied and Associated Powers publicly arraign William II of Hohenzollern, formerly German Emperor, for a supreme offence against international morality and the sanctity of treaties" and a "special tribunal will be constituted to try the accused." Articles 228 and 299 continued, "The German Government recognizes the rights of the Allied and Associated Powers to bring before military tribunals persons accused of having committed acts in violation of the laws and customs of war," and the Commission on the Responsibility of the Authors of the War and on Enforcement of Penalties would organize proceedings against the former German emperor, Wilhelm II.[4] However, few trials took place and the sentences that were handed out were light; the Netherlands refused to extradite the Kaiser, making the issue of his adjudication moot. The United States consciously chose not to pursue trials for fear of violating principles of sovereignty and creating the impression that justice was only for the victors—a common theme in many critiques of international justice. In fact, some Americans did not support the initiative; for instance, the secretary of state at the time, Robert Lansing, was an ardent supporter of sovereignty and its interpretation that only sovereigns are responsible to their own subjects. Moreover, as US president Woodrow Wilson commented, responsibility for the conflict resided in the unstable political relations on the continent: "the whole European system bears the deeper guilt of the war—its combination of alliances and agreements, a developed web of intrigue and espionage, which assurance drew the whole family of nations into its web."[5]

In 1920, in Turkey, as part of the Treaty of Sèvres, the victors called for the adjudication of Turkish leaders who directed the Armenian genocide, but without success. The formation of Turkey out of the ashes of the Ottoman Empire galvanized Turkish resistance against meaningful trials, thereby preventing any sort of legal determination. In the end, Turkey held its own "Istanbul Trials," but the handful of sentences rendered were light. Part of the subtext of the exercise was a denial that crimes against humanity had been committed upon Armenians between 1915 and 1917, a denial that remains today in official Turkish government pronouncements.[6] And the 1923 Treaty of Lausanne, which granted a "Declaration of Amnesty" for offenses during the war, further underscored a dearth of possible legal remedies, and the desire to turn a page on the past.

Between the world wars, there were two failed but noteworthy attempts to create a permanent international criminal court. In 1920, the judicial advisory committee for the first international court to adjudicate legal disputes between states—the Permanent Court of International Justice (PCIJ) created in 1922—recommended that it also try individuals for international crimes. The League of Nations, however, rejected the proposal. In 1934, a Bulgarian nationalist killed the Yugoslav king and French foreign minister, which led Paris to propose that the league prosecute terrorism. A treaty was drafted to criminalize it under the domestic law of signatories and to create a permanent court, but again nothing resulted.

In this same period, however, the 1928 Kellogg-Briand Pact supposedly made war illegal. Some have argued that the principles within this international legal instrument established jurisprudence in setting out criminal behavior, which undermined subsequent claims that the law was *ex post facto* and that there were no legal grounds for prosecution after World War I. However, even at the time, observers recognized that the dramatic verbiage was more stirring than effective. Sheldon Glueck, criminologist at Harvard Law School, commented at the time, "The Pact sounds too much like a pious wish expressed in rather pompous terminology. The more I read it in the light of recent history, the more it seems to laugh in my face as a piece of ghoulish and dishonest international law mumbo-jumbo."[7] The 1929 Geneva Conventions also made some effort to promote compliance through criminal penalties but with soft language. Article 29 reads, "Parties shall also propose to their legislatures should their penal laws be inadequate, the necessary measures for the repression in time of war of any act contrary to the provisions of the Charter."

After WWII, in Germany from November 1945 to October 1946, the Trials of the Major War Criminals before the International Military Tribunal (IMT) were held at Nuremberg. The basis for these trials was primarily the crime of aggression—that Germany attacked other states. Crimes against humanity, such as extermination of minority populations, had not been clearly enumerated beforehand and, surprisingly, legal proceedings did not address them in substance. Second, although there were persistent worries about sovereignty as well as accountability for Allied forces, no soldiers from the winning side were brought before tribunals despite having killed civilians. US president Dwight D. Eisenhower was especially concerned about the fate of professional soldiers, who followed the orders of political leaders. In Japan, from May 1946 to November 1948, the International Military Tribunal for the Far East judged Japanese war criminals. These trials raised essentially the same issues as those in Nuremberg.

The complete Allied victory in 1945 made possible the international prosecution of senior war criminals. The IMT and IMTFE initiated the modern era of international criminal law by rejecting the notion of collective responsibility and taking the radical step of holding leaders accountable for acts committed while agents of the state—thereby rejecting immunity. They also developed substantive criminal law by spelling out crimes against humanity, which incorporated emerging human rights norms into IHL. After WWI, the central focus of prosecutions had been legal violations of conduct during war, mostly relating to treatment of soldiers on the battlefield or as POWs; but after WWII, a specific class of offenses gained attention: abuses against civilians.

The experience of Nuremberg motivated the ratification of the Genocide Convention in 1948—the absence of that specific crime had meant that those responsible for the Holocaust could only be prosecuted for "persecution" (part of crimes against humanity). The definition of war crimes in the Nuremberg Charter was codified and further developed in the 1949 Geneva Conventions and 1977 Additional Protocols, which criminalize specific acts in war ("grave breaches") and call for the prosecution or extradition of violators. The tribunals' judges also generated procedural law by establishing the judicial processes that would apply during the trials, based on the Allies' domestic criminal law.

Some objected to the content of the decisions and sentences because they did not reach a verdict commensurate with the magnitude of the crimes. Others, however, objected to the legality of the process for three reasons: First, the jurisdiction was a violation of sovereignty and not negotiated but imposed. Second, the laws were not on the books until after crimes were committed (*ex post facto*) and were therefore illegitimate. Third, the trials constituted "victor's justice," such that the losers (in Germany and Japan) faced justice whereas the winners were ignored and effectively absolved—for instance, there were no trials for the UK's firebombing of Dresden (February 13–15, 1945), the US atomic bombing of Hiroshima (August 6, 1945) and Nagasaki (August 9, 1945), or the Soviet execution of Polish soldiers at Katyn (April–May 1940). Telford Taylor, a

US prosecutor on leave from the Supreme Court, complained, "The laws of war do not apply only to the suspected criminals of vanquished nations. There is no moral or legal basis for immunizing victorious nations from scrutiny. The laws of war are not a one-way street."[8] The US military understood the politics; General Curtis LeMay, head of the US bombing campaign against Japanese cities, stated, "I suppose if I had lost the war, I would have been tried as a war criminal. Fortunately, we were on the winning side."[9] The accusation of "victor's justice" rang true because of inadequate protection for the accused; the Allies selected the judges; the principle of non-retroactivity was ignored for mass atrocities; and judgments, including death sentences, were final and without appeal.

After these tribunals completed their work and the Genocide Convention was signed in December 1948, the issue of war crimes almost vanished until the 1990s. As the Cold War deepened, neither side wanted to delineate principles or legal commitments. While public international law applies largely to states, there are two primary exceptions: piracy (outlawed for more than 200 years) and rebel groups in armed conflict. In fact, IHL's provisions apply to all belligerents, and the Security Council has applied wide-ranging sanctions on such nonstate actors as the National Union for the Total Independence of Angola starting in the early 1990s.[10] As such there traditionally has been little accountability for individuals for breaches of international law until the controversial exception of the council's targeting individuals (in governments and in nonstate groups) with sanctions but without a process to determine wrongdoing. Moreover, state responsibility is not criminal—it carries no penalties such as imprisonment for officials.

By contrast, international criminal law is a mixture of international humanitarian and human rights law with domestic criminal law that provides for individual accountability. IHL proscribes certain behavior during armed conflicts, has been drawn on by all international tribunals since Nuremberg and Tokyo, and provides a clear concrete element of contemporary international criminal law. The post-Nuremberg broadening of international criminal responsibility to include actions outside of and during armed conflict against one's own citizens reflects the incorporation of international human rights law. Applying domestic criminal law and trial procedures has filled gaps in an international legal system established for a different purpose—the consensual regulation of the international behavior of states. The range of offences consists of war crimes, crimes against humanity, genocide, torture, terrorism, and aggression. The post-WWII tribunals and the ad hoc ones for the former Yugoslavia and Rwanda have prosecuted the first three, which are known as "core mass atrocity crimes."

The term "international criminal justice" describes the judicial mechanisms for holding individuals accountable, including via state prosecution for crimes committed within its territory, or under universal jurisdiction if committed elsewhere. One of the main reasons for international tribunals is the failure of domestic courts to pursue gross abusers of human rights.

The Nuremberg and Tokyo tribunals heightened temporarily an interest in international criminal law and a possible permanent court. In 1947, General Assembly resolution 177 requested the International Law Commission (ILC), a subsidiary body, to survey the criminal law developed by the IMT.[11] In 1948, it passed resolution 260 to study a possible court, which the ILC's 1951 report recommended.[12] The ILC also drafted a statute in 1953.[13] However, the General Assembly postponed consideration, primarily due to disputes about the definition of aggression and the basis for establishing jurisdiction.

The momentous political changes after the Cold War rekindled interest in enforcing international criminal law. Trinidad and Tobago led a coalition of sixteen Caribbean and Latin American countries that encouraged the General Assembly to request the ILC to study creating a court to combat drug trafficking (aspects of transnational jurisdiction seemed problematic), which was approved in resolution 44/39. The ILC also continued research into a draft code of crimes[14] and produced a draft court statute in 1994.[15] Building on the momentum of the ad hoc Security Council tribunals, this draft became the basis for the ICC statute in 1998.

Some have looked to the UN system to address the issue, although the world organization's Charter is silent on the issue of criminal tribunals. However, there is one avenue that held such a possibility; under Article 41, the Security Council has the authority to pursue measures other than force to promote and protect international peace and security—and the argument could be made that justice connects in this way. But this path has only been followed by the Security Council to authorize the creation of courts or refer cases to courts, not for the Security Council to actually engage in the administration of justice.

In the discussion of key cases of the 1990s, we encountered the first two tribunals created since WWII, those created by the Security Council in 1993 and 1994, respectively, to try individuals for mass atrocities committed on the territory of the former Yugoslavia after 1991 (ICTY, in The Hague, the Netherlands) and during the year of Rwanda's genocide (ICTR, in Arusha, Tanzania). Later the council modified these courts, and also has been intermittently and variously involved in the creation of "hybrid" international-domestic tribunals.[16]

The end of superpower rivalry paradoxically led to both a growth in intrastate conflicts in the 1990s and improved prospects for conflict management. We learned that the early post–Gulf War euphoria about the possibilities for robust Security Council action quickly soured in the wake of the 1993 debacle in Somalia, and the inability to end the war and atrocities in the former Yugoslavia and the genocide in Rwanda further dampened the short-lived enthusiasm. Rather than military action, the Security Council decided to use Chapter VII to create tribunals to prosecute those responsible for atrocities in these wars.

The Security Council's deliberations illustrated the renewed possibilities to initiate international action, judicial as well as other Chapter VII measures; it is important to consider these in addition to the details of the ad hoc tribunals. Resolution 780 of October 1992 requested that the secretary-general create a commission of experts to examine evidence of gross violations of international humanitarian law in Yugoslavia, which recommended the creation of an ad hoc international tribunal. The commission stated that the customary law of war crimes establishes a legal basis for universal jurisdiction, and the Genocide Convention (Article VI) for an international tribunal.[17] Not all members of the council, including the permanent ones, were initially on board. The United States favored a judicial approach, the United Kingdom was wary of the consequences for a peace deal based upon negotiating with war criminals, and China consistently expressed reluctance based on its defense of sovereignty. Nevertheless, Security Council resolution 808 asked the secretary-general to develop specific proposals. His report included a statute for the tribunal,[18] which the council approved unanimously in May 1993 by resolution 827. In December of that year, in a significant indication of the broad state support for this unprecedented political and legal move, the General Assembly welcomed the court's creation in resolution 48/88 and encouraged the contribution of resources for its effective functioning.

In April 1994, the Security Council condemned the violence and breaches of international humanitarian law in Rwanda, but its reluctance to confront the tragedy militarily was evident from a presidential statement—less authoritative than a resolution—that avoided the word "genocide."[19] Mounting criticism and fatalities led the council to request the secretary-general to draw up contingency plans.[20] A report issued in May by a special rapporteur, who was appointed by the Commission on Human Rights[21] to investigate allegations of genocide, encouraged the council to acknowledge the gravity of the situation by using the "G" word, which appeared in resolution 925 in June. The following month, resolution 935 requested the secretary-general to create a commission of experts to investigate the alleged breaches of humanitarian law. The interim report of the commission of experts recommended the establishment of an international court,[22] leading the council to establish the Rwanda tribunal in November 1994 by resolution 955 months after the killing ended. Unlike the ICTY statute, the US and New Zealand governments drafted the ICTR's, with assistance from the new Rwandan one. That post-genocide, Tutsi-dominated government was an elected council member at that time; it voted against the creation of the ICTR because it did not have a provision for the death penalty and was not based in Rwanda.

The legal basis for the tribunals was contentious because the UN Charter does not explicitly authorize the Security Council to establish judicial bodies. The objection that the council was acting *ultra vires*—beyond its legal authority—was raised during negotiations over both ad hoc tribunals, especially by China and Brazil. But Charter Article 39 gives the council the right to act in response to threats to international peace and security— as perceived by the council itself—effectively the power to define what counts as a threat and an acceptable response.

There have also been war crimes hearings without actual trials (that is, enforcement components) that gave amnesty for acknowledging crimes, as was the case in post-apartheid South Africa (the Truth and Reconciliation Commission) and post–civil war El Salvador (the Truth Commission).[23] There are also a few states (for example, Spain and Belgium) that have pursued foreign war criminals—that is, invoked universal jurisdiction in regard to national jurisprudence, although with limited success. Lastly, in addition to the ICTY and ICTR, the Security Council has also created a handful of war crimes tribunals constructed to address particular situations with a mixture ("hybrid") of international and national judges (e.g., for Sierra Leone, East Timor, Kosovo, Lebanon, and Cambodia).[24]

These precedents were consequential, especially the ICTY and ICTR. But despite their ad hoc character, their creation suggested that the moment was propitious to pursue an older notion, a permanent international criminal court.

The Rome Statute and the ICC's Formation

In many ways, the ICC is the culmination of previous efforts to bring war criminals to justice. It was first conceived as a follow-up to the Genocide Convention, whose Article 6 states that genocide could be prosecuted "by such international penal tribunal as may have jurisdiction with respect to those contracting parties which shall have accept its jurisdiction." Around that same time, the General Assembly commissioned the ILC to study the possibility of organizing a permanent war crimes tribunal. Despite a formal proposal crafted in 1954, it was undercut by Cold War divisions and remained on the drawing boards.

After the Cold War, there was a renewed interest. In the summer of 1998, the UN Diplomatic Conference on the Establishment of a Permanent International Criminal Court was convened in Rome; it was attended by 160 states, 33 IGOs, and 236 NGOs. In mid-July, the gathering produced the treaty that is the ICC's legal basis; the final vote for its creation was 120 states for, 7 against, and 21 abstentions. A court with universal jurisdiction was to be based in The Hague to prosecute four crimes. The first is genocide, which is the intent to destroy, in whole or in part, a national, ethnic, racial, or religious group. The second is crimes against humanity, or the widespread or systematic attack, with prior knowledge, directed against any civilian population. The third is war crimes, which are grave breaches of the Geneva Conventions and other serious violations of the laws and customs applicable in international armed conflict and in conflicts "not of an international character" listed in the Rome Statute, when they are committed as part of a plan or policy or on a large scale. The fourth is aggression; at the time of the Rome gathering, this specific crime was undefined. It remained so until a conference reviewed the document in 2010 and agreed to a definition that basically refers to a use of force that is in breach of the UN Charter—the planning, preparation, initiation, or execution of an act of using armed force by a state against the sovereignty, territorial integrity, or political independence of another state. However, its provisions only came into effect in 2017.

After sixty states ratified it, the Rome Treaty came into effect on July 1, 2002. The ICC only covers crimes committed after this date (i.e., they cannot be pursued retroactively) and only on the territory of states that are party to the treaty (having ratified it) or if the perpetrator is a national of the state that is party to the treaty. Non-party states can accept the court's jurisdiction to investigate particular allegations. The Security Council also can authorize action when universal jurisdiction pertains. In addition, the ICC prosecutor can receive approval from a pre-trial chamber to pursue an investigation. In general, the court's jurisdiction is informed by the principle of "complementarity," whereby it must be demonstrated that existing national jurisdiction is unable or unwilling to prosecute.

The ICC remains controversial.[25] As of the end of 2016, 124 states were signatories. States disapproving of the ICC are not as numerous, but they are powerful. On-the-record opponents include Russia, China, India, Israel, and the United States.

The United States has been particularly outspoken in resisting the ICC, despite initially being a supporter and having led the way for Nuremberg, Tokyo, and the ad hoc tribunals. During the negotiations, the United States objected to the court's jurisdiction (that nationals of a non-signatory state could be prosecuted if crimes were committed in the territory of signatory state); the prosecutor's role (too potentially independent); and the definition of the crime of aggression (too vague). At the end of his term in 2000, President Bill Clinton signed the agreement although he did not submit it to the Senate for ratification because it was clear that there would be no approval. After coming into office, President George W. Bush publicly renounced the ICC and took the highly unusual step of "unsigning" the treaty in May 2002 shortly before it was to come into effect. John Bolton, who would later become Bush's ambassador to the UN, argued in 2002, "The ICC is an organization whose precepts go against fundamental American notions of sovereignty, checks and balances, and national independence. It is an agreement that is harmful to the national interests of the United States, and harmful to our presence abroad."[26] To that end, if the ICC should take root, Bush pushed the Security Council to grant the United States (and others who had not committed to the treaty) temporary immunity. In July 2002, the Security Council granted it for one year.

However, Bush worried that the ICC could still potentially try US citizens if another country handed them over; thus he signed the American Service-Members Protection Act—the so-called "Hague Invasion Act"—that spelled out the use of force to liberate any US soldier detained by the ICC. At the same time, Washington hoped not to jeopardize the potential to call upon the ICC, and an amendment to the bill states, "Nothing in this title shall prohibit the United State from rendering assistance in international efforts to bring to justice Saddam Hussein, Slobodan Milosevic, Osama bin Laden, other members of Al Qaeda, leaders of Islamic Jihad, and other foreign nationals accused of genocide, war crimes or crimes against humanity." Furthermore, the Bush administration initiated bilateral immunity agreements (permitted under the Rome Treaty's Article 98) with states in which US troops were deployed. They provide that no American soldier should be sent to The Hague. Moreover, Washington threatened to cut off foreign aid to any state that would not sign such an agreement. This arrangement has resulted in "status-of-forces" agreements with more than 100 states with a clause against sending Americans to the ICC.[27] In short, the United States is party to treaties that require its compliance with IHL, but it is exempt from sending its soldiers to The Hague to face criminal proceedings.

In another potentially negative development, African states originally were among the ICC's most enthusiastic supporters—spurred originally by the 1994 horrors in Rwanda and earlier by apartheid—but have begun expressing second thoughts about sitting heads of state as targets. Since 2012 Chief Prosecutor Fatou Bensouda has opened investigations into the situations in northern Uganda, the DRC, and the Central African Republic (CAR) upon the requests of those countries' governments, into Darfur and Libya upon the request of the Security Council, and into Kenya *propio motu* by the prosecutor. The first chief prosecutor, Luís Moreno-Ocampo (2003–2012), had submitted a request to investigate the post-election crisis crimes that unfolded in Côte d'Ivoire in late 2010 and early 2011. The court also issued arrest warrants for Sudanese president Omar al-Bashir and Libya's Gaddafi as well as Kenya's president, Uhuru Kenyatta. The warrant against al-Bashir is the only one currently in effect as Gaddafi is dead and the one against Kenyatta was withdrawn for insufficient evidence.

Action against sitting heads of state makes for political complications, exacerbated by the regional breakdown of states parties: thirty-four are in Africa, twenty-eight are from Latin America and the Caribbean, nineteen from Asia and the Pacific, eighteen in Eastern Europe, and twenty-five are from Western Europe and other states. While African complaints that ICC prosecutions unfairly single them out can be countered by the fact that most of the cases were brought to the court by the continent's governments, and because the chief prosecutor is herself African, nonetheless the accusation of Western bias continues to resonate in the battle to strip impunity from those who commit genocide, war crimes, crimes against humanity, and now aggression.

The ICC as an International Organization

There are four avenues for bringing a case to the ICC: a government that has ratified the Rome Statute, the Security Council, the prosecutor's office (with approval from a pre-trial chamber), and ad hoc self-referral by a government that has not ratified the Rome Statute. No two ICC judges are from the same country, and with a staggered rotation, each serves a nine-year term. The court is presently comprised of nineteen judges—it usually has eighteen, but one more remains on the bench as her term has expired but she is presiding over an ongoing case. The geographic breakdown for judges is Western Europe, five; Eastern Europe, three; Africa, four; Asia, three; and Latin America and the Caribbean, three. Seven women and twelve men serve on the bench.

The ICC's detention facilities are in a Dutch prison in Scheveningen. It consists of twelve cells that presently hold those facing charges. Some also contain those being held for other courts, such as Charles Taylor of Liberia (who is being tried by a special court in Sierra Leone).

As of 2016, the ICC has ongoing proceedings against twenty-two (there can be more than one defendant in a case) in nine situations—among them four states have referred situations occurring in their territories (Uganda, Democratic Republic of the Congo, Central African Republic, and Mali), three investigations were opened *proprio motu* by the ICC Prosecutor (Kenya, Côte d'Ivoire, and Georgia), and two situations have been referred by the Security Council (Darfur/Sudan and Libya). The cases under consideration were Uganda, two; DRC, five; Darfur, Sudan, five; CAR, one; Kenya, three; Libya, one; Côte d'Ivoire, three; and Mali (no case yet, but the investigation began in 2012). The ICC was also undertaking preliminary investigations into nine other situations: Afghanistan, Burundi, Colombia, Gabon, Guinea, Iraq/UK, Nigeria, Palestine, and Ukraine. The ICC rejected an appeal by the Palestinian Authority to investigate war crimes during the 2008 Gaza intervention, as neither Israel nor Palestine had joined the ICC at that time—the latter became a member in April 2015.

In terms of performance, the cases of twenty-three separate individuals have been brought before the ICC; six are in custody, but thirteen remain at large. Of those in the system, nine are in the pre-trial phase, five are at trial, and one is in an appeal. With respect to completed proceedings, despite nine convictions, only five cases are at the closed stage, meaning a conviction and sentence or an acquittal becomes final—in two instance charges have not been confirmed (unless there is new evidence the case is closed), similarly one case has had the charges withdrawn, one case has had the charges vacated, and one person has been acquitted. Three, all from Africa (two from the DRC, one from Mali) have been found guilty and presently are in the "reparation phase."

The broadening of the ICC's jurisdiction to cover the crime of aggression could expand the court's future work. At the 2010 Review Conference of the Rome Statute held in Kampala, "aggression" was defined to mean a use of force in breach of the UN Charter (invasion, bombardment, blockades, attacks, or allowing a state to be used as a base); and individuals who are involved in planning, preparation, initiation, or execution can be held accountable. As a result of thirty countries having ratified it, this new standard goes into effect in 2017. But a compromise was also struck whereby the ICC may act on the crime of aggression when the Security Council refers the matter to the ICC or the alleged aggressor and victim states are parties to the Rome Treaty—states that are not party, or do not accept its jurisdiction are exempt. Furthermore, states also may opt out of this provision.

In chapter 3 we discussed the experience with ad hoc tribunals in the former Yugoslavia and Rwanda. Table 5.1 summarizes those experiments side-by-side with war crimes prosecutions by the ICC.

Table 5.1.　War Crimes Prosecutions

	Courts		
	International Criminal Tribunal for the Former Yugoslavia (ICTY)[a]	*International Criminal Tribunal for Rwanda (ICTR)*[b]	*International Criminal Court (ICC)*[c]
Duration in years	24 (ongoing) 1993–2016	21 1994–2015	15 (ongoing) 2002–2016
Indictments	161	93	39
Fugitives	0	3	13
Acquitted	19	14	1
Convicted and sentenced	83	62	3
Cumulative costs (estimates)[d]	$2.5 billion	$2 billion	$1.75 billion

[a]ICTY, Facts and Figures, accessed January 1, 2017, http://www.icty.org/en/content/infographic-icty-facts-figures.
[b]ICTR, "The ICTR in Brief," accessed January 1, 2017, http://unictr.unmict.org/en/tribunal.
[c]ICC, ICC homepage, accessed January 1, 2017, https://www.icc-cpi.int.
[c]This data is based on recent budgets of these organizations and builds on Daniel McLaughlin, *International Criminal Tribunals: A Visual Overview* (New York: Leitner Center for International Law and Justice, 2015), 7, 27, and 72; ICC, "The Cost of Justice," accessed January 1, 2017, http://www.icty.org/en/about/tribunal/the-cost-of-justice; The Justice Hub, "The 2016 ICC Budget—More Money, More Problems," accessed January 1, 2017, https://justicehub.org/article/2016-icc-budget-more-money-more-problems.

Conclusion: Evaluating the ICC's Prosecution of War Crimes

In reflecting on the ICC and war crimes tribunals more broadly, they can be interpreted as barometers of humanitarianism. They speak to the inspiration and genesis of humanitarian innovation (tribunals and courts arise in the aftermath of traumas) and humanitarianism's place and power in international politics. At the same time, they also are a testament to the continued existence of the ugly reality of humanitarian failure in not originally protecting the victims from the perpetrators being pursued.

The interpretation of the comparative data presented above in table 5.1 requires answers to five sets of queries, which serve to conclude this chapter. First, why are they created when they are created? There are several schools of thought that interpret the rise of war crimes tribunals, each drawing on different approaches to international relations. Returning to the earlier discussion, realists argue that the end of the Cold War signaled the end of the resistance by great powers to the idea. Liberal institutionalists contend that civil society pressures (NGO activism) prompted its creation. Constructivists look at the power of ideas and new mediums that brought greater attention, including the so-called CNN effect (the forging of a global audience). Post-colonialists spotlight that

Western powers have established the ICC as a new legal means to punish non-Western leaders as well as institute Western-styled legal principles. Critical humanitarians would emphasize that the ICC is a coping tool for addressing mass atrocities (without tackling the underlying structural problem of why and how atrocities arise) that placates the consciences of those who were unwilling to stop atrocities but afterward sought to punish perpetrators. In addition, they posit that punishing individuals would not ameliorate the suffering of victims while the process could whitewash others who are culpable, including by having a system of laws that merely moderates bad behavior without actually preventing or stopping even worse behavior in the future. The definition of humanitarianism is relevant for regulating types of behavior and normative frameworks, for instance, in promoting individual criminal responsibility.

Second, what are the advantages of war crimes tribunals? The ICC's permanence signals the end of ad hoc, start-from-scratch processes that were impediments in several situations—notably that laws are instituted *ex post facto*, which violates key rights and due process principles, especially non-retroactivity. Adherence to the rules of the ICC promotes respect for law generally and improves long-term prospects for human rights protection.[28] The ICC may contribute to an enduring peace by giving some satisfaction to victims. Finally, some argue—although it is impossible to prove what does not happen—that it acts as a deterrent to potential criminals or accessories by eliminating a guarantee of impunity as any criminal will one way or another face adjudication and punishment in some way.[29] In the end, the ICC is the figurative and literal court of last resort for mass atrocity crimes—a powerful symbolic role that at least creates the opportunity to enhance the chances for justice.

Third, what are the disadvantages of the ICC? The list is lengthy, beginning with its limited jurisdiction; only those who sign the treaty are subject to its purview, unless the Security Council decides to act. Its selectivity in choosing cases to prosecute appears to reveal bias toward the West and rings "imperialism" in some ears. Not only is there "victor's justice" whereby the powerful do not face criminal sanctions, but prioritized cases may be perceived as serving the interests of great powers. As Danilo Zolo writes, "There is justice as tailored to the major powers and their political and military authorities, who enjoy total impunity for war crimes—and above all wars of aggression . . . disguised as humanitarian wars in defence of human rights or preventive wars against 'global terrorism.'"[30] Testimony holds the potential to embarrass or incriminate other states and therefore diminish support for legal solutions. Tribunals also can be viewed as inefficient and costly—particularly after wars when many other essential expenditures are required. Some have pointed to the huge ICC expenditures (some $1.75 billion; currently about $150 million annually), which seem incommensurate with only three convictions amidst a growing rebellion about its reach. Accountants, for instance, might balk at the price tag of nearly $600 million per conviction; by contrast, the ICTY's and ICTR's were a "bargain." Indeed, although the ICTY and ICTR have spent more than the ICC and have narrower jurisdictions, they have been more efficient in terms of adjudication—more trials, acquittals, and convictions. Moreover, they also have fewer fugitives, which may signal better law enforcement and perhaps greater respect from local populations who often help track down suspects. However, in some ICC cases, suspects have willingly surrendered themselves, which suggests their possible belief in a fair trial.

Fourth, what if the ICC undermines peacebuilding? Those facing war crimes trials may be more likely to continue fighting and committing atrocities if they have no political means of ending the war that will spare them legal prosecution. In an ideal world, peace and justice go hand in hand, but it often seems that the pursuit of one interferes with the other. This potent critique is often echoed within war-torn countries themselves; outsiders emphasize justice but those who bear the costs of war are often more willing to accept the injustice of war criminals going free if the war ends sooner.

Fifth, what if the ICC undermines the fundamental building block of international society? The most critical lingering debate about international judicial pursuit by the ICC concerns state sovereignty because its operations are predicated on the concept that the court stands above the state. As such, developments, especially in Africa, as this book was going to press were unsettling for those dedicated to global accountability. Although non-African cases are under consideration, the only individuals convicted to date have been Africans (among them the former DRC vice president), as are all others currently indicted. Although the current chief prosecutor is Gambian and the African cases have mainly been requested by African countries, dissatisfaction nonetheless festers. In October 2013, the AU's fifty-four members rejected a motion that African states withdraw from the ICC, but it nonetheless called for cases against sitting heads of state to be deferred until they left office. In January 2016, one of those scrutinized, Kenya's president Uhuru Kenyatta, proposed that all AU members withdraw as a bloc; his proposal was applauded but no action followed. However, in October 2016 alone, three African states (Burundi, South Africa, and Gambia) voted to do so; a subsequent change in government caused Gambia to pull back from the announced plan, and a South African court declared its withdrawal "unconstitutional and invalid." But the damage was done, and in November, Russia also decided to cut its ties with the court—symbolically and symmetrically significant—to join the earlier Bush administration's "un-signing" of the Rome Statute. Moreover, the prospect for more contention and the unraveling of this legal regime appears likely. For instance, having become a UN non-member observer state in 2012, the Palestinian Authority formally joined the ICC in April 2015 and has formally lodged two cases against Israel, the construction of settlements and the conduct of the 2014 war in Gaza. This tactic is bound to raise predictable hackles in Washington and Tel Aviv.

In addition to earlier unanswered questions, what the future holds for this bold international legal experiment is even more unclear when considering the following. Will the criminalization of aggression have an impact on the doctrine of preemption—that is, under what conditions can force be used other than self-defense after an actual attack? Further, what role should the Security Council play with respect to the ICC? What role does the ICC play in deterring war criminals? Some contend that deterrence cannot entirely be recognized as legal or "prosecutorial," but rather "social"; if so, how can this be measured and is the effect discernible? Can actors authorized by the Security Council be subject to ICC jurisdiction—that is, will the ICC adjudicate UN peacekeepers who commit war crimes? If so, how will this affect the UN's ability to field peace operations? What role does the ICC play in issues of counterterrorism?[31] What are the legal and political ramifications of dubbing acts of terrorism war crimes? Can a legal definition of terrorism under international humanitarian law be determined?

Along with earlier discussions of ad hoc tribunals for the former Yugoslavia and Rwanda, this chapter undoubtedly leads the reader to ponder: What is now and what will be the ultimate impact of trials by permanent and ad hoc courts? Drawing up a balance sheet at this juncture requires defining subjective and preliminary measures for success or failure. It also requires a calculator that assigns values to the factors accounting for contradictory outcomes and trends. The mathematics are daunting.

6

Humanitarianism in the Post-9/11 World

Afghanistan, Iraq, Libya, and Syria

The rubble of the UN headquarters in Baghdad following a suicide bomber attack on August 19, 2003, which killed twenty-two, including the secretary-general's special representative for Iraq, Sergio Vieira de Mello, and wounded over one hundred people. (UN photo)

Responses to the humanitarian disasters of the 1990s stirred constant debates as humanitarians struggled to be relevant in settings featuring mass atrocities by government and armed nonstate actors; since 2001, the challenges and associated controversies have only been compounded by a marked increase in violent extremism. The rise of militant Islamic terrorist organizations, potently signaled by the 9/11 attacks, refashioned global politics and wars in Africa, the Middle East, and southwest Asia. Humanitarianism, in turn, has been buffeted by a new wave of crises, security threats to personnel, and political pressures to integrate into great power interventions. This chapter examines the four most turbulent cases of the post-9/11 period and considers peculiar challenges that have reshaped humanitarianism: the context of counterterrorism in Afghanistan, the civil war in Iraq, the Arab Spring in Libya, and endless atrocities in Syria. The issues have revolved around relief (humanitarian space, access, security for aid workers, and aid economies); rights (IHL, especially the problems of "illegal combatants"); rescue (just war variants, including R2P); and refuge (displacement and population flows). What, if anything, is new? What legacies loom?

Afghanistan: Counterterrorism and Asphyxiated Humanitarianism

Long before the terrorist attacks of September 11, 2001, and the war and occupation that followed, Afghanistan (see map 6.1) suffered from poor humanitarian conditions that reflected poverty and the catastrophe of Soviet occupation that General Secretary Mikhail Gorbachev called Moscow's "bleeding wound."[1] Earlier Afghanistan was regularly in the crossfire of competing interests that sought to resolve conflict by force. In the nineteenth century, two great powers struggled over control of Afghanistan—Britain and Russia pursued influence in southwest Asia as part of an imperial "Great Game." Although by the early twentieth century imperialist forces left and the state of Afghanistan was consolidated under a monarchy, the country again became a pawn in the US-USSR confrontation during the Cold War. In July 1973, a former prime minister ousted the monarchy but was in turn assassinated in April 1978. This

Map 6.1

led to a new faction of Communist-oriented military officers taking over, thereby bringing to power the People's Democratic Party of Afghanistan (PDPA). However, it was immediately threatened by other elements within Afghanistan that did not want a Communist government. In late December 1979, the PDPA invited the USSR to send troops to secure its rule. The Soviets would occupy Afghanistan from 1979 to 1988 and fight an Islamic-based insurgency (the *mujahadeen*).

This war produced sizable displacement; soon millions of Afghans were either internally displaced or in refugee camps in Pakistan and Iran. The camps in Pakistan housed about 3 million Afghans and became bases for the insurgency, giving them an opportunity to receive medical attention, recruit new militants, and attract assistance from the Pakistani government as well as the United States, which was looking to counter Soviet influence.[2] Washington funded specific humanitarian agencies that supported their interests—mainly CRS, CARE, and the IRC. Other humanitarian agencies operating in the camps, including UNHCR and the WFP, also played into politics in that they provided aid to tribal leaders—mostly Pashtuns as Tajiks and Hazaras received far less—who inflated beneficiary counts to receive more aid and also channeled it exclusively to their supporters. Not only was this massive relief operation not neutral; it was also among the first major systematic instances of unauthorized access because the Afghan and Soviet authorities did not consent. After a protracted war of more than nine years, the USSR was bled dry—militarily, economically, and politically. On February 15, 1989, the last Soviet troops left Afghanistan. The total fatalities for the armed conflict were about 26,000 Soviet troops and around 1.3 million Afghans. Moreover, millions of Afghans remained displaced.

While there was some rejoicing at the defeat of the Soviet Union, Afghanistan remained war-torn for much of the 1990s. The power vacuum left by the retreat of the USSR created space for local warlords—who had helped expel the Soviets—to exert their influence, often backed by new ethnic-based militias. The result was a patchwork of authorities and armed groups struggling for political control and tax revenues, including involvement in drug trafficking (growing poppies and processing them into opium). Frustration at the chaos and violence of the warlords, as well as distaste at the growth of the drug trade, led many to turn to religious authorities to forge a new governing regime. In 1994, the Taliban emerged (a "*talib*" is a wandering cleric) as a movement of students and religious figures seeking to bring order to Afghanistan by cracking down on warlords and drug traffickers and instituting an Islamic government. The Taliban grew in popularity, size, and power; by 1996 they had captured Kabul, the capital.

During the civil war of the mid- to late 1990s, humanitarians worked to aid and resettle the displaced from the previous conflict and assist new victims. From the point of view of the aid community (not just humanitarians, but also those involved in development work more broadly), there were two problems: too much aid was ending up in the hands of belligerents and fueling the conflict, and opposition to what was seen as Western influences was creating resentment. Thus, in 1997 the UN conceived of the "Strategic Framework," to bring together aid programs, coordinate a "do-no-harm" approach, and promote local solutions. However, with attention focused on other disasters—in the late 1990s Kosovo and East Timor received the lion's share of resources—Afghanistan was neglected as donors provided only about 40–50 percent of what had been requested by aid agencies.

Consequently by the year 2000, Afghanistan remained a humanitarian disaster; the UNDP rated it among the worst places in the world.[3] Few had access to clean water, sanitation, health care, and food. About 5 million of a population of some 26 million were receiving international assistance, including the millions who were still either internally displaced or refugees. Life expectancy in Afghanistan was a paltry forty-five years.

Given that Al Qaeda had been hosted by the Taliban and used Afghanistan as a base of operations, following the 9/11 attacks and with the unanimous support from the Security Council, the United States invaded Afghanistan in early October 2001.[4] The numbers of casualties and displaced increased; meanwhile humanitarian space shrank as the Taliban could not guarantee the safety of humanitarian workers, which led the UN, the ICRC, and several other NGOs to withdraw. The phase of the war that deposed the Taliban was relatively brief compared to the ongoing and protracted armed conflict—Kandahar, the center of the Taliban's organization, fell to US-led forces within two months. For the duration of this episode, October to December 2001, only twelve US soldiers lost their lives. However, the Afghanis paid a significantly higher price; a minimum of 3,500 were killed and 6,200 wounded. Furthermore, additional displaced populations (about 1.2 million) added to already high numbers. Similarly, another 2.5 million were added to the 5 million who already required international assistance to survive.

Since then both sides have endured significant casualties. As of January 1, 2017, the United States had lost 2,392 soldiers out of 3,528 total coalition casualties. Overall, by December 2016, more than 110,000 Afghanis had been killed, of whom more than 30,000 were civilians. The humanitarian situation was perilous: as of the end of 2016, out of a population of 27 million, at least 1.2 million were internally displaced, and more than 8 million required food, health care, and/or protection. The Obama administration, which had previously campaigned on withdrawing and winding down US involvement, announced in July 2016 that US forces would remain to assist with counterterrorism; approximately 8,400 US soldiers remained on the ground when the Trump administration assumed power.

Since 9/11, there have been numerous pledges for humanitarian and development aid to Afghanistan, but they have been modest by comparison to other disasters, and of the promises made, few have been kept. In January 2002, pledges were made for $5.2 billion over five years; but in terms of numbers of victims this was about 25 percent of what was spent per person in Rwanda, Cambodia, East Timor, and Kosovo. In totaling up US expenditures in Afghanistan, the war effort cost nearly $600 billion (or about $17,000 per Afghan). In terms of "reconstruction" and humanitarian aid, nearly $110 billion had hit the books by the end of 2015, but much of these resources went directly to counterterrorism and counter-narcotics programming as well as to provide security for aid workers. Despite this massive inflow into Afghanistan since 2001, humanitarian conditions in the country remain desperate. Data from 2016 show that over one-third of the population live in poverty and nearly another one-fifth live just above that.

As to the state of humanitarian dynamics in Afghanistan, the situation is grim in three ways. First, humanitarian space is limited; attacks by militants have pushed agencies to remain sequestered in their cities and other fortified areas. Humanitarian space has also been undermined by the US military's delivering of aid, which compromises humanitarianism and perhaps is best illustrated by the deployment of US civil-military units, Provincial Reconstruction Teams (PRTs). They blur the distinction between security and humanitarian actors.

Second, aid workers continue to be targeted. In November 2009, the UN basically cut its presence by half due to threats, although some staff returned in early 2010. The yearly figure in Afghanistan has been rising since the post-9/11 invasion. From the late 1990s through 2000 a total of just over a dozen aid workers were either wounded or killed in attacks. Since then, the numbers show an appalling rise detailed in table 6.1. Nearly 1,100 aid workers have been victimized in Afghanistan since 9/11. The annual number has declined from the peak in 2013 because aid agencies withdrew personnel, leaving fewer on the ground to be exposed.

Third, the aid economy has been troublesome. A substantial portion of aid for Afghanistan has gone to Western agencies to pay for home offices and staff salaries. Beyond such expenditures that overstate the actual value of disbursements, aid agencies also cause prices for such items as real estate and food to rise in response to an increase in demand, thereby driving up the cost of living for already impoverished Afghans.

Although much attention has been given to Afghanistan, its eastern neighbor, Pakistan, also presents shockingly difficult humanitarian

Table 6.1. Aid Workers Wounded or Killed in Afghanistan, 2001–2016

2001	6
2002	8
2003	22
2004	40
2005	35
2006	55
2007	48
2008	63
2009	62
2010	123
2011	92
2012	105
2013	167
2014	127
2015	101
2016	26

Source: The Aid Worker Security Database, accessed January 2, 2017, available at https://aidworkersecurity.org.

challenges. Formed in 1947 as a Muslim state for populations that had been grouped into India as a British colony, Pakistan has remained a significant source of political tensions, if not outright hostility, with India. Much of this can be attributed to Muslim-Hindu cultural strife and India's disputed occupation of Kashmir.

Following 9/11 and the US invasion of Afghanistan, many of the Taliban, the religious movement comprised mostly of ethnic Pashtuns, sought refuge across the border in Pakistan where other Pashtuns welcomed and supported them. This theater of operations is often termed "AfPak," and both countries present similar challenges with respect to the erosion of humanitarian space. Al Qaeda's leadership, too, gravitated to Pakistan; it was considered a place to operate without direct interference from US military forces and to spread their ideology of global jihad. Osama Bin Laden located Pakistan as the center of jihad struggle and amalgamated all of Pakistan's enemies to nurture support for his cause. In 2006 he denounced "a Crusader-Zionist-Hindu war against Muslims." Shortly thereafter in 2007 a group calling itself "Al Qaeda in India" announced its presence. Islamic militants in Pakistan are a cause for concern for the central government and its Western allies. Pakistan's population is nearly six times larger than Afghanistan's, and so intervention to defeat terrorists and insurgent groups and rebuild governance in the far western reaches appears untenable.

Aside from extremist Islamic terrorism, Pakistan has also been beset by a series of natural disasters, including earthquakes and floods. A 2005 earthquake in the northwest displaced millions. Humanitarian aid helped tend to the displaced population and has also had an impact in positively reshaping views about aid agencies. The massive floods in the summer and fall of 2010 harmed a huge number of Pakistanis—an area of the size of Italy was damaged, 20 million were affected (including 1,800 dead), and 2 million dwellings destroyed. In addition to being forced from their homes because the floodwaters receded slowly, farmers missed the planting season, which drastically undercut food supplies.

Despite sizable and seemingly ever-growing humanitarian needs, the space for assistance has shrunk significantly in the past few years. Table 6.2 indicates that the danger to aid organizations has increased as the intensity of the war has escalated starting in 2007, notably with a pronounced turn to drones after 2009.

One notable cause of attacks was that the CIA recruited a Pakistani doctor to gather DNA evidence of bin Laden's presence through a hepatitis B vaccination project; the doctor was giving shots and keeping needles to test if any of the vaccinated children were bin Laden's. This violation of patient confidentiality and political common sense has led to outrage in Pakistan against humanitarians. The ICRC, which has been working in Pakistan since 1947 and fields one of its largest operations there, halted most of its programs in August 2013 due to deteriorating security. Table 6.2 illustrates the spike in successful attacks on aid workers that year. However, humanitarian work continues to be carried out primarily by the

Table 6.2. Aid Workers Wounded or Killed in Pakistan, 2001–2016

Year	Count
2001	1
2002	0
2003	0
2004	2
2005	0
2006	0
2007	20
2008	28
2009	40
2010	28
2011	29
2012	25
2013	41
2014	18
2015	2
2016	0

Source: The Aid Worker Security Database, accessed January 2, 2017, available at https://aidworkersecurity.org.

Pakistani military but with modest inputs from the World Health Organization (WHO), UNICEF, and MSF. In short, the humanitarian footprint in Pakistan is dwindling, which accounts for the decline in the victimization of aid workers, and what remains is mostly dominated by the military.

Iraq: Civil War and Tainted Humanitarianism

Despite having experienced colonialism and occupation by a variety of imperial powers (Ottoman and British), by the late twentieth century Iraq was a moderately wealthy and stable country (see map 3.1). Development primarily resulted from oil exports but also modest agricultural and some industrial development. Further, although governed by monarchy or military dictatorship since its inception, Iraqis fared reasonably well in socioeconomic terms. In 1990, before the Persian Gulf War, the country ranked ninety-first on UNDP's Human Development Index (HDI), placing it roughly in the middle tier.[5] However, the war took a heavy toll; a UN report suggested that Iraq was back in "the stone age."[6] Moreover, a sanctions regime in the 1990s had serious humanitarian consequences, and by 2000 Iraq had fallen to 126th on the HDI. In addition, food imports had become increasingly necessary but were curtailed by the sanctions regime. As a result, the Security Council created the Oil-for-Food Program to allow Iraq to generate revenue to afford importing foodstuffs, but by the end of the 1990s, nearly 60 percent of the population had come to rely on food aid through OfFP. Additionally, following the Persian Gulf War and the uprising of the Kurds in the north and the Shiites in the south, the Hussein regime severely repressed and forcibly displaced populations: somewhere between 600,000 to 800,000 Kurds in the north, and 100,000 to 300,000 primarily Shiites in the south.

While the United States did not oust Saddam Hussein from power during the Gulf War, it remained concerned about Iraq's WMD potential. The sanctions regime put in place after the 1990–1991 armed conflict was intended to persuade or force Hussein to disarm and destroy his chemical weapons, which had also been used during its war with Iran from 1980 to 1988 as well as against Kurds in that same period. The OfFP was designed to prevent using export receipts to acquire nuclear weapons. In addition to sanctions, the UN had also imposed inspections to monitor compliance. In 1998, Hussein announced that he would not allow inspectors to continue their work; in short order the United States and the United Kingdom responded with air attacks to push Iraq to allow them. The public and policy preoccupation with WMD skyrocketed after 9/11, and the Bush administration focused intensely on Iraq's potential to acquire them and pressured the Security Council to demand that Iraq disclose its weapons programs. Iraq complied but only to a degree; its documentation made no mention of chemical, biological, or nuclear capabilities.

In early 2003, the Security Council once again faced a decision about whether to intervene. Washington contended that there were three reasons to go to war: First, collective security had to be enforced as Iraq was in violation of Security Council resolutions 687 (the terms of settling the earlier Persian Gulf War) and 1441. Second, preemptive self-defense was required because countries with WMD must be stopped before they attack. Third, Saddam Hussein's attacks against Kurds amounted to genocide.

However, others countered that Iraq should not be attacked for three reasons: First, there was no link between Al Qaeda and Iraq, and Security Council resolutions pertaining to terrorism provided no authorization to attack states that did not harbor terrorists. Second, many feared the Bush doctrine of preemption and wished to avoid granting this permission to violate sovereignty. Third, the inspections were working; inspectors had found no WMD in Iraq, and ongoing efforts prevented Iraq from developing them.

When the Security Council considered the issue, the only supporters to attack Iraq were the US, the UK, Spain, and Bulgaria. Because Washington could not mobilize even the minimum required number of nine votes (out of fifteen) and faced certain vetoes, the draft resolution was withdrawn, and the Bush and Blair administrations proceeded anyway. On March 17, 2003, they issued an ultimatum to Saddam Hussein to step down within forty-eight hours or be attacked. On March 19, "the coalition of the willing" launched its attack without Security Council approval. Within a brief period, the Hussein regime was dismantled and defeated. On May 1, Bush declared "mission accomplished." From March 17 to then, 140 US soldiers were killed. The toll for Iraqis was 13,000 dead and 260,000 displaced. During this phase of the war, a major humanitarian disaster was averted; no mass displacement happened and no famines or epidemics occurred. Nevertheless, the situation was precarious.

While the war between the United States and the Hussein regime ended quickly, the conflict morphed into a civil war involving Kurds, Sunnis, Shiites, foreign forces (including private military corporations), and a newly created pro-US central government. This conflict caused a colossal humanitarian problem; substantial numbers were killed and displaced, and humanitarian space was circumscribed. Under the Fourth Geneva Convention, occupying powers are obligated to maintain order and safety as well as provide food and medical supplies in territories under their control. The US-led coalition furnished some assistance but also relied on funds left over from the OfFP; and it lobbied the Security Council to lift the sanctions so that new exports could also contribute. From May to July, the Iraqi state began to crumble—not simply because the Hussein regime had been unseated, but because the governmental institutions of Iraq itself were markedly weakened as social services were eroded or collapsed. During June and July looting and insecurity predominated with a major impact on humanitarian conditions: for instance, child malnutrition almost doubled from 4 to 7.7 percent as aid agencies truncated their operations and several withdrew altogether.

In July and August, the US-led forces and the UN took steps separately to support the delivery of humanitarian assistance, including rebuilding governance in an effort to sustain social services. On July 13, the Coalition Provisional Authority (CPA) was established to administer the country and prepare for a new transitional government. The CPA's oversight of basic law and order was viewed as an essential first step in moving beyond war, occupation, and the worsening humanitarian crisis. On August 14, the Security Council passed resolution 1500, which established the UN Assistance Mission for Iraq (UNAMI) to phase out OfFP and coordinate relief work. However, in the late summer and fall, humanitarian workers in Iraq and, indeed, the entire international humanitarian system, would be profoundly shaken by two events. First, on August 19, UN headquarters in Baghdad was bombed, killing twenty-two, including the special representative of the secretary-general, Sergio Vieira de Mello. This violence had immediate material impacts with the withdrawal of two-thirds of UN staff from Iraq; it also had deep symbolic significance as de Mello was considered among the most dynamic people in the humanitarian sector and the UN. Second, on October 27, a white ambulance with a red-crescent symbol was used as a truck bomb and detonated inside the ICRC compound, killing eighteen. In many ways, these two strikes were the humanitarian system's equivalent of 9/11—an overwhelming shock that altered conceptions of war and victimization; the notion that the values of humanitarianism or its symbols protected aid workers was buried in the rubble.[7]

The civil war has more flowed than ebbed since the 2003 invasion; the counterterrorism activities of the United States and its allies destroyed the state and unhinged Iraqi society. There have been some periods of reduced violence and consolidation of new governing authorities in Baghdad under a Shiite-led regime. Counterterrorism, particularly against Al Qaeda in Mesopotamia (AQIM), was at first virtually impossible as the CPA dismantled the Iraqi military, which led many Sunni battle-hardened soldiers to gravitate to opposition forces that were a blend of nationalist insurgents and transnational jihadists. Not until Washington began to differentiate between counterterrorism and counterinsurgency—and, more importantly, to partner with local Sunni forces (the "Anbar Awakening") that also resisted AQIM and other transnational Islamic fighters—did counterterrorism begin to succeed. The crowning moment was killing AQIM leader Abu Musab al-Zarqawi in an airstrike in June 2006.

Since 2014, the conflict in Iraq has also taken on a new dimension with the rise of the militant Sunni organization al-Dawla al-Islamiya al-Iraq al-Sham (Daesh)—which is usually translated from Arabic and shortened as "the Islamic State," "ISIS," or "ISIL"—and its considerable presence in northern and western Iraq (and discussed in greater detail below for Syria). Beyond fueling, if not escalating, violent Sunni-Shiite conflict, Daesh has triggered significant displacement.[8] Since the summer of 2016, the United States and the Shiite-led government launched a campaign against Daesh positions near the oil-rich areas of Mosul in the north and attempted to cut off the flow of arms, material, and combatants coming across the Anbar province in the west. Starting in mid-October, a major offensive began to liberate Mosul, which led Daesh forces to commit outright massacres of civilians and use them as human shields. As this book goes to press, some 110,000 have been forced from the area, but far more are anticipated as facilities to house more than 500,000 are under construction.

The past decade and a half, as well as the present moment, of war and humanitarianism in Iraq is far from auspicious. The human cost has soared since 2003. As of the end of 2016, total coalition fatalities were 4,832 (of whom more than 4,512 were American) in addition to upwards of 40,000 wounded—if including soldiers with post-traumatic stress disorder are included, the numbers would be at least tenfold. For Iraqis, the price has been extremely high. Estimates range from between 170,000 to 190,000 for violent deaths to substantially more than 1 million if disease and hunger are included in the tabulation. Furthermore, other aspects of the humanitarian situation are dismal. Out of a population of 36 million, 3.1 million are internally displaced, at least 2.5 million are refugees (mostly in Syria and Jordan), and 11 million need relief aid. Aid workers have also been victims of the violence—table 6.3's data begin in 2001 to show the contrast in periods: the tail end of OfFP, the initial invasion in 2003, and after the withdrawal of most US troops at the end of 2011.

The discussion of Iraq's humanitarian plight would be incomplete without a brief discussion of using public international law to hold violators of IHL accountable for their actions, which concentrated on bringing Saddam Hussein to justice. This idea was not at or even near the top of the agenda for quite some time. Hussein had assumed leadership of Iraq in 1979 and been involved in a variety of acts that undoubtedly constituted war crimes. However, he was never actively considered for prosecution until after his government was overthrown, and he was captured by US forces on December 13, 2003.

Table 6.3. Aid Workers Wounded or Killed in Iraq, 2001–2016

2001	0
2002	1
2003	49
2004	30
2005	9
2006	18
2007	7
2008	0
2009	1
2010	9
2011	0
2012	0
2013	1
2014	0
2015	0
2016	1

Source: The Aid Worker Security Database, accessed January 2, 2017, available at https://aidworkersecurity.org.

One of the first issues was who could, or should, adjudicate Saddam's crimes. Some were concerned about the death penalty; the United States was sympathetic to this idea. But European and other states opposed it. The issue became moot because Hussein faced Iraqi, not international, justice: in May 2004 the CPA devised the Iraqi Special Tribunal for Crimes against Humanity, whose temporal jurisdiction spanned July 17, 1968 (when the Ba'ath party came to power) until May 1, 2003 (when the war officially ended). At the time, many were concerned that this legal process was still being directed and carried out by internationals more than Iraqis. Accordingly, the process was basically put on hold until after a new Iraqi government was formed and the CPA handed over power. On July 1, 2004, two days after the transition, Saddam was arraigned for crimes against humanity: killings of religious figures in 1974; massacres of Shiites in 1982; forced displacement of and atrocities against Kurds from 1986 to 1988 (including the use of chemical weapons); the invasion of Kuwait in 1990; and the suppression of Shiites and Kurds in 1991.

In October 2005, the trial began with obvious political and legal problems. Hussein repeatedly refused to acknowledge the jurisdiction of the court, often noting that it had been installed by occupying powers after an illegal invasion. Further, he had no legal representation, and Iraqi judges had little familiarity with IHL. The standard of evidence was questionable given that documentation gathered through coercion was permitted. These problems led several Western human rights organizations to object to and not support the work of the tribunal. In addition, domestic Iraqi politics influenced the tribunal's administration. For instance, the prime minister replaced an administrator, who was a potential political rival, with a member from his own party to prevent the position from building political support for the opposition. Finally, staff turnover complicated the procedures; one judge was replaced, and one judge and two defense attorneys were assassinated during the trial. Nevertheless, Saddam was found guilty and received the death penalty; he was hanged on December 30, 2006.

Libya: The Arab Spring and Reborn Humanitarianism

In early 2011, inspired by the successes of Arab Spring demonstrations that had led to the removal of dictators in other parts of North Africa—including neighboring Tunisia and Egypt—a widespread protest movement erupted in Libya against the authoritarian regime of Colonel Muammar el-Gaddafi. Unlike the sectarian divide between Sunnis and Shiites that ripped apart Iraq or the ethnic cleavages that contributed to divisions in Afghanistan, in Libya (see map 6.2) more than 90 percent of the population are both Arab and Sunni, with Berber minority populations. The central tension is mainly based on tribal and regional affiliations, but the country was also further polarized between those who supported the colonel's autocratic rule and those who opposed it. Gaddafi had come to power in 1969 when he led a coup against the monarchy. Oil wealth, nationalist sentiment, and high-profile anti-Americanism sustained his rule for decades. Through a combination of carrots (allocation of economic resources and political patronage) and sticks (harsh repression), he maintained his grip on power. In particular, his use of oil wealth to fund social services also contributed to the quality of life of Libyans—the 2011 HDI ranked Libya at 64 of 187 countries[9]—which bought a degree of stability. Nevertheless, surging enthusiasm fueled by the Arab Spring raised the prospect of ending Gaddafi's dictatorship; on February 14, 2011, the first major protests began in the eastern city of Benghazi.

In the following weeks, the Gaddafi regime issued threats of atrocities—his son, Saif al-Islam Gaddafi, the heir apparent, promised "thousands" would die and "rivers of blood" would flow if the protests did not stop; the colonel himself called for attacks on protesters and referred to them as "rats" and "cockroaches" while vowing to "cleanse Libya house by house." The initial brutal crackdown killed nearly 1,000 in the first few weeks. Both the League of Arab States and the AU condemned Gaddafi's response and suspended Libya's membership in their respective organizations. At the UN, the Security Council exhorted the government "to

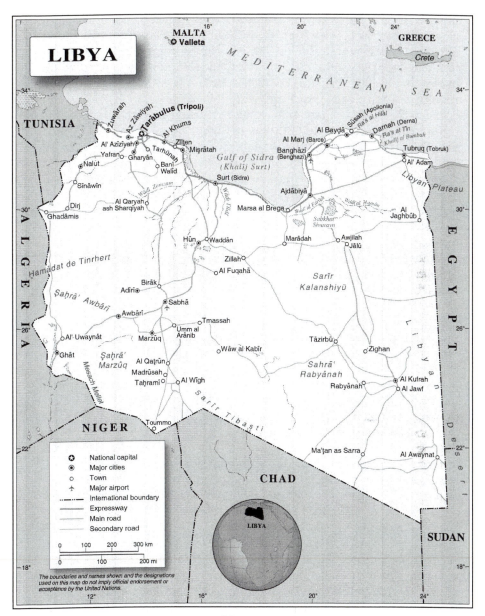

LIBYA

MALTA
○ Valleta

GREECE
Crete

M E D I T E R R A N E A N   S E A

TUNISIA

Zuwārah
Az Zāwiyah
Ţarābulus (Tripoli)
Al Khums
Zlīţen
Al' Azīzīyah
Tarhūnah
Yafran
Gharyān
Nalut
Banī Walīd
Sīnāwin
Wādī Zamzam
Al Qaryah ash Sharqīyah
Dirj
Ghadāmis

Mişrātah

Gulf of Sidra
(Khalīj Surt)
Surt (Sidra)

Al Marj (Barce)
Al Baydā
Sūsah (Apollonia)
Ra's al Hilāl
Darnah (Derna)
Ra's at Tīn
Khalīj al Bunbah
Banghāzī (Benghazi)
Tubruq (Tobruk)
Al' Adam

Libyan Plateau

Ajdābiyā

Marsa al Brega
Wādī al Fārigh
Wādī al Hamīm
Al Jaghbūb
Sabkhat Shunayn

ALGERIA

Hamādat de Tinrhert
Şaḥrā' Awbārī
Adīrī
Birāk
Awbārī
Al'-Uwaynāt
Ghāt
Şaḥrā' Marzūq
Marzūq
Sabhā
Umm al Arānib
Tmassah
Al Qaţrūn
Madrūsah
Ţahramī
Al Wīgh
Mesach Mellet
Toummo

Hūn
Waddān
Zillah
Al Fuqahā

Marādah
Awjilah
Jālū

Sarīr Kalanshiyū

Wāw al Kabīr
Tāzirbū
Zighan

Sahrā' Rabyānah
Rabyānah
Al Kufrah
Al Jawf

EGYPT

Libyan Desert

NIGER

Sarīr Tibasti

Ma'ţan as Sarra
Al Awaynat

CHAD

LIBYA

SUDAN

Legend:
- ✪ National capital
- ◉ Major cities
- ○ Town
- ✈ Major airport
- International boundary
- Expressway
- Main road
- Secondary road

0   100   200   300 km
0   100   200 mi

The boundaries and names shown and the designations used on this map do not imply official endorsement or acceptance by the United Nations.

Map 6.2

meet its responsibility to protect its population."[10] The Office of the High Commissioner for Human Rights (OHCHR) also chastised the regime and reminded member states of the "responsibility to protect," and for the first time the Human Rights Council (HRC) referred to the responsibility to protect, in resolution S-15/1, which led to General Assembly resolution 65/60 suspending Libya from the HRC.

By late February, criticism of Libya was widespread, including from the Libyan ambassador to the UN, who defected. Abdurrahman Mohamed Shalgam, in tears, testified before the Security Council on February 25: "They demonstrated peacefully . . . [and] they were killed. . . . Muammar Qaddafi and his sons are telling the Libyans, 'Either I rule you or I kill you,' . . . [I plead] to the United Nations, please save Libya." The next day, Security Council resolution 1970 imposed an arms embargo and travel ban, and froze the bank accounts of Gaddafi's family and inner circle. Furthermore, the Security Council also referred the situation in Libya to the ICC, only the second time for such a step. Although Moscow agreed to sanctions, during debates about the resolution's text, Russia was adamant that force not be used and opposed the establishment of no-fly zones, which had been deployed in places like Iraq and Bosnia in the 1990s. Moscow's representative commented that the resolution "does not enjoin sanctions, even indirect for forceful interference in Libya's affairs, which could make the situation worse."[11]

In late February and early March, the violence escalated. Although the rebels had taken over Benghazi and Tobruk, Gaddafi's forces recaptured these cities and were poised to crush the rebellion. On March 7, the Gulf Cooperation Council (GCC) requested the Security Council to condemn crimes against civilians and authorize the use of force to prevent Gaddafi from using his airpower, particularly the use of heavy arms and the recruitment of mercenaries. By this point, more than 1 million needed humanitarian aid. In the Security Council's chamber, the debate about next steps unfolded. The government contended that "Libya's actions are a legitimate response against terrorism as it seeks to defend itself and to prevent terrorism from spreading in the Mediterranean region and al-Qaida from infiltrating Europe."[12] Moreover, Libya argued that Security Council resolution 1970 violated international law and the UN Charter, and it also set "a dangerous precedent." Lastly, Libya asked if responding to an insurgency was the double standard for Security Council intervention, why was it unprepared to act in Palestine, Uganda, Kashmir, Angola, or Chechnya?

But the Security Council was unmoved by these arguments—indeed, it was reacting to the simultaneous diplomatic offensive by the Libyan government along with Gaddafi's continuing threats to his opponents[13]—and its March 17 resolution 1973 called for "all necessary measures" to protect civilians, including a ban on flights in Libyan air space.[14] This language was UN-ese developed in the 1990s for coercive military action; but given Russia's fears about sovereignty, language was inserted specifically stipulating that the operation would exclude "a foreign occupation force of any form on any part of Libyan territory." Thus, the resolution provided for air strikes against heavy equipment (tanks and artillery) in Libya but no foreign boots on the ground.

For the first time the world organization authorized the use of "military force for human protection purposes" (in the ICISS's mouthful) against the wishes of a functioning state. By contrast and before even the report from the commission, the Security Council's authorization for Somalia in 1992 was for intervention in a political vacuum (i.e., there was no government), and consent for France's intervention in Rwanda in 1994 was given by an interim government before a new Tutsi government had been recognized. Resolution 1973 was passed unanimously, with ten affirmative votes (all the African members, Nigeria, South Africa, and Gabon, as well as Bosnia, Colombia, France, Lebanon, Portugal, the United Kingdom, and the United States) and five abstentions (Brazil, China, Germany, India, and Russia).

Reflecting widespread international political sentiments, diplomats were outspoken. Bosnia-Herzegovina remarked that Benghazi could potentially develop into "a situation not unlike Srebrenica." The UK's delegate would later similarly comment that the UN "stopped Benghazi from joining Srebrenica and Rwanda in history's painful roll call of massacres the world failed to stop." But there were also serious reservations; those who abstained questioned the merits of using force. Brazil said, "Our vote today should in no way be interpreted as condoning the behavior of the Libyan authorities or as disregard for the need to protect civilians and respect their rights. . . . [but] we are not convinced that the use of force as provided for in paragraph 4 of the resolution will lead to the realization of our common objective—the immediate end to violence and the protection of civilians." Russia noted: "We are consistent and firm advocates of the protection of the civilian population. Guided by this basic principle as well as by the common humanitarian values that we share with both the sponsors and other council members, Russia did not prevent the adoption of this resolution. However, we remain convinced that the quickest way to ensure robust security for the civilian population and the long-term stabilization of the situation in Libya is an immediate ceasefire." And China commented that it was "gravely concerned by the continuing deterioration of the situation in Libya. We support the Security Council's adoption of appropriate and necessary action to stabilize the situation in Libya as soon as possible and to halt acts of violence against civilians. . . . China is always against the use of force in international relations. . . . China has serious difficulty with parts of the resolution."[15] Cuba opposed the action entirely and stated, "The United States and NATO, supposedly to avoid a massacre, launched a military attack against a sovereign State without there being any threat to international peace and security, and unleashed a 'change of regime operation.'"[16]

The operation began on March 19, 2011—ironically, the eighth anniversary of the US invasion of Iraq in 2003, which also contributed to a sense of déjà vu among opponents. Washington, and to a lesser extent Paris and London, initially took the lead (Operation Odyssey Dawn) but within two weeks handed over operational control to NATO (Operation Unified Protector). This was supplemented with military support from the region (by Qatar, the United Arab Emirates, and Jordan); there was also a surprising degree of support from other NATO allies—Denmark and Norway together destroyed as many targets as Britain; Belgium, Denmark, and Norway dropped as many bombs as France. During the chaos of the conflict, the ICRC was careful not to be seen as taking sides and negotiated access with both government and rebel factions. By late May, military momentum had shifted to the rebels, who by late August had seized Tripoli. Gaddafi managed to avoid capture and hid in the southern deserts of Libya until he was killed in Sirte on October 20—some argued that his brutal execution tarnished 2011's singular human rights accomplishment.[17] The next day NATO declared the operation over, and within a week the Security Council lifted the no-fly zone and ended the mandate of civilian protection. While some have judged the R2P operation in Libya as a success in averting immediate massacres by the Gaddafi government, others point to the long-term instability that has resulted—indeed, the country has been wracked by civil war almost continuously since shortly after the initial end of hostilities.

The contours of humanitarian space since 2011 can be gleaned from the toll on aid workers in table 6.4. In the decade prior to 2011, no aid workers had been wounded or killed in Libya except for an episode in 2010 when nine aid workers were kidnapped going to Gaza but which

Table 6.4.   Aid Workers Wounded or Killed in Libya, 2011–2016

Year	Count
2011	2
2012	9
2013	1
2014	1
2015	3
2016	0

Source: The Aid Worker Security Database, accessed January 2, 2017, available at https://aidworkersecurity.org.

took place in Libyan waters. However, in the immediate aftermath of the 2011 operation to oust Gaddafi and subsequent civil war, the number of aid workers victimized grew.

One should recall that the intervention in Libya as in Kosovo took place from the same altitude (i.e., bombers at 25,000–35,000 feet). But Kosovo's aftermath included substantial military, administrative, judicial, and economic support whereas virtually nothing followed in Libya. The West had obviously forgotten Colin Powell's Pottery Barn rule in the run-up to the 2003 invasion of Iraq: "You break it. You own it."[18]

An additional note regards IHL. The ICC has pursued charges against Gaddafi and several of his top lieutenants. However, for Gaddafi himself the ICC is irrelevant because he was killed; but for his sons (Saif al-Islam and Mohammed) and his top aide (Abdullah al-Senussi), the warrants remain outstanding because Libya is not party to the ICC; more importantly, the government does not want outsiders to administer "justice" on behalf of Libya. There is an obvious dilemma. On the one hand, the ICC represents a foreign entity that could suggest Libya's inability to adjudicate war crimes appropriately. On the other hand, the ICC's power comes from universal acknowledgement of its principles, including due process. Ultimately, the ICC is unlikely to try these suspects because the Libyan government appears more interested in publicly humiliating show trials and revenge than justice. But the idea that the ICC achieves justice and order even in the face of horrific war crimes would send a moral and political message. Many humanitarians wish to nurture the court and IHL by insisting that the ICC's role is imperative because otherwise "victor's justice" will prevail and weaken humanitarianism's relevance.

The ideological fireworks over R2P ignited from the outset in debates over whether to intervene in Libya with critics from the Global South charging that it was a "Trojan Horse" for Western imperialism. Rhetorical flourishes from such usual suspects as Cuba, Venezuela, Sudan, and Zimbabwe continued. The hackles raised by South Africa's President Jacob Zuma were typical of this critique: "We strongly believe that the resolution is being abused for regime change, political assassinations, and foreign military occupation."[19] Criticism continued after regime change in Tripoli as buyer's remorse set in, with Brazil taking the lead during the 66th session of the UN General Assembly in fall 2011: "the international community, as it exercises its responsibility to protect, must demonstrate a high level of responsibility while protecting" (RwP).[20] Tautological, ambivalent, and ultimately mischievous, this framing nonetheless also reflected the norm's perceived pertinence and power even for the hegemon from Latin America, a region known for its anti-imperial views.

While the supporters of the intervention on humanitarian grounds could and should have maintained a more consistent argumentation in relation to the original mandate,[21] nonetheless the feigned surprise about regime change is hard to fathom. International action should alter behavior by a pariah regime—in this case, causing Gaddafi to halt abuse and negotiate an end to repression and violence. However, if no change in behavior occurs—and in Libya it did not and undoubtedly was an implausible prospect—a change in regime should not have come as a surprise but as the logical outcome of deploying R2P military force. Critics forget the noteworthy regime changes with dramatically positive humanitarian consequences in 1978 and 1979: the elimination of the Khmer Rouge in Kampuchea and removal of Idi Amin in Uganda after military interventions by Vietnam and Tanzania, respectively. Fewer crocodile tears were shed in the Global South for halting mass atrocities in the 1970s.

Moreover, claims of a "moral hazard" to employing R2P in Libya—an incentive structure that favors provoking atrocities—are questionable. Kuperman has posited that

> The biggest misconception about NATO's intervention is that it saved lives and benefited Libya and its neighbors. In reality, when NATO intervened in mid-March 2011, [Gaddafi] already had regained control of most of Libya while the rebels were retreating rapidly toward Egypt. Thus, the conflict was about to end, barely six weeks after it started, at a toll of about 1,000 dead, including soldiers, rebels, and civilians caught in the crossfire. By intervening NATO enabled the rebels to resume their attack, which prolonged the war for another seven months and caused at least 7,000 more deaths.[22]

However, the factors that drove the conflict were not that Western intervention was imminent but rather the continued monopolization of politics by Gaddafi and his violent repression. Additionally, there was no way to know whether Gaddafi would have settled for merely repelling the rebel forces or engaged in a far more brutal crackdown. If his previous behavior was any indication, bloody reprisals were more likely; thus, the real moral hazard for the West and the UN would have been to refrain in the hope that the situation would stabilize peacefully, without intervention.

It is important to return to politics and our original question of "why Libya?" A massacre was certainly prevented in Benghazi in March 2011. Gaddafi's ugly verbal pyrotechnics—which recalled Rwanda's 1994 tragedy by hurling the same ethnic epithets as those of the murderous Hutu regime, like "cockroaches" and "rats"—was a wake-up call and activated R2P. On the regional side, the motives also included mutual rivalries; participating governments arguably abhorred Gaddafi more than they cared about the population of Benghazi.

The twenty-two-member Arab League's plea to the UN to impose a no-fly zone against Libya was decisive; it was accompanied by backing from the Organization of Islamic Cooperation (OIC) and the GCC, but with some initial foot-dragging by the AU (which Gaddafi had financed handsomely). Washington, London, and Paris enthusiastically voted for the authorization and then gave meaning to resolution 1973 to protect civilians with overwhelming air power. The earlier resolution 1970 had unanimous support, and it was significant that no country voted against resolution 1973—the perceived costs of noncompliance apparently outweighed at least temporarily any benefits, even for Beijing and Moscow.

The international military action against Libya marked a turning point in the post-9/11 intervention slump. As the Working Group on R2P chaired by Madeleine Albright and Richard Williamson noted, "Libya was a textbook application of R2P principles." However, their report continues, "Collective military action to enforce R2P will be rare,"[23] which certainly summarized accurately what has happened since—R2P in Libya was the exception, not the rule. And this generalization undoubtedly will not change with the election of Donald Trump.

The crippling backfire from the 2011 intervention in Libya has cast a pall over the operation and, for some, on the future of R2P. The overthrow of Gaddafi, while noteworthy and hailed by many in Libya and elsewhere, has given way to a civil war with vicious rival militias. The two principals are the Libya Dawn movement, which is from Misrata and has some Islamic factions and business groups behind it, and the Dignity group from Benghazi, under Khalifa Haftar. There is also a Daesh branch, the "Tripolitania Province," growing and operating.

Moreover, the humanitarian crisis shows little indication of abating, which challenges agencies to gain access to the displaced and others in need. A 2015 report noted that "an estimated 20% of hospitals and 18% of primary health care facilities are not functioning. 60% of hospitals were closed or made inaccessible at least once during the six month period from April to October 2015 due to the conflict."[24] By the end of 2016, out of a population of about 6 million, almost 700,000 were internally displaced and at least 1.3 million required assistance.

As the situations in Tripoli and elsewhere across the Middle East continue to unfold, acute dilemmas remain for humanitarians and policy makers—who to save, how to save them, and who should do the saving. Each is intensely politically charged, especially in war zones. Blowback is inevitable, and turmoil is guaranteed in countries without a tradition of elections or civil society, especially without significant investments in a post-conflict society. All decisions have unintended and perverse consequences; it is unreasonable to think that R2P actions would be immune. That said, the ongoing tumult in Libya would argue that the original third component of R2P, the responsibility to rebuild, should be reemphasized so that interveners heed Powell's Pottery Barn wisdom and participate in post-intervention peacebuilding.

Syria: Endless Atrocities and Stillborn Humanitarianism

Many of the issues in Afghanistan, Iraq, and Libya arise again in Syria (map 6.3), where the civil war grew from local dissidents as part of the 2011 Arab Spring protest wave; anti-government agitation was directed at a long established authoritarian regime. The Assad family has ruled Syria since Hafez al-Assad, then defense minister, seized power in 1970. His son, Bashar, took over in June 2000 when his father died. In mid-March 2011, the first large-scale anti-government actions took place in the city of Daraa. Since then the initial uprising morphed into a modest, then full-blown civil war and then a regional and global proxy war. Humanitarian conditions reached deplorable levels and continue to deteriorate for the population of 23 million: by late 2016, estimates indicate close to a half-million dead, 6.3 million IDPs, 4.8 million refugees (mostly in Jordan and Turkey), and 13.5 million in need of assistance (including 4.9 million in hard-to-reach areas).[25]

Responding to the humanitarian challenges of the Syrian conflict has been tortuous. The HRC has repeatedly condemned the Assad government, and the UN Joint Office on the Prevention of Genocide and Responsibility to Protect has issued a host of statements calling for immediate end to possible crimes against humanity. But in terms of enforcement, the results have been virtually nonexistent because of deadlock within the Security Council. While some point to the fallout from Libya, the double-vetoes by Moscow and Beijing have been as adamant as those earlier in Kosovo. While endless atrocities demand a response, there has been a profound lack of will to stand up for previous commitments to avert atrocities; with nervous handwringing in the West coupled with active blocking by Russia and China, what is not displayed is a "responsibility to protect," but an irresponsibility to deflect.

The conflict raged in summer of 2011—on August 3, the Security Council unanimously denounced "widespread violations of human rights and the use of force against civilians by Syrian authorities," and on August 23, the Human Rights Council similarly condemned crimes against humanity in Syria. By the fall, mounting political will at the UN emerged to do something about Syria. Finding the appropriate "something," however, proved elusive. The debate in September 2011 is a microcosm of the dynamics of deadlock. Damascus reiterated that there was no need for an R2P operation: "Syria exercised its responsibility to protect citizens. It acted to guarantee their safety and stability."

Russian and Chinese intransigence have blocked authorizing anything resembling an R2P operation, officially because of unease about what transpired in Libya. Russia's permanent representative, Vitaly Churkin, remarked:

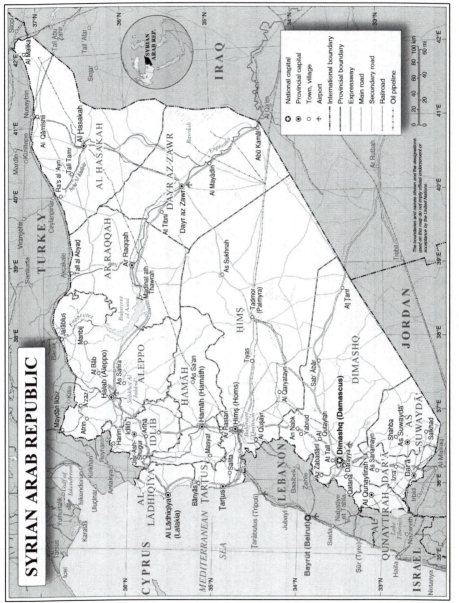

Map 6.3

Chapter 6

Our wording proposals on the inadmissibility of external military intervention are not taken into account. And that, in view of the well-known events in
North Africa, cannot but make us wary. . . . The situation in Syria cannot be
considered in the Security Council in isolation from the Libyan experience.
The international community is wary of the statements being heard that the
implementation of the Security Council resolutions in Libya as interpreted
by NATO is a model for its future actions to exercise the "responsibility to
protect." It's not hard to imagine that tomorrow "united defenders" may
begin to apply this "exemplary model" in Syria as well.[26]

In response, Britain's foreign minister called Russia's (and China's)
vetoes of an R2P operation for Syria "deeply mistaken and regrettable."
Other states also had reservations, and here the RWP influence is pertinent. For instance, South Africa noted that previous Security Council texts
"had been abused and implementation had gone far beyond mandate,"
and the council "should not be part of any hidden agenda for regime
change." Furthermore, such criticism has also come from those within
the humanitarian sector who worry that R2P exceeds the premise of humanitarianism—the title of a 2012 piece by David Rieff goes to the heart
of such critiques: "Save Us from the Liberal Hawks: Syria's a Tragedy. But
It's Not Our Problem."[27]

An important part of the international concern over Syria—and the one
issue that has galvanized action—revolves around the presence and use
of chemical weapons. In June 2013, France and the United Kingdom, followed later by the United States and the UN, confirmed the use of sarin
gas in March and April. Until then, approximately 60,000 individuals
had already been killed by this war. A mass chemical weapons attack on
August 20 killed more than 1,300 in a suburb of Damascus and aroused
international attention. In response, on September 26, Security Council
resolution 2218 authorized a joint mission between the UN and the Organization for the Prohibition of Chemical Weapons (OPCW) to remove
chemical weapons from Syria. This operation began on October 1 and ran
through June 23, 2014, which completed the removal of stocks disclosed
and discovered—although verification is still ongoing and there remain
manufacturing facilities that have not been inspected. In terms of crimes
against humanity and war crimes, what could have been less discrimi-
nating than chemical weapons? While their use could well have justified
an R2P response, they did not. However, critics of the Security Council's
ineptitude must admit that when its permanent members decide to use
it—and apparently the existence of WMD was uniformly viewed as a
threat to all—the contested body works.

A political and military, and in effect a humanitarian, turning point
in the conflict in Syria—which would, as discussed earlier, also have
an impact in Iraq—was the January 2014 emergence of Daesh, a radical

militant Sunni organization. About a decade in the making, it emerged from the cinders of AQIM, a subsidiary of the central Al Qaeda organization based in Afghanistan-Pakistan, which was dismantled by the US-led counterterrorism campaign in Iraq. In 2011, fragments of AQIM merged with militant Sunni groups in Syria to form Daesh under the leadership of Abu Bakr al-Baghdadi. In 2013, Daesh made its presence felt by securing what has become its capital, Raqqa. This area became a staging ground for a January 2014 offensive, and its forces conquered a large swath of territory spanning northern and eastern Syria and into western and northern Iraq—an area bigger than the United Kingdom. However, in 2015, Daesh would lose about 40 percent of this territory due to counterattacks by Syria (backed by Iran and Russia), Iraq (supported by Iran and the United States), Turkey, and Kurdish forces. Over the course of 2016, Daesh forces have been pushed back even further; as noted, in Iraq, they have been contained around Mosul with some pockets in the northern and far western parts of Anbar province, although in Syria they continue to have a sizable presence to the north and east, with their military forces and political apparatus entrenched around Raqqa. Aside from the waves of displacement unleashed by the violence of its armed forces, Daesh raises once again the prospect of mass atrocities as a tactic, particularly the genocide against Yazidis, an ethnic Kurdish minority that practices its own religion.[28] It also underlines the obvious limits of humanitarians, who can neither stop Daesh nor readily secure access to their victims.

With respect to emergency relief, aid agencies have struggled mightily to attain access to vulnerable populations. In July 2014, in Security Council resolution 2165, cross-border convoys of emergency aid were approved without the prior approval of the Syrian government, which has not given consent. But other thorny challenges remain for the members of the international humanitarian system. Daesh not only imposes a militant form of Islam but also prides itself on being anti-Western and thus actively attacks aid agencies and has executed aid workers. Daesh's strategy involves seeking to eliminate competition for political support by being the sole provider of humanitarian assistance in war-torn areas. It also was responsible for mass human rights violations, which included slavery and the recruitment of child soldiers in addition to genocide. Estimates are that the numbers of Daesh forces have declined by perhaps 75 percent from their peak so that by December 2016, between 12,000 and 15,000 militants remained in action across a significant span of territory across northern Syria and western and northern Iraq.[29] Beyond these areas, affiliated groups have sprouted in Libya, Egypt, and Afghanistan; they have pledged their allegiance to Daesh and carried out similar attacks against Western interests, including humanitarian workers.

Moreover, another challenge imperiling aid work in terms of safety and access stems from Russia's active entry into war in 2015. Negotiating access is even more difficult as Syria's leverage has greatly increased with the military backing of Russia. In February and again in March, Russian air power hit hospitals operated or supported by MSF. Once again, within this perspective, aid agencies are viewed as part of the Western footprint. From late February 2016 to late April 2016, there was a cease-fire between the rebel groups and the Assad regime (though fighting with Daesh continued unabated), which was short-lived; the government resumed a siege of Aleppo until it defeated the armed opposition based there in December and allowed it to evacuate its supporters to areas in the north.

The erosion of humanitarian space is perhaps most palpable in attacks on hospitals. Overall, the data on attacks of aid workers tell what is becoming a familiar tale of violence to deter, harass, victimize, and repel humanitarian agencies. In the period 2001–2010, there were no aid workers killed or wounded in Syria, but this began to change in 2011 as table 6.5 shows. The mounting insecurity has led to agencies withdrawing staff, which likely accounts for the decline in numbers since 2013.

The allure of "neo-imperialism" continues to distract and resonate despite evidence across the Global South favoring humanitarian intervention under appropriate circumstances, including the African Union's Constitutive Act's robust Article 4(h). "Though some critics fret that RtoP could prove to be a humanitarian veneer by which powerful states could justify military intervention in the development world, more often the problem has been the opposite," former UN special adviser on R2P Edward Luck writes. "The capable have stood by as the slaughter of civilians unfolded. . . . They have looked for excuses not to act, rather than for reasons to intervene."[30]

That certainly encapsulates the politics for the moment behind our original query, "why not Syria?" States for the most part remain on the sidelines while vigorously condemning Syria's bloodbath and watching successive agreements go up in flames. The anemic international response

Table 6.5.   Aid Workers Wounded or Killed in Syria, 2011–2016

2011	3
2012	25
2013	70
2014	42
2015	13
2016	21

Source: The Aid Worker Security Database, accessed January 2, 2017, available at https://aidworkersecurity.org.

to Syria's plight has confirmed that norms do not an effective operational advance make. UN member states increasingly are willing to condemn abhorrent conduct but often remain unable to agree on a common course of action even in the face of mass atrocities.

The first year of Assad's murderous repression resulted in "only" 12,000 victims, which led the Arab League and UN to appoint a joint envoy, former UN secretary-general Kofi Annan. At that modestly optimistic moment, the first two points of what turned out to be his dead-on-arrival six-point plan were a cease-fire and humanitarian access; the Security Council approved sending some 300 unarmed monitors to replace a handful of Arab League ones. Futile diplomatic dances took place in Moscow and Geneva as fatalities mounted. Fed up with his "mission impossible," in August 2012 a depressed Annan resigned his post and concluded in an op-ed in the *Financial Times*: "President Bashar al-Assad must leave office."[31] The Security Council saw no point in renewing the mandate of the observers but approved a replacement envoy, the former Algerian foreign minister and UN veteran negotiator, Lakhdar Brahimi. While numbers are hard to pin down in such circumstances,[32] the seemingly indefatigable UN troubleshooter plodded along despite the death toll going from perhaps 25,000 when he was appointed to some 160,000 in May 2014 when his frustration led to his resignation. Another UN veteran, Staffan de Mistura, took over the thankless task.

Syria was distinctly more complicated, chancy, and confused than Libya. Whereas the latter's relatively cohesive opposition movement was run from inside and spoke with one voice, the former's is based outside as well as inside of the country, dispersed geographically, and divided politically. The most visible and central opposition group in exile, the Syrian National Council, was divided. Invariably, successive efforts to cobble together a more unified resistance movement ended in acrimony and failure. Moreover, instead of the situation seen in Libya where virtually an entire country (other than those on his payroll) mobilized against Gaddafi, a substantial number of Syrians supported the regime or remained on the sidelines waiting to see who would prevail. The Assad government has sufficient firepower and support among minorities to keep fighting. By contrast to Libya's virtual single ethnic group (Arabs and Arabized Berbers, almost all Sunni Muslims), Syria's diversity is striking: Arabs constitute 90 percent of the population, but there are substantial numbers of Kurds, Armenians, and others. In terms of religion, Sunni Muslims are about three-quarters of the population, and another 15 percent are Alawites (an offshoot of Shiite Islam), Druze, and other Muslim sects; in addition to possible inter-Muslim divides, there is a possible cleavage with the Christian 10 percent of the population. Unlike the largely desert-like Libya with a few isolated cities, Syria's dense urban areas mean that effective surgical airstrikes were unlikely while significant civilian deaths guaranteed. Rather than Libya's small mercenary army that quickly defected or departed, the Syrian armed forces essentially remain well equipped, disciplined, and loyal. Meanwhile, Moscow supplied all manner of weapons to the Assad regime, which also had support from Iran as well as Shiite fighters from Iraq and Lebanon.

Despite ongoing negotiations launched in spring 2013 by then US secretary of state John Kerry and Russian foreign minister Sergei Lavrov, the war has continued apace and taken on the character of a sectarian regional battleground, with arms from Europe and the United States being openly supplied. The government and the opposition both believe in a military victory, but neither seemingly has the capacity to overwhelm the other. The entrance of serious Russian military assistance in 2015 seemed to change the game in the Assad regime's favor. An agreement between Turkey and Russia in December 2016 may further strengthen Assad's hand by ensuring that opposition forces are pushed to the Turkish border. The Trump administration's launch of Tomahawk missiles in April 2017 hardly clarified matters. However, emergency relief increased somewhat over the past two years, although not what was necessary for the access supposedly required by Security Council resolutions.

In January 2014, a gruesome trove of 55,000 photographs taken by an anonymous defector—a military policeman called "Caesar"—surfaced with numbers inscribed on 11,000 bodies on the eve of "Geneva II." Three distinguished international lawyers commissioned by the Qatari government verified them. The actual rather than merely moral costs of inaction became clear with Nuremberg-like evidence of war crimes. Atrocities are widespread, but the regime leads in this macabre competition—they "far outweigh" the atrocities committed by the opposition according to then UN high commissioner for human rights Navi Pillay.[33] Assad and his generals eventually must be on The Hague's docket, accompanied by some members of the armed opposition. In May 2014 Moscow and Beijing once again vetoed a resolution, this time a gently worded French one to refer the evidence to the ICC.

The current toll is overwhelming. A situation that seemingly could not get worse continues to do so. Sustained stalemate and slaughter are the likely scenario unless a post-Assad, power-sharing agreement can be found. The election of Donald Trump adds additional uncertainty to the equation. Such an arrangement would require a negotiated exit for Assad that could be supported by the West, Russia, China, and Iran. Given the accounts to be settled, no such agreement would be credible without foreign soldiers (perhaps a combined UN and Arab League deployment). The difficulties of ending atrocities were not made easier with the fifty-country coalition's bombing against Daesh that began in September 2014 in Iraq and was extended to Syria. While Daesh's grisly massacre of civilians—Kurds, Yazidis, Shiites, and moderate Sunnis—provided a feasible humanitarian justification, R2P hardly entered the picture because the intervention was consensual. The major justifications were geopolitical—Daesh threatens anyone with a stake in stability in the Middle East.

That said, the responsibility to protect is a principle and not a tactic, and the principle remained intact in Syria even if action was considerably less robust than the initial efforts against Libya. As indicated in chapter 4, R2P has been cited in some fifty Security Council resolutions and been the basis for such government initiatives as establishing focal points and participating in the "Friends of R2P" in New York. As a reflection of change, France has been asked to return militarily to its former colonies: Côte d'Ivoire in 2011 to overthrow an incumbent president who had lost an election and started a civil war;[34] the Central African Republic starting in 2013 to counter the CAR's genocidal chaos, which became part of a UN hybrid force with the African Union to protect civilians; and in Mali in 2013 along with troops from the fifteen-member ECOWAS to counter Islamist extremists. The transformation of international attitudes is remarkable if we contrast the deafening silence for the 1982 massacre by Hafez al-Assad of some 40,000 people in an artillery barrage of Hama with the hostile condemnations of his son's machinations: the UN's Joint Office on the Prevention of Genocide and R2P called for a halt to crimes against humanity; the Human Rights Council routinely condemned the crimes with crushing votes and published a report detailing extensive crimes; the United States, the European Union, and other states imposed sanctions; the Arab League condemned the actions, formulated a peace plan, and sent human rights monitors; and the UN General Assembly condemned the violence and supported the peace plan with a two-thirds majority and subsequently even more overwhelmingly (only 12 of 193 states voted against the resolutions) condemned Assad's mass atrocities and called for his departure.

In terms of altering humanitarian calculations, the value of a functioning Security Council was demonstrated in halting Colonel Gaddafi's murderous initial designs on Benghazi while Syria highlighted the costs of a malfunctioning one. But even here, when the politics were right and the need arose for a face-saving way to dispose of chemical weapons, the universal UN authorized it and worked with the OPCW.

While of slim solace to Syria's victims and their families, these clarion calls reaffirmed R2P. In comparison with Libya, the "why not" in Syria was clear: the politics in the country and at the UN were different as well as the geography and the demography; the military challenges were tougher; and the costs of coercion clearly outweighed potential benefits.

Aidan Hehir speaks of the "permanence of inconsistency" to characterize the politics of R2P—or indeed of anything.[35]

Conclusion: Revisiting Humanitarian Action and Intervention

Six distinctive aspects of post-9/11 humanitarianism become evident after exploring the four cases in this chapter. The first is the shape and size of humanitarian space, which is shrinking under the siege of the GWOT; there is little respect for aid agencies and concern over their influence, which undermines access.[36] The situation in Afghanistan has become prototypical. One practitioner summarized:

> In general, but particularly pronounced at local level, there is deep and prevalent hostility towards aid organisations and a general difficulty in distinguishing between different actors (NGOs, UN agencies, the UN Assistance Mission in Afghanistan (UNAMA), for-profit contractors, PRTs, and so on). The Taliban who criticise aid organisations are not just accusing them of being "spies" or siding with the government, but are also critical of their perceived lack of a principled approach and effectiveness. Elders, while generally not as hostile towards aid agencies, often shared many of the Taliban's criticisms: uneven distribution of aid in favour of more peaceful areas, corruption and a lack of respect for Afghan culture.[37]

Limited access reflects several factors. There is a conflation of all Western-based actors—neither belligerents nor local populations distinguish between foreign military forces and aid workers. An Afghan observed, "You cannot tell the difference between our tribes, so how can you expect us to tell the difference between yours. As far as we are concerned they are all foreign soldiers who are Christians and they are in our country."[38] In addition, aid agencies are vulnerable symbolic targets for militants. Refusing Western assistance sends a powerful message (and deepens dependence on local, possibly Islamic, providers of social services); an even more shocking message results from violent attacks on them.

Little can be done about attacks on aid workers. "Talking to the Taliban has often been seen as taboo by many humanitarian actors, and viewed by the government and military forces as an act of collaboration with the enemy. Although attitudes have changed in recent years, few aid agencies are willing to talk about this subject publicly."[39] We are still desperately looking for better answers to: Should the response be to use military tools or try to construct a political solution? What are the impacts of different security arrangements? In the context of multiple humanitarian agencies pursuing their own approaches, can this problem be addressed coherently?

The second distinctive aspect regards distorted aid economies; in each of the cases aid has become a key political resource and provided leverage. Here as in earlier crises, assistance can be manipulated by directing it toward friends and away from foes. Moreover, it can be especially problematic when aid goes to feed or care for militants who seek to continue war. The use of refugee camps as recruitment stations or hospitals for armed groups is pervasive. Also, as discussed, the OfFP featured a type of "humanitarianism" that entails victims essentially paying for their own relief, certainly another version of a perverse aid economy. Again, analysts and aid workers continue to ask: How can aid operations be structured to ensure that relief goes where it is intended? How much aid diversion is tolerable? Should "do no harm" protocols be invoked to insist upon withdrawal from areas where aid deliveries have become fundamentally corrupted?

The third aspect arises from R2P. Before trying to probe paralysis in Syria, we should recall how legacies shape our views. Michael Oren, Israeli ambassador to Washington, commented: "In my meetings with American policy makers, I often detect a conversation between ghosts. The ghosts of Afghanistan and Iraq are vying with the ghosts of Rwanda and Kosovo."[40] Contestation necessarily greets efforts to distill lessons. On the one hand, Afghanistan and Iraq demonstrate that wars are easier to start than to finish, and that it is easier to destroy an old order than build a new one. On the other hand, Rwanda and Kosovo show that genocide and ethnic cleansing beg for timely international responses, or later there will be even greater costs, including purely humanitarian ones.

The painful irony of the 2003 invasion of Iraq is that its justification was fictitious claims of stopping the development of WMD by the Saddam Hussein regime, which subsequently morphed into an ostensible effort to liberate populations suffering grievous human rights violations. What is especially puzzling is that the scale and scope of atrocities in contemporary Iraq may have actually worsened after over a decade of occupation. In other words, the 2003 invasion has fostered conditions that now require an R2P rescue. Moreover, the regime's actual earlier use of chemical weapons against Kurds—perhaps from 1985 but certainly by 1988—received no commentary at the time but could have justified outside intervention.

Nevertheless, we have not heard the death knell of R2P. When the politics are right, humanitarian intervention happens. Double standards, properly understood, relate to dissimilar treatment of similar cases; but cases are inevitably different: Syria is not Libya, just as Côte d'Ivoire is not Sri Lanka, and the CAR is not Burma. Selective responses are inevitable.[41]

That said, Libya was not an aberration.[42] Indeed, NATO's precedent-setting action in Kosovo was surely not the last of its kind, although the argument would be on firmer grounds had the Libyan intervention been followed by comparable Western stabilization efforts and peacebuilding. The Independent International Commission on Kosovo appropriately characterized it as "illegal but legitimate."[43] It was a justified departure from the Charter regime because the Security Council confronted then what it has in Syria, predictable paralysis and big-power vetoes. Both Kosovo and Libya were feasible, and both were justified, although Kosovo suffered from the lack of the Security Council's legal imprimatur, and Libya from a failure to follow through.

These cases help us move beyond our earlier theoretical normative discussion. In the abstract, R2P indicates that state sovereignty is no longer absolute but contingent on responsible behavior. If a government violates IHL, and in particular, if it permits atrocities or perpetrates abuse, the Security Council may act. But the council also may not. Consistency is a fool's errand. Political interests vary from case to case. Militarily coming to the rescue, even for human protection purposes, is an unlikely option for democracies. Foreign ventures risking lives with few vital interests at stake are a tough sell; politicians in democratic states fear that they will be held accountable at the ballot box for ventures that do not clearly suggest success.

R2P's central challenge is not inadequate normative consensus. The red herring of imperialism is often tossed into the diplomatic pond although, as Michael Walzer notes, "It is more often the case that powerful states don't do enough, or don't do anything at all, in response to desperate need than that they respond in imperialist ways."[44] There is ample evidence across the Global South to sustain military humanitarianism under the appropriate circumstances; in this respect, the overwhelming support by countries in the region for outside intervention in Libya *and* Syria is noteworthy.[45]

Despite counterintuitive arguments that it would be useful to excise military intervention from the R2P repertoire,[46] it is time for policy and decision makers to acknowledge that there was not too much military intervention for human protection purposes but rather nothing significant between Kosovo in 1999 and Libya in 2011. However, a specific emergency shocks the conscience, and however hard or soft the applicable public international law, humanitarian space will open and vulnerable civilians will be aided when the conditions are right: political will and military capacity ultimately determine whether, when, where, and why to protect and assist affected populations. In Libya, additional support came from R2P's moral and legal dimensions that dovetailed with political and military ones. Rather than speaking truth to power, R2P's value added was speaking truth *with* power. In Syria, only the moral dimensions were compelling; therefore civilians were slaughtered or fled while politicians pontificated and strategists preached that goals were unreachable and no obvious exit was apparent.

Syria certainly shames the international conscience, but Ramesh Thakur counsels: "it would be premature to conclude that R2P can be branded 'RIP.'"[47] Human abattoirs are not inevitable, but it seems that we utter "never again," time and again. As the political-humanitarian crossroads at Benghazi revealed, we are capable of uttering "no more Holocausts, Cambodias, and Rwandas"—and occasionally meaning it. The question is, under what conditions? And the answer to that is always, "when the politics are right." Humanitarianism is normatively, organizationally, and materially capable of walking through that door, but politics must first open it.

The fourth distinctive aspect concerns the application of IHL for conduct in war. For some, this has meant considering whether Al Qaeda and more recently Daesh and other terrorist groups should be prosecuted for war crimes. Attacks on civilians and aid workers certainly make the case compelling, but in terms of jurisprudence there must also be declared wars. While many terrorists formally and proudly renounce IHL as Western propaganda, it nonetheless is troubling to consider some conduct by those fighting terrorists. The United States has primarily looked to military solutions in waging the GWOT, but the applicability of IHL is pertinent, particularly whether to hold trials for suspects and captured terrorists. Shortly after the 9/11 attacks in November 2001, US president George W. Bush ordered military commissions for terrorists. The uncertain legal grounding and mechanisms for such an initiative led the administration to erect a facility at its military base in Guantánamo Bay—outside the jurisdiction of US civil law. The first group of detainees arrived in January 2002. By late 2002, 680 were being held at the extraterritorial base in Cuba.

The legal maneuvers for detainee terrorists and terrorist suspects at Guantánamo began in earnest in 2002. White House Counsel Alberto Gonzales initiated this process in a January 2002 memo where he deemed the Geneva Conventions "quaint" and contended that they did not apply to "unlawful combatants."[48] In February, Bush decided that none of the detainees at Guantánamo would receive Geneva Convention protections. Others in the administration were concerned; Secretary of State Colin Powell (a former military commander and secretary of defense) claimed that not respecting the Geneva Conventions would "reverse over a century of US policy and practice." But the Department of Justice nevertheless ruled that the Taliban and others were not entitled to "prisoner of war" status. Moreover, in July the Bush administration authorized the use of waterboarding and other "enhanced interrogation techniques," and in December the Department of Defense authorized interrogation techniques such as stress positions, nudity, and the use of dogs to intimidate detainees—what some might consider torture.

Critics have argued that the system was dangerous and normalized a "state of exception."[49] Not only was the use of torture counter to American principles, but also the international political repercussions were viewed as devastating to Washington's image because many detainees were either innocent or incarcerated with insufficient evidence. A scathing 2004 report documented US torture and led to a crackdown that has likely reduced the practice, although for the remainder of the Bush administration instances of waterboarding and stress positions were authorized explicitly.[50] A 2004 Supreme Court ruling determined that Guantánamo Bay was under US military jurisdiction and detainees were entitled to "contest the factual basis" for their detention. Afterward a significant number (about 600) have either been released or transferred to other jurisdictions (usually their home country). At the end of 2016, sixty remained imprisoned with only a handful slated to have their cases heard, and the rest to be detained indefinitely on murky legal grounds. Again, the election of Donald Trump as the forty-fifth US president raises numerous disconcerting questions about the future if he makes good on his campaign promises about using torture and sending new detainees to Guantánamo Bay.

Additionally, there are war crimes committed in combat, not just in the treatment of those detained after armed hostilities. Two examples are telltale. The October 2015 attack in Kunduz, Afghanistan, on an MSF hospital by US special forces was a clear breach of IHL. Similarly, Russian airstrikes in Syria have routinely hit hospitals, as have Saudi ones in Yemen. When great or not-so-great powers wage war in the name of counterterrorism, ignore fundamental principles, and are not held accountable, the prospects for humanitarianism dwindle.

The fifth distinction results from humanitarian responses themselves. In addition to safeguarding humanitarian space, what can agencies do to remain true to their principles? It is useful, for instance, to consider what agencies are doing to respond to non-permissive operating environments. One possibility is a "back-to-basics" approach as recommended by Nicolas de Torrente and others.[51] As long ago as 2009, Christophe Fournier, MSF's international president, argued in a speech to NATO officials:

Our ambition is a limited one. Our purpose is not to bring war to an end. Nor is it humanitarian to build state and government legitimacy or to strengthen governmental structures. It's not to promote democracy or capitalism or women's rights. Not to defend human rights or save the environment. Nor does humanitarian action involve the work of economic development, post-conflict reconstruction, or the establishment of functioning health systems. Again, it is about saving lives and alleviating suffering in the immediate term. This marks a fundamental difference between our two ways of thinking. What you do in Afghanistan today is for the Afghanistan of tomorrow. What we do in Afghanistan today is for today. We heal people for the sake of healing people.[52]

This recommendation requires promoting "acceptance" among local populations, which is humbler and less provocative than many efforts, and its modesty qualifies under David Rieff's "bed for the night."[53] It may also involve greater engagement with belligerents on both sides. A related modality is to "bunkerize"—that is, humanitarian work stays within the confines of hospitals, displacement camps, and aid compounds, thereby limiting the exposure and vulnerability of staff. However, it also prevents them from assisting communities where most victims reside. At the other end of the operational spectrum are many of the efforts documented here, a militarized form of humanitarianism.

There are trade-offs, often difficult or imponderable. In particular, the character of civilian-military interactions has an impact on the nature of humanitarian work. But what exactly? And which model of humanitarian action, under which conditions, is the most meaningful, vibrant, effective, and durable?

The sixth and final aspect concerns the views of local populations, which are virtually impossible to discern on the ground in war zones and frequently overlooked in academic and journalistic accounts. For the most part, agencies operating on GWOT battlefields are viewed with suspicion.[54] However, it should be noted that in the Middle East and North Africa there is distinctive understanding of humanitarianism that developed as a reaction to the increased role of Western NGOs—"Islamic relief" has a different approach; solidarity (not universality), justice (not neutrality), and religion-based (not secular). More research is needed on how contrasting versions of humanitarianism play out in disasters.[55] How do locals understand the work of humanitarian agencies? Do they simply see Westerners? Do they only focus on receiving aid and do not care how or by whom it is delivered? What do recipients indicate about humanitarian action, law, and intervention under the GWOT's parameters? What is the meaning of continually shifting world politics and the impact on humanitarianism?

This conclusion is more extensive than those of earlier chapters because the quandaries resulting from these four cases very much haunt today's international humanitarian system. The usual interpretations can be applied throughout; realism's obsession with great power string-pulling; liberalism's hope for efficient assistance to foster justice and order; constructivism's teasing out the new social construction of humanitarianism in the context of the GWOT; Marxism's cynicism at relief propping up areas immiserated and made vulnerable by capitalism and where possible fostering markets; feminism's worry about the marginalized and how their numbers ultimately may be increased through aid; and post-colonialism's concern with fronting and reiterating Western imperialism.

However, beyond these blanket statements, the approach of critical humanitarianism may be more fruitful; it recognizes the power of humanitarianism for better and worse. Most importantly, it remains sensitive to the possible objectification of recipients and endeavors to find ways to engage meaningfully in contemporary and future catastrophes so that humanitarians come to the rescue but do not lose their souls in the process.

7

Humanitarianism
Forgotten and Forsaken

*Darfur, South Sudan, Uganda,
and Neglected Victims*

Feeding center as part of Operation Lifeline Sudan in Ajiep, Sudan (August 27, 1998). (UN photo/Eskinder Debebe)

In This Chapter

- Darfur: Humanitarian Sideshow
- South Sudan: Born into Crisis
- Uganda: A Moving Humanitarian Target
- Sexual and Gender-Based Violence: A Blind Spot
- Conclusion: Marginalized Disasters, or Humanitarianism Lost in Translation

In contrast to the previous chapter that concentrates on the contemporary configurations of humanitarianism, war, and politics in an age of terrorism, this one shines a spotlight onto crises that dwell in the shadows because they are not actually part of the GWOT. Although some have at times garnered attention, they remain fundamentally abandoned by distracted, disinterested donors and their citizens who devote few resources to emergencies in which national interests and great powers are not engaged; the mechanics of how particular crises become forsaken is detailed further in chapter 9's discussion of media and markets. There is another twist to who is ignored arising from differences within populations afflicted by emergencies: those who have varied needs and create special challenges for humanitarians. There are classes of people, if not entire populations, who live in reprehensible conditions with few or no prospects for outside assistance or even sustained media attention.

There is a double focus: cases of countries that are neglected, in the Sudan and neighboring Uganda; and an investigation of a category of frequently disregarded victims—of sexual violence. Space does not permit discussing the multitude of other forgotten crises or victims—for instance, Haiti, CAR, Yemen, Colombia, North Korea, or Myanmar—as well as such categories as child soldiers or the disabled. This chapter's illustrations typify the larger issues under the premise of neglect. The core questions include: What is the nature of "neglect"? What are the causes and consequences of low-visibility crises, and how do they differ from high-profile ones? What are the challenges of delivering aid in neglected humanitarian disasters or to ignored victims?

The character of humanitarianism is shaped by resource allocations in the international system; more resources are suggestive of high priorities, and the determinative criteria for allocations indicate the influence of knowledge (consciousness) and norms (conscience). The politics that underpin this influence are manifest in responses and the quality of humanitarianism. The notion of "neglect" should be problematized to identify how it is engendered and to what effect. "Marginalized" captures how neglect is imposed. Is neglect the product of other pressing concerns overwhelming such cases, or does it happen because no one gives a damn? Thus, some crises are not really "forgotten" (international organizations of all stripes clearly know about them) but rather "forsaken" (victimization is the inevitable product of too many crises, political attention deficit disorder, and a form of compassion triage that ranks crises). This brief survey examines neglect as a reflection of victims being ignored by powerful actors and of the hierarchy embedded within the international humanitarian system.

Darfur: Humanitarian Sideshow

Most of the international attention on Sudan since its independence in 1956 has concerned the armed conflict between the North and the South, which had been ruled as distinct territories by the United Kingdom but were then grouped into a single post-colonial state (see map 7.1). Decades of strife were driven by clashes between the Arab, Muslim North (presently under the leadership of the National Congress Party, NCP) that controlled Khartoum and the government, and the Christian and animist rebel groups in the South led primarily by the Sudan People's Liberation Movement (SPLM). Sporadic violence turned to war in 1983. Recent estimates are that this war has killed around 2.5 million people and displaced 4.6 million more from a total population of what in 1983 was around 22 million.[1]

Suffering was heightened by a massive famine that resulted from the war; the government had used food as a weapon by depriving rebel areas of basic sustenance as well as agricultural resources (such as seeds, fertilizers, and pesticides); the violence also often prevented farmers from working the land. Aid agencies were eager to respond, which resulted in the path-breaking 1989 Operation Lifeline Sudan (OLS). It was the first time that the UN was the lead agency in a civil war; in previous disasters, sovereignty had prevented the UN from such a visible role because to deal directly with the armed opposition an intergovernmental organization would have been seen as challenging state authority. OLS brought together the UN system as well as some thirty-five NGOs and thus was ahead of its time in integrating relevant actors into a common framework. The result of this type of political engagement was to create humanitarian "space" including establishing "corridors of tranquility."[2]

Nevertheless, the lethal combination of war and famine in the late 1980s eventually killed 400,000–500,000 Sudanese. This brief overview of the North-South civil war not only introduces the history of humanitarian crises and action in Sudan itself but also the essential contextual backdrop necessary to grasp the nature of international responses in the western part of the country, Darfur. A premium was placed on ensuring that the ruinous North-South armed conflict (which still occasionally flares

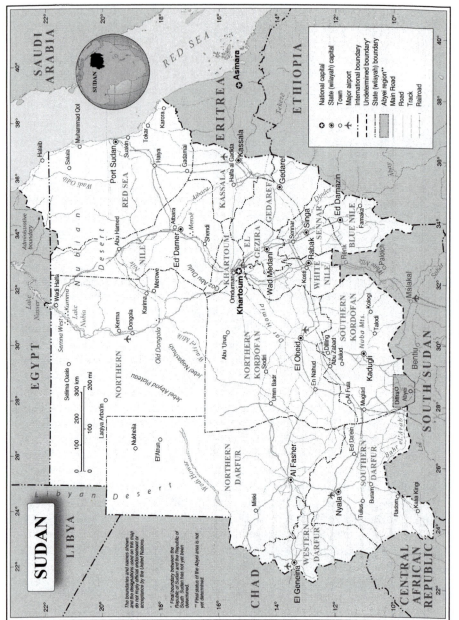

Map 7.1

between two states, Sudan and South Sudan, discussed below) does not resume. In short, addressing Darfur's woes was marginalized.

Darfur is roughly the size of Texas, whose population of 27 million is four and a half times Darfur's 6.2 million. The Darfuris are Muslim but not Arab, although other Sudanese populations are Muslim and Arab. Darfur itself was an independent Muslim sultanate until 1916 when it became a British colony, and in 1956 it was incorporated into a newly independent Sudan. Like the rest of the country, Darfur suffered serious famines in the 1980s. Later, a drought led Darfuri agriculturalists and Arab nomads (raisers of livestock) to armed clashes over the use of land for farming versus grazing.

By the dawn of the twenty-first century, at least twenty-six Darfuri rebel groups crystallized. The two most prominent were the Justice and Equality Movement (JEM) and the Sudanese Liberation Movement/ Army (SLM/A). In February 2002, rebels burned a government garrison. In April 2003, the SLA attacked a government airfield at El Fasher (the capital of North Darfur), destroying helicopters and jets as well as killing seventy-five soldiers. This strike created a new sense of urgency in Khartoum, where the government responded by sponsoring the *"janjaweed,"* or Arab militias. The government allowed them to confiscate land in exchange for their help in putting down the rebellion. During the winter of 2003–2004, the violence peaked and resulted in 600,000 displaced people. In April 2004, the government and several major rebel groups signed the N'Djamena Humanitarian Ceasefire Agreement. In addition to stopping the violence, it called for the AU to deploy forces to protect observers from the African Union Mission in Sudan (AMIS). However, the flawed agreement failed to clarify restrictions regarding armed movements in designated areas. Moreover, the AMIS operation suffered from too few troops, poor logistics, and inadequate funding.

Despite growing international outrage, the response was anemic. In May 2004, the UN high commissioner for human rights stated that these actions "may constitute war crimes and/or crimes against humanity," and later that month the Security Council condemned the violence by the government and the *janjaweed*. In July, the US Congress voted 422 to 0 for a resolution that declared the situation in Darfur "genocide," and Secretary of State Colin Powell echoed this sentiment in his September testimony.[3] However, he also said that "no new action is dictated by this determination"—thereby softening what many believed was the "hardest" of international legal documents, the Genocide Convention. Security Council resolution 1556 called for the government to disarm the *janjaweed*, and the special representative of the UN secretary-general negotiated safe zones with Khartoum's consent. Nevertheless, the humanitarian crisis continued, and by late 2004 more than 1 million Darfuris had been displaced, including 200,000 into neighboring Chad. On January 25, 2005, the UN-sponsored International Commission of Inquiry into Darfur released its report, which avoided the word "genocide" but instead referred to "crimes under international law." By February, 3 million Darfuris required international assistance.

In March, Security Council resolution 1590 authorized a new operation, the UN Mission in Sudan (UNMIS), whose primary focus was to keep the peace in southern Sudan but which did not address Darfur. A few days later, resolution 1591 imposed travel bans and froze the assets of key individuals implicated in human rights abuses, but no embargo was placed on Sudan's most valuable export, oil. In order to promote the prosecution of war criminals, the subsequent Security Council resolution 1593 referred Darfur to the ICC, all the while the war continued. At the end of August 2006, Security Council resolution 1706 for the first time explicitly referenced the "responsibility to protect" and authorized UNMIS to take over from AMIS subject to Khartoum's consent—China and Russia as well as rotating member Qatar abstained. But the resolution's passage became moot because the government did not approve the operation, the first time that UN peacekeepers had been authorized but not deployed. In July 2007, the Security Council tried again; resolution 1769 authorized a joint UN-AU operation, and the United Nations / African Union Mission in Darfur (UNAMID) supplanted the under-resourced and ineffective AMIS. Initially 26,000 troops and an annual budget of $1.5 billion were approved, but by December this plan was scaled back to about one-third of the original authorization.

Meanwhile the ICC pursued war crimes charges against the leadership of Sudan and the *janjaweed*. In March 2009, the court issued a warrant for President Omar al-Bashir on seven counts: five for crimes against humanity and two for war crimes; but by a vote of 2–1 the judges rejected genocide by citing inadequate evidence. Such human rights groups as the Enough Project and advocates as South African Archbishop Desmond Tutu strongly favored the controversial warrants. But surprisingly, several notable humanitarians opposed them because of the concern that the ICC warrants would anger Khartoum, which could expel NGOs and thereby diminish or even prevent essential relief. As feared, just five days after the warrants were issued, the so-called Ministry of Humanitarian Affairs wanted to "Sudanize" humanitarian operations within a year. Ultimately thirteen NGOs were pressured and subsequently withdrew, which resulted in 1.1 million victims without food, 1 million without water, and 1.5 million without health care.

Others criticized the warrants from a peace and security perspective. In southern Sudan, they could produce a backlash that would trigger a resumption of the war. Post-colonial critics argued that the warrants were racist because ICC prosecutions were aimed only against Africans. Furthermore, considerable frustration was apparent with the ICC itself because its warrants were not implemented. In December 2014, the new chief prosecutor Fatou Bensouda—herself an African from Gambia—suspended the genocide case against al-Bashir. Her logic was that the great powers, and even the not-so-great ones, had done nothing to secure his arrest despite the ICC's eight written requests to the Security Council. In 2011, the ICC had issued additional warrants against Sudan's defense minister, Abdel Raheem Muhammed Hussein, for war crimes and crimes against humanity in Darfur in 2003 and 2004, as well as against two Darfuri rebel leaders (Abdullah Banda and Saleh Jerbo).

In 2017, life in Darfur remains precarious. Although much of the damage has already been done and UNAMID currently has almost 14,000 troops (fewer than the authorized nearly 16,000), sustained violence and displacement continues—in fact, almost a third of the total displaced have fled from attacks in the past few years. In addition to at least 300,000 dead, humanitarian conditions remain abysmal for more than 6 million Darfuris. Over half of the nearly 2.5 million who have been forcibly displaced live in government-controlled camps, and approximately 3.3 million require emergency aid.[4] Humanitarian space is tenuous given that relief has been imperiled since the March 2009 forced withdrawal by agencies; in February 2014, the Sudanese government ordered the ICRC to halt work despite its annual assistance to some 1.5 million people, leaving UNAMID as the main humanitarian presence. Aid workers and peacekeepers alike have been targets. UNAMID forces have sustained more than 230 fatalities since 2008, and over that same period nearly 200 aid workers have been victimized.

South Sudan: Born into Crisis

The crisis that had been part of the North-South struggle in Sudan has also endured, albeit in a different form. After over twenty years of conflict and extensive UN diplomacy, the civil war ended in January 2005. The peace treaty, the Naivasha Accords, stipulated that the North withdraw its forces from the South, and that the NCP and SPLM form a unity government for six years, after which a referendum would be held to determine whether the South would secede. The February 2011 referendum resulted in a resounding 98+ percent of the population in the South voting for independence. The creation of the UN's 193rd member state of South Sudan on July 9, 2011, has not, however, led to the end of war or humanitarian crises in either Sudan itself or South Sudan (see map 7.2).

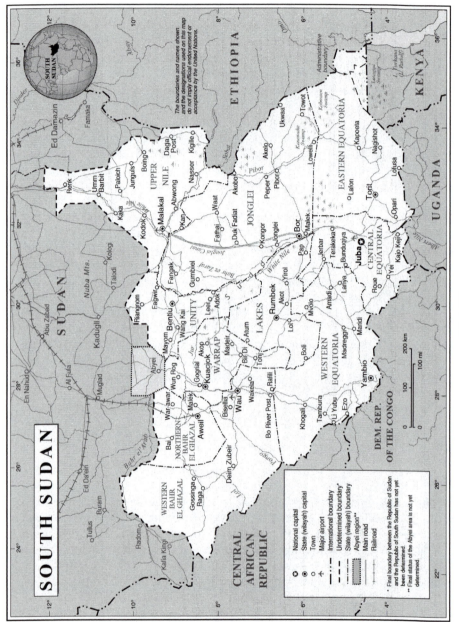

Map 7.2

Three overlapping drivers of violence and non-permissive environments are evident: First, tensions have long existed between the populations in the northern and southern parts of what was once a large single country known as "Sudan." This conflict has some cultural and religious elements—a massive country was lumped together by British colonialists who drew boundaries that assembled diverse peoples and societies. Second, Sudan and South Sudan have remained at odds over the division of oil resources (centered on the town of Abyei) and debt (which was $38 billion at the time when South Sudan gained independence). Third, along the border and within South Sudan there is strife. In Sudan itself, in the states of South Kordofan and Blue Nile, opposition movements to the central government that had fought with the South during the civil war continue to oppose the government, but they also feel betrayed by South Sudan for abandoning them. There is also ethnic conflict within South Sudan, particularly in Jonglei state between Lou Nuer and Murle ethnic groups, but also more broadly between the Nuer and the predominate Dinka population.

The birth of South Sudan has nourished two security and humanitarian crises, and the UN has dispatched two peacekeeping operations. In June 2011, shortly before South Sudan became independent, the UN Interim Security Force for Abyei (UNISFA) was established to prevent a military confrontation between Sudan and South Sudan through demilitarization. On the same day that South Sudan became independent, the UN also launched the UN Mission in South Sudan (UNMISS) to observe and maintain peace within the new country. This operation has nearly 14,000 uniformed personnel, which since its inception has suffered forty-six fatalities. Although its original mandate was to assist with nation-building, in May 2014 the Security Council shifted the mandate to civilian protection.

South Sudan's internal armed conflict also exacerbates the humanitarian disaster.[5] Most notably Nuer militias have been fighting with the Dinka-led government. Peace talks led to an agreement in May 2014 and another cease-fire in February 2015, but brutal fighting continues. Some aid agencies remain in South Sudan—UNICEF, WFP, CARE, Oxfam, IRC, Jesuit Refugee Service, among others—but humanitarians have confronted severe challenges. In addition to the violence that stymies access and the inaccessible parts of the country during the rainy season, political problems have produced government bureaucratic constraints, which have levied exorbitant taxes on relief and otherwise made operations ever more difficult.

In addition, and even more troubling, South Sudan raises structural problems at the heart of forgotten disasters; even when international efforts materialize, they may be eclipsed by local needs and hostile actors.[6]

Since 2011 more than 100,000 have been killed. By the end of 2016, with a population of more than 11 million, estimates were that 4.8 million people needed assistance, more than 3 million had been displaced (more than 1.8 million internally) while more than 1.3 million had become refugees.[7] Darfur has achieved notoriety for its slow-motion genocide and persistently poor humanitarian conditions—the crisis began in 2003 and has quietly churned along, cumulating widespread catastrophe. However, South Sudan is more neglected than Darfur despite how quickly the crisis unfolded and inflicted casualties. Additionally, it is presently far more dangerous for aid workers, who since 2011 have experienced 240 acts of violence.

The seemingly endless series of humanitarian horrors emanating from this state born into continuing but forgotten humanitarian agony in 2011 became even more troubled in 2016 as a series of negotiations between rivals collapsed and exposed more citizens to deprivation. In fact, troops under the command of South Sudan's president, Salva Kiir, had been fighting supporters of rebel leader and former vice president Riek Machar since civil war erupted anew in December 2013, with both sides whipping up animosity directed at the other's ethnic group. Machar was dismissed in July 2016 after yet another ignominious event and once again civilians unsuccessfully sought shelter in the UN compound, and UNMISS supposedly deployed to protect civilians failed to respond.

Ignoring warnings and seemingly unable or unwilling to respond to murder and rape, including of foreign aid workers, less than a mile away, the Security Council added 4,000 soldiers in August 2016 as the secretary-general ordered an independent investigation about the UN's unwillingness to respond. For years, the UN has documented atrocities as well as the lack of political will to do anything about them, including the inability of its peacekeepers to stop them. Perhaps South Sudan was no longer totally "forgotten," however, because amidst fears of genocide in late 2016, the Security Council considered sanctions.

Uganda: A Moving Humanitarian Target

Following independence from Britain in 1962, Uganda's brief experiment with democracy was disrupted by Idi Amin's overthrow of president Milton Obote in January 1971 (see map 7.3). As a member of the Kakwa ethnicity, Amin brutally repressed supporters of Obote, including the Acholi minority from the north. An intervention from October 1978 to April 1979 by Ugandan rebels supported by Tanzanian troops ousted Amin. Obote returned to the presidency in 1980; but in 1985 he was again deposed, this time by Tito Okello, an Acholi. In 1986, however, Okello's government was removed when Yoweri Museveni, from the Banyankole ethnic group,

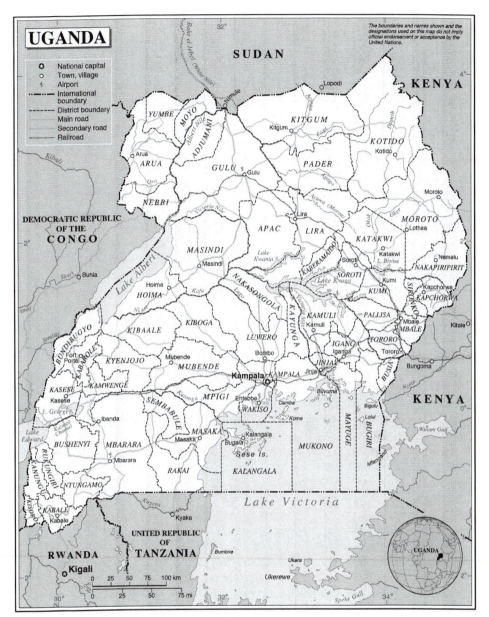

Map 7.3

carried out a coup. This triggered an insurgency among the Acholi. One of the insurgent groups was formed in 1989 by a then twenty-five-year-old spiritualist, Joseph Kony—the Lord's Resistance Army (LRA).

The LRA was never numerous but has always been a thorny problem, mostly because of Kony's sinister tactic of capturing and raising children as part of his movement.[8] In the early to mid-1990s, the LRA had somewhere between 3,000 and 4,000 fighters, including child soldiers, who mostly operated out of the southern part of then Sudan—which the Khartoum government allowed because Uganda was supporting the Sudan People's Liberation Army in southern Sudan. In order to counter the LRA's influence and control the Acholi population, in 1996 Kampala began to build "protected villages," essentially concentration camps in the Gulu district (one of the areas predominately populated by the Acholi). However, the LRA continued to prove troublesome; in March 2002 after Museveni had won another election, he ordered "Operation Iron Fist." The counterinsurgency campaign was to obliterate the LRA and Acholi resistance and included the extension of "protected villages" to Pader and Kitgum districts. The number of IDPs soared—between 1.6 and 2 million (about 94 percent of the Acholi population)—and the conditions in the camps steadily worsened. By 2006, mortality rates were three times those in Darfur. The LRA, whose number of fighters had dwindled to 1,500, fled to Sudan.

In addition to the military campaign, some members of the Ugandan government pursued negotiations with the LRA. However, in December 2003, Museveni referred the situation in northern Uganda to the ICC, which in October 2005 issued warrants for Kony and four other LRA commanders. Consequently, within the LRA there was division over how to negotiate an end to the conflict, with some wanting a negotiated settlement but others a guarantee that they would not appear on the ICC's docket. In 2008, the government and the LRA reached a deal whereby Uganda was to establish a special court to adjudicate war crimes and request the withdrawal of its ICC warrants; however, the ICC has not complied.

Starting in summer 2006, the armed conflict effectively subsided in northern Uganda as negotiations between Kampala and the LRA progressed. However, in December the government lost patience and embarked on a new campaign (Operation Lightning Thunder) to capture LRA commanders. But the operation was unsuccessful and instead resulted in a dispersal of the LRA and their flight to southern Sudan, the DRC, and the CAR—where they basically have remained. Between defections, deaths, and surrender by various contingents, the LRA now has about 200 fighters and perhaps 400–600 child abductees.

The war in Uganda involving the LRA ran from 1986 to 2006, but it is now essentially over as the LRA concentrates on survival and not victory. In April 2017 the Ugandan government ended its hunt, although Kony is thought to be trying to rebuild his organization.[9] The toll was substantial though concentrated. Since 1987, at least 100,000 have been killed, 60,000–100,000 abducted, and 2.5 million displaced. Uganda has a population of more than 37 million but the Acholi ethnic group, which bore the brunt of the burden of this violence, now only numbers about 1.7 million, many of whom were displaced and lost livelihoods. LRA and government war crimes both contributed. The 2012 Kony campaign by the NGO Invisible Children briefly brought greater attention to the former and renewed a narrative to foster global action. However, the withering of the LRA as a military threat and its relocation has wound down the humanitarian crisis in Uganda, which has created conditions conducive to "forgetting" the crisis, especially with more attention being focused on the neighbors, CAR and DRC.

Sexual and Gender-Based Violence: A Blind Spot

One class of war victim has often been marginalized and given less attention than those killed or displaced: those who suffer sexual and gender-based violence.[10] This type of victimization tends to be more likely in emergencies, as an IFRC report summarized: "women and girls are at a higher risk of sexual violence, sexual exploitation and abuse, trafficking, and domestic violence in disasters."[11] Although rape is the best known, SGBV is cast more broadly to include coerced undressing and non-penetrating sexual assault (for example, mutilation).[12] Sexual violence can be an act of torture but can also be part of a longer-duration pattern, such as sexual slavery. This type of violence primarily victimizes women and girls, but men and boys have also been afflicted.[13] Three key issues warrant consideration.[14] The first is staging: some acts of sexual violence are private, but others are inflicted publicly to humiliate the immediate victim and also traumatize the community, which underscores the political and social impacts of sexual violence. The second concerns the perpetrators: some acts are carried out by individuals but others by groups, thus raising the question of whether sexual violence is an individual crime or has been strategically organized. The third relates to patterns because sometimes all the main belligerents engage in the practice (symmetric) while in other situations only one side does (asymmetric).

Sexual violence was common in wars of the twentieth century. In World War II, belligerents from both sides carried out systematic, strategic sexual violence against their opponents. Germany organized military brothels in Eastern Europe. Soviet forces engaged in widespread rape in conquering Germany, especially Berlin. Japan committed rape extensively in its campaign against Nanjing in 1937–1938 and coerced 200,000 in East and Southeast Asia to serve as "comfort women."

In the 1960s, US forces in Vietnam were implicated in several episodes of sexual violence, including the My Lai massacre. In 1971, during the Bangladesh war of secession the Pakistani army was responsible for a campaign of mass rape that victimized at least 200,000. During the 1980s, sexual violence was a tool of government forces in counterinsurgency campaigns in El Salvador and Peru.

In the 1990s, widespread instances occurred. In Sierra Leone, sexual violence did not explicitly target certain ethnic groups; it was indiscriminate but prevalent. Two of our earlier cases featured countless instances of sexual violence: Bosnia-Herzegovina from 1991 to 1995 was characterized by both public acts to humiliate opponents and rape camps run by Serbs, Muslims, and Croats; and Rwanda in 1994 revealed sexual violence as a main Hutu tactic against Tutsis. The practice has now become routine, appearing in innumerable ongoing conflicts, such as in Darfur where the genocide is gendered[15] as well as in the Kivu region of the DRC and the assault on the Yazidi minority in Iraq.

Some success has occurred in identifying sexual violence as criminal, including the June 2008 Security Council resolution 1820 that condemned sexual violence as a tactic of war and affirmed it as a war crime, but in practice the issue is not routinely addressed in internationally mediated peace processes.[16] Since 2010 a special representative of the secretary-general has been tasked with bringing more attention to the appalling phenomenon.

We would be remiss to end this section without mentioning the less widespread but perhaps most unforgiveable of neglected cases, namely crimes committed by UN peacekeepers. Few cases have drawn as much and as damning attention as the sex abuse that arose in spring 2014, when allegations came to light, again, that international troops serving in the CAR had sexually abused children in exchange for food or money.

While seemingly nothing could be more important or obvious than ensuring accountability for those whose job description is to protect and not abuse civilians, perhaps most appalling in the 2014–2015 scandal was the history of UN inaction. In response to the 2004 allegations of sexual misconduct by peacekeepers in the DRC, the secretary-general invited Prince Zeid Ra'ad Zeid al-Hussein—then the permanent representative of Jordan and now the UN high commissioner for human rights—to act as his Advisor on Sexual Exploitation and Abuse by UN Peacekeeping Personnel. In 2005 he presented *A Comprehensive Strategy to Eliminate Future Sexual Exploitation and Abuse in United Nations Peacekeeping Operations*. The so-called Zeid report recommended standard rules for all peacekeeping personnel, the establishment of a professional investigative process, and the institution of relevant "organizational, managerial and command measures."[17] He further argued that those guilty should be subject to disciplinary action and held financially and, where appropriate, criminally accountable.

Given the symbolic and actual importance of UN peace operations, these measures were essential steps toward professionalism. Zero tolerance toward such actions is certainly required. Echoing previously reported abuse in Haiti, Liberia, and the DRC, subsequent reports about UN operations added troops from several African countries to the list of dishonor after finding that children displaced by war were molested and raped while the UN remained silent on the sidelines. Finally, in August 2015, the secretary-general asked the UN's CAR chief of mission—Babacar Gaye, a retired Senegalese general and veteran UN administrator—to resign after yet another Amnesty International report publicized new allegations of abuse.

This virtually unprecedented action by a secretary-general suggested that perhaps the world organization was finally willing to address the fact that almost 500 such allegations had been reported between 2008 and 2013. While Zeid's efforts had failed to halt abuse, a growing political willingness surfaced to enact his envisioned reforms. Hence, it was ironic that the 2015 human rights whistle blower, Anders Kompass, was working for Zeid in the OHCHR when he was suspended for leaking a confidential and unredacted report on abusive peacekeepers. But the UN Appeals Tribunal issued an order immediately to lift his suspension as the decision was "prima facie unlawful."[18] After having his name cleared, he resigned in May 2016, pointing out that not only had efforts on the ground been ineffective, but also impunity existed for peacekeepers *and* the higher echelons of the UN civil service.[19] Clearly Zeid's earlier efforts had started but failed to staunch the culture of impunity.

In fact, remarkably little has been done to counter SGBV aside from traditional cultural admonitions and brief references in international humanitarian law—for instance, the ICC has taken up the issue several times (Articles 6, 7, and 8 of the Rome Statute refers to instances of SGBV). Out of 300 peace agreements for forty-five conflicts in the first twenty years since the end of the Cold War, only eighteen address sexual violence specifically. But a sign of progress in this area was that both the ICTY and ICTR extended the overlooked earlier work by the wartime UN War Crimes Commission.[20] Moreover, the October 2000 Security Council resolution 1325 was the first council resolution specifically to consider the impact of war on women.[21] A study of the decade after the passage of the resolution showed some progress in such areas as the role of women in politics and the promotion of gender equality, but also much work to be done with respect to gender-sensitive security sector reform and SGBV more generally.[22]

Violence, sanctions, and poverty have disparate impacts on women; the council lent considerable legitimacy to reform efforts.[23] To take stock after fifteen years and six additional resolutions, the Security Council approved a high-level review to assess national, regional, and global progress on the original resolution. Radhika Coomaraswamy—previously special representative of the secretary-general on children and armed conflict and special rapporteur on violence against women—led the advisory group and commented, "It is truly a frightening phenomenon when your protector becomes a predator."[24] While strides were observed, mainstreaming of gender in peace operations still had not become standard practice, and the funding for programs supporting women in peace and security efforts remained "abysmally low."[25]

A promising development took place in March 2017 when António Guterres proposed stopping the reimbursement of countries that failed to investigate claims against their soldiers in UN peace operations and to place that money into a trust fund to assist victims. A related measure was to insist that all UN personnel acknowledge in writing that they understood the organization's policy against exploitation and abuse. He also called for a high-level meeting on sexual exploitation and abuses during the general debate of the General Assembly.

The primary vehicle since July 2010 for empowering women within the system now is UN Women. The General Assembly broke the mold and merged four smaller bodies to support implementing standards and meeting obligations under national and international law. "While donors are not prioritizing gender equality," UN Women has emerged as pivotal for international peace and security.[26] It has a seat at the high table for decisions about security and justice, SCBV, post-conflict humanitarian planning, and peacebuilding. The participation by UN Women was an encouraging institutional consolidation to improve the security of women; it serves as a model of sorts for other consolidation in the byzantine UN system. Nonetheless, the modest role of women within the world organization purportedly committed to gender equality clearly is another reflection of bias. One former senior staffer, Karin Landgren, calculated that in 2015, men were appointed to 92 percent of senior positions.[27] Again, Secretary-General Guterres has announced gender parity as a goal during his mandate.

Why has so little seemingly been accomplished to address SGBV? First, a cultural taboo on discussing such violence makes it awkward to put the topic on some political agendas or even conduct research on the scope and nature of the problem as a step toward addressing it. Second, there has been surprisingly little political activism on the issue—some aid agencies have begun, but it is rarely the central focus of advocacy or programming. Third, a lack of conviction continues about the issue's relevance in resolving conflict or making peace; in spite of progress in the ad hoc tribunals, it is by far the least condemned war crime. Fourth, there is an ongoing debate about whether SGBV is the product of opportunities presented to individuals or an incentive to combatants by their leadership as part of a strategy. Most approaches tend to conceive of it as the former and are unwilling to consider it as the latter.

Conclusion: Marginalized Disasters, Humanitarianism Lost in Translation

This chapter's reflections about marginalization bring attention to humanitarian dynamics for two levels (geopolitical and geographical) and for types of victims. First, the discussion of Darfur, South Sudan, and Uganda show that some humanitarian disasters receive far less attention and fewer resources than the louder and more prominent ones discussed in the previous chapter. To illustrate marginalization's material dimensions, we contrast various crises and assistance in 2013 and 2014, noting the differences between estimated aid requirements versus what actually was delivered. Table 7.1 shows the amount of money spent per person for the visible actions in Syria in contrast to two of our cases and two other largely forgotten ones.[28]

The data tells a complicated story of neglect and surges in media attention. It is perhaps unsurprising that no aid levels reach what is truly needed for a crisis; but those who left Syria received far more than those who remained. Access in Syria is limited, but the states that bear the burden of hosting the displaced also emphasize their own problems as much as the plight of vulnerable populations. Moreover, donor fatigue may have set in as requirements keep increasing and allotted funds decline—thus forsaking may be in the offing. Also noteworthy are disparities between populations in Syria and those in Haiti and CAR; aid levels

Table 7.1. Survey of Aid Per Capita in Humanitarian Crises, 2013 and 2014 ($)

	2013		2014	
	Required	*Actual*	*Required*	*Actual*
Syria SHARP	207	141	243	119
Syria RRP	559	406	576	363
Sudan	229	128	147	82
South Sudan	357	258	474	425
Haiti	169	80	398	203
CAR	122	62	309	219

Note: "Syria SHARP" refers to "Syrian Humanitarian Response Plan," which is aid going into the country, whereas "Syria RRP" refers to "Syrian Regional Response Plan," which goes to Syrians who have fled the country.

Source: Global Humanitarian Assistance Report 2015 (Somerset, UK: Development Initiatives, 2015), 26.

in Syria rose markedly in 2014 but only as the crisis worsened and needs increased. Finally, South Sudan is a surprising instance of an upswing in needs that is close to being met. However, when looking at the history of assistance there—which remains apparent with aid levels in 2013–2014 that went to Sudan—the drama of the initial crisis catalyzes interest and support but it is hard to sustain; if history repeats, they are likely to trail off. Data from 2015 confirm this hunch; many of the well-known crises have some shortfalls in meeting needs, but not of the magnitude seen in forgotten crises. For example, the Syria Regional Response Plan has mobilized 65 percent of its needs, but the CAR Regional Response Plan a paltry 4 percent.[29]

Another data set that verifies the existence of neglect is the European Commission's Department of Humanitarian Aid and Civil Protection (ECHO) annual production of its "Forgotten Crisis Assessment" (FCA) index.[30] Emergencies are evaluated in terms of their vulnerability, media coverage, and donor interests (evident in levels of aid and qualitative analysis). Since 2004, crises that have paradoxically become infamous due to being neglected have appeared a considerable number of times on the list—Sudan (5), CAR (5), and DRC (3).[31] At the same time, several other countries have experienced even more severe neglect and appeared numerous times: Algeria (13), Myanmar (13), India (12), Colombia (10), Bangladesh (9), Yemen (8), and Nepal (8).

Moreover, certain categories of victims receive too little attention and assistance to address special needs; SGBV is emblematic. The IASC has asked that agencies include a gender marker in their budgets to monitor responses. Table 7.2 indicates that funding over the last few years has increased considerably for SGBV—the 2012 total of $48.5 million almost doubled to $92.6 million in 2013 and $107.3 million in 2014—and may even be greater than these figures because sometimes SGBV programming may be part of other activities. However, other data shows that the commitment to tackle gender issues, including SGBV, may have peaked and is declining.

Humanitarianism has a strange character in forgotten and forsaken crises. Whereas liberalism promises an efficient provision of services to all crises that have an impact on the collective good, realism points to the interests of great powers, particularly with respect to security, as the

Table 7.2. Humanitarian Assistance Marked as Gender-Related, 2011–2014

	2011	2012	2013	2014
Humanitarian aid not coded for gender	71%	56%	56%	64%
Humanitarian aid coded as making "significant" or "principal" contribution to gender equality	16%	23%	24%	20%

Source: *Global Humanitarian Assistance Report 2015* (Somerset, UK: Development Initiatives, 2015), 87.

most influential factor in determining the international humanitarian system's agenda. Skewed results but at least some assistance is delivered; aid levels may be relatively modest in comparison to those in the armed conflicts of direct interest to major powers, but nevertheless aid still exists even in crises in which few or none of their vital interests are present. "Humanitarian realism" accepts a more modest humanitarianism in areas not central to world order. By contrast, more critical perspectives, such as Marxism, argue that humanitarian aid blunts the impact of the conflict and contributes to keeping it out of the limelight; hence, humanitarianism in forgotten crises may play a role in keeping them off the political radar.

Feminism as a tool of analysis is particularly salient for this chapter because it asks why and how marginalization occurs. It offers insights in explaining SGBV by noting the structural position of women, but it also often draws on the concept of "intersectionality," or the compound effect of multiple identities—in this case, gender, race, and class—to bring to the fore why vulnerabilities arise, endure, and matter.[32] Feminism also raises the delicate issue of whether there is voyeurism in analyses, or whether studies define the issue as a medical one in order to obscure the political dimensions.[33] However, constructivism and post-colonialism, too, furnish useful insights about forgetting and forsaking. Beyond material interests, a compelling story can lead to "discovery" of a crisis. The illustration of the Save Darfur Movement in 2005–2007 is telling. In making the call for R2P in Darfur, this human rights group painted a simplistic picture of Arab versus African and misstated facts. InterAction, a hub for more than 180 US-based NGOs, complained that Save Darfur's approach would only harm prospects for a negotiated settlement. However, the inaccuracy of the narrative helped—that is, it helped Save Darfur's fundraising. Such analysts as Mahmood Mamdani argue that many organizations reproduce colonial relations under the guise of human rights and humanitarianism because only the West matters in the framing.[34] The message behind Save Darfur is that only when a Western organization dramatizes the plight of victims to Western audiences is the humanitarian impulse activated, especially the use of military force for human protection purposes. This sequence strips agency and value from afflicted populations and at the same time morally and materially enriches Western agencies.

The debate as to whether genocide was committed in Darfur is another illustration of possibly dangerous tactics to elevate a particular humanitarian crisis. Application of the term "genocide" is riddled with politics. First, does it fundamentally connote either a racially pejorative interpretation of conflicts (e.g., only barbaric cultures produce such extreme violence), or does it ultimately only cater to reaching for military solutions? In other words, post-colonial thought would recognize "genocide" as a useful construct for blaming racial strife on the victims and empowering the West to act. The legal implications of terming large-scale acts of violence "genocide" make such a determination significant. But a "moral hazard" may result that encourages troubling behavior by populations being victimized; to confront marginalization, they may endure or even solicit atrocities to stir responses.[35]

The impact of marginalized humanitarianism is not solely fewer resources and more victims. Critical humanitarianism underscores the impact on the perceptions about aid and aid workers. Humanitarianism is predicated on what Nicholas Wheeler called "saving strangers"—that assistance is not self-interested and thus not given for material gain or ethnic or religious advantages.[36] The dramatic variations in the levels of visibility and kinds of assistance in response to different crises indelibly color the character of humanitarianism.

To be forgotten or forsaken is a political condition that inhibits, minimizes, or otherwise distorts humanitarian action; but it also erodes political support even for areas where political will usually is available. This crucial reality about the politics of outsiders may make it impossible for Western agencies to have an effective presence in non-Western settings. Crises marginalized by structural biases of great powers or an inability to craft a narrative that inspires may be further marginalized by portrayals of aid workers under attack or the futility of efforts. The outcomes of neglect underpin chapter 9, which analyzes the macro-political and economic filters that characterize the business and contribute to this neglect. But first we consider another variant of the forgotten and forsaken in humanitarian crises, those forcibly displaced.

8

Humanitarian Limbo

Displaced Populations, Prolonged Suffering, Contested Camps

A wide view of the UN/NGO compound where the American Red Cross, Turkish Red Crescent, World Food Programme, World Health Organization, EC Humanitarian Aid Office, United Nations Office for the Coordination of Human Affairs, and others share space to coordinate the humanitarian effort for victims of the earthquake that hit Pakistan on October 8, 2005, in Muzaffarabad (October 24, 2005). (UN photo/Evan Schneider)

In This Chapter

- The Problem of Forced Displacement
- Fixing the Problem
- The Problem with Fixing the Problem
- Europe's Contemporary Crisis
- The Meaning of "Refugee-Terrorist"
- Conclusion: Displacement, Domination, Dysfunction

---

orcibly displaced populations inhabit a peculiar sociopolitical space; special rights are accorded, including assistance and protection (both legal and physical), and governed by emergency authority to save lives. The humanitarian sector in particular, but the UN and other global governance actors more generally, have struggled with the nagging problem of how to address the plight of such victims—how to aid those escaping violence, famine, or other scourges. Displacement demands a humanitarian response, but at the same time, the interlocking problems of enduring crises alter the prospects for return by the displaced and undermine the potential for resettlement. The result is shunting populations off to camps that often are systems of control and sources of strife.

This chapter probes the politics of coming to the rescue of the displaced, specifically examining the thorny netherworld of uncertain human rights while receiving aid—a humanitarian limbo. The central questions that inform our analyses include: What is the nature of the challenge of displacement? Who is a "refugee"? What are the options for addressing displacement? What is a "camp"? What criteria determine practices in deploying, designing, and operating camps?

The Problem of Forced Displacement

There is no single "problem" of displacement but many. Indeed, the phrasing itself is revealing because the issue showcases the misconception of singularity or consensus in defining the problem. There are many different actors and agendas, which is an overarching problem—one of misunderstanding and talking past one another. Here it is useful to unpack the general scope of displacement along with the perspectives from host states, humanitarian agencies, and the displaced themselves.

To begin to understand why displacement represents such an enormous contemporary challenge, it is necessary to appreciate the history and growing scope and intensity of the problem. Populations have always been on the move; in fact, nomadic lifestyles have been common, and a few groups like the Tuareg continue today. And migration has routinely been a livelihoods strategy, whether it was to follow seasonal foods or pursue work in other parts of the world. However, for humanitarianism, the concern that crystallized in the past century and a half was centered on armed conflicts and natural disasters. In particular, both international and civil wars have almost always triggered displacement, but economic and technological constraints meant that forcibly displaced populations were usually relegated to remaining within or proximate to the national territories where they experienced displacement.

Here we repeat a major distinction about such individuals that sometimes is disregarded in the popular treatment of humanitarianism: "internally displaced persons" have been uprooted but remain within their national political jurisdiction; but "refugees" have crossed a national border. Indeed, the designation of "refugee" comes with a set of prescribed rights under IHL, whereas IDPs remain subject to the rules of their home state. Those who cross a border but are not officially deemed "refugees" are illegal migrants, and like IDPs they have no international legal protection.

In the twentieth century, massive or intense wars coupled with greater global communication and transportation connections inspired and enabled greater mobility even among the poorest displaced populations. During and following World Wars I and II, huge numbers of people were on the move. As discussed, new laws and organizations were devised to assist them; but aside from the previously mentioned constraints that limited many from pursuing refuge, there were also political negotiations to promote resettlement within countries, reapportion territories, or even create new countries. After WWI, for instance, borders changed and a bevy of new Eastern Europe countries were established to give homelands to nations lacking states. Examples include Serbs fleeing Austrian forces; Germans displaced by Russia from East Prussia; Belgians uprooted by Germany; Armenians escaping Ottoman areas; Russians, Poles, Latvians, Lithuanians, Ukrainians, and Jews in flight. In all it is estimated that roughly 10 million were displaced across Europe, including the USSR, or about 2 percent of a total population of 480 million.[1] Following WWI, Europe's displaced received assistance to remain within Europe and help rebuild; there were seemingly few places to which to flee with much of the entire continent afflicted by war.

The post-WWII period witnessed even more significant forced displacement—perhaps 10 percent of the total population, with estimates of between 40 and 55 million out of some 540 million.[2] Among them were Germans expelled by Soviet forces, Ukrainians and Belarussians deported from Poland, and Jews fleeing the continent. Furthermore, many people trapped behind the Iron Curtain in Central and Eastern Europe sought to move to the West but were limited by the politics of the Cold War—the Soviets did not want to lose populations, especially scientific talent. In addition, the repressive political conditions of Soviet-styled Warsaw Pact countries also fostered continued displacement. For instance, when the Soviet Union repressed an attempted revolution in Hungary in 1956, more than 200,000 fled to the West. Similar waves followed Soviet incursions in Czechoslovakia in 1968 and Poland in 1979.

Beyond the macro-struggle of the so-called superpowers, other conflicts and natural disasters in what was to become the "Third World" assumed increasing importance beginning with the greatest recorded mass migration of some 15 million people after the 1947 creation of India and Pakistan. The scale of such post-colonial reckoning continued when East Pakistan became Bangladesh in 1971 and another 10 million people fled violence. To such numbers would be added the "boat people" from Vietnam (1975–1979) and those later from violence in Cambodia (1978–1979) and Ethiopia (1980–1985). Indeed, the overall numbers jumped markedly in the late 1970s–1980s—from 1976 to 1982, the number of refugees under UNHCR's jurisdiction almost quadrupled, from 3 to 11 million.[3] At the end of the Cold War another wave of displaced populations hit Europe. In 1989, 1.1 million fled from Eastern to Western Europe. The breakup of Yugoslavia in 1993 added another 700,000 to Western Europe. The other crises in the 1990s and early twenty-first century, discussed in chapters 3 and 6, triggered additional waves worldwide.

The numbers of forcibly displaced have been steadily growing as seen in table 8.1. While recent growth has been primarily in IDPs, refugee num-

Table 8.1. Forced Displacement, 1996–2015 (in millions)

Year	Internally Displaced Persons	Refugees and Asylum-Seekers	Total
1996	19.5	18.0	37.5
1997	17.0	17.0	34.0
1998	19.0	16.5	35.5
1999	20.0	17.0	37.5
2000	21.5	17.5	39.0
2001	24.5	17.5	42.0
2002	24.0	16.5	40.5
2003	23.0	16.0	39.0
2004	24.0	16.0	40.0
2005	22.0	15.5	37.5
2006	23.0	16.0	39.0
2007	25.5	17.0	42.5
2008	25.5	16.5	42.0
2009	26.5	16.5	43.0
2010	26.5	16.5	43.0
2011	26.0	16.5	42.5
2012	26.5	16.5	43.0
2013	34.0	18.0	52.0
2014	36.5	22.0	58.5
2015	40.8	24.5	65.3

Source: UNHCR, *Global Trends: Forced Displacement in 2015* (New York: United Nations, 2016), 6.

bers have also increased. The most recent global data for 2015, the latest record-breaking year, show approximately 65.3 million out of a world population of 7.4 billion—or one in every 113 citizens of the world—have been forcibly displaced (up from 59.5 million the previous year). The ghastly math indicates that twenty-four people fled each minute in 2015, which is four times faster than ten years earlier. Of the 65.3 million, only about one-third are refugees (21.3 million), and far more (around 40.8 million) are IDPs. In 1982, when IDP data were first gathered, there was one IDP for every ten refugees; at present, the ratio reversed twentyfold such that it now stands at about 2:1.[4] Moreover, these appalling figures did not include almost 20 million displaced by natural disasters and development projects.[5] There are also about 3.2 million asylum seekers in the pipeline and 10 million "stateless" (without status or documentation).

The major source countries of today's displaced are found in table 8.2. The "top ten" account for nearly one-fifth of the global total. Other major suppliers are also war-torn and economically blighted areas, including Yemen, Burundi, Ukraine, and Central America.

Despite the abundance of media attention to the influx of refugees into Europe, 86 percent had fled to such poor and middle-income countries as Ethiopia, Jordan, and Turkey. Table 8.3 considers the size of refugee populations but calculates the relative burden of respective hosting countries. These data show that some countries carry a much heavier burden not only in terms of the actual numbers of refugees but also in relationship to their populations—Lebanon and Jordan are the most notable, but Turkey and Chad also register high percentages. Moreover, the table also indicates how many of these host countries have very limited capacities to assist refugees. Furthermore, some the countries shoulder a disproportionate burden, including several that are classified as "least developed" (Ethiopia, Uganda, DRC, and Chad).

Table 8.2. Top Ten Refugee-Source Countries, 2015

Syria	4,872,000
Afghanistan	2,666,000
Somalia	1,123,000
South Sudan	778,000
Sudan	629,000
DRC	541,000
CAR	471,000
Myanmar	451,000
Eritrea	411,000
Colombia	340,000

Note: The data include refugees and people in refugee-like situations, with a global total approaching 64 million.

Source: UNHCR, *Global Trends: Forced Displacement in 2015* (Geneva: UNHCR, 2015), 62–66.

Table 8.3. Top Ten Refugee-Host Countries, 2015

Country	Number of Refugees	Size of Population	Refugees as Percent of Population (%)	Refugees as Percent of World Refugee Population (%)	GDP per capita ($)	GDP as Percent of World GDP (%)
Turkey	2,600,000	80,275,000	3.24	3.98	20,400	1.394
Pakistan	1,600,000	202,000,000	.79	2.45	4,900	.813
Lebanon	1,200,000	6,240,000	19.23	1.84	18,300	.072
Iran	1,000,000	82,800,000	1.21	1.53	17,300	1.204
Ethiopia	750,000	102,375,000	.73	1.15	1,800	.141
Jordan	700,000	8,185,000	8.55	1.07	10,900	.723
Kenya	600,000	46,800,000	1.28	.92	3,200	.124
Uganda	500,000	38,320,000	1.30	.77	2,000	.069
DRC	400,000	81,330,000	.49	.61	800	.054
Chad	400,000	11,850,000	3.38	.61	2,600	.026

Source: Data compiled from UNHCR, *Global Trends: Forced Displacement in 2015*, 15; Central Intelligence Agency, *The World Factbook*, https://www.cia.gov/library/publications/the-world-factbook.

Another element central to contemporary displacements is their increasingly lengthy duration. Instances where 25,000 people or more have been displaced for more than five years are referred to as "protracted refugee situations" (PRS). The number and average length of these situations have been steadily growing. In 1993, there were twenty-seven PRS averaging nine years, whereas by 2003, the thirty-three PRS were averaging seventeen years.[6] As of 2014, there remained thirty-two PRS, eleven lasting over thirty years, twelve lasting twenty to twenty-nine years, and nine lasting ten to nineteen years.[7]

As far as the states that host displaced populations are concerned, dealing with forced displacement involves the violation of border controls and accompanying burdens. There is a considerable range of economic challenges.[8] Addressing the basic needs of displaced populations is costly; the draining and often open-ended commitments of resources can be politically unpopular. Additionally, spending within these states by relief agencies can spur inflation and spike exchange rates. Agencies also may recruit skilled and talented local workers, whose employment can lead to "brain drain." In terms of economic fallout from humanitarian assistance, there may also be an informal or parallel economy whose participants pay no taxes. Moreover, corruption can manipulate aid and alienate local populations. The interests that become vested in the relief economy also seek to continue the crisis to keep the resources flowing—or in David Keen's adaptation of Clausewitz, "war may be the continuation of *economics* by other means."[9]

Host states also perceive the threat of sheltering displaced populations—whether as refugees, but especially as migrants—as having political and cultural impacts with possible implications for fomenting nationalism.[10] The prospect of migration, or permanent resettlement, particularly raises the issue of identity and the capacity of the state to control its territory. Furthermore, host states also worry over issues related to population flows, such as the spread of disease witnessed during the 2014–2015 Ebola crisis, in addition to the often trumped-up but nevertheless real concern over an opening for criminal elements.[11]

Displacement presents aid agencies with a different albeit related set of three challenges. First, the lack or politicization of the legal definition of "refugee" and "migrant" is problematic; each connotes a distinct set of rights with varied responsibilities. Although there is an international convention and a UN organization on "refugees" (UNHCR) that can effectively enact a specific definition by taking up action, contestation over the term puts such undertakings on weak legal ground and can contribute to more of an ad hoc performance than a common agreed standard. Other agencies, such as the ICRC and Save the Children, engage in similar practices of asserting norms beyond law. "Migrants" suffer from the dearth of an agreed international definition, and moreover there is no single document covering their status.

Second, the uncertainty surrounding jurisdiction and roles is manifest in resource allocations. Agencies frequently struggle to raise funds in the context of scarcity and competing priorities; demand for relief is simply higher than the supply of funds. Regardless of promises made at the time when crises erupt and subsequent pledging conferences, dramatic shortfalls often follow. Part of the explanation comes from competing crises. For instance, in responding to the crises in the DRC, appeals are made for peacekeeping and development as well as humanitarian relief; meanwhile, the DRC competes for resources with Syria, Somalia, and other crises. Furthermore, there is competition among agencies that may have competitive programming. For instance, one agency may propose in-country assistance whereas another pitches aid for refugees—both are displaced and require help, but fundraising strategies may conflict. In Syria in 2015 for instance, less than half the estimated necessary resources were available; in fact, globally only $25 billion of the estimated $40 billion were mobilized.[12]

Third, agencies also face challenges in operationalizing their responses as per their mandates. Besides the shortage of funding, insecurity results from working in dangerous, volatile environments. A central operational challenge derives from the ethics, politics, and realities of relief—to engage in humanitarian practices in circumstances that are fundamentally inhumane. An agency identifies itself as humanitarian, but what if, as Barbara Harrell-Bond so pertinently asked, its work fosters, enables, or contributes to non-humanitarian outcomes, including making them worse?[13] Agencies confront the ultimate dilemma: to stay to ease the crisis despite the prospects that additional suffering could result, or to restrict operations to clear-cut and relatively unproblematic situations that risk reducing an agency's overall impact.

For those uprooted, the problem of displacement reflects the litany of horrors that accompany flight. The sweep of humanitarian needs is great: food, medicine, shelter, sanitation, protection, and the list goes on. Populations are destitute and vulnerable, and the trauma of displacement deep. In addition to what is generally a loss of virtually all material possessions and perhaps also an affliction of physical and psychological wounds, including the condition of "liminality," popularized by Victor Turner.[14] In this way, the displaced are mentally trapped between two places—neither in the place where they once resided nor in the place where they now find themselves. The challenge to maintain a cultural, national, economic, or political identity in the confines of liminality is overwhelming, and the displaced may be compelled to adopt a de-humanizing identity, "refugee" or "displaced."

Fixing the Problem

The international humanitarian system has attempted to tackle the problem of displacement in a variety of ways: articulating rights, supplying relief, and providing protection. The first global and intergovernmental initiative to concentrate on this kind of victimization was in 1921 when the League of Nations established the Office of the High Commissioner for Refugees. This effort was primarily designed to address those fleeing during the early years of the Russian Revolution (1917–1923) and the breakup of the Russian empire. By the late 1920s and early 1930s, the challenge of resettling such large numbers of displaced populations prompted debates about whether to simply send them back to where they came from, but this approach was contentious because often there was no agreement that a particular crisis had ended and that violence would not await returnees. The international humanitarian system responded by agreeing to protect the displaced from being forced to return (*non-refoulement*) and acknowledge their right to resettle. Article 3 of the 1933 Convention Relating to the International Status of Refugees stated:

> Each of the Contracting Parties undertakes not to remove or keep from its territory by application of police measures, such as expulsions or non-admittance at the frontier (*refoulement*), refugees who have been authorised to reside there regularly, unless the said measures are dictated by reasons of national security or public order. It undertakes in any case not to refuse entry to refugees at the frontiers of their countries of origin.

WWII led to a consolidation of the relief and refugee regimes. In 1946, the vehicle for the distribution of assistance, the United Nations Relief and Rehabilitation Administration (UNRRA), was transferred to the "temporary" International Refugee Organization (IRO). However, disputes arose over the term "displaced person." The UNRRA and IRO were enmeshed in Cold War politics and disagreed on a strategy—the IRO, sponsored by the United States, promoted resettlement, while the UNRRA, which was viewed after the war as more closely coinciding with Soviet interests, advanced repatriation. This deadlock required negotiating a new international agreement with a mandate for a new international organization. At the same time, human rights and humanitarian activists were working to promote norms that would foster resettlement, including Article 14 of the Universal Declaration on Human Rights: "Everyone has the right to seek and to enjoy in other countries asylum from persecution."

After the war, Hannah Arendt worried that refugees were in an untenable position: stuck between the "abyss of nationalism" that would provoke hostility in the places to which they fled and repatriation to face the dangers that caused them to flee in the first place. She articulated the core problem: populations would either return or receive asylum, but the latter would entail long-term commitments by host states and pressures on the displaced population to adapt.

> The first great damage done to the nation-states as a result of the arrival of hundreds of thousands of stateless people was that the right of asylum, the only right that had ever figured as a symbol of the Rights of Man in the sphere of international relationships, was being abolished. Its long and sacred history dates back to the very beginnings of regulated political life. . . . The second great shock that the European world suffered through the arrival of the refugees was the realization that is was impossible to get rid of them or transform them into nationals of the country of refuge. From the beginning everybody had agreed that there were only two ways to solve the problem: repatriation or naturalization.[15]

In 1951, the Convention Relating to the Status of Refugees became the legal basis for creating the Office of the United Nations High Commissioner for Refugees. However, the convention circumscribed the legal definition of a "refugee" to basically only someone in Europe displaced before January 1, 1951. Aside from this temporal and spatial configuration, the convention intentionally did not apply to war criminals, those who commit serious nonpolitical crimes, the Palestinians receiving assistance from the UN Relief and Works Agency for Palestinian Refugees in the Near East (UNRWA), and refugees who have equivalent status as a national in their country of asylum. The main principles of the 1951 convention are *non-refoulement*; no penalties for illegal entry; and a guarantee of many social, economic, and political rights (including education, religion, access to courts, freedom of movement).

Article 33's key first paragraph spells out that states may not force refugees to return to places that they escaped: "No Contracting State shall expel or return ('*refouler*') a refugee in any manner whatsoever to the frontiers of territories where his life or freedom would be threatened on account of his race, religion, nationality, membership of a particular social group or political." However, the next paragraph allows states to refuse refugee status on grounds of security: "The benefit of the present provision may not, however, be claimed by a refugee whom there are reasonable grounds for regarding as a danger to the security of the country in which he is, or who, having been convicted by a final judgment of a particularly serious crime, constitutes a danger to the community of that country."

The protection outlined in the 1951 convention is legal, not physical. UNHCR's mandate is structured to promote three sorts of durable solutions: voluntary repatriation (return to country of origin); local integration (permanent settlement in country of asylum); and resettlement (in a third country). When UNHCR began operations in 1951, it was expected to complete its work in about three years. Unrealistic optimism also characterized UNRWA's establishment in December 1949 to deal with the immediate aftermath of the end of the British mandate in Palestine. It, too, was supposed to last for three years—until Israel took over responsibility in 1952—but is still present and helping the fourth generation of displaced Palestinians.

But the problem of forced displacement was not merely a temporary, post-WWII phenomenon for UNHCR, any more than the presence of Palestinian refugees was a short-term problem for UNRWA. Displacement has persisted much longer and become far more pervasive. It also took on new forms, such as the emergence of "stateless" people, those who not only have been displaced but have no legal standing even in their territory of origin, first referenced in the 1954 Convention relating to the Status of Stateless Persons. In 1961, another international agreement was reached, the Convention on the Reduction of Statelessness, to provide a means to legally register this particularly administratively vulnerable population. Of greater significance was the pressure to reconsider "refugee"—the 1951 Convention was far too limited; the problems of refugees were neither short-term ("temporary"), nor were they restricted purely to Europe. Therefore, in 1967 a new Protocol Relating to the Status of Refugees was signed amending the 1951 Convention to encompass a worldwide mandate without time limits. In many ways, it simply reflected ongoing practice as UNHCR had informally been working in places like Tunisia and Hong Kong. Regional instruments that recognized the rights of refugees were also developed, such as the Organization of African Unity's (OAU's) 1969 Convention Governing the Specific Aspects of Refugee Problems in Africa, and the 1984 Colloquium on International Protection of Refugees in Central America, Mexico, and Panama.

UNHCR remained the linchpin of the refugee regime. During the Cold War, however, the organization's scope was limited and only able to provide protection once displacement had occurred. Former high commissioner Sadako Ogata notes:

> UNHCR essentially waited on the other side of an international border to receive and to protect refugees fleeing conflicts. This approach was determined by the very concept of international protection of refugees which would come into play if, and only if, victims of persecution or violent conflict fled their homeland. It was also dictated by the concept of state sovereignty and the consequent reluctance of intergovernmental organizations, such as UNHCR, to be seen as being too involved in the internal conditions of countries of origin that might give rise to refugee movements.[16]

The Executive Committee of the high commissioner's Programme Standing Committee similarly points out:

> From the time of its establishment in 1951 until the early 1980s, there was a
> broad international consensus that UNHCR could respect its humanitarian
> and non-political status by confining its activities to countries of asylum and
> by responding to refugee movements once they had taken place. Any effort to
> address the conditions giving rise to forced populations displacements within
> countries of origin . . . would have involved the Office in functions which fell
> beyond the scope of its Statute, and were therefore impermissible.[17]

Yet broadening UNHCR's mandate neither solved nor stopped displacement. Starting in the late 1970s, displacement in the Third World began growing rapidly, which added to charges under UNHCR's purview.
The growth of the organization was also fostered by many countries that
did not want to bear the costs of hosting or incorporating refugees; thus,
they empowered the agency to foster repatriation.

While UNHCR's conventional response was to push for repatriation,
some humanitarians began to call for other actions, which began in the
late 1980s with the appointment of Jean-Pierre Hocké. After initially lob-
bying for the return of refugees as part of reforming UNHCR, his staff revolted against policies for Ethiopia and the "boat people" from Vietnam.
Subsequently, the organization shifted from focusing entirely on legal aid
and emergency response to refugees to concentrating on root causes of
displacement.[18] Thinking and practice of UNHCR took another turn starting in 1990 under the leadership of Sadako Ogata. Over her decade as
high commissioner, she worked to create a "protection mandate" for UN-
HCR that would afford the displaced security within their own country
and thereby undercut the need to become refugees. Whereas the tradition
of UNHCR had brought people to safety, Ogata sought to bring safety to
the people, which produced the concept and practice of "safe havens."[19]

According to this newer thinking, operationalizing UNHCR's "protection mandate" necessarily involves working with militaries as a tactic to
enable an overall strategy of limiting displacement. This was pioneered
with the UNPROFOR mandate in Bosnia and deepened over the decade
with UNHCR's working with NATO for logistics support. However, even
where there were few security forces, UNHCR promoted repatriation,
taking this approach to Hutus in what was then eastern Zaire after the
1994 Rwandan genocide. When they were displaced in the midst of the
Tutsi rebellion that overthrew the Hutu government, UNHCR proposed
returning the Hutus to Rwanda. In this period, UNHCR's policy of addressing long-term causes of conflict to facilitate return, a practice known
as "preventive protection," argued that keeping populations safe in their
own lands was the most effective approach. After Ogata's departure,

two of her successors, Ruud Lubbers (2001–2005) and António Guterres (2005–2015), similarly pursued return-centered policies, although in principle the three "durable solutions" routinely proposed by UNHCR remain voluntary repatriation, local integration, or third-state resettlement.[20]

Fixing the problem of displacement also involves the design of human settlements. From this perspective, refugee camps and other organized centers that provide temporary shelter and emergency assistance are powerful instruments for managing the displaced. Anne Stevenson and Rebecca Sutton have reviewed the field manuals of three major humanitarian agencies—UNHCR's *Handbook for Emergencies*; MSF's *Camp Planning Guidelines*; and the Norwegian Refugee Council's *Camp Management Toolkit*. They judge that these agencies nurture settlements and meet basic needs but are intrinsically disrespectful, disempowering, and alienating for those whom they are intended to serve.[21] The manuals do not foster or even allow participation in designing and building facilities and the environment around them. In fact, they engender a type of class hierarchy among camp residents based on proximity; those in more remote parts have less access to resources.

The ideal model proposed in these manuals' designs are refugee camps predicated upon families or households. The formula creates a camp of around 20,000 people (about 30–45 square meters/person)—a size that is above all functional for the logistics of distributing basic services and materials as well as structured to be secured and controlled should the occupants violently resist or attempt to leave. In general, the process by which camp space is allocated is unclear, although the manuals usually call for centralizing service delivery (e.g., one marketplace, one health center, etc.) without recognizing the value for camp dwellers to determine finding space for common areas, such as places to socialize. However, giving greater power to refugees to structure their own spaces is not without controversy because of potential corruption or manipulation. Nevertheless, in recent years there has been greater demand for agencies to democratize or at least increase the ownership of the displaced in the spatial governance of camps.[22] But this too should be considered critically, as some of the impetus behind promoting self-governance is to shift responsibility for the welfare of refugees to the refugees themselves.[23]

In contrast to refugees, migrants (those whose relocation has been or become legal) are supposed to be covered, as are all citizens, by a more explicit albeit still patchwork of international human rights agreements—for example, the two covenants on civil and political rights and on economic and social rights—as well as a few more tailored ones such as the 1990 UN Convention on the Protection of the Rights of All Migrant Workers and Members of Their Families. There is also the International Organization for Migration (IOM), which has operated autonomously since 1951, primarily promoting rights and coordinating the policies of states for migrants. There are obvious difficulties in determining the status of refugees versus migrants along with their overlapping needs—for instance, the influx of both refugees and migrants entailed much duplicative paperwork and administration in the facilities in southern Europe's ongoing crisis. IOM is not officially part of the UN system but cooperates closely with UNHCR. Proposals for merging the two agencies remain on the drawing boards even after the September 2016 New York Summit when IOM became an independent organization within the UN system.[24]

The Problem with Fixing the Problem

Making better camps does not address the need for camps, and indeed, it may quell or tamp down pressure to halt forced displacement. By operating displacement camps, aid agencies are in effect colluding with a system that accepts displacement, caters to it, and may even thrive from it. Agencies may uncritically espouse a "victim strategy" that seeks merely to tend to suffering and not tackle its root causes, which Rony Brauman argues inexorably reduces individuals to their biological essence and strips them of their rights.[25] In other words, in the name of humanity, humanitarian organizations save people, but the structures produced in saving them govern the displaced inhumanely. He contends that aid workers are akin to "zookeepers" and need more actively to express solidarity and recognize the humanity of those whom they help.

Moreover, camps also create a vehicle for managing populations—sometimes directing them to areas where they are less threatened, other times harnessing them for their financial and human resources. Ethiopia's mid-1970s practice of population transfers—ostensibly to move civilians into places where there was greater access to aid, security, water, and agricultural resources—was, in fact, crucial in the government's counterinsurgency strategy. Starting in 1979, there were camps in Thailand along the Cambodian border where Khmer Rouge fighters escaped and regrouped after the Vietnamese intervention. These camps were controlled by the Thai military and provided a new infusion of consumers and resources for the Thai economy.[26] They also enabled the Khmer Rouge to "tax" goods. This case also divided humanitarians; MSF refused to work with actors associated with the Khmer Rouge and boycotted the camps, but Oxfam worked through the new government. More painfully, camps hosting Afghans, Eritreans, Namibians, Palestinians, and Hutus (from Rwanda) were staging grounds for recruitment (hence "refugee-warriors").[27] In sum, camps are opportunities for political authorities to pursue strategic interests and challenges for aid agencies because working in them can make them complicit.[28]

[In addition to host countries and local interlocutors, great powers also can utilize the infrastructure of humanitarianism to pursue other goals.] Mark Duffield contends that this is part of the merging of security and development in order to manage at-risk and risky populations.[29] Michel Agier launches a similar broadside in seeing "humanitarian government" as the "left hand of empire."[30] In his interpretation, controlling migration is part of a containment strategy in the aftermath of military interventions. For him, care and control are two sides of the same humanitarian coin. Those that staff humanitarian agencies subscribe to a common *modus operandi* in organizing camps, with professionals establishing parameters for security, logistics, surveillance, construction, and dimensions. There is implicitly an agreed upon body of knowledge about humanitarianism among agencies. Nevertheless, camps become important areas for spotlighting the contested nature or politics of humanitarianism: there is the discretionary power of administrators in these "spaces of exception" (a place where the usual rules and rights do not apply), often in an extraterritorial jurisdiction as camp areas legally and practically operate beyond existing formal political geography, and where populations are relegated to survival as the priority. But at the same time, there are "forms of resistance" to what is essentially a type of imprisonment and repression. There are cases of populations in camps reclaiming their agency, protesting conditions, and resisting the "victim" label.

Didier Fassin provides another critical perspective on refugee camps.[31] He follows in the footsteps of the classic work of Giorgio Agamben on the "bare life": "The camp is the space that opens up when the state of exception begins to become the rule"[32]—meaning that there is no humanity accorded in this place that exists outside the normal bounds of politics and society. Fassin problematizes "the camp" and its processes to analyze the "filtering" and security function that humanitarianism has come to perform for power. He tells the story of a woman who fled Haiti after being raped and is diagnosed with HIV. She is refused asylum in France on political grounds (they are not convinced that her displacement is the result of politics) but is granted it on the merits of medical claims (repatriation would imperil her access to adequate medical care). This sort of classification schema begets a perverse logic of sympathy for a specific type of ailment but a disavowal of a basic right to protection. From this angle, humanitarianism can become an obtuse blend of "compassionate repression."

[Thus, the problem of fixing the problem of camps is that it renders humanitarianism an attendant to disaster, one that does not question the reasons for disasters that cause displacement. Furthermore, rather than risk being overwhelmed by the tides of those in need, it participates in defining worthy victims and confining them while the stilted, politicized process plays out. Additionally, some observers contend that even programming aimed at rectifying injustices may reproduce them—for example, one study of gender mainstreaming in a Kenyan refugee camp found that gender asymmetries were reinforced or even worsened by aid efforts.[33] For the most strident critics, the camps represent a humanitarianism devoid of dignity and humanity, and anything that eases the acceptance of camps undermines the very premise of humanitarianism.

Europe's Contemporary Crisis

During the Cold War when displacement in Europe primarily involved the West automatically welcoming anyone fleeing Soviet oppression, the situation was not presented as a dire burden. However, after European integration advanced and expanded membership in the 1980s and 1990s—of which the Schengen regime on migration established in 1986 is a cornerstone—displaced populations coming to Europe from outside the West pose quite different challenges. The perception is not only that they bring diseases and crime as well as compete for jobs and drain social services, but also that they are a threat to Europe's identity. As such the issue of displacement, along with the broader question of migration, has been securitized. In short, refugees and migrants are no longer portrayed in terms of human rights but rather as connected to economics, terrorism, and security. Entering "Fortress Europe" is arduous for the vulnerable, particularly as European governments cooperate to enact "filtering" at or beyond the borders of Europe: the Polish border, Greek islands, Ceuta and Melilla (Spanish North African territories), Albania and Croatia, and Libya and Morocco.

The alarmist dread surrounding the displaced in Europe purportedly revolved around the large numbers. In earlier periods when wars and famines in distant places impelled displacement, populations moved mainly nearby to proximate locations. Even after the end of Cold War and for a decade or so thereafter, only a trickle made their way to Europe. However, the magnitude of the crisis in Syria, and to a lesser extent in Libya, Iraq, and Afghanistan, has convinced those suffering in these areas that it is too dangerous to remain either in their home or neighboring countries. They perceive that these respective wars will not end; in the remote event they do, livelihoods or culture will not return to the pre-crisis state of affairs.

Accordingly, and along with economic migrants, refugees are chasing a dream of living in peaceful, prosperous Europe, a life viewed, or at least imagined, through worldwide media exposure. New routes that do not entail a lengthy, dangerous journey at the hands of smugglers across the Mediterranean but rather a relatively quick island hop from western Turkey to Greece have spurred flows. The numbers are considerable by recent European standards of migration. In 2014, 216,000 arrived in Europe. In 2015, there were more than 1 million: 800,000 from Turkey to Greece, and 150,000 from North Africa alone; nearly 4,000 drowned. In 2016, nearly 350,000 came, with more than 5,000 killed in the process. The lower numbers reflect a March 2016 deal between Turkey and the EU's twenty-eight member states—Turkey will maintain the refugee camps and receive those who had made it into Europe in exchange for about $6.3 billion through 2018 and support on other issues, such as easing travel of Turkish nationals into the EU or refraining from public criticism of the war against Kurds in the southeast.

Aside from containing refugees in Turkey, there is no vision for stopping the flows into Europe, and refugees still come through other routes, mostly from North Africa. With no end in sight to the war in Syria, the potential is high for substantial continued flows, especially as whether and how long Turkey is able and willing to maintain its camps so that Europe does not have to host displaced population is unclear. The situation is likely to remain politically explosive for two reasons. First, in setting up camps and resettlement networks, humanitarian agencies are bringing foreign populations into countries that are seeing a surge in nationalism and xenophobia. Second, the fracture in refugee policy in the European Union lies at the intersection of the divide over issues of identity, economy, and security.

The Meaning of "Refugee-Terrorist"

Western governments readily interpreted the revelation that one of the terrorists in the November 13, 2015, attacks in Paris had transited through a Greek island as a refugee as signaling a need to respond with more bombing against Daesh and fewer admissions of refugees. The label "refugee-terrorist" demonizes foreign "others" as, on the one hand, needy and, on the other hand, violent. But this myopia concentrates on security and makes an erroneous, counterproductive prescription. In the short term, military solutions may curtail terrorist violence by Daesh beyond territory that it controls—although it may not, as "lone wolf" operatives in the West have demonstrated in San Bernardino, Orlando,

Nice, and Berlin. However, it ignores the long-term structural problem, namely that the current humanitarian response often is embittering populations that it aims to serve.

To begin, the "refugee-terrorist" configuration has precedents, although seeing the origins requires recognizing that the term "refugee" is by no means an exclusive identity. In other crises, those who have experienced displacement have often later engaged in violence, particularly against those supposedly responsible for their displacement. Examples of what have been previously dubbed "refugee-warriors" include the Pashtuns from Afghanistan who regrouped in camps in Pakistan to fight the Soviet-backed government of the 1980s, and the Hutus who fled Rwanda and regrouped in Zaire's camps and continued the war against the new Tutsi-led government in the mid-1990s.

In Syria and Iraq, however, there are additional elements that have kindled the "refugee-terrorist" phenomenon. First, there is a sense of displacement experienced by Daesh members, not in a geographic but a cultural sense because a cosmopolitan, secular, globalized world seems to marginalize or reject their values. For militants, the battlefield no longer features conventional frontlines but instead concentrates on taking the fight to the homeland of the opponent. The aim is not simply to kill or harm civilians but also to instill a sense of terror and provoke a reaction that polarizes targeted societies, which in turn will implement self-fulfilling policies that substantiate the enemy as evil. In a maneuver that could be characterized as a form of post-colonial political jujitsu, the terrorist who used "refugee" status to gain entry into Europe used a security vulnerability of the West born out of liberal internationalism's idea of how to address (and contain) the problem of displacement.

In addition, the terrorist who posed as a refugee also leads to terrorizing legitimate refugees. Western governments crack down, stripping refugees of basic human rights in an attempt to more effectively manage the displaced and protect their own citizens. This chain of events could have an incendiary effect on refugees. In the minds of many displaced persons from the areas currently controlled by Daesh, the West is responsible—the war that began in Iraq in 2003 and its subsequent chaos enabled extremists to build their power and influence. Now that they have become "refugees," the West further demeans them by forcing them to live a degrading, bare subsistence life, forever under surveillance, subject to hostility and scapegoating, and brutalized by repressive police. This re-victimization of refugees creates another opportunity for terrorists to organize; they can make the case that even when the displaced have physically relocated in the West, they will never be treated humanely, let alone accepted as citizens.

The tragedies are manifold. A misguided response to "refugee-terrorists" will exacerbate violence, worsen conditions for refugees, and play into the hands of terrorists. Only when security gatekeepers in the West fail do we discuss the allocation of alienation, scarcity, and strife worldwide; this dynamic reflects and contributes to marginalization and resentment by many non-Westerners. Until the West acknowledges and respects the legitimate needs of refugees not only for asylum but also for rights and dignity, every fix is temporary and tackles symptoms while fueling another cause for conflict. The spotlight on "refugee-terrorists" underscores the spread of xenophobia and framing humanitarianism as a security liability to push for using aid architecture to control displaced populations more strictly. The term reifies the politicization of humanitarianism into a configuration of supporting a security-based approach to humanitarianism and provokes a political and cultural divide between refugees and host societies.

Conclusion: Displacement, Domination, Dysfunction

Displacement is fraught, and so too are proposed solutions. Managing the survival of displaced populations invariably occurs in locations with limited resources, and where the application of political will—usually in short supply—requires domination. Operating under these conditions or contributing to this outcome is dysfunctional for humanitarianism.

Six factors account for this outcome. The first concerns definitions, and in particular "what is a refugee?" It lingers after almost seven decades since the ratification of the convention that founded UNHCR. The stakes are high. In fact, as a recent review by MSF of the international humanitarian system's response to displacement in South Sudan, eastern DRC, and Jordan found, "Status [of displaced populations] was the principal determinant of assistance, rather than need or vulnerability."[34]

However, there is little incentive and much opposition to fleshing out a definition, let alone broadening it, because doing so is likely to create ever-greater commitments for states. The absence of a new comprehensive and accurate definition reflects an underlying consensus. There is great variation in determining status, with some countries conducting individual assessments and others enacting group classifications to separate the "legal" from the "illegal," the welcomed from the resented. There are also designations of types of refugees that show the changing nature of flows and may connote differentiated responsibilities. For example, urban and out-of-camp refugees may stand outside aid and protection systems. In essence, if populations do not cooperate and stay in camps, they may not receive the obligatory assistance that comes with being a "refugee." Since 2009 UNHCR has expanded protection for urban refugees. However, in light of resource and power constraints, its policy mostly defers to governments. The organization comments that "national and local authorities have a primary role to play in providing refugees with protection, solutions, and assistance."[35]

A related definitional debate centers on "what is a camp?" Is it a temporary shelter to aid the displaced? Or is it a political creation providing a base for the displaced to be manipulated or controlled by the host state and its allies? Or is it a beachhead from which the displaced navigate entry illegally or carry out violence? Given constraints and diverse agendas, can camps be truly "humanitarian"?

The second factor regards who bears the burden for refugees. A model of how the presence of displaced populations influences host states was sketched, as was the contemporary European context. However, despite the gnashing of teeth and associated rancor, it is not Europe that is most affected by displacement but rather the Global South. When people escape violence in a developing country, the vast majority of refugees relocate to a different country in the Global South—we noted earlier that in 2015 nearly 8.5 of every 10 were located there.[36]

The third factor reflects that managing the displaced requires and reiterates power. As Agier has written, "Every policy of assistance is simultaneously an instrument of control over its beneficiaries."[37] States worry about destabilizing population flows and therefore have approached addressing displacement as a type of containment, including the location of refugee camps[38] and the biometric tracking of aid recipients.[39] Support for security of the displaced in the country where they have been displaced (UNHCR's "preventive protection") is a means to keep the displaced where they are, a safe distance from potential host states. As Jennifer Hyndman argues:

> Emerging national and ethnic divisions of power in the post–Cold War period have generated strategies of containment that serve to keep refugee and internally displaced people "over there," far from the borders of charitable donor countries in the West. Since 1990, particular strategies have been employed to curb refugee flows through such measures as preventive protection and through the extended use of technically temporary refugee camps.[40]

Moreover, the power expressed in managing the displaced is crucial for states and humanitarian agencies as it becomes part of their *raison d'être*—without displacement, these bureaucracies would not be able to lodge a claim for resources or acquire the authority they have.

This power should be understood in the context of forcibly displaced victims who come under the power of actors that routinely deny them rights, regardless of the claims about keeping them alive; as such, they suffer a second victimization. Arendt notes that statelessness leads to a loss of the "right to have rights,"[41] but humanitarian remedies do not prioritize recovering or grounding the legal and political status of the displaced. Instead, the international humanitarian system is preoccupied with maintaining "bare life" and at the same time depriving the saved of rights, which Agamben contends excludes them from political life and inflicts social death.[42] This line of argument posits that the inhumane conditions inflicted on refugees render them less than human—the term "relief camp" can be an oxymoron because camps do not fundamentally relieve the source of suffering but may substitute one indignity for another.

The fourth factor pushes us to acknowledge that the focus on root causes or the structural underpinnings of displacement is paradoxical and depends on how the problem is defined: Is it that displacement occurs in the first place? Or is it that the displaced seek to come to host countries? Safe zones in areas in crisis seem to address the second root cause. However, if it is the first, then the question must be asked, who is responsible for displacement? If there is trail of causality that leads back to the West, then such culpability requires the West to open its doors or at least its collective pocketbook. What is the more sensible political, economic, and social calculus for the West—to provide resources to establish, promote, and secure free and prosperous states or on occasion manage hundreds of thousands of displaced, possibly temporarily? In the math of a politicized world order, however, the piecemeal handling of symptomatic displacement may be more expedient than the hard work of solving the root causes of displacement and certainly far more palatable than opening the door to permanent resettlement.

The fifth factor necessitates asking what follows. Humanitarianism offers relief in emergencies, but the longer term is another story. The displaced have economic needs and require resources to foster integration. Some refugees have shown that they are remarkably capable of generating the means of survival and even prosperity—refugee economies can be quite vibrant. But that is not always the case, and humanitarian responses must be careful not to undermine their initiative and agency.[43] There is a distinction between development and humanitarian concerns, albeit a hazy one, and the former do not really fall into the domain of humanitarian agencies. But is giving relief and protecting human rights in a disaster not a promise for help all along the way to resettlement or return?

A related and qualifying note for the longer run is another tragic and frequently unacknowledged truth: the displaced who have been traumatized and lost everything in a cataclysm often do not recover, even those who receive assistance. Those who are viscerally linked to their previous lives may find it impossible to build a new one—older individuals, in particular, simply are less likely to adjust. In other words, usually an

unspoken element of sacrifice in camps means that only children ultimately have a chance to be saved. Camps are short-term solutions that
leave long-term scars, and older generations are likely to fare worse while
youth tend to be more resilient.

The sixth factor concerns whether aid agencies can do more about the
larger structural issues of camps that haunt the sector. Humanitarians
do not want to make camps too attractive or they can create a form of
moral hazard with a perverse incentive structure; and so, becoming and
remaining a refugee, not independence and resettlement, are logical outcomes. Yet, inhumane camps are unacceptable. The issue gets to the chief
concern: are the camps a preserve or a perversion of humanitarianism?
With better design, camps can be more comfortable for the displaced, but
whose interests and welfare are ultimately served by this exercise? Should
humanitarian agencies get out of the camp business?

Despite a liberal vision that international organizations ensure rights,
the reality of Western and great-power influence underscores post-
colonial or realist, respectively, interpretations of outcomes. However, the
independence of organizations—for example, in classifying populations
as refugees—recalls constructivism's salience. But feminism and critical
humanitarianism perhaps offer the most analytical traction in recognizing
how the displaced become and remain marginalized and are in effect re-
marginalized by the regime intended to address displacement.

The phenomenon of seemingly endlessly displaced populations and
growing international mechanisms designed to ease but not alleviate
pain—as well as allow states to absolve themselves of responsibilities
for the displaced—are at the center of rethinking humanitarianism.
While the sector is committed to helping the displaced, if the execution
of its duties makes it complicit in rights violations, humanitarianism
loses its coherence and casts aid agencies into a limbo of their own: they
are presented with a dilemma of participating in a world order that
saves but subjugates.

Managing displaced populations through such structures as camps
gives rise to distinct realities depicted by Agier: "On the one hand, a clean,
healthy and visible world; on the other, the world's residual 'remnants,'
dark, diseased and invisible."[44] The growth of displaced populations and
the longevity of camps demonstrate the widening chasm between the
sanitary, lavish world of the privileged and the despoiled, scarcity-riven
one of the marginalized. Ironically and tragically, aid agencies operating
camps in some ways and sometimes can be contributors.

9

The Humanitarian-Industrial Complex

Media and Markets

Secretary-General Ban Ki-moon records a video message for Instagram at the Support Syrians Conference in London. Joined by world leaders, the secretary-general called for protection and assistance for the millions of people caught up in the world's biggest humanitarian crisis (February 4, 2016). (UN photo/Eskinder Debebe)

Modern mass media provide global stages on which the humanitarian narrative is shaped, disseminated, and performed—on platforms from radio to cable television to Internet forums and social media. Irrespective of claims to the contrary, humanitarian organizations are not apolitical, nor are they immune to market pressures. Earlier we mentioned the influence of media and markets, but here we offer a more systematic treatment. Information technologies have assembled a worldwide audience that influences the triangulation of humanitarianism with war and politics because of the direct, as well as inadvertent, impact of communications on defining images and messages that shape resource allocations and perceptions.

The depiction of the media's relationship to humanitarianism as technical and functional ignores political dimensions (i.e., the capacity of aid agencies to affect the character and composition of action in the field and headquarters). Four media and communication capacities help shape humanitarianism's practices and power. First, they can provide early warning about natural disasters or mass atrocities—for example, sending an alert regarding the arrival of hurricanes, tsunamis, and locusts as well as the whereabouts and movements of hostile military forces and war criminals. Second, they can verify the locations of victimized and vulnerable populations as well as shelter and hospitals. Third, in coordinating work among agencies and connecting field missions and headquarters, they can transmit requirements and share operational plans between aid workers to foster cooperation and avoid redundancy. This information is also useful in soliciting and informing donors. Fourth, preventive war media capabilities might be considered part of the humanitarian toolkit, such as jamming hate radio or blocking social media that contributes to mass atrocities.

This chapter explores the media-market-humanitarianism link by analyzing the changing politics of the dominant narrative—specifically how an issue becomes "humanitarian," and how it ranks in comparison with other issues in catalyzing responses—and the infusion of commercialism into humanitarianism. To begin, media has become a form of power for organizations as eliciting mercy is critical to mustering resources. However, the construction of the narrative is contested, and different actors may appropriate the appellation "humanitarian" to further their own interests.

A supplemental element to the focus on image-making is how it translates into altering the product—in this case, humanitarianism and its position in the marketplace of ideas and politics. Combining in a single expression "humanitarian business" will be seen by many as provocative, but it is also accurate.[1] It is jarring for those who idealize the enterprise because the adjective has essentially indisputable positive connotations while the noun usually is associated with ruthless wheeling and dealing and is at odds with the values and self-image of true believers. The adjective is rooted in morality and principle—the parable of the "Good Samaritan" jumps to mind. The objective is noble: to help people whose lives are at grave risk, heedless of who they are, where they are located, or why they are in need. Aid agencies are only interested in the welfare of those in their care and are unaffected by political and market factors in the countries that provide or receive relief. If humanitarian action claims the moral high ground, "business" is customarily seen to occupy less lofty territory. In contrast to humanitarians, businesspeople operate in an arena where typically deals are cut, money buys access, the common good is ignored, talk is cheap, and tough decisions about profit margins overlook the human costs when necessary.

The day-to-day functioning of aid agencies intersects in a myriad of ways with home and host governments, with armed insurgents as well as military peacekeepers and local populations; most crucially, it confronts the priorities of potential funders. As agents engaged in resource acquisition and distribution, where they get their resources and how and to whom they deliver aid can have significant political consequences, particularly in war zones, which is where the bulk of the business takes place. For aid workers, it is difficult to ignore proverbial bottom lines—there are financial strings that tug and restrict the enterprise.

This chapter begins with a look at media power, or the phenomenon of constructing narratives—the process and impact of "humanitarianizing" an issue—which includes the niche of celebrity humanitarianism. Then it investigates marketization bolstered by the power of the media that have altered the behaviors and sales pitches of agencies as well as attracted new actors. Before turning to conclusions about the state of humanitarian narrative and power, it briefly examines the overlapping of marketization and militarization of humanitarianism in the context of aid agencies hiring private security contractors. Four questions drive this analysis: What are humanitarian narratives and how are they constructed? How and why are they meaningful? What is the scope and significance of the humanitarian-industrial complex? What are the trade-offs between the marketplace and humanitarian action?

The Media: Mercy as Spectacle

A major factor explaining variations in humanitarian responses relates to the construction of the humanitarian narrative—the stories about means and ends, successes and failures. It explains why there is an "emergency," and the logic driving humanitarian behaviors. The narrative generates and sustains political will and economic wherewithal from individual and institutional donors. It is instrumental in manufacturing attention or neglect—raise or lower the visibility of "forgotten" and shame or embrace the dismissal of "forsaken" crises. The narrative fluctuates with tragedies and triumphs, which influences the reception to appeals for funding and for cooperation on the ground. For example, the narrative of the Holocaust during WWII was that there was not adequate information among humanitarian actors to gauge what was transpiring; but after the war, the narrative changed to the "spirit of Nuremberg" and the lament of "never again," which continues to affect politics and to inspire war crimes tribunals elsewhere. By contrast, the narrative of Rwanda is brooding; action came late and was manipulated by those who had perpetrated the genocide; the terrible results, years later, propelled a narrative of limiting humanitarianism or tethering it to political goals.

How is a humanitarian narrative constructed? In the field of critical security studies, the Copenhagen School has outlined a model of "securitization," which explains how an issue moves from the realm of politics to security within which emergency conditions compel a different set of norms and behaviors. Borrowing from that blueprint and drawing on the sensibilities of critical humanitarianism, a model of "humanitarianization" explains how an issue comes to be considered as genuine—that is, accorded the normative and political benefits that follow from such a classification. To that end, narratives provide a framing for action or indifference. The elements consist of norm entrepreneurs seeking to mobilize, sometimes also interested in attracting material support, along with an audience (who furnish the political will and material resources to carry out responses). The media plays a pivotal role by propagating the narrative and amplifying normative sensitivities.

Humanitarianization not only highlights the interjection of normative meaning into behaviors but also impels certain actions. Thomas Haskell has explored a humanitarian "recipe," a specific sequence of steps to alter the course of events.[2] To realize these recipes—and, indeed, humanitarianism itself—four preconditions are required. The first is the ethics of helping strangers, which requires compassion. The second is a belief about the causes of an evil event that have contributed to a disaster. The third precondition involves a technique for intervening, a plausible policy and path to address injustice that could range from sending money to authorizing military force. The fourth is that the failure to act constitutes a suspension of routine; the crisis prevents, at some level, living a normal life, and the horror is too great to not respond.

Michael Ignatieff further problematizes the role of the media in constructing narratives by examining the "stories we tell."[3] First, he contends that there are limits to our empathy, meaning that we care most about those who are connected to us through history, tradition, creed, and ethnicity. The differences between an "us" and a "them" can therefore justify disregard. A 2016 survey of almost 18,000 people in sixteen countries— some in the West, and some in war zones—concluded that "people living in the P5 countries and Switzerland are generally more tolerant of civilian casualties and deprivations than people living in countries affected by armed conflict." Similarly, when it came to attacks on aid personnel, "Nearly six out of ten respondents perceive that the death or injury of humanitarian workers as they are delivering aid in conflict zones as wrong, but in a lower proportion than deprivation of food, medicine or water and attacks on the architectural heritage. The proportion is higher among people living in countries affected by armed conflict."[4]

Ignatieff suggests that the emotion of pity is structured by our similarities or closeness to others: the notion that we are tied together through the recognition of a shared humanity is a modern myth. For a humanitarian response to be manifest, we require a story that turns strangers into neighbors. This view builds on a lengthy philosophical tradition, including Aristotle who argued that proximity matters, that we only pity those whom we know. More recently, the idea of "distance" has been articulated to refer to those to whom we are connected versus those to whom we are not—there is not only spatial distance (physical detachment) but also social or cultural remoteness. There is selectivity in media coverage of crises generally, but also with respect to the presentation of specifically humanitarian issues.

Prior to the system's inception in the nineteenth century, humanitarianism had unfolded in virtually all cultures, which have versions of compassion, charity, mercy, and equivalents of Western just war. The identification of an issue as humanitarian to mobilize resources is not new, but in the contemporary period the networks influencing humanitarization include new media actors that determine and influence the audience. The conventional understanding is that the media creates attention for crises and therefore triggers a response. This view dates from the earliest international communication systems, such as telegraph, and grew in significance with the diffusion of radio, television, and later cable and satellite communications, and most recently with the Internet and social media. Formation of a global audience began in the post-WWII period; photojournalism in this period shared powerful humanitarian narratives, such as the 1972 image from the Vietnam War of nine-year-old Phan Thi Kim Phuc burned by napalm. The role of the media in humanitarianism has received greater attention since the 1990s when the "CNN effect" (or the "BBC effect") was noted; and it has grown astronomically with the rise of social media. Some journalists have consciously pursued producing messages that inspire, practicing a "journalism of attachment," which Martin Bell has defined as "a journalism that cares as well as knows; that is aware of its responsibilities; that will not stand neutrally between good and evil, right and wrong, the victim and the oppressor."[5]

While images of disasters and victims tend to elicit strong feelings in viewers, not all reactions are similar. Some individuals react with pity and empathy; some with anger toward perpetrators; some with guilt for their own comfort and lack of response; and some with a sense of helplessness.[6] Feelings are crucial because they often shape responses—do we give to charity, seek vengeance, focus on ourselves, or become paralyzed? Psychology, sociology, anthropology, and media studies have explored the techniques of crafting images that explain, evidence, and expand on a narrative to mobilize societies.

What message is the takeaway? Most media narratives are underpinned by a message that inspires committing resources, perhaps even expanding the range and goals of humanitarianism. For example, showing well-fed, grateful aid recipients in the process of transitioning to new lives would communicate successful programming. However, other messages could signal a catastrophic flaw to relief operations in a war zone and call for humanitarians to withdraw. Here the narrative may portray corrupt, disinterested, or overwhelmed aid workers—images of land rovers ferrying staff between cloistered compounds while those needing aid beg for help in the background—or alternatively an interlocutor (such as a militia or criminal enterprise) exploiting assistance as seen in images of bags of rice piling up behind armed thugs as well-to-do warlords enjoy luxuries.

Six narratives dominate contemporary media coverage of humanitarian action; the first four describe the nature of the victims, and the other two depict those coming to the rescue. The first includes innocent victims and evil perpetrators, the most widespread classic juxtaposition in armed conflicts. This narrative has been used since antiquity to justify aid and force. Built into it is the heroic element and sense of agency ascribed to the audience; their actions have impact, they can save lives. It resonates with liberalism's and constructivism's beliefs in institutions and organizations as embedding norms and creating opportunities beyond the constraints of established power structures.

The second revolves around the basic equality of suffering as both sides endure human rights violations. This narrative proclaims unending needs, which may inspire either a call for more resources or exhausted retreat.

The third narrative is related, namely that there are no good guys, only bad guys. This portrayal stresses the manipulation of emergency relief and suggests that such conditions foster a counterproductive performance that demands withdrawal.

The fourth involves "Acts of God," which often accompany disease and famine, and it also decontextualizes a crisis by ignoring significant military, governance, and economic factors. Human-made causal factors of droughts and floods tend to disappear in media treatments that emphasize the dramatic, not the quotidian.

The fifth narrative is a self-congratulatory victory lap of sorts that portrays a sense of the heroic in promoting the agency or donor that saves victims from evil. It seeks to empower viewers or listeners to at least donate, if not act. There is a variant that accompanies just war rhetoric and modern technology by which advanced Western military forces conducting armed operations utilize precision munitions and other special techniques to limit civilian casualties. This variation calls for no action but deference because technology will respect proportionality and quickly defeat forces committing mass human rights violations.

The sixth narrative points to a defective international humanitarian system—accompanied by a note of despair and plea for change. It questions the lack of efficiency or even corruption of aid agencies. This critique has come from many quarters, from powerful states that see agencies as financial burdens to Marxists and post-colonialists who see humanitarian narratives as sustaining class or Western identities.

Although there are episodic deviations, some patterns are apparent as seen in a review of the narrative that humanitarians themselves have historically disseminated versus those claiming to be members of the movement. They are fundamentally for the audience and not for the victims, who tend to remain voiceless. Communicated within the narrative are the governing relations between the audience and victims—what Ignatieff delineates as "zones of safety" and "zones of danger."[7] The first was the imperial narrative at the dawn of the era of modern international communications in the nineteenth century. Humanitarianism in this period was presented as part of the gift of Western civilization to barbarian lands. The narrative was that it pacified and acculturated savages, with some discourse emphasizing the role of Christianity and saving souls.

Earlier the dominant narrative was renewal and progressive optimism. Humanitarianism's role in contributing to the better treatment of wounded and captured soldiers and the provision of relief during the late nineteenth century and throughout the world wars of the first half of the twentieth century was improved medical technologies, a plethora of new international agreements, and the development of agencies and infrastructure. In the post-WWII period, rival Cold War narratives surfaced. A US-USSR ideological competition for the mantle of humanitarianism emerged as part of a proxy war with the future of world order at stake. Each side articulated a vision to bolster relations with the Third World. The West's version was a liberal narrative that decolonization and assistance would lead to progress and development. In contrast, the Socialist internationalist narrative portrayed humanitarian aid as building global bonds to resist capitalist exploitation.

By the late 1980s and early 1990s, the narrative of the Cold War shifted. The Soviet implosion and the appearance of a unipolar international system coincided with a surge in the availability of information, communication, and networking technologies, which altered relations between audiences and victims. The 1991 Persian Gulf War and the start of operations in the Balkans and Africa to quell crises in more muscular ways than before also stoked enthusiasm for more robust humanitarianism. This period produced a globalization narrative that emergency relief could facilitate the transition to development and contribute to lasting peace. However, the disasters and failures of the mid-1990s spawned a chaos narrative for the Global South that limited leverage for humanitarianism. This reaction characterized Somalia in 1993 following the failed attempt to arrest Mohamed Aidid and the consequent firefight of "Blackhawk Down" or the Battle of Mogadishu. The images of the bodies of US soldiers dragged through the streets eroded support for humanitarian operations; and the media kindled and fed the "Somalia Syndrome," or Washington's reluctance to engage in military humanitarianism without state consent.

Yet the more successful cases of humanitarian protection in Kosovo and East Timor, among others, fueled the growth in aid budgets and renewed the vibrancy of the humanitarian ethos. Revisiting the "never again" humanitarian narrative in the late 1990s became a staple reflecting the sentiment that all lives have meaning, and that what happens elsewhere in the world matters closer to home. Humanity is bound by moral linkages; the suffering of others is an injustice against us all. The narrative obliges a sense of responsibility in the audience.

The most recent dramatic narrative shift followed 9/11. The GWOT narrative conflates humanitarian agencies and Western powers, with the former seen as "force multipliers" or supplements for the West's pacification of troubled regions. Additionally, this narrative often pairs the suffering on both sides of a conflict in an image of equality of victimization—a common practice in 2001 when many media sources juxtaposed the terrorist destruction with US-led attacks in Afghanistan. In some instances, the emphasis was more on victimization of the West; something similar has occurred in media coverage of refugee and migrant flows into Europe and attacks on and executions of expatriate aid workers. Media treatments of different terrorist attacks in Beirut, Kabul, Ankara, and Istanbul versus those in Paris and Brussels display the power of the GWOT narrative. The former situates terrorist attacks as a normal part of conflict-ridden areas that host timeless grudges, whereas those in Europe are presented as exceptional because they not only are rare but also underscore the unequivocal innocence of those harmed. The possibility that terrorists were mixed with refugees and detailed stories of the relatively few Westerners killed in attacks compared to those from and in the Global South dominated the headlines. The Western reading of this narrative as vulnerability also caters to the Global South's perception of humanitarianism as a Western conspiracy. Such decontextualized images as that of Alan Kurdi (a two-year-old whose dead body washed up on the beach in Turkey) being spread worldwide with no analysis of responsibility has heightened resentments across the Global South.

Narratives influence audiences and potentially prompt humanitarian responses, but they should also be understood as a form of market priming—capturing attention to generate resources also sells goods to the public and donors, in this case aid and protection. In an era that fosters an aesthetic and culture that craves surprise and outrage, there is a business here as Susan Sontag has argued: "The hunt for more dramatic (as they are often described) images drives the photographic enterprise, and is part of the normality of a culture in which shock has become a leading stimulus of consumption and a source of value."[8] Guilt may compel, but suffering sells.[9] This approach is troubling for agencies—to be marketers of misery, to profit from pain. Humanitarians must walk a fine line because, as James Dawes states, "The disconcerting paradox of humanitarian work is this: it is sometimes impossible to distinguish the desire to help others from the desire to amplify the self, to distinguish altruism from narcissism."[10]

Agencies have often established guidelines for media images, for example Save the Children UK's 1991 "Focus on Image" and CARE's "Brand Standards." The General Assembly of European NGOs updated their 1981 "Code of Conduct on Images and Messages" in 2006 because "the reality of our world today [is] that many of the images of extreme poverty and humanitarian distress are negative and cannot be ignored." It continued that, regardless, "images and message should seek to present a complete picture of both internal and external assistance and the partnership that often results between local and international NGOs."[11] Narrative construction and audience relations have become an essential ingredient of humanitarianism.

Celebrity Humanitarianism: Mercy as Accessory

A strange modality of the humanitarian narrative has arisen with the growth of a relatively recent phenomenon, celebrity humanitarianism, in which the star becomes a storyteller, a disseminator of the humanitarian narrative. The celebrity can be a participant in public events, organize a personal charity campaign, or lobby on behalf of salient issues. For example, in the 1950s, Danny Kaye and Audrey Hepburn were symbolic pioneers for UNICEF. In 1984, Bob Geldof assembled the landmark "Band-Aid" concert, which more than 1.5 billion people watched and mobilized funds for famine relief in Ethiopia. It was the first instance of a real-time global fundraising campaign with simulcast musical performances in London and Philadelphia. Geldof revisited his success in 2005 with Live 8 concerts seen by over 3 billion. More recently, Angelina Jolie is a special UNHCR envoy, and George Clooney has been outspoken in spotlighting the plight of Darfur. Meanwhile, Sean Penn joined forces in Haiti beside former US presidents Bill Clinton and George W. Bush—the latter being part of a more widespread trend of "diplomatic afterlives."[12] Some from the Global South have also gained celebrity and used their fame to promote humanitarian causes, such as Malala Yousafzai of Afghanistan, who has become a symbol for female education.[13]

On the one hand, celebrities and their influence can help bring attention and funding to what are often neglected or under-resourced disasters. On the other hand, as Ilan Kapoor outlines, celebrity humanitarianism may play a role in legitimating a form of liberal capitalism.[14] In any case, the message is an oversimplified narrative. Celebrities promote their own "brand" and an image of Westerners caring about afflicted populations. It is impossible to know someone's true motives, but Kapoor notes several structural features of celebrity humanitarianism that may give pause. First, they are essentially unaccountable elites; they use their fame as they see fit and are rarely punished for manipulations or missteps. Second and more pronounced in his indictment, celebrity humanitarianism does not confront the power structures that give rise to the power of celebrities and glorify capitalism while reproducing inequality. Celebrity humanitarians rationalize and trumpet their privileged position through token acts of charity that do not raise the issue of fame and power while still receiving benefits such as tax credits and free, positive promotional advertising.

Despite contradictions and these dynamics, are the problems associated with celebrity humanitarianism justified by raising awareness and additional resources?

The Market: Mercy as Commodity

Humanitarianism has traditionally been defined by its disinterested motivation in responding to wars and a cultural valuing of human life unconnected to power politics or economics. The emergence of the international humanitarian system in the late nineteenth century coincided with the expansion of liberal projects, including the growth of a capitalist world economy. Liberal economics is predicated on the production of profit, arguing that individual freedom and interdependence culminates in efficient markets. Starting in the late 1970s and taking hold more firmly since the end of the Cold War, governments worldwide have become enamored with "neoliberalism"—a belief that private capital can provide public services at least as and perhaps more efficiently than government bureaucracies. The spread of this ideology has also given impetus to states to distance themselves or even withdraw from humanitarian tasks that they have been reluctant, if not altogether unwilling, to undertake. Thus, there has been a push to subscribe to a "new public management agenda" that necessitates marketizing humanitarian action and allowing the private sector to participate in the provision of this service. Within aid agencies this idea has generally been viewed with suspicion or as outright sacrilege. But the efficiency of market-based actors and the scarcity of funding have motivated changes in attitudes and behavior.

Humanitarianism subsists in a marketplace of ideas within a world order. How should those made vulnerable by war and other emergencies be protected? What versions of humanitarianism are culturally popular? Hugo Slim has remarked that humanitarianism begins with "selling the idea of restraint and compassion in war."[15] The sector is a peculiar type of market. In fact, it is an unusual "quasi-market" prone to many asymmetries.[16] The producer-consumer relationship is different from conventional markets. Producers (aid agencies) sell to buyers (donors) but deliver to consumers (aid recipients). Meanwhile the consumers—ultimately, victims are clients—do not directly purchase a service or good, but donors choose and finance the purchase of goods and services delivered by humanitarians.

While aid agencies are often beholden to donors for funding, in other ways they have power in the international humanitarian system because donors usually lack the ability to determine the impact of their funds independently from what agencies tell them. According to a principal-agent model of the donor-aid agency relationship, humanitarian organizations have a vested interest in not disclosing information that would alienate donors or cause them to hesitate. Contrary to many other markets, completely marginalized in the process are the consumers/"beneficiaries"/recipients/

victims who have little or no voice. Such disconnects and asymmetries in information and influence undermine pure market principles.

Furthermore, distortions in the humanitarian marketplace also result from other structural imbalances. The market is an oligopoly with few sellers; there are a relatively small number of large service providers—for instance, the UN system, the ICRC, MSF, CARE, and Save the Children. It also is an oligopsony with a few major buyers—in 2014 seven governments and international organizations accounted for well over 60 percent of funding. The dearth of actors has opened the door for greater involvement by for-profit firms. Hence, in considering the commodification of mercy, it is important to note two levels of marketization: humanitarians behaving as market-based actors and market-based actors behaving as humanitarians.

The first form is brought to the fore by Thomas G. Weiss in his depiction of agencies obsessed with autonomy despite the obvious advantages of central coordination of responses.[17] The Good Samaritan accurately characterizes the aspirations of numerous aid workers, who can but should not be oblivious that marketing images are valuable in an expanding and competitive global business in which numerous suppliers vie for market shares. While funding is more abundant than ever, resources are still "scarce" in comparison with mushrooming needs. The term "business" will unsettle humanitarians but their success involves the four "Ps" of a first-year marketing course: product, price, place, and promotion.[18] Marketization in the globalizing world of the twenty-first century means that everything has a price—from access to moral authority to lives. In effect, there is a global commodity chain for mercy: an agency manages production of a value or public social good (in this case the welfare of disaster victims) through its network of service providers and staff, and outreach to donors and the public.

Earlier we saw that institutional innovations in the humanitarian system usually followed wars when horrors exposed the inadequacies of responses. However, the end of the Cold War resulted in no immediate transformation of international institutions but rather a huge sigh of relief. Yet it unleashed armed conflicts and led to the eruption of crises held in check by East-West tensions; and it also resulted in the proliferation of humanitarian agencies and opening resource floodgates. We reiterate briefly and extend what we wrote earlier, namely that during the first two decades of the post–Cold War era, budgets of humanitarian agencies registered a fivefold increase from about $800 million in 1989 to some $4.4 billion in 1999, followed by an additional quadrupling to $16.7 billion in 2009. After peaking at just over $20 billion in 2010, the figures drifted downward but then increased dramatically to $22 billion in 2013 and $25 billion in 2014.[19] Nevertheless the January 2016 report of the High-Level

Panel on Humanitarian Financing indicated that the $25 billion in 2014 fell short of the $40 billion needed.[20] Growth has continued but there remains a gap between what is provided and what is required as demonstrated by the fact that despite a record $28 billion in 2015, the 45 percent shortfall in the UN's coordinated appeal—the amount requested was $19.8 billion, but $8.9 billion was absent—was also the largest to date.[21]

While the number of UN organizations has not grown, their budgets have (accounting for about two-thirds of total Development Assistance Committee [DAC] humanitarian disbursements); disconcertingly, the UN system is still run like the small conference-servicing body that it used to be.[22] As many as 37,000 international NGOs are relevant for what Linda Polman calls "the crisis caravan,"[23] even if only a handful of the 2,500 mainly humanitarian ones are truly significant. Activities by giants like ICRC (including its 190 national societies) and World Vision (respectively, almost $2 billion and $1 billion annually) clearly dwarf most NGOs and even some UN organizations. Typically, about one-quarter of annual total humanitarian assistance disbursements are from private sources.

Over the past decade, governments have disbursed over $110 billion for humanitarian assistance. In 2010 and 2011, they provided about $14 billion per year, $13.2 billion in 2012, and $16.4 billion in 2013; and private voluntary contributions reached a peak of $6.3 billion in 2010 (roughly $4 billion in 2012 and $5.6 billion in 2013), up from $3.0 billion in 2007.[24] Moreover, over the last half-decade UN peace operations have added another $8 to $10 billion annually, with most soldiers deployed in countries with large humanitarian allocations. While these resources are not strictly relief aid, they often contribute to distribution in providing logistical pipelines and protection. Whereas sixteen mainly Western states pledged their support to Bosnia in the mid-1990s, a diverse group of seventy-three attended the 2003 pledging conference in Madrid for Iraq, and ninety-two responded to the December 2004 tsunami. OECD governments almost doubled their assistance between 2000 and 2010 from $6.7 billion to $11.8 billion, which stood at $14.1 billion in 2013. Meanwhile, the contributions from non-DAC donors between 2011 and 2013 increased from $.8 billion to $2.3 billion, representing about 15 percent of total official humanitarian aid, double the percentage from 2011.[25]

How many individuals work in this arena? Estimates of aid workers, including cleaning personnel and drivers in field offices as well as CEOs in headquarters, may total more than 200,000 people.[26] But Peter Walker and Catherine Russ are undoubtedly closer to the mark: "We have no idea." Nonetheless, their ballpark estimate is 30,000 professionals (both local and expatriate) worldwide directly engaged in relief operations.[27]

Global bottom lines of some $18–28 billion in recent years with personnel spread across the planet helping 75–100 million people would strike most observers as a substantial business. The culture of humanitarian cooperation is actually one of humanitarian competition. Alexander Cooley and James Ron point to the impact of the "contract culture" that is "deeply corrosive" of the humanitarian soul. What they have termed "the NGO scramble" for resources calls into question two conventional interpretations of such entities. First, more actors supposedly demonstrate the vitality of civil society. Cooley and Ron, however, argue that more actors in fact create more uncertainty and competition. Second, marketization produces efficiency and effectiveness, but as Cooley and Ron point out, it is also mostly maladjusted: "dysfunctional organizational behavior is likely to be a rational response to systematic and predictable institutional pressures."[28] In essence, they argue that a materialist framework for understanding the behaviors and outcomes by transnational NGOs identifies the rationality of agencies in responding to marketization pressures.

Put another way, there is competition among agencies for attention and funds that reflect reliance on donors. Rony Brauman points out, "As the NGOs are happy to repeat, 'the needs are limitless.' This slogan provides a good interpretation of the humanitarian feeling, which is by definition unlimited because its object is the suffering of humanity, and it offers a prime fuel for organizational growth."[29]

Alex de Waal provides a clear explanation: agencies have their "soft" interest of delivering humanitarian relief, but they also have a "hard" interest of organizational survival.[30] These objectives should not and cannot be disaggregated; agencies point out that they need to survive and thrive to be able to respond to the next disaster. Thus, there has been a disturbing preoccupation with "market share" and "branding." Neil Wright, former head of UNHCR's Yugoslav liaison unit, observes: "NGOs don't want to be coordinated. They depend on being able to sell, to market the performance of their activities in order to get more donors. And that is positive, the more NGOs doing that, the wider the net is trawled to bring in resources to carry out humanitarian activity."[31] Marketization has transformed humanitarian agencies into operating like for-profit actors with detrimental effects on the values, coherence, and efficacy of humanitarian action in crises. A 2012 report comments:

> The rhetoric of the principles of humanitarian action plays an important part in humanitarian actors' efforts to mark out and protect for themselves a distinctive market niche—as well as a distinctive political and operational space. Yet in practice, different humanitarian agencies take different positions with regard to these competing sectors and actors; some, for instance, are willing to engage directly with peace-building or state-building activities, while others insist on a more purist and isolationist approach to humanitarian engagement. This explains the ease with which aid agencies come to-

gether to create a common discourse of principled humanitarian action, and the difficulty they have in replicating this discourse in practice.[32]

The second form of marketization is the movement of for-profit contractors into the humanitarian business. Stephen Hopgood, reflecting on Ignatieff's pronouncement of a "revolution of moral concern," argues that what in fact has transpired amounts to the "commodification of moral concern under globalization."[33] Hopgood points out that under neoliberalism, aid agencies have embraced business language and now readily use terms like "clients," "brand," and "accountability." His prime illustration is the case of Wal-Mart with respect to responding to Hurricane Katrina, which pummeled New Orleans and the Gulf Coast in 2005—if Wal-Mart delivers relief, does that make it a humanitarian organization? To what extent is it acceptable for nonprofit aid agencies to hire or work with for-profit actors so as to produce more economical humanitarian outcomes? For example, contracting for logistics and transportation may be less expensive than humanitarian agencies' maintaining their own fleet of aircraft or ships that may not be needed regularly. If a for-profit firm can deliver goods faster and at less cost, should they not be considered an acceptable mechanism?

To be clear about the trade-offs, the advantage of participation by for-profit firms in the humanitarian sector is that they supposedly improve efficiency. Business management techniques save time and money, which in turn saves lives. There are three disadvantages, however: First, business-oriented humanitarian action exacerbates marketization; aid agencies compete with one another and with the for-profit sector for donor support. Second, humanitarian action by business may be a part of "market priming," the creation of new markets for companies that may subsequently displace more value-oriented humanitarian agencies and local capacities. This claim has been made for some time about US food aid programs as a method of stimulating demand for US grain products. Third, the values of business contrast with those of humanitarians, who view beneficiaries as having intrinsic value, not as a means to profits. Business humanitarianism also implies a worrisome incentive structure that has a vested interest in suffering; more disasters mean more victims, and more victims mean more profits, or at least a larger bottom line.

We would be remiss in discussing humanitarian business not to quickly identify two problems for aid workers within the local economies where they operate. First, it is virtually impossible not to work with "spoilers,"[34] but humanitarians must pay special attention not only to inadvertently enhancing the legitimacy of illegitimate actors, but also to materially sustaining them. Humanitarian aid is fungible and can relieve belligerents of some burdens of waging war, thereby improving their capacity to continue fighting by diminishing the demands of governing and reducing the costs of sustaining casualties. In addition, "corruption," relabeled the "cost of doing humanitarian business," consists of humanitarians' purchasing access. Estimates of such payments range from 15 to 80 percent of the total value of relief shipments. A 25–30 percent "tax" seems to be a working average, which was the documented figure for the share claimed by Indonesian soldiers in Aceh and local armed actors throughout the former Yugoslavia.[35]

Second, outside agencies may constitute virtually the entire local monetized economy. International salaries ten to thirty times as high as the equivalent position in the non-aid local economy are attractive not only to skilled workers, technicians, and those with language skills but also to drivers, guards, gardeners, cooks, and cleaners. Moreover, inflation often arises along with the accompanying costs of prostitution, drugs, contraband, and other harmful social mores. Moving from the "economics of war" to the "economics of peace," Graciana del Castillo reminds with regards to her analysis of Afghanistan and Liberia, is implicitly perhaps the toughest of challenge for peacebuilding.[36] Situating a constructive economics of humanitarianism in this transition also is essential.

All in all, it would not be unfair to point to the existence of a "humanitarian-industrial complex"—a network of the business sector providing services to humanitarian agencies immersed in their own marketplace—that at present likely has more profit-motivated actors than ever before. Two signs are indicative of mushrooming marketization. First, aid agencies are "branding" their activities to better attract donors. Second, there has been a sizable growth in for-profit actors servicing the sector. Thinking in economic terms for a moment, if business has a comparative advantage in logistics and efficiency, what specifically is the comparative advantage of humanitarian agencies? How can it be measured? Who should be doing the measuring? And should private contractors be a part of humanitarian responses? Are business-humanitarian partnerships possible or passable? As Hopgood challenges us to ask, should we dare to say "no" to Wal-Mart?

In 1998, the "Sphere Project" (an initiative of many agencies through InterAction and the Steering Committee for Humanitarian Response) released the *Humanitarian Charter and Minimum Standards in Disaster Responses*,[37] which called for quality and accountability in humanitarian action in the wake of the Rwandan crisis. It rejects market-based actors because its sensibilities dictate that humanitarianism is about "being," not just "doing"—humanitarianism is a quality to the process, not simply a rationalized outcome—and that at a basic level, markets do not provide dignity to victims. Is this view antiquated? Does it sacrifice needed capabilities that undermine responses and the best interests of victims to preserve a cultural monopoly for aid agencies? Or does it necessarily reify key values in working with victimized populations?

Private Security Contractors: Mercy and Mercenaries

Another extraordinary configuration of humanitarianism, war, and politics embellished by marketization consists of hiring private security contractors (PSCs) by aid agencies. Several factors explain the emergence and expansion of this practice since the 1990s. The insecure operational environments encountered by aid workers in such places as Somalia and Rwanda were viewed through the new public management agenda.[38] Agencies were looking for cost-effective security tools, and private sector providers of security could sell their services in the humanitarian marketplace. Neoliberal ideology shaped budgets of states in the Global South, which contributed to security problems in areas hosting humanitarian crises, and it also shaped budgets of international organizations looking to reduce expenditures.

Further, the independent and rapidly deployed capacities of PSCs also appealed to the insecurity of agencies, which were otherwise forced to rely on weak, sometimes incompetent or belligerent, state armed forces; fickle militias; and slow-moving, easily rattled UN forces. Some humanitarians, however, opposed agency-PSC interactions—there is a long tradition of opposing mercenaries.[39] The issue exposed a cultural debate within the sector as Abby Stoddard, Adele Harmer, and Victoria DiDomenico observe:

> One side sounds the alarm that the privatisation of security seen in military and diplomatic ventures has begun to creep into relief assistance, evoking images of armed international mercenaries and the prospect of a highly militarised, unprincipled and unaccountable humanitarian response. The other side dismisses it as a non-issue or at best a "sideshow," arguing that humanitarians' use of these entities is minimal and too circumscribed to warrant attention.[40]

The critique regards the inevitable political blowback that undermines any temporary increase in operational security. In this view, the noblest of humanitarian ends are undercut by crass and ultimately counterproductive violent means. In this way humanitarianism is a process that agencies seek to dominate. Practitioner Tony Vaux and colleagues comment:

> Aid agencies, NGOs in particular, like to rhetorically monopolise the high ground. The mere suggestion that commercial companies may have expertise and a quality of services that is equal to, if not better than, that of charitable

organisations, can lead to outcries of indignation. There is an implicit, and sometimes explicit, argument that all profit motivated organisations are by definition "unprincipled" whereas all not-for-profit organisations are on the contrary by definition "principled."[41]

In 1994, the then head of UN peacekeeping, Kofi Annan, was confronted with the challenge of militarized displacement camps, which the Hutu *génocidaires* were using to intimidate civilians, recruit militants, and continue the conflict with the new Tutsi-led government in Rwanda. The future secretary-general "considered the possibility of engaging a private firm. But the world may not be ready to privatize peace."[42]

This view was becoming more widespread when an abrupt change occurred in the late 1990s, which has since accelerated.[43] The number of incidents against aid workers grew in number and visibility—for example, we should recall the earlier depictions of attacks on UN and Red Cross and Red Crescent compounds and vehicles; the Aid Worker Security Database has documented that at least 4,079 aid workers have been victims from 1997 through the end of 2016.[44] For all the discussions about security sector management and reform—part of a larger conversation about the protection of civilians in non-permissive operating environments—adequate means of providing security for aid personnel were largely absent. In addition to a normative imperative to respond quickly even under violent conditions, agencies also had an organizational imperative to be present in crises. An essential element of overall fundraising often required agencies to leap before looking. "Humanitarian organisations' motivations and rationales for using PSPs [private security providers] are based on immediate exigencies, often not conducive to thoughtful policy decisions, or on untested assumptions regarding cost and liability that may not stand up to scrutiny."[45]

The current degree of reliance on PSCs is hard to calculate because many agencies are uncomfortable releasing this information—because of its possible impact on recruitment and contributions.[46] However, studies from 2006 and 2009 show sizable amounts:[47] about 25 percent of high-end firms and more than 50 percent of military support and logistics firms reported working for humanitarian clients. While not an everyday occurrence, almost every aid agency has paid for security at some point—in 2007, 22 percent of agencies reported using armed security services. The cultural taboo about hired guns—specifically hiring PSCs—has been evaporating, especially with the establishment of a regulatory regime that accepts its legitimacy while restricting the practice. Since 2010, the signing of the International Code of Conduct for Private Security Providers has made arrangements more politically palatable. In June 2012, the UN drafted a system-wide policy on using PSCs approved by the Inter-Agency Security

Management Network. Examples of UN humanitarian agencies using PSCs include OCHA, whose policy calls for "reputable" firms; UNHCR's "ladder of options," which resulted in hiring ArmorGroup in Kenya; and the WFP's using private guards for relief supplies. Such NGOs as the IRC Caritas have used PSCs. As World Vision's security manual summarizes, "The rules of security have changed. And so must our practices."[48]

One illustration is MSF, which once opposed PSCs but more recently has altered its policy to use them.[49] Earlier Fiona Terry, a former MSF research director, had argued, "If humanitarian action has been reduced to a logistical exercise, better to contract a supermarket chain to deliver aid with the protection of DSL [Defense Systems Limited] and at least avoid the humanitarian pretense."[50] Other humanitarians continue to object, but only a handful of agencies have been explicit in their disavowal. For example, Save the Children's Nick Downie, head of security for the emergencies team, writes,

> I am concerned that our reputation and community perceptions of our work are at risk when we work with PMSCs [private military and security companies]. Equally, I am worried that inappropriate engagement with PMSCs will lead to us becoming more insecure. Many aid workers assisted by PMSCs are already, and will become more, vulnerable because of this engagement. . . . I prefer active avoidance rather than associating with this globally resurgent-armed actor.[51]

For like-minded agencies, PSCs are intrinsically incompatible with humanitarianism, and the associations of one agency can contaminate the perception of the entire sector.

What do aid agency–PSC interactions indicate about the nature of humanitarianism? To start, privatizing the creation of fortified humanitarian space is the apotheosis of two strands in humanitarian thought—militarization and marketization—which suggests experiments. Security capacities expand the possibilities for protection. However, other interpretations identify structural limitations. PSCs do not address the source of insecurity but try to limit the consequences. Although perhaps some lives are saved with the presence of PSCs, violence and victimization are usually displaced. Instead of the humanitarian worker injured or killed, it may be the PSC or locals who have gotten caught in the crossfire, which among other things can obscure the actual human toll of aid operations.

Moreover, hiring PSCs legitimates them and therefore helps rehabilitate their image; they become a moral part of the humanitarian narrative. This arrangement also contributes to the perception of agencies as too prone to emphasize military responses to humanitarian crises. It casts agencies in a poor light because PSCs are usually guarding staff or materials, which ipso facto suggests greater interest in their own security than in confronting the same insecurity felt by vulnerable populations—a key element of humanitarian solidarity.

In short, PSCs may be valuable to augment short-term security, but their backgrounds and the incentive structure that governs their actions erode humanitarian foundations. Perspectives have changed considerably in the past two decades, from when Annan said the world "wasn't ready" to an almost ordinary option. What was once seen as politically inflammatory is now cast as eminently practical. This phenomenon in many ways is representative of the current dilemma of what humanitarianism is—that is, a contested conversation about its technical mechanics and impacts versus its politics, methods, and message.

Conclusion: Humanitarianism's Value and Humanitarian Values

The intertwined influences of media and markets clash with traditional humanitarianism—is the quality of mercy in intentions, behaviors, or outcomes? Can other agendas blend with humanitarianism without hijacking it? Here the power of narratives has been discussed with respect to enabling the work of agencies but also modifying their images to reflect fundraising and commercial realities. The perspectives of critical humanitarian studies, and a survey of the practical challenges to agencies as storytellers, have been central to our analysis.

Agencies are heavily invested in the humanitarian narrative, which is essential not only for access but also for funding. The received wisdom regarding humanitarian narratives parrots realism, contending that they echo the whims of the great powers—what becomes recognized widely as a humanitarian issue is about dominance. Marxists and post-colonialists respectively attribute the successful humanitarianization of an issue to economic class power or Western influence. However, in more concrete terms the media and relief agencies are responsible for etching the narrative because the behavior of aid workers creates images from which the media select and popularize. The narrative is rhetorical but has political implications; it describes the values and mission of operations and consequently becomes a key to achieving consent on the ground. The norm entrepreneurs are endemic to constructivism and have discernible behavioral repercussions.

Drawing on feminism and critical humanitarianism and their focus on the voiceless, several other angles on power become apparent when exhibited by the state and the politics of humanitarian narratives. They may have an unwanted palliating effect, in fact, routinizing three previously objectionable premises. The first is that a humanitarian narrative that does not ask why there is suffering, not merely how to cope, normalizes disasters. It may also celebrate the role of donors and aid workers, privileging self-congratulations over the limits of their activities. In a related fashion, some critics note that the portrayals of new technologies, both military and medical, sanitize impressions of wars and responses. For instance, precision munitions ("smart bombs") present a reality in which the "bad guys" are removed while local innocents and "good guys" are spared; but this antiseptic view can increase receptivity to the potential use of military force. Narratives can also symbolically demonstrate a commitment and possibly absolve responsibility for not doing more, what could be described as a humanitarian "fig leaves" or "alibis."[52]

A second premise is that new media technologies have not solved the problem of distance between zones of danger and of safety. They have not fundamentally reduced "moral distance" because they do not readily translate into moral relationships.[53] In fact, media coverage not only does not establish a new relationship, it may ingrain biases. Media can have the effect of skewing our vision of the world in at least two ways. Media may turn moral narratives into entertainment in order to increase viewer ratings and revenues. The old journalistic adage of "if it bleeds, it leads" accentuates what could be considered "humanitarian pornography." Essentialist depictions or crude caricatures of good and evil predominate and draw audiences; they do not reveal the truths about crises. Moreover, media may turn political narratives into humanitarian dramas. The media often erase politics and portray crises as "natural" disasters. They concentrate on the consequences of conditions and not their causes. For example, famines become unavoidable tragedies rather than being recognized as strategic choices of the powerful.

The problem of over-generalizations—media clichés such as the abandoned orphans or courageous journalists who get the story right while under fire—is that they can easily be manipulated and misused. Moreover, they may contribute to "compassion fatigue." In other words, if moral narratives become routine and repetitious, they lose salience and traction. Humanitarian crises can make for good viewing, but they often savage the dignity of victims and ultimately may numb potential donors and responders.

A third premise centers on understanding the economics of humanitarianism. "Disaster capitalism"[54] is how Naomi Klein has christened the market ideology that profits from such crises. The humanitarian-industrial complex includes actors and firms from the media to logistics and security companies, from multinational agribusiness to farmers and IGOs and NGOs. Part of the media's influence includes entertainers and other celebrities who "produce" humanitarianism by pitching purchases that are treated as proxy for humanitarian acts. Compassion is channeled into consumption and validated in a tax deduction.

While humanitarianism aims to reduce suffering, a certain degree of suffering must exist to maintain the raison d'être of aid agencies. The horrors of wars and natural disasters become opportunities for profit, and the bigger and worse, the more profit and institutional security. In brief, the marketplace creates perverse motivations and incentives.

The media cannot be entrusted to compose the humanitarian narrative, or political and economic pressures may corrupt the process and product. Agencies themselves must become storytellers; they must define themselves or face being defined by the media. However, humanitarians confront four dilemmas in their media relations. First, should they use well-worn but effective stereotypes to project the image of a disaster and elicit desperately needed funds? Is it acceptable to give in to duplicity and profiteering to get resources that enable effective responses? One challenge is that narratives are perceived so differently—beauty or beast depending on the eyes of the beholder. Further research is necessary about what sorts of appeals work better with which audiences. Do gender, age, culture, or class determine reactions?

Second, agencies often have a public story that avoids taking sides and confronting perpetrators who might imperil staff and access to victims. At the same time, relief agencies may have a private story for donors, governments, and journalists in which blame is apportioned and politics identified. Is this hypocritical? Is there a need to harmonize narratives, especially to remain true to doing justice to the suffering? Or is it acceptable to obfuscate the story to placate the powerful and maintain humanitarian access?

Third, how much attention—meaning staff and resources—should agencies allocate for massaging public relations? Should humanitarians invest in the media at the expense of other programming? What precisely is the payoff? Public relations can be expensive and hard to justify, and it is unclear how to weigh its impact.

Fourth, in several crises the media have contributed to armed conflicts by helping to spread perceptions that incite or inflame belligerents. In such cases, should agencies act, or endorse others to act, to control the dissemination of incendiary communications? To what extent is this type of information another form of imperialism?

Humanitarian narratives are a cornerstone of the system. Marketization, including the behavior of the media, has a paradoxical impact on humanitarianism. In one sense, it creates new opportunities for attention and resources; but in another subtler, albeit nefarious and debilitating sense, it subverts and endangers. There is a value to the humanitarian narrative—it can inspire action, assign responsibilities, inform policy, and alter stereotypes—but primarily it can only be justified if its products are value-based. Markets and media have created a more powerful humanitarianism, but also one more prone to manipulation.

10

Humanitarianism Unbound

Public Health Disasters and Environmental Emergencies

Hurricane Sandy passed to the west of Haiti on October 25, 2012, causing heavy rains and strong winds, flooding homes, and overflowing rivers. Residents wave at the approaching helicopter of a humanitarian assessment mission of the UN Stabilization Mission in Haiti (MINUSTAH) to their island off the southwest coast of Haiti (October 26, 2012). (UN photo/Logan Abassi)

In This Chapter

- Infectious Diseases and the Humanitarian Agenda
- HIV/AIDS and Ebola
- Public Health Challenges and Humanitarianism
- The Humanitarian Impact of Environmental Crises
- Climate Refugees
- Environmental Challenges and Humanitarianism
- Conclusion: If Humanitarianism Bends, Does It Break?

Humanitarian culture can be broad in casting the range of rights, needs, and activities that contribute to the protection of vulnerable populations. Although such long-term structural afflictions as poverty are often catalogued as a development activity, there are also instances in which issues other than those war-born pose an acute emergency. Regardless of sources, the debilitated and displaced warrant a "humanitarian" response. This perspective has recently been injected into public health and the environment. In fact, the existential threat from these sources could be larger than the traditional focus of the international humanitarian system, war.

To that end, this chapter considers the breadth of humanitarian ambitions and reach by using illustrations of responses to infectious diseases and climate change. Three queries drive this analysis: How and why do diseases and environmental emergencies constitute humanitarian crises? How and why have humanitarian agencies reacted to non-war-based humanitarian crises? What are the consequences of incorporating public health and ecology into humanitarianism?

Infectious Diseases and the Humanitarian Agenda

The concern with human welfare that broadly underscores the humanitarian agenda can expand the horizon of aid agencies into the realm of public health—the science and methods of preventing disease—from control of the spread of infections through sanitation, education, and health services. In addressing war, they have confronted epidemics because many fatalities in the context of armed conflicts result from disease. The significance of infectious diseases became another form of emergency over which the international humanitarian system has gained jurisdiction. Furthermore, the variation in access to public health is a form of injustice that, whether precipitated and prolonged by armed conflicts, has routinely added a layer of crisis. The association with war in terms of casualties and fatalities may compel responses, but humanitarianism's increased concern with long-term structural problems that contribute to crises may also have motivated this mandate expansion.

Diseases can create economic and social development problems. For example, with respect to Ebola, the impact could be seen in economic decline as fewer domestic workers produced less and worries arose when foreign workers returned home. In Sierra Leone, one prediction suggested a 4 percent drop in GDP. This consequence has also been seen in regard to human immunodeficiency virus and acquired immune deficiency syndrome (HIV/AIDS). Alex de Waal has outlined a "new variant famine" thesis, which holds that HIV/AIDS has fostered food insecurity because it often kills agricultural workers, "exactly those capacities that enable people to resist famine. AIDS kills young adults, especially women—the people whose labor is most needed."[1] Consequently, public health can become a humanitarian crisis. Although responding to such disasters is not characterized by the same intensity of fraught politics found in helping war-torn areas, humanitarianism's approaches to address infectious diseases nonetheless have their own unusual political dynamics. The issue of bio-weapons or the use of infectious disease as weapons would bring together both the politics of war and disease in a humanitarian response.

Infectious diseases present three sorts of problems: medical, logistical, and organizational. The first is essentially a technical question regarding the biology of sickness and addressed by epidemiology—virulence (how deadly a disease is) and transmissibility (how easily it transmits to another host). Medical science has the technology and knowledge to show how diseases spread via the lack of immunity that humans have to powerful incapacitating viruses. Often diseases "spill over" from animal hosts in a process called "zoonosis."[2] Roughly 60 percent of all human infectious diseases originate with animals, including viruses ranging from bubonic plague to influenzas to Lyme disease. When a zoonic transmission occurs and the species barrier is "jumped," the impact in illness requiring hospitalization is greater, especially as it often becomes more virulent after the "jump." The second aspect, logistics, then becomes substantial, which leads to questions about budgets and donor priorities. The third problem is organizational in that humanitarians are tested by the magnitude and nature of needs in public emergencies that question the range of their mandate and abilities.

Infectious diseases have been problematic since antiquity. Records indicate that smallpox was a widespread blight as early as 1350 BC in Egypt. There were bubonic and pneumonic plagues in ancient Greece (430 BC), early Christendom in the Roman and Byzantine Empires (165–180 and 531–750), throughout Europe in the 1340s–1350s, and in parts of China in 1910–1920.[3] The most notorious of these was the transmission of the "Black Death" (1347–1351), which has been considered fallout from the first biological weapon; it resulted when Mongol invaders catapulted plague-infected bodies over the walls of the fortified settlement of Caffa, a Genoese settlement in Crimea.[4] This tactic caused the population to flee along Black Sea routes to the Mediterranean and Europe. Other early illustrations of mass infectious diseases are smallpox outbreaks in the Americas during the sixteenth century and Australia in the eighteenth.

Historically, epidemics were addressed through state-centered interventions. For example, during the plague of the fourteenth century, Venice quarantined areas to prevent the transmission and impact of the infectious disease. It was not until the mid-1800s that an organized global response to such pandemics arose. On par with other developments to improve human welfare in the nineteenth century, an international organization to address infectious diseases was established in 1851. The First International Sanitary Conference was held in Paris and led to a convention to control the spread of so-called Asiatic diseases—cholera, plague, and yellow fever—that maritime traffic transmitted. Waves of cholera epidemics were ubiquitous in the nineteenth century: in India (1816–1826, persisting until the early twentieth century); Europe and the United States (1829–1851); Russia (1852–1860); Spain (1854–1855); Europe and Africa (1863–1875); and Europe, the Americas, Japan, and Persia (1880s and 1890s). Ten other conferences were subsequently held between 1851 and 1903 to develop procedures to contain diseases, which produced International Sanitary Regulations in 1903 and the Office International d'Hygiène Publique in 1907. Meanwhile in the Americas, in 1902, the International Sanitary Office of the American Republics was formed.

In 1919 after WWI, the Health Organization of the League of Nations was founded to coordinate efforts to counter infectious diseases, which at that time focused on influenza and typhus. At the national level, states began to invest more into public health infrastructure to monitor and combat the spread of infectious disease in a world increasingly integrated through commerce and communications. There was also an international agreement on banning the use of diseases as a weapon: the 1925 Geneva Protocol for the Prohibition of the Use in War of Asphyxiating, Poisonous or Other Gases, and of Bacteriological Methods of Warfare.

In 1948, the three global agencies for addressing different aspects of public health issues—Office International d'Hygiène Publique (organized agreements and shared medical, epidemiological, technical information), the League of Nations Health Organization (commissions on diseases and reports on crises), and the UN Relief and Rehabilitation Administration (on-the-ground operations)—were consolidated into a new UN specialized agency, the WHO.[5] This new entity was charged with monitoring the spread of diseases and building political consensus on how to respond. Its early activities focused on tuberculosis, malaria, and smallpox. It is governed by the World Health Assembly, in which three delegates from each state participate (with one vote). The executive board consists of thirty-two members, of which three have always been members of the Security Council.

The WHO has also overseen the establishment and revisions of International Health Regulations (in 1951, 1969, 1973, 1981, and most recently in 2005) and regulated a range of products, from infant formula to tobacco. In 1998, the WHO established the Global Outbreak and Alert Response Network (GOARN), which tracks diseases through more than 110 real-time networks and organizes the collaboration of more than 200 technical institutions and 600 partner organizations; between 2000 and 2015, it responded to more than 130 international public health emergencies. The WHO's two-year budgets have fluctuated in recent years. In 2010–2011 it was $4.54 billion; it dropped in 2012–2013 to $3.959 billion and rose slightly in 2014–2015 to $3.977 billion. For 2016–2017, it is $4.384 billion.

After the Cold War, global cooperation on public health expanded. The UNDP prioritized it as part of the emerging framework of "human security"—"health security" was one of seven key priorities. Other UN initiatives to address public health challenges of infectious diseases included the Millennium Development Goals (MDGs). These eight goals set specific benchmarks of progress for a wide range of socioeconomic problems that were to be achieved by 2015. Goal #6 delineated the UN's goals for combating infectious diseases with three targets: to lower HIV/AIDS by one-half and reverse its spread; to achieve universal access to treatment for HIV/AIDS for all those in need by 2010; and to halt and reserve incidences of malaria and other major diseases. Along with setting these goals in 2002, member states also set up the Global Fund to Fight AIDS, Tuberculosis, and Malaria, which annually raises about $4 billion to fight these maladies. With the expiration of the MDGs at the end of 2015, the UN Summit on the seventieth anniversary approved the Sustainable Development Goals (SDGs), which include Goal #3: "Ensure healthy lives and promote wellbeing for all at all ages." This goal calls for the end of epidemics (including HIV/AIDS, tuberculosis, and malaria, along with tropical diseases, waterborne diseases, and other communicable disease) by 2030.

HIV/AIDS and Ebola

Pandemics kill and uproot millions each year, oftentimes more than armed conflict, though on occasion the two go hand in hand. A brief look at two cases of widespread transmission of disease illustrates the nature of that particular infection and the politics of humanitarian involvement in public health. We could have examined a large sample and variety of other even more lethal diseases—for example, tuberculosis, malaria, and influenza—but we concentrated on these two because they exhibit contrasting sets of challenges: HIV/AIDS creates long-term health problems for those afflicted, whereas Ebola ravages far more quickly and kills many immediately.

Since first documented in the early 1980s (although some scientists estimate that it has existed since the early twentieth century in parts of western Africa), more than 70 million have been infected with HIV/AIDS, which has killed around 35 million and orphaned between 11 million and 18 million.[6] Attempts to counter the spread of HIV have met some success. In 1990, the rate of new infections was just under 2 million per year, which peaked at 3.5 million in 1996 and declined over the last few years to around 2.1 million. But the number of those dying each year grew considerably over the 1990s, from 250,000 annually in 1990 to 1.6 million in 2000. In the twenty-first century, the yearly fatality rate reached its height in 2005 when 2.4 million died; it has since decreased markedly, registering around 1.1 million deaths in 2015. Today, it nonetheless remains the world's most deadly infectious disease. Overall, however, the number of those living with HIV has steadily grown—in 1990, 7.3 million, then more than doubling within four years to 15.9 million in 1994, and then almost doubling again in about eight years, as 2002 data show a population of about 30 million. Currently almost 37 million live with HIV.

While the global statistics regarding declining numbers of infections is encouraging, considerable regional variations persist. During the period 2000–2013, for instance, the Caribbean, southern Asia and the Pacific, and southern Africa have seen a decrease of about 49 percent. Latin America, western and central Africa, and Southeast Asia have seen much smaller declines or even stagnation. Western and central Europe along with North America have seen a substantial drop. However, in Eastern Europe, East Asia, the Middle East, North Africa, and central and western Asia, the numbers increased. Seventy percent of all who are infected reside in sub-Saharan Africa. Aside from combating the spread of infection, efforts are also being made to give greater access to medical treatments. In 2003 only about 800,000 people received antiretroviral therapy (ART), and in 2010, 7.5 million had access, but by the end of 2015 the number had soared to 18.2 million, or nearly half of those afflicted.

A viral hemorrhagic fever, Ebola, likely transmitted by fruit bats and by way of monkeys, was first discovered in what was then Zaire in 1976. Viral hemorrhagic fevers (VHFs) are highly contagious viruses that attack multiple organs, causing hemorrhages. They weaken the entire vascular system, leaving the body too weak to regulate itself. Other VHFs include

Rift Valley fever, Marburg virus, Lassa fever, and Bolivian hemorrhagic fever. In the case of Ebola, it debilitates its victims by liquefying organs and causing death. It usually burns out quickly—it is intense but does not spread far. From 1976 to 2014, there were about two dozen outbreaks that infected on the order of 2,400, killing some 1,650 individuals. However, the most recent outbreak that began in December 2013 was many times more lethal, persistent, and far-reaching. As of late March 2016 when the epidemic ended, 28,646 cases and 11,323 deaths were documented. These were mostly concentrated in Sierra Leone (14,124 cases, 3,956 fatalities), Liberia (10,675 cases, 4,809 fatalities), and Guinea (3,811 cases, 2,543 fatalities).[7] Not only was there a concentration in a few states but also variations in mortality rates; Ebola was significantly more deadly in Guinea, likely due to less adequate or accessible public health infrastructure. Global concerns over Ebola led to the September 2014 Security Council resolution 2177 that recognized the disease as a "threat to international peace and security." These words are the UN Charter's trigger for action by the council, which for the third time had made such a declaration about a health crisis. As for HIV/AIDS, the correlation between war-torn societies and disease was too evident for the Security Council's permanent and elected members to overlook.

Public Health Challenges and Humanitarianism

The depth of public health challenges and their pertinence for humanitarians in war zones can be illustrated further by examining the politics and economics of aid provision. Given tight budgets and other resource constraints, public health programming may compete with responses to war victims. At the local level, there is often a shortfall in funds to pay for life-saving treatments, let alone investing in research or infrastructure. Therefore, often agencies are obliged to make hard choices among initiatives. Representative of such dilemmas is a tale about an aid worker in Haiti who was struggling to make a triage decision about the pluses and minuses of authorizing an expensive ($20,000) life-saving treatment for a single child versus the value of using the sum to help numerous children.[8] Irrespective of the entry of humanitarian agencies into public health, overwhelming needs are coupled with too few resources, which make such decision making as commonplace as it is painful and bring to the fore the politics of triage.

Similar tensions about inequalities are also manifest at the global level. Public health systems are fundamentally state-based and serve their own populations; international mechanisms are significantly smaller and weaker. For example, the WHO's annual expenditures of about $2.2 billion a year should be compared with those of 2016 by the municipal health agency for New York City of about $1.35 billion. Thus, Western countries spend far more on public health for their own populations than is allocated to tackling global public health. Indeed, Sara Davies argues that the West's support of the WHO is self-interested in seeking to stop the spread of disease to the West, not necessarily prevent wider outbreaks in target countries.[9]

Political-economic problems are further complicated by profit motives and the pharmaceutical industry. Drugs are expensive to invent and sometimes to produce. Medicines are frequently patented, meaning that an individual or company owns its design outright. An annex of the 1994 Marrakesh Agreement establishing the WTO has a provision regarding the Trade-Related Aspects of Intellectual Property Rights (TRIPS), which ensures that inventors receive a twenty-year monopoly on their inventions, allowing them to charge whatever they wish for the medicines that they have developed. However, the November 2001 Doha Agreement, still not final, sought to make the provision on patents not binding until 2016. In any case, countries such as Brazil, Thailand, and South Africa have manufactured less costly generic versions of drugs.

Another challenge coming from the embrace of public health by aid agencies is the entanglement in the politics of global health security. The earliest international work on public health served empires that were more concerned with the spread of infectious diseases from colonies to the metropole than with their eradication. The establishment of monitoring and quarantining systems became and remains a method for surveillance and control. Similarly, when humanitarians take on public health, they become politicized. Who gets access to public health may be contested, particularly in areas of scarcity. In addition, the information gathered in conducting such work enables aid agencies to produce specialized knowledge that is useful to global security governance; this result too may corrode humanitarianism.[10]

Ultimately, infectious diseases pose a profound challenge not only because of the human misery that they create and the opportunities for surveillance and control, but also because they lead to questioning the value of humanitarian activities. As Jean-Hervé Bradol has shown, such concerns are emblematic of MSF's shifting policies and priorities for public health.[11] In the 1970s, MSF sought to move beyond patient care and promote public health more broadly. However, by 1992 the organization's charter no longer emphasized public health. At the heart of this change was that by taking on public health, MSF had fewer resources to devote to the direct delivery of medical assistance in emergencies. The goal of "health for all people of the world by 2000" was articulated at the 1978 Alma-Ata Conference and was certainly a noble aspiration. The practice of MSF in the 1990s was to be involved in every phase of public health—patient care, public health administration, international organization and national government policy formulation, pharmaceutical company advocacy, and public debate. As part of its attempt to confront the root causes of humanitarian crises, such an ambitious program spread efforts too thin and detracted from the MSF's comparative advantage in war zones.

The expansion of humanitarianism from war-born emergencies to systems of human welfare is logical given contemporary requirements. However, organizational politics and turf-consciousness often can get in the way of sensible solutions. The quarrel over the role and extent of directing operations to public health lingers within the international humanitarian system.

The Humanitarian Impact of Environmental Crises

Although the formal structures of humanitarianism are rooted in responding to wars, natural disasters and ecological issues also qualify, and many also strike war-torn societies. For example, the May 1970 earthquake in Peru (killing 30,000) and the November 1970 Bhola cyclone that hit eastern Pakistan (killing 250,000–500,000) provided an additional momentum for MSF after its founding following the Biafra War.[12] The magnitude of forced displacement from natural disasters has become a trigger for concern and action, especially as environmental emergencies now generate an even larger demand than armed conflicts, although those displaced usually can return more easily than those fleeing war zones. In 2013, data showed that 8.2 million were newly displaced by war whereas 22 million fled natural disasters.[13] Another data set showed that in 2014 almost 60 million were displaced by persecution, violence, conflict, or human rights violations, but more than 140 million were buffeted by natural disasters. Indeed, since 2008 an average of 22.5 million people are displaced each year by weather-related disasters.[14] The top five countries were China (58 million), Philippines (10 million), India (5.7 million), Burkina Faso (4 million), and Sri Lanka (3 million).

The very character of environmental problems makes them difficult because they are diffuse (cover a wide area); usually transnational (cross jurisdictions of states); long-lasting (lengthy gestation period); frequently ambiguous in origins (hard to identify the responsible party); and usually without consensus about solutions (losses by some but gains by others).

Aside from the complex challenges of scale and political dissonance, humanitarians face the legal and cultural question as to whether addressing these situations under the mantle of humanitarianism is permissible and warranted. Environmental crises are in every sense emergencies, but they lack the violent drama associated with wars. Those displaced—for example, after the nuclear disaster in Chernobyl or the chemical one in Bhopal—may remain long-term IDPs or refugees.

Humanitarians have frequently recognized extreme environmental disasters as a direct concern—earthquakes, hurricanes, tsunamis, etc.—and hence provided relief services to supplement state responses. The challenges posed by environmental emergencies revolve around authority and capacity, on the one hand, and political consequences, on the other. The jurisdiction for disaster responses lies primarily with governments, but what role do agencies have where there is no clear agreement or support by governments? Additionally, from where do the financial resources for humanitarian responses come in order to help allay natural disasters? Moreover, whose political agendas are furthered by humanitarian responses to environmental crises that move populations or shape their recovery? The political tenor of these queries resembles many comparable ones from humanitarians in wars.

By contrast to routine worries about insufficient funds that bedevil many humanitarian responses, in the singular case of the Indian Ocean tsunami that struck on December 26, 2004, the consequences of resource mobilization proved more significant.[15] In the wake of a tremendous loss of life—perhaps as many as 227,000—and millions displaced, some $13.5 billion in assistance flooded the region, the most generous amount ever mobilized for a single disaster. When the crisis erupted, there were UN development activities in several of the affected countries. These operations immediately shifted to humanitarian delivery, which showed the proclivity for "mandate-stretch" by international organizations in such situations—chasing newly available resources—as well as the blurring of distinctions between humanitarians and other actors, including military and commercial. Furthermore, although overall resources were not problematic, their allocation and deployment were. Locals were not consulted about recovery strategies, and oftentimes agencies did not possess knowledge of local economic and political conditions. In the end, much aid was delivered but sometimes with negative impacts: political influences steered assistance into helping those who were already better off—which restored lives, but ones of profound economic inequality. Furthermore, weak local capacities to prevent and respond to natural disasters, a major contributor to the crises in the first place, were not addressed by aid, so additional dependency resulted. In short, humanitarian action in environmental emergencies remains frantic and vexing.

To return to the issue of authority and jurisdiction, participation is often not problematic because exigencies tend to open access for aid agencies; usually they quickly receive consent. However, where the environmental disaster itself is human-made, such as the overuse of water, an industrial accident, or the emission of a toxic agent, or there is no official acknowledgement due to ignorance and fear of legal culpability, the politics change. Indeed, they complicate humanitarian responses, which resemble the contested politics endemic to operating in war zones. A humanitarianism concerned with tackling not only the emergency phase but also root causes has become widespread. And in ecological disasters the same issues recur that are confronted in addressing armed conflicts: access, refugees, and criminal accountability.

Building on the issues of consent and force to protect vulnerable populations associated with humanitarian intervention, a parallel can be drawn by applying these same concerns to responding to conditions affected by environmental emergencies. In the scenario whereby environmental problems with humanitarian repercussions require a security solution, in referencing issues of *jus ad bellum* from just war theory, does the environment constitute a "just cause" for armed intervention? Could there thus be a "green" dimension to R2P? In other words, could there be a "responsibility to environmentally protect"?

The notion of intervention is invariably and endlessly controversial—it violates state sovereignty, requires resources, inflicts a human toll, and may not ultimately achieve its intended outcome. Moreover, in terms of the environment, different sorts of challenges may require different sorts of responses. The criteria for relying on different components of the humanitarian toolkit become harder to discern in environmental emergencies. The scale of death and destruction is a perennial consideration, but with respect to intervention, so too are the politics of causality; an environmental disaster must be clearly connected to a violator, whether by intent or negligence.

It is hard to determine when an environmental crisis that becomes an "emergency" in a humanitarian sense would justify intervention. Some violations are clearer—for example, a country with a nuclear power plant that is on the verge of meltdown. Less clear would be toxic wastes illegally dumped or overfishing when a government has been unresponsive. Grayer still are atmospheric environmental emergencies, such as acid rain or global warming. Some ecological problems indirectly affect the humanitarian agenda but do not readily appear on it because they do not register as being significant for the "emergency" phase of survival that defines humanitarianism. For example, it would be a stretch to argue for an environmental crisis such as the loss or extinction of endangered species, which may have a deleterious long-term impact on sustainability to environments on which all life depends.

Some obstacles to a "green" or environment-driven humanitarianism that connects ecology with humanitarian conditions are rooted in the sector, notably sensitivities within humanitarian culture to restrict its agenda to the immediate and clearly verifiable plight of victims, and an agency imperative not to organizationally overstretch. However, others reside with states, whose routine invocation of sovereignty can be paralyzing. International regulations for protecting the environment parallel what humanitarianism routinely encounters in protecting people—namely, the claim by states to exclusive authority. Following WWII and the wave of decolonization that swept through the Global South, the environment was understood as another area in which the West exploited former colonies. In 1962, the host of newly independent states successfully pushed for General Assembly resolution 1803 (XVII), which protected the right of a state to exercise control over its natural resources. This principle was reaffirmed at the 1972 Stockholm United Nations Conference on the Human Environment. Much like human rights, the environment customarily takes a secondary position to sacrosanct sovereignty.

However, the accepted role of humanitarianism in confronting the casualties of armed conflicts is spelled out by IHL, which has banned ecological manipulation as a practice of war. The 1976 UN Convention on the Prohibition of Military or Any Other Hostile Use of Environmental Modification Techniques (ENMOD) concentrates on the environment as a potential victim of war; it specifies that military tactics "having widespread, long-term or severe effects" to the natural environment are illegal. Among the influences leading to this treaty was its possibility for constraining the great powers from engaging in this practice as the United States had in Vietnam with mass defoliation campaigns and weather manipulation. The further embedding of this environment-humanitarian norm can be seen the 1994 Guidelines for Military Manuals and Interactions on the Protection of the Environment in Times of Armed Conflict prepared by the ICRC and the UN's General Assembly, which responded to the systematic burning of oil wells by Iraq in Kuwait during the 1991 Persian Gulf War.

Not only have the environmental aspects come to be addressed by the international humanitarian system, but also the available tools have been broadened. Humanitarianism finds a role in contributing to disaster risk reduction and articulates the issue in the moral terms of its culture.[16] The blending of environment into humanitarianism was hinted by the 2001 ICISS document in discussing criteria to satisfy just cause to intervene: "overwhelming natural or environmental catastrophes, where the state concerned is either unwilling or unable to cope, or call for assistance, and significant loss of life is occurring or threatened."[17] This diplomatic sleight of hand finessed the issue, but over a decade and half later, the politics remain opaque and the issue lurks. Indeed, Lloyd Axworthy, who as Canadian foreign minister launched the ICISS in 2000, has become a partisan of applying R2P to climate change.[18]

Based on the humanitarian principles in international agreements, some activists and scholars such as Robyn Eckersley contend that a new set of international norms should inform reactions to environmental disaster.[19] She identifies three modalities of protection, which echo humanitarian sensibilities. The first is "ecological intervention" or the use of force to protect the environment. Her logic seeks to satisfy the criteria of morality, legitimacy, and legality. The second concerns "ecological defense," or an intervention to protect human populations disrupted by environmental deterioration. Hers is akin to the notion of R2P but fundamentally different because the victim is not only human. Ecological defense is more directly analogous to R2P in that it reaffirms state sovereignty—it asserts that states bear the primary responsibility for treatment of their environs—and emphasizes human victims rather than states that cause environmental harm. The third revolves around "crimes against nature," which call for a criminal tribunal to prosecute "ecocide," or "widespread, long-term and severe damage to the natural environment." Eckersley's definition extrapolates from the 1976 ENMOD treaty but is broader; ENMOD only applies to destroying environmental resources during war, and this notion would pertain at all times.

Not all bad environmental behavior will necessitate an operational response, to be sure, from humanitarian agencies. To gauge which type of response is appropriate, a typology of three environmental harms is helpful. The first concerns environmental emergencies as a part of human rights violations because this type of disaster aggregates problems and brings additional concerns to motivate an adequate response. The second regards trans-boundary environmental emergencies, for which the UN Charter prescribes two possible ways to respond: a state can defend its environment as part of self-defense (Article 51); and the UN Security Council can define an environmental crisis as a security threat (under Article 39), and thus legally authorize an intervention within a state to thwart ecological danger. The third concerns internal environmental emergencies with no threat to humans, for which a response requires a morality beyond one based on "humanity"—some would say it demands acknowledging humanity's anthropocentrism, and which would be the most contentious form of ecologically motivated uses of force.

The first two scenarios connect the environment to human rights and security threats that have become an essential component of the humanitarian agenda. The third shows the limits of that agenda.

Climate Refugees

One case in the environment-humanitarian nexus merits particular attention because of affinities with earlier discussions, namely climate change as a source of forced displacement.[20] In 1985, the UN Environment

Programme (UNEP) popularized the term "environmental refugees" to refer to those who fled droughts, floods, sea rise, and other natural disasters: "those people who have been forced to leave their traditional habitat, temporarily or permanently, because of a marked environmental disruption (natural and/or triggered by people) that jeopardized their existence and/or seriously affected the quality of their life." However, this compilation of labels for many varieties of environmental "disruptions" is unhelpful because each requires a tailored response. Nevertheless, and despite a handful of doubters, including US president Donald Trump, there is virtual unanimity among world-class scientists on the Intergovernmental Panel on Climate Change (IPCC) as to the veracity of this claim. Human-made climate change is the most prominent environmental crisis behind increasing flows of vulnerable populations. With its relatively rapid onset in geological time and altering of weather, climate change has led to floods from rising seas; droughts inducing desertification, crop failures, and malnutrition; heat waves causing heat stroke and skin cancers; higher temperatures and wetter environs enabling more insect-transmitted and water-borne diseases; and coral bleaching contributing to the depletion of fisheries. The December 2015 Paris Agreement aiming to lower emissions has led to modest optimism, but it fundamentally accepts warming of two to three degrees Celsius. In short, the issue impels humanitarian responses because at this point the world cannot realistically stop climate change; the best it can hope for is to adapt and mitigate its effects.[21]

As the impacts of climate change have grown more acute, the growing numbers of forcibly displaced people, especially those from small island states (e.g., Tuvalu, Kiribati, and the Maldives) and eroding coasts (e.g., Bangladesh), have been the first to experience this phenomenon. Estimates predict an enormous surge in the number of "eco-refugees." Although as early as 1990 the IPCC predicted that significant migration would result from climate change, a dispute over the methodology of a 2005 report by Norman Myers has slowed scientific work and humanitarian activism on the issue. He calculated that in 1995, 27 million traditional refugees were almost matched by 25 million environmental refugees. Myers then estimated that the growth in environmental degradation would likely mean that by 2050 there would be 200 million climate refugees.[22] A 2005 UNEP map showed 50 million displaced by environmental sources in 2010. Since then other studies have led to different estimates—some higher, some lower—but all posit dire forecasts. The IPCC's 2007 report presents evidence that an increase of two to three degrees Celsius could cause 800 million to 1.8 billion to face water shortages.[23] In 2011, for instance, the American Association for the Advancement of Science predicted that by 2020 some 50 million environmental refugees were likely. A 2015 study calculated that on average

26.4 million people have been displaced by sudden onset environmental disasters each year since 2008.[24]

The enormous scope of humanitarian needs posed by such crises and calculations about them is daunting. To make matters worse, the resulting displacements are likely to be permanent—for instance, in cases of sea rise, there is nothing to return to; therefore, resettlement is the only option. Given the peculiar circumstances of victimization (sometimes slow onslaught), the potential for consuming available resources (the requirements might dwarf those of war-born crises), and the fear of precedents (agencies may not want to make a growing and unceasing commitment to populations that would then fall under their mandate), the international humanitarian system generally has veered away from dubbing climate change a "humanitarian" crisis as seen in the controversy over the expression "environmental refugee."

We should recall that the designation "refugee" creates an entitlement to certain protections and assistance under IHL. Hence, it is worth noting the 2010 UN decision to stop using the expression "environmental refugee" and avoid "climate refugee," and instead use "environmental migrants" or "environmentally displaced persons" (favored by UNHCR, IOM, and the Refugee Policy Group).[25] Additionally, although UNHCR's *Guiding Principles on Internal Displacement* refers to "natural or human-made disasters" as triggers for displacement, they emphasize state, not international, responsibility; moreover, they are not legally binding. Climate displacement is a reality, but humanitarians are seemingly divided over whether their organizations have the authority and capacity to confront this crisis; this ambiguity is underscored by the lack of a legal discourse to define and address it.

Environmental Challenges and Humanitarianism

The issues arising from responses by the current range of aid agencies to environmental emergencies resemble those regarding humanitarian involvement for infectious diseases, but with some key differences. The challenge of ecology, or ensuring livable environs, is centered on the politics inherent in humanitarianism regarding its meaning and the allocation of its material resources. Environmental regulation as a humanitarian practice may be construed as a reflection of colonialism. Advocacy and demands for binding treaties that place the onus on the Global South can be viewed as preachy, domineering, and estranging. However, relief that does not alter the relative positions of the powerful in local societies, including the role of the state, has uncritically been accepted as "humanitarian." At a more provocative level, the deployment of an environmentally based R2P could be painted as Western political notions and interests determining local governance under the premise of humanitarian protection.

Should humanitarianism expand its reach to the environment, or would that go too far beyond the existing consensus? If environmental protection is the criteria for motivating humanitarian responses, there are virtually an endless number of crises that require responses, including grave ones that would necessitate intervention. Such an approach would quickly consume all the resources in the international humanitarian system and leave nothing for other crises.

Vagueness on the border between environmentalism and humanitarianism could lead to selective application; and as critical humanitarian commentary would point out, also would connote an implicit unevenness of the value of lives. For example, the repercussions of climate change are experienced unevenly; those in coastal areas of Asia and Africa are and will be more immediately and greatly harmed. As such, some climate activists have displayed a curious logic of sacrificing certain populations, such as those of Tuvalu, in the hope that it bolsters the formal recognition of climate refugees—a scenario termed "wishful sinking."[26] A humanitarianism that steers away from environmental issues can be a comment on which strangers are worthy to save. From a similarly critical perspective, a humanitarianism that tends to the victims of human-made disasters can help sustain the systems that perpetuate them. There is less pressure to move away from environmentally insensitive development when the humanitarian sector is easing its impacts.

Nonetheless, to ignore the negative and growing impacts of environmental emergencies will be impossible; the needs simply will be too great. But to tackle them will entail vast resources, which cannot be deducted from the already inadequate ones devoted to helping war victims.

Conclusion: If Humanitarianism Bends, Does It Break?

Promoting the survival of vulnerable populations in crises is central to humanitarianism, but the nature of any crisis determines what specific institutions are deployed and what resources are mobilized. Public health, environmental emergencies, and armed conflicts can each be threatening, but war has been the focal point for humanitarianism; but this emphasis has obscured the frontiers of engagement by a variety of aid agencies. The structural problems of public health systems have humanitarian impacts but are customarily recognized as the province of development agencies or others that tackle long-term issues. Environmental emergencies may be riper for humanitarian responses, but the issue of tackling root causes when so-called natural disasters are facilitated or exacerbated by human-made factors may raise hackles about administrative authority. Humanitarian culture and discourse are not dissimilar from organizations responding to public health and environmental issues—surviving in crises. But will addressing these themes and the populations affected by them make humanitarianism unbound? Would humanitarianism be liberated or dangerously overreaching?

Scholarly perspectives could add a dimension to our analysis of the relationships of public health and the environment to humanitarianism. Realism and liberalism offer their standard perspectives: the former contends that the expansion of the humanitarian field occurs at the discretion of great powers, while the latter would interpret it as another illustration of more efficiently managing global problems. However, interpretations from unconventional schools of thought provide more insights for these core debates about humanitarianism's essence. The Marxist view can be seen in terms of causes, casualties, and the distribution of assistance. In many instances, political economy structures them. The poor tend to be most vulnerable; their access to public health infrastructure and environmentally clean areas and resources is limited, and therefore, they tend to bear the burden of health and environmental disasters. When aid does arrive, wealthier populations are more likely to reap its benefits. Postcolonial and feminist thought helps illuminate disparities and dependency. The case of the responses to the 2004 Indian Ocean earthquakes and tsunamis demonstrates how humanitarian action can be less effective than it should be as well as nefarious when there is too little local ownership. Moreover, technology for sanitation and clean water can create chains of dependency for the Global South. Constructivism can explain how rhetoric helps reinvent the scope of the international humanitarian system. How (or whether) the term "humanitarian" and its related vocabulary (specifically the designation "refugee") are used with regard to this chapter's themes is crucial to judging the adequacy of international responses. Critical humanitarianism observes that there is a key normative element that directs humanitarianism to concentrate on victims of war and natural disasters over those resulting from public health and environmental problems—that the appetite for assisting or saving victims of violence and "acts of God" is greater than for other afflictions even if suffering is suffering and death is death regardless of the source.

In practical terms, public health and environmental emergencies raise three concerns for humanitarians: First, how can we resolve tensions between addressing public health or ecology versus other essential and defined goals? For instance, should aid agencies send help to a government facing an epidemic or drought even though it has committed major human rights violations and ruthlessly pursued a war? If a government is corrupt and may use the assistance to further its own political interests by only allowing medicines to its supporters, is humanitarianism not undermined? Second, should humanitarian agencies be involved in public health and environmental emergencies as part of their routine programming? Does responding to them deprive the international humanitarian system of resources critical to responding to armed conflicts? Should humanitarians concentrate on the specific niche of mitigating suffering caused by war where few institutions can act and leave other crises to different types of social welfare agencies? Third, if there is no international political consensus about whether or how to respond to a crisis, then what? If a state will not address a life-threatening problem within its own borders, who should? As the Security Council has agreed that infectious disease (HIV/AIDS), pandemics (Ebola), and climate change are threats to international peace and security, should this principal UN organ expand its purview more regularly to include interventions linked to health and environmental threats? As indicated, one of the R2P architects, Lloyd Axworthy, has become increasingly committed to the importance of reacting to both health and climate challenges with an approach akin to that of R2P.[27]

And so, how far can humanitarianism bend before it breaks? While there has been much stretching of war-born humanitarianism, politics and funding have imposed limits. There is no consensus among humanitarians or even great powers about public health and environmental emergencies as humanitarian challenges. The core question is what the tipping point means—will needs tip the sector into acting or will by acting in this area capsize it?

11

The Study and Practice of Humanitarianism

Making Sense and Finding Meaning in Saving People

After suffering displacement in Afghanistan, new residents arrive in the Roghani Refugee Camp in Chaman, a Pakistani border town (December 1, 2003). An aid worker guides the new arrivals, with soldiers in the background. (UN photo/Luke Powell)

In This Chapter

- Condition of the Humanitarian Sector
- The Revolution in Humanitarian Affairs
- Lessons from Loss or Lessons Lost?

This analysis of humanitarianism has examined the phenomenon to see its extensive and exceptional connections to war and politics, as well as its evolution, not only to comprehend dynamics and changes but also to understand the practical implications for aid agencies and their personnel. Simplistic conceptions of humanitarianism—notably the benevolent and heroic aid workers who invariably save aggrieved yet innocent and powerless victims from unfailingly evil villains—are a disservice. Those who require assistance should not also have their dignity violated with cliché caricatures that are a product of appropriating the narratives of the needy and at the same time setting an impossible standard for humanitarians. Instead, more subtlety and nuance are required to explain the intersection of the ethics of care and the politics of emergencies. Armed conflicts and compassion are central elements in triggering humanitarianism, but legalities, organizational imperatives, and cultural moorings also inform humanitarianism's fundamental and indispensable social relationship.

A central foundation for our work is that knowledge of humanitarianism, and by implication the contribution of scholars, is consequential because analyses have structured what is known, and such knowledge shapes what is possible and what are understood as lessons. Making sense of humanitarianism enables finding its meaning and contributes to saving people, both in terms of improving their material well-being but also in recognizing and restoring their dignity. The perspectives and data in previous chapters raise scholarly puzzles and practical problems, and here we summarize and speak to both. What is humanitarianism? Why and how did it develop and change? What is its impact? How does it have meaning? What role do aid workers have in defining humanitarianism? Our conclusion reviews and probes what the present suggests about the changing nature of humanitarianism, its relationship to war and politics, and its challenges.

Condition of the Humanitarian Sector

To gauge contemporary reality, we analyze recipients and donors and situate them with respect to needs, available resources, and agency roles. Here we provide a snapshot of the nuts and bolts of the international humanitarian system. The data are essentially informed estimates because there often are no exact survey data or time series, and there can be substantial variations reflecting different methodologies by different agencies.[1] Therefore, our or anyone's data primarily capture recent characteristics and trends rather than provide a quantifiably unassailable depiction. Nonetheless, such data are a sufficient basis to hazard suggestions. Some have appeared earlier, but the repetition here allows this chapter to stand on its own.

Needs

At the end of 2015—the last year for which full data exist—there were more than 65 million displaced by conflict and another nearly 90 million due to natural disasters; this subset is from the overall 677 million people who are at risk and living in politically fragile or environmentally vulnerable places.[2] Although some of those displaced or otherwise directly affected had access to resources that enabled survival, and in a few cases recovery, most were not positioned to receive aid. Entering 2016, some 125 million people were in desperate need, of whom only about two-thirds were assisted. By the second half of 2016, those in need of aid had climbed to more than 130 million, while those receiving it had risen to almost 97 million.[3]

Recipients

A closer look at recipients of humanitarian assistance reveals the protracted nature of the crises that receive the most aid. "Risk aversion was pervasive within the NGO community, not only in relation to security but also to programming, meaning that agencies were choosing to prioritise the easiest-to-reach over the most vulnerable."[4] In addition, the most favored recipients are not necessarily the countries in greatest need or the most deserving; the data underscore that helping in emergencies does not inevitably address root causes or promote development solutions. Many emergencies last years, even decades. Table 11.1 depicts the top ten recipients, 2005–2014.

Although the onset of sudden large-scale crises sometimes rockets a country up in the rankings—such as the Indian Ocean tsunami of 2004, Haiti's earthquake in 2010, or Japan's Fukushima nuclear disaster in 2011—many of the largest recipients have been long and chronically in crisis. Indeed in 2014, 91 percent of official humanitarian assistance was directed to long- and medium-term disasters.[5] On a related note, the top

Table 11.1. Top Ten Recipients of International Humanitarian Assistance, 2005–2014 (Aid in $ million)

	2005	2006	2007	2008	2009	2010	2011	2012	2013	2014
1	Sudan $1,494	Sudan $1,499	Sudan $1,448	Sudan $1,505	Sudan $1,555	Haiti $3,244	Pakistan $1,361	South Sudan $875	Syria $1,855	Syria $2,008
2	Indonesia $962	oPt $601	oPt $635	Ethiopia $954	oPt $1,219	Pakistan $2,217	Somalia $1,073	Syria $774	oPt $793	South Sudan $1,501
3	Pakistan $899	Lebanon $598	DRC $451	Afghanistan $935	Ethiopia $747	Sudan $977	oPt $930	oPt $675	Sudan $736	Iraq $1,166
4	Iraq $721	Indonesia $572	Iraq $395	oPt $676	Afghanistan $699	Ethiopia $685	Afghanistan $675	Somalia $589	South Sudan $664	Palestine $1,155
5	Ethiopia $709	Pakistan $504	Afghanistan $355	Somalia $646	Pakistan $634	oPt $660	Ethiopia $693	Pakistan $537	Jordan $650	Jordan $895
6	Sri Lanka $617	DRC $472	Lebanon $353	DRC $573	DRC $623	Afghanistan $620	Japan $604	Ethiopia $488	Lebanon $484	Philippines $847
7	oPt $383	Iraq $437	Bangladesh $350	Myanmar $525	Somalia $611	DRC $501	Sudan $548	Afghanistan $487	Somalia $458	Lebanon $554
8	Afghanistan $349	Afghanistan $384	Ethiopia $334	Iraq $406	Iraq $508	Kenya $305	Kenya $538	DRC $472	Ethiopia $457	Ethiopia $539
9	DRC $331	Ethiopia $383	Somalia $299	Zimbabwe $360	Zimbabwe $427	Chad $297	Haiti $537	Sudan $447	Afghanistan $450	Afghanistan $532
10	Zimbabwe $232	Somalia $349	Pakistan $270	China $$39	Kenya $426	Somalia $256	South Sudan $495	Lebanon $412	DRC $449	DRC $529

DRC: Democratic Republic of the Congo
oPt: occupied Palestinian territories

Sources: Global Humanitarian Assistance Report 2015, 139; Global Humanitarian Assistance Report 2016, 54–55.

ten crises usually receive 25–35 percent of global totals, often worsening those that had been critical prior to 9/11; many others reflect different factors and predate 9/11. Thus, international humanitarian assistance has by no means been wholly hijacked to focus on terrorism.

Donors

There is also great continuity among donors. Many states ranked in the top ten have been in that position for years, and all are members of OECD's DAC, primarily a group of thirty-five wealthy Western states. Table 11.2 reflects contributions to humanitarian assistance through such UN mechanisms as UNHCR, OCHA, UNRWA, WFP, UNICEF, IOM, and FAO.

The United States and northern European countries remain the largest contributors to this system—in 2014, for example, OECD/DAC members accounted for $17.6 billion of the $25.1 billion total, whereas other governments contributed just $2.6 billion or less than half of the flows from private donors of about $5.5 billion.[6] While the purity of their humanitarian motives can be queried, the OECD/DAC ensures the annual availability of substantial humanitarian resources. However, some new donors are starting to disburse significant sums through the humanitarian channels of the UN system as seen from the figures for the United Arab Emirates (UAE), Saudi Arabia, and Turkey. Changes in humanitarian assistance indicate recognition of the importance of a crisis, although for these three countries their proximity, political links, or religious ties to Afghanistan, Iraq, and Syria are more obvious explanations for their significantly increased giving. At the same time, it also represents support for international organizations as delivery vehicles. Moreover, rankings do not necessarily reflect compassion levels because populations and other aid should also be considered. For example, in looking at the data for 2014 and 2015, a different perspective is visible in table 11.3, which shows that the largest donors are not always the most generous in per capita terms. In recent years, new donors from the Middle East (Saudi Arabia, Turkey, UAE, and Qatar) contributed a relatively larger share of their resources when measured this way.

Table 11.2. Top Ten Donors to International Humanitarian Assistance, 2005–2015 (Aid in $ million)

	2005	2006	2007	2008	2009	2010	2011	2012	2013	2014	2015
1	US $3,969	US $3,436	US $3,317	US $4,746	US $4,703	US $5,170	US $4,491	US $4,064	US $4,767	US $5,961	US $6,422
2	EU $1,706	EU $1,853	EU $1,653	EU $1,953	EU $1,605	EU $1,723	EU $1,825	EU $1,832	EU $1,970	UK $2,345	Turkey $3,176
3	UK $923	UK $1,156	UK $822	UK $973	UK $1,110	UK $1,014	UK $1,254	UK $1,210	UK $1,865	EU $2,258	UK $2,822
4	Japan $851	Germany $822	Germany $648	Germany $727	Sweden $723	Sweden $809	Sweden $880	Germany $848	Germany $1,059	Germany $1,230	EU $1,988
5	Germany $782	Netherlands $656	Sweden $610	Sweden $682	Germany $713	Germany $782	Germany $850	Sweden $838	Japan $878	Sweden $933	Germany $1,490
6	Norway $684	Sweden $641	Norway $563	Saudi Arabia $643	Spain $610	Canada $590	Japan $802	Japan $575	Sweden $821	Japan $882	Sweden $1,178
7	Netherlands $450	Norway $546	Netherlands $548	Netherlands $616	Netherlands $513	Norway $568	Norway $587	Norway $552	Canada $655	Saudi Arabia $755	UAE $1,059
8	Sweden $589	France $449	Canada $377	Spain $588	Norway $504	Japan $562	Canada $543	Canada $532	Norway $628	Canada $747	Japan $1,020
9	France $380	Spain $359	Spain $376	Norway $517	UAE $477	Spain $510	Australia $495	Australia $467	Netherlands $449	Norway $639	Canada $873
10	Italy $363	Canada $358	France $375	Canada $453	Australia $450	Netherlands $486	Spain $456	Netherlands $456	France $422	Netherlands $538	Netherlands $868

EU: European Union institutions
UAE: United Arab Emirates

Sources: Global Humanitarian Assistance Report 2015, 138; Global Humanitarian Assistance Report 2016, 46.

Table 11.3. Top Ten Donors Compared by Volume versus Percentage of Gross National Income, 2014 and 2015

	2014		2015	
	Amounts ($ millions)	*Percentage of GNI*	*Amounts ($ millions)*	*Percentage of GNI*
1	US $5,961	Kuwait .24%	US $6,422	Turkey .37%
2	UK $2,345	Luxembourg .17%	Turkey $3,176	Kuwait .33%
3	Germany $1,230	Sweden .15%	UK $2,822	UAE .25%
4	Sweden $933	Denmark .14%	Germany $1,490	Sweden .19%
5	Japan $882	Norway .12%	Sweden $1,178	Luxembourg .15%
6	Saudi Arabia $755	UAE .10%	UAE $1,059	Denmark .15%
7	Canada $747	Saudi Arabia .10%	Japan $1,020	Norway .14%
8	Norway $639	Ireland .09%	Canada $873	UK .10%
9	Netherlands $538	UK .09%	Netherlands $868	Netherlands .10%
10	Denmark $486	Qatar .08%	Norway $737	Switzerland .09%

Sources: Global Humanitarian Assistance Report 2015, 42; Global Humanitarian Assistance Report 2016, 46–47.

Unmet Needs

Despite the growth and sizable amount of resources for the international humanitarian system—from around $1 billion in 1990, to $5 billion in 2000, to $20 billion in 2010, and $28 billion in 2015—total funding is still inadequate. Not only do requirements exceed anticipated resources, but often donor pledges go unfulfilled. In 2015 only 45 percent of needs identified and to be addressed by the UN were covered ($10.8 billion was funded, but $8.9 billion remained unmet). This is not new, but after modest improvements, recent gaps have been glaring. Table 11.4 depicts data for UN-coordinated appeals and the ongoing problem of shortfalls. Moreover, donor credibility suffers when needs are neglected and even inadequate commitments are ignored.

Table 11.4. Funding and Unmet Requirements of UN-coordinated Appeals, 2006–2015 ($ billions)

	2006	2007	2008	2009	2010	2011	2012	2013	2014	2015
Required Funding	$5.9	$5.5	$8.1	$10.0	$12.9	$9.5	$10.0	$13.2	$20.3	$19.8
Actual Funding	$3.9	$4.0	$5.7	$7.1	$8.0	$5.8	$6.2	$8.5	$12.4	$10.8
Unmet Funding	$2.0	$1.6	$2.3	$2.8	$4.9	$3.6	$3.8	$4.6	$8.0	$8.9
Unmet Funding as Percent	33.9%	29%	28.4%	28%	38%	37.9%	38%	35.8%	39.4%	44.9%

Source: Global Humanitarian Assistance 2016, 37.

Agencies

For the most part, disbursements have been through international organizations. In 2014, they accounted for over half (about $13 billion) of the approximately $25 billion spent by the entire humanitarian system. The IFRC spent nearly $2 billion, NGOs almost $8 billion, and the private sector and others above $2 billion.[7] Furthermore, among intergovernmental agencies, a considerable concentration exists. Table 11.5 shows that in 2014 six UN organizations alone accounted for 46 percent of all humanitarian disbursements.

Table 11.5.   Donor Government Funding to the Six Largest UN Humanitarian Agencies, 2010–2014 ($ billions)

Agency	2010	2011	2012	2013	2014
Office of the Coordination of Humanitarian Affairs	$0.2	$0.3	$0.3	$0.4	$0.3
Food and Agriculture Organization	$0.1	$0.2	$0.2	$0.2	$0.3
World Food Programme	$2.6	$2.8	$2.5	$3.3	$3.8
UNICEF	$0.6	$0.7	$0.5	$0.7	$1.0
UN Relief and Works Agency	$0.6	$0.6	$0.6	$0.7	$0.9
UN High Commissioner for Refugees	$1.6	$1.6	$1.7	$2.3	$2.5

Source: Global Humanitarian Assistance 2016, 68.

Concentration within the nongovernmental portion of the humanitarian sector can also be seen in table 11.6. The 2013–2015 data show that international NGOs, primarily incorporated in the West, continue to dominate. However, NGOs from the Global South are growing in salience, and the emphasis on channeling resources through national and local NGOs is also increasing.

Table 11.6.   International Humanitarian Assistance Channeled to NGOs, 2013–2015 ($ in millions and percent of aid through NGOs)

	2013	2014	2015
International NGOs	$2,434.6 (84.3%)	$4,577.7 (88.3%)	$3,190.2 (76.6%)
Southern International NGOs	$29.1 (1%)	$22.5 (0.4%)	$124.3 (3.0%)
National NGOs	$40.0 (1.4%)	$36.9 (0.7%)	$80.0 (1.9%)
Affiliated National NGOs	$37.1 (1.3%)	$44.4 (0.9%)	$48.7 (1.2%)
Local NGOs	$9.2 (0.3%)	$5.6 (0.1%)	$7.6 (0.2%)
Undefined	$337.2 (11.7%)	$499.6 (9.6%)	$715.8 (17.2%)

Source: Global Humanitarian Assistance 2016, 71.

Although the resources predominately come from the West, there are new players shaping the sector, and more particularly influencing where and how aid is directed. While the exact procedures and parameters are yet to be negotiated, the Grand Bargain of the World Humanitarian Summit in 2016 requires donors and agencies to channel 25 percent of global humanitarian assistance through local and national organizations by 2020. Nevertheless, there remain significant gaps in funding that belie the limits and fragility of humanitarianism. While crises burgeon, a yawning chasm between what is promised and what is delivered not only threatens the day-to-day practice of humanitarianism; it haunts its very premise.

The Revolution in Humanitarian Affairs

The introduction to this book signaled that our cardinal point of departure would be the changes in formal humanitarianism because the pressures and challenges of the past twenty-five to thirty years threaten a transformation that heralds uncertainty for its viability and value. The timeless question of "what is humanitarianism?" is thus necessarily supplemented with "what has humanitarianism become?" and "what is the impact of this altered humanitarianism?" To put it more starkly, "is humanitarianism still humane?" Here we step back from the micro-level and the quantifiable to examine the macro-level and the meta-issue of "revolution"—we also return to the schools of international relations to spotlight ways of understanding change. Four facets get to the crux of understanding changes in the meaning of humanitarianism: ethics and principles; space and security; economics and markets; and perceptions and relationships. And they suggest substantial enough shift to permit us to point to "transformations" and even "revolution."

Ethics and Principles

Humanitarianism can be interpreted as a philosophy of bettering the conditions of humanity, a conventional interpretation born of liberalism. This is often couched broadly, which contributes to the confusion over definitions—with some concentrating on providing basic material needs, others cast it as more ambitiously embracing the liberal agenda to include a wide range of rights. Considering changes in humanitarian ethics leads to a stalemate of sorts; the debate remains between counter-revolutionary minimalists (who emphasize survival of afflicted populations, the proverbial "bed for the night") and revolutionary maximalists (who endeavor to integrate the entirety of human rights into the DNA of humanitarianism, as long as it "does no harm").

A more practical and ethical distinction situates understanding the moral evolution of ethics by scrutinizing institutions of the international humanitarian system, which takes an avowedly more political angle. Humanitarianism, like virtually every other worldwide social phenomenon, is political—always has been, always will be. The question, however, concerns the character of its politics and role in organizational ethics. This preoccupation with power derives from the realist perspective and considers change from the point of view of the distribution of power, highlighting great powers in particular. The inception of the international humanitarian system reflected such politics in the 1860s, which carved a niche for the ethics of care in tending to wounded soldiers and providing some protection for those captured. The devastation of wars, especially in the two world wars, became so widespread that politics formally expanded to encompass civilians as a focal point for assistance and protection. The ethics of humanitarianism during the Cold War reflected the East-West rivalry, with both sides wanting to capitalize on the legitimacy of the idea of aiding the vulnerable, if not outright coming to their rescue.

In the post–Cold War era, when the great powers concurred on the deployment of resources, usually to instill stability without having to devote military assets, the ethics of humanitarianism were altered to enable aid, sometimes using force to achieve that goal. After 9/11, despite a brief honeymoon between the great powers as they saw common cause in the GWOT, unity was shattered by the 2003 intervention in Iraq, and ever since international politics has been more contentious among the great powers. The selective application of R2P is telltale—in 2011, why Libya and why not Syria? The whims of great powers continue to figure prominently in realizing humanitarian ethics, and to that extent, there is more continuity than change.

Beyond philosophy and great powers, humanitarian ethics should also be viewed in terms of cultural proprietorship. While the international humanitarian system was established in the West and at the behest of Western powers, voices from the Global South often are adamant in recalling that many of the values of humanitarianism are not uniquely Western. Post-colonial theory articulates the inherent biases in portrayals and practices of international humanitarian agencies, so that non-Western organizations must adopt the discourse and practices of the West to be recognized as "humanitarian."[8] The increase in local and international NGOs in the Global South with a growing reach and especially in the emerging powers underscores that contestation over humanitarian ethics is not simply a matter of theatrical debates and symbolic gestures, but materially, the Global South is increasingly positioned to contribute to the determination of humanitarian ethics. As not only hosts of the vast majority of crises and the first line of defense for refugees but also as the location for new donors, the Global South's views are now an essential part of conversations about refugee rights, distributive principles in relief operations, and the use of force to protect vulnerable populations. While a brewing shift in power relations within the international humanitarian system is on the horizon, decisive change has not yet occurred; the West's voice still dominates debates.

Space and Security

In operationalizing the ethic of care in war zones, the means of delivery necessarily raises the issue of insecurity. Whether it is the liberal vision of bringing human rights or the realist one of protecting interests, the post–Cold War era has witnessed more deployment of military force to achieve humanitarian goals—from securing space in which aid is distributed to halting mass atrocities and tackling their root causes, including regime change. Traditionally, humanitarian space was predicated on state compliance, and as long as they were the principals in war zones, humanitarians were protected. That is, various UN logos and especially the ICRC's emblems were recognized and respected.[9] The "new wars" of the 1990s and the post-9/11 conflicts associated with violent extremism, however, often have belligerents who neither follow IHL nor consent to humanitarian operations. Asymmetrical warfare that targets civilians and aid workers, in addition to co-optation of humanitarian agencies by operating in the context of counterinsurgency or counterterrorism, can constrict or warp humanitarian space.[10]

In fact, in many cases, targeting aid workers is a means for belligerents to send a political message. Table 11.7 shows distressingly large numbers of aid workers harmed in humanitarian crises over the past decade and half. Heightened danger is evident and may impede recruitment and deployment. Simultaneously, within areas riddled with disorder and insecurity, corruption and criminal behavior add extortion and predation to the list of existential threats habitually faced by aid workers. The most recent attempt to address this problem was the 2016 Security Council resolution 2286, which calls for greater accountability for attacks on aid workers. The agreement about the significance of the problem, however, is not matched by agreement about how to move forward and actually guarantee the security of aid personnel.

Insecurity has forced agencies to confront seemingly impossible options: to stay and accept the dangers, leave, or devise new methods for protecting personnel. The first option of business-as-usual is not viable because emblems and logos no longer provide an effective means of protection despite the fervent hopes of traditionalists. The second option, withdrawal, is also problematic. Ethically, aid agencies are reticent to

Table 11.7.   Aid Workers Victimized, 2000–2016

2000	91
2001	90
2002	85
2003	143
2004	125
2005	172
2006	240
2007	220
2008	278
2009	296
2010	254
2011	309
2012	277
2013	475
2014	329
2015	287
2016	199

Source: The Aid Worker Security Database, accessed January 2, 2017, https://aidworker security.org.

turn away from crises; how is it possible to help without being present? Also, donors are far less likely to fund an agency that is not visible, which provides a significant incentive to stay the course, especially in light of heightened competition for funding.

The third option of new modalities of aid delivery is where there has been considerable change; it has been readily pursued by the revolutionary-minded. Two new practices have been instituted, sometimes simultaneously. The first involves a "bunkerization" or "hardening" of potential targets as well as lowering their profile to make them more elusive. This may involve increasing the presence and force capabilities of guards (including hiring private security capabilities), adding fortifications to agency compounds, and using unmarked vehicles for aid deliveries. A 2014 MSF report examined the hazards of "bunkerization" and noted how it fostered a sense of distance from the local population.[11]

The second entails "localization" whereby international aid workers are removed and local aid workers play larger roles in order to promote and substantiate the perception of assistance as being locally sourced, or at least administered, which is presumed to convey robust local support. In addition, "remote management" decreases the exposure of expatriates.[12] Although such changes may have possible upsides, the downside is that they may be part of an incremental strategy of disengagement or ultimately make it easier.

However, both bunkerization and localization are myopic. While they may decrease casualties among aid workers, they do not fundamentally change the local security environment; the vulnerable remain vulnerable. Furthermore, these tactics displace the threats and dangers from expatriate to local personnel. The ultimate impact is to foster a cultural distinction between aid workers; as post-colonial theory would underscore, non-Western actors pay the price while Western aid workers reap the benefits. Therefore, the major change is an increase in threat levels, whether politically or economically motivated; both terrorists and criminals seem to thrive on the presence of aid operations. However, more than the threats themselves, the perception of dangers has grown and alters security practices and the distribution of casualties.

Economics and Markets

Ethics inspire, security enables, but money realizes aid operations; here humanitarianism has been transformed over the past three decades or so. The development of new donors and agencies along with new organizational philosophies has altered the landscape. The spread of neoliberalism throughout the 1980s and 1990s encouraged the germination of a marketplace of ideas in humanitarianism (i.e., agencies pursued their own interpretations of ethics and tactics in defending their programming to donors). As such, agencies were "marketized," and liberal political economic prescriptions led them to develop their respective niches as aid providers. They embraced business language and practices that potentially revolutionize the sector. "Recipients" became "consumers," "branding" became ubiquitous, and concerns over market share propelled programming and promotion.

In addition to the marketization of the sector, there was also the "commodification" of humanitarianism more broadly. The focus on cost-effectiveness rather than on values or character led to for-profit service providers—from logistics to security. In the neoliberal perspective, aid resembles other goods or services and can most efficiently be allocated through market mechanisms. Although the ICRC, the UN, and NGOs remain the largest channels for humanitarian assistance, business has made significant inroads. In this way both the neoliberals and Marxists agree that the commodification of humanitarian aid as a service and the marketization of agencies constitute a radical change, although they obviously disagree on its merits. The former contend that a more streamlined and productive humanitarianism has resulted. By contrast, the latter hold a dim view of such developments and attempt to counter such a dramatic change by pointing to economic competition's detrimental impact on decision making, which compels abandoning "unprofitable" emergencies (those where there is no "market" for addressing a specific crisis) or risk losing market share or even bankruptcy as donors look elsewhere. Moreover, Marxists cynically view economic opportunism as riding on the coattails of disasters.

Perceptions and Relationships

Ethics, security, and economics are the superstructure of humanitarianism. But they do not constitute its essence; the sine qua non of humanitarianism is relationships among people. How do they treat one another? Besides rhetorical posturing and interests, do they manifestly value one another? By measuring the quality of interactions with an eye toward the protection and promotion of humanity and dignified lives, how can the meaning of humanitarianism and questions of changes best be understood?

The first true revolution in humanitarian affairs was institutionalization, the very creation of a formal system of organizations to save people. Although the sentiment of helping the less fortunate is a staple of many cultural traditions, it was initially authorized as an official international collaborative effort by Western states. The establishment in 1864 of the first agency, what would become the ICRC, was pivotal. Liberal traditions of mutual respect for the freedom of individuals, in this case by giving assistance through cooperative methods to those in emergencies, led to the development of the international humanitarian system, both laws and institutions. Beyond the generalities of liberal principles, that an idea, especially one predicated on normative values such as justice and mercy, could become embedded into sociopolitical life (i.e., recognized by states) attests to a realignment of power—it bespeaks the salience of constructivist interpretations that emphasize how beliefs can be translated into behaviors that reshape material realities. The Geneva Conventions, beginning in the late nineteenth century, are a social product that has fundamentally altered how militaries and governments operate. Thus, the founding of the international humanitarian system is a heightened acknowledgement of the value of human life, is evocative of normative power, and is indicative of changed relationships among people.

The second historic change in relationships central to humanitarianism was the expansion in categories of victims and recipients. At the outset, the official domain of humanitarian agencies was tending to soldiers, but not long thereafter it incorporated aid to POWs. Following World War II, the Geneva Conventions expanded to include civilians caught in conflicts. Additionally, the initial postwar mandate for the refugee regime was quickly extended to forcibly displaced populations worldwide, not just those uprooted by WWII. Lastly, the specific refinement of categories of aid recipients that recognizes their individualized needs, such as child soldiers or victims of sexual violence in war, is another marker of a radically changed humanitarianism. The possible expansion to cover refugees and IDPs displaced by climate change demonstrates the value of feminist and post-colonial critiques in problematizing why some emergencies are recognized but others are not. Their logic is that privileging classes of victims and marginalizing others—even going so far as not to identify them as such—is symptomatic of a politically motivated bias.

Creating more capable organizations and expanding their coverage have advanced the humanitarian cause, but amidst the preponderant issue of juxtaposing lofty promises and bull-headed practices. Critical humanitarianism illuminates by asking observers to bear in mind the integral quality of humanitarianism as valuing people and scrutinizing the actual relationships that emanate from the international system. From this perspective, three sets of relationships are crucial to understanding revolutionary change.

The first can be termed "structural" and reflects the conditions under which humanitarians operate. The external relations of aid agencies—with donors, states, multinational corporations, and gatekeeping armed nonstate actors—influence funding, logistics, access, and protection. Prototypical of the challenge of working with belligerents is defining humanitarian space. In Syria, MSF provided GPS coordinates of its hospitals, thinking that this procedure would shield them, but paradoxically it may have made targeting them all the easier. The main challenge is the instrumentalization of humanitarianism by which external actors use agencies as tools not necessarily to provide relief and protection but rather to pursue their own interests. Such external actors may seek to manage populations or acquire knowledge to better manage them, which can turn humanitarians into agents of surveillance who then contribute to an unjust world order. This interpretation is commonplace among realists, but the critical humanitarian view emphasizes how this prospect undermines why belligerents and recipients may be wary of manipulation.

A second set of relationships is "sectoral," or interactions among aid agencies. The problems of coordination in the context of competition over resources and differences in interpretations of ethics undermine the coherence of responses; they also have a deleterious effect on how agencies are viewed. This reality is reinforced, and sometimes exacerbated, by a divide between aid agencies and personnel from the North versus those from the Global South.[13] Agencies based in the latter receive far less funding. Moreover, the modification in security tactics that removes expatriates (primarily Westerners) from field work and shifts the onus to locals reveals a stratification that does not reflect the reputation of an agency or its budget but rather accentuates the nationality and cultural affiliation of respective aid workers. This problem can also be seen in knowledge production; a huge proportion of the scholarship and policy research on humanitarianism is conducted by Westerners. This differentiation of aid workers and the dominant decibel levels of Western researchers—what followers of Edward Said might dub a humanitarian "Orientalism"—further erodes the soul of humanitarianism.

The third set of relations is of the greatest significance and labeled "seminal"—the individual experiences of aid workers and recipients. In many ways, everything else—legal precedents and wrangling, behind-the-scenes dealings, bureaucratic bargaining, organizational collaborations, and media spotlights—is tangential to the direct interface. The quality of interactions between providers and beneficiaries is the fulcrum of the relationship. If we somehow disaggregate and step away from the "external" and the "sectoral" relationships and their impact on the "seminal," we can get to the heart of the problem, what anthropologists call "fetishism." Beyond the mad dash for funding and trepidation toward risky environments, aid workers can undermine their relationships with recipients by placing their own routines and public images above the requirements for succor and acknowledgement of local worth. In the event that aid personnel are disrespectful of local customs or express a sense of self-congratulation, humanitarianism can resemble voyeuristic tourism.

The discourses and practices of aid workers matter to the dignity of those afflicted by disasters. A narrative that spotlights the role of humanitarians or indelibly brands affected populations as "victims"—however helpful to elicit greater funds—is demeaning and undignified; moreover, it deprives individuals of their voices. However unintentional or unanticipated, such vocabulary nevertheless adds to a power imbalance and aggravates victimization. This supreme tension is well characterized by Tony Vaux's description of an aid worker as "the selfish altruist," someone who is psychologically secure in aiding others.[14] To Vaux and others, to give is to receive. The danger, however, is that the compunction to give, or to be seen as giving, can overshadow the act itself and thereby poison relationships. In other words, the danger is that the act of giving is celebrated, but the situation itself is disempowering.[15] Stated another way, the vulnerable do not want aid as much as they want a change in the conditions that make them dependent on aid. The principle of "accountability" is representative of this top-down perspective—that is, the term usually refers to the needs of donors to evaluate how agencies perform, or for agencies to see how recipients utilize aid. Accountability, however, has not provided a check on agencies and donors by those in need. Furthermore, this self-centered focus on the aid provider is also apparent in security practices that insulate aid workers from attacks by having them stay in fortified compounds, but that also isolate them from the communities in which they work.[16] The result can be a lack of familiarity and connection that sows additional misunderstandings and mistrust.

Examples of significant pathologies and dysfunctions unfortunately abound: cultural contestation tearing the sector apart; mission creep; the defense of principles as ends in themselves; one-size-fits-all solutions; and echo chambers immune to outside criticism and inputs. In the 1990s, the Iraqi sanctions regime that gave humanitarian aid but in effect required recipients to pay for it themselves through revenue gained by selling their natural resources (oil); Rwandan refugee camps that served as bases for those who committed genocide and sought to continue the war; and the "well-fed dead" in the Balkans who showed the inadequacies of relief aid without effective protection. Syria is another case of perverse humanitarian politics. The continual speeches and fanfare surrounding events since 2011 are illustrative: the ongoing European refugee crisis and electoral blowback, the World Humanitarian Summit in Istanbul in May 2016, and the UN Summit on Refugees and Migrants the following September. Donors, refugee-transit states, and refugee-hosting states all made pledges accompanied by applause worldwide. Yet those in the crises were not only absent from policy deliberations, they were also objectified and deprived of agency by being portrayed as forever helpless and needy. In brief, the displaced have been displaced from the conversation on the displaced. Critical humanitarianism, in contrast, insists on making how vulnerable populations feel about responses and responders *the* baseline metric. It is one thing to physically save people from massacres and famines; but it is another to ensure that the process grants them respect and saves them psychologically and socially. Critical humanitarianism views the revolution in humanitarian affairs as coming with a price, ultimately one that on many occasions has alienated aid workers from recipients.

Lessons from Loss or Lessons Lost?

The loss of lives, resources, and reputations over the course of humanitarian operations, adjudications, and performance assessments often has spurred efforts to learn lessons as well as augment their in-house data-gathering and interpretation. While efforts at learning have become more customary, has the substance of lessons been learned or lost? We conclude by distilling knowledge produced and dissecting knowledge-production proficiencies by practitioners and by scholars, accompanied by diagnoses and prescriptions for what ails aid agencies and their personnel.

Humanitarian Wisdom and Intelligence

The history of humanitarianism is filled with successes of saving vulnerable populations, but it has also had its share of failures—inefficiencies, corruption, manipulation, turf wars, inequalities, abandonments, attacks on aid workers, and unjust outcomes. Since the debacles of the 1990s prompted serious reevaluations of principles and practices, there have been numerous attempts to tease out lessons. Current conventional thinking denotes the three quintessential lessons discovered over the past thirty years:

- *"Humanity" remains the bedrock principle of humanitarian action*: The protection of human lives and dignity cannot be compromised, but there is flexibility regarding such other traditional principles as neutrality, impartiality, and independence. Objectification of people is inherently antagonizing.
- *Competition undermines coherence*: While aid agencies frequently have reasons to operate independently—for instance, reflecting differences in interpretations of ethics, or desires to project autonomy and profile—the result can be a disconnected and deficient humanitarian footprint that ultimately represents less than the sum of the parts. This generalization also rings true for courts, tribunals, and truth-and-reconciliation commissions.
- *Perceptions are performance*: Regardless of actual behavior, images are decisive. The views not only of vulnerable populations but also of belligerents, donors, and publics are central to realizing humanitarianism. Poor perceptions or publicity of the sector impose limits. When the value of humanitarianism is seen as low, skewed, or not cost effective, budgets dry up and consent is withdrawn.[12]

These lessons, however, are fundamentally contextual; they are the product of a specific historical experience, and translating them for programming in other emergencies can be problematic. Cookie-cutter lessons are clearly inappropriate and even dangerous. Local realities must be appreciated and reflected, and policies subsequently customized and refined. Failures in programming—by individuals, organizations, or the system as a whole—often reflect a dearth of local knowledge, intelligence, and analytical capabilities.

Misunderstanding the operational environment, the donor marketplace, and structural conditions is debilitating. Already a decade ago, we characterized the "fog of humanitarianism"—noting its similarity to the "fog of war" that breeds uncertainty and confusion among soldiers in battle—and identified six obstacles that impede the development of adequate information and analytical tools within aid agencies. We believe that humanitarian wisdom resides in recognizing the following challenges:

- *Organizational inertia*: Organizations thrive on routine and many actors have little or no interest in changing existing practices. Academic research is often seen as disconnected from on-the-ground reality. Humanitarian culture has often come to mean a categorical view that anyone suffering in an emergency anywhere is a worthy potential recipient, and nothing more needs to be known. This tenet may be compounded by a lack of feedback from failure to gather appropriate data on operational settings or recipient views.
- *Poor information management and dissemination*: Organizations may not possess a mechanism capable of collecting data, or processing and sharing it, or disseminating targeted information from partners.
- *Limited human resources and attrition*: Organizations often have too few staff to dedicate to analytical tasks, and their boards may look upon such "research" as frivolous. But quality data collection and analysis requires trained professionals, and there may be too few with requisite skills on the payroll within the organization. Additionally, those who gain experience in conducting this type of work may move on—burnout rates particularly in field postings are high. Organizations have little experience in recruiting and retaining such analysts.
- *Costs*: To establish and maintain a humanitarian intelligence capacity can be seen as too expensive by overseers or by donors. Such a "luxury" can appear as undermining the premise of putting people first. Ironically, many of the same donors demand information to hold agencies accountable. Further, data collection can be treacherous, especially in war zones, and researchers may pay with their lives.
- *Medical over political triage*: The standard operating procedures within aid agencies foster an all-hands-on-deck culture—act now, ask questions later. They are functionally geared to react to emergencies more than analyze the political context; the pace and timetable of research does not fit the temperament of practitioners.
- *Image*: Humanitarian intelligence, including performance reviews, may generate unseemly findings, which can act as a disincentive or exacerbate public relations problems with parliaments or the public. A typical reaction is to refrain from looking for failures—or worse, hiding them—even though they often hold key insights. The truth hurts psychologically, but it can also hurt financially or worse if it provokes outrage that fuels violent attacks.[18]

However, there have been notable advances in learning lessons, which often have highlighted the need for greater situational awareness (including early warning) and led to developing a capacity for humanitarian intelligence. A path-breaking move in this regard was the Joint Evaluation of Emergency Assistance to Rwanda that assessed responses to the 1994 genocide. Within a few years other such efforts at periodic organizational reviews began, such as the IFRC's Sphere Project and MSF's *Avenir*. In recent years, humanitarian intelligence capacities have received much greater attention and resources. A pioneer in this regard has been the hub of agencies participating in the Active Leaning Network for Accountability and Performance in the Humanitarian Action (ALNAP), which has partnered with the Sphere Project along with the Humanitarian Accountability Partnership International, People on War, and others. Following in these footsteps, there have been initiatives to promote humanitarian innovation:[19] MSF, Mercy Corps, Oxfam, CARE, and the ICRC have developed analytical capacities.

Within the UN, OCHA, UNICEF, and WFP have established policy review mechanisms and branches for cultivating creativity, such as ReliefWeb Labs and Innovation Labs. The Good Humanitarian Donorship (GHD) principles, initially endorsed by the EU and seventeen other donors in 2003, underline the importance of coherence and effectiveness of humanitarian action, and in particular donor and not just recipient accountability. As a follow-up in 2007, the Humanitarian Response Index (HRI) was begun in order to promote the GHD principles and practice—and thereby contribute to greater transparency, accountability, and impact. The HRI is an independent mechanism to measure and publicize the individual performance and commitment by government donors. The private sector has also participated, with companies such as DHL Logistics partnering with OCHA, and private foundations, such as the Gates Foundation helping to sponsor research about how to improve operations. Increasingly, scholars and think tanks also conduct research in this area, exemplified by the Overseas Development Institute and the Centre for Humanitarian Dialogue. And to bring different actors and elements together, there are also open platforms for sharing information, such as Humanitarian Data Exchange.[20] Lastly, included in the Grand Bargain of the 2016 World Humanitarian Summit was a pledge "to publish timely, transparent, harmonized and open high-quality data on humanitarian funding by mid-2018" and to incorporate "gender and age markers" to more clearly identify recipients and needs as well as a "localization marker" to indicate through which channels aid is distributed.[21]

Despite progress, three challenges nevertheless remain. First, the knowledge produced must be problematized and expanded. Quantitative data is a form of abstraction that does not, and cannot, reflect subtler yet meaningful qualities crucial to humanitarianism. There will always be debates over the best metrics for measuring needs and performance, but transparency in methodology, and the explication of its assumptions and limits, can sharpen their utility and ease controversies. Second, intelligence must be humanitarian in content as well as form—that is, the methods for gathering and using it must also be thoughtful, sensitive, and considerate. Organizations should not give access to their information to those who apply it for anything but humanitarian purposes. This admittedly fine line necessitates that agencies be wary of being transformed into surveillance tools. Part of the task here is to grasp the politics of knowledge and knowledge production so that the humanitarian narrative cannot be appropriated for other purposes.

Third, and perhaps most importantly, the actual durability of so many initiatives is in question if such efforts remain on the periphery rather than at the center of priorities for individual organizations. In this regard, an indication of the need for changing the dominant culture was the Emergency Capacity Building Project (ECB), a decade-long effort financed mainly by the Bill and Melinda Gates Foundation to which we referred briefly above.[22] In 2004 the emergency directors from seven of the largest NGOs—CARE International, Catholic Relief Services, International Rescue Committee, Mercy Corps, Oxfam GB, Save the Children, and World Vision International—met to discuss persistent problems. An initial ECB report identified key gaps constraining the ability to provide timely, effective, and quality responses. Between 2005 and 2013, some twenty publications resulted. However, learning requires not only diagnoses and prescriptions but also investments and implementation. Yet the dominant humanitarian culture resists cures for what ails the system. Frenzied fervor to react to crises is a laudable hallmark of commitment, but such relentlessness can be reckless when it hinders organizations from devoting energy and their own discretionary resources—not just those of the Gates Foundation—to understanding specific tactics and tailoring subsequent responses accordingly. Indeed, devoting precious core resources would be a concrete indicator of the seriousness of purpose about learning by management and staff.

In short, conventional wisdom is innately historically specific and requires updating. Ralph Waldo Emerson's observation that "Each age . . . must write its own books; or rather, each generation for the next succeeding" accurately conveys that adaptation is vital to relevance.[23] The right lesson must be extracted and transmitted, otherwise it is not learned, but lost. The knowledge problem in the "fog" is inextricably linked to the performance problem, a "quicksand of humanitarianism": the more an organization struggles to act on its impulses, the more deeply it may find itself mired in troubling political, economic, and social quandaries partially of its own making. For humanitarianism to remain possible, it must be appropriate; the development of humanitarian intelligence is critical.

Humanitarians Anonymous

Our research about humanitarianism, war, and politics included analyzing the challenges of continuity and change. A profound sense of anxiety and anguish exists among practitioners who ask, "What can be done?" Their concerns are palpable for the fate and future of humanitarianism. Despair is natural and reasonable—after all, space is shrinking, access is imperiled, atrocities are unfettered. Meanwhile, gross characterizations seek to denigrate or manipulate the sector from outside, and more painful still, condemnation comes from inside by those who are rightly irate or disappointed at disorganization, dysfunction, and estrangement. The 1990s judgment from the then UN high commissioner for refugees, Sadako Ogata, that "there are no humanitarian solutions to humanitarian problems"[24] provides the backdrop here for our final comments about the flagging morale and self-doubt that question the merits of humanitarianism at the end of the twenty-first century's second decade. The resolve to right wrongs with mercy and justice endures, but it often is eclipsed by the agonizing grief over what humanitarianism has wrought, and how it is perceived. Has the solution become part of the problem?

As this book goes to press, we note with deep concern the toxic shifts in the domestic politics of many of the countries that have traditionally supported humanitarian action. The ascendance of nativist and xenophobic political parties adds to the angst with the prospect of cutting humanitarian aid or attaching strings to it. New leadership proudly and publicly shuns IHL in the pursuit of enemies whom they dub "subhuman."

It is therefore not surprising that the present mindset of humanitarians evinces survival. True believers see contemporary challenges as par for the course and greet ongoing changes with a shrug. More alarmed voices cry out, but even they basically continue to operate within long-established assumptions and arrangements. Given the flaws, fragmentation, and distortions in humanitarianism that are recognized by practitioners and pundits alike, to continue to champion traditional humanitarianism is puzzling. From a psychological point of view, a competent therapist would observe that defending an activity that is widely viewed as dysfunctional demands treatment.

Humanitarians need to think about how to reinvent their work and themselves. It is time for proponents of all stripes to join in common cause, to share their collective struggles, and to forge a new identity at the system, organization, and individual levels. The twelve steps of Alcoholics Anonymous (AA) can inspire a shorter program of introspection by the extended, dysfunctional humanitarian family. It is helpful to recall that AA's official mediation is the "Serenity Prayer" attributed to the US's most prominent twentieth-century theologian, Reinhold Niebuhr: "God, give us grace to accept with serenity the things that cannot be changed, courage to change the things that should be changed, and the wisdom to distinguish the one from the other."

Niebuhr's 1943 counsel that pragmatism is part of wisdom and that personal responsibility for action is essential is the basis of our proposed six steps for those in treatment, the distraught community within the sector who require "Humanitarians Anonymous":

1. *Admit a higher power*: Ethics can be powerful but are no match for politics. Opportunities to act are context specific, but every effort should be made to follow a common standard with the hope of re-configuring power.
2. *Take an inventory*: Agencies must know their capacities (resources and tools) and situate their comparative advantages. Aid organizations may seem weak relative to great powers, but in comparison to recipients they have tremendous leverage. Humanitarian power has an impact, for better and for worse.
3. *Acknowledge mistakes*: Agencies should call attention to their own poor performance not as a sign of weakness, but because contrition is a confidence-building measure.
4. *Make amends*: Accountability has been minimal. When mistakes or malfeasance occur, agencies should provide redress. Agencies cannot rectify past errors or damage, but intent and symbolism matter.
5. *Develop sensitivities*: The analytical capacities of agencies are woefully underdeveloped, not only for risk analysis but also for monitoring and evaluation. Greater investment is essential; humanitarians must understand the situation before they act on it.
6. *Express values*: With global communications, replete with Internet traffic and social media, the means of making (and remaking) the humanitarian narrative is readily at hand. The image and mantle of humanitarianism is the greatest asset of aid agencies, and they should not only practice what they preach, but preach what they practice.[25]

Recovery is never easy. The first thing to do is to admit the existence of the problem, and humanitarians long ago crossed that threshold. But so far they have been far more focused on coping with symptoms than on addressing the causes of problems or grappling with the despair within the sector. Acknowledging foibles and failures is the only way for humanitarians to once more begin the hard work of earning back trust and reclaiming their rightful role in saving both the lives and dignity of vulnerable populations. Self-awareness and candor are a prerequisite for respect. True humanitarians cannot define themselves as saviors but rather admit their own biases and vanity as linked to the act of aiding.

This recognition does not belittle their efforts, but it respects the desire of the assisted to know those who come to their rescue. Humanitarians cannot deny the politics of humanitarianism, but they can come to terms with it and engage in a conversation with those whose material and moral sustenance are the purpose of the enterprise.

The goal of humanitarianism is to save people. Yet before UN agencies and NGOs can effectively resume pursuing this vital and valiant objective, they must first save themselves by accepting that their staff are human and, in the process, rediscover their own humanity.

Notes

Introduction

1. *Global Humanitarian Assistance (GHA) 2016* (Somerset, UK: Development Initiatives, 2016), http://www.globalhumanitarianassistance.org/report/gha2016.

2. Thomas Aquinas, *Summa Theologica*, 2a2ae, Question 30, "Mercy."

3. Michel Foucault, *Security, Territory, Population: Lectures at the Collège de France 1977–1978* (New York: Palgrave, 2004).

4. Marcel Mauss, *The Gift: Forms and Functions of Exchange in Archaic Societies*, rev. ed. (1925; repr., London: Cohen & West Ltd, 1966); Edward P. Thompson, *Customs in Common* (New York: New Press, 1991); and James C. Scott, *The Moral Economy of the Peasant: Rebellion and Subsistence in Southeast Asia* (Princeton, N.J.: Princeton University Press, 1976).

5. Muriel Rukeyser, *The Speed of Darkness* (New York: Random House, 1968).

6. Aldous Huxley, "A Note on Dogma," *Proper Studies* (London: Chatto and Windus, 1927).

7. Thomas S. Kuhn, *The Structure of Scientific Revolutions*, 3rd ed. (Chicago: University of Chicago Press, 1996).

Chapter 1: Humanitarian Culture, Traditions, and Theories

1. Craig Calhoun, "The Imperative to Reduce Suffering: Charity, Progress, and Emergencies in the Field of Humanitarian Action," in *Humanitarianism in Question: Politics, Power, Ethics*, ed. Michael Barnett and Thomas G. Weiss (Ithaca, N.Y.: Cornell University Press, 2008), 73–97.

2. David Rieff, *A Bed for the Night: Humanitarianism in Crisis* (New York: Simon & Schuster, 2002), 57–89.

3. Walter Benjamin, *Theses on the Philosophy of History*, VII (1940; first published, in German, 1950, in English, 1955).

4. Michael Ignatieff, *Human Rights as Politics and Idolatry* (Princeton, N.J.: Princeton University Press, 2001); and *The Lesser Evil: Political Ethics in the Age of Terror* (Princeton, N.J.: Princeton University Press, 2004).

5. John Stuart Mill, *On Liberty*, ed. Elizabeth Rappaport (Indianapolis, Ind.: Hackett, 1978), chapter 1, para 10.

6. Hans Morgenthau, *Politics Among Nations: The Struggle for Power and Peace*, 5th ed. (New York: Knopf, 1978), 4–15; Dale C. Copeland, *The Origins of Major War* (Ithaca, N.Y.: Cornell University Press, 2000); John Mearsheimer, *The Tragedy of Great Power Politics* (New York: Norton, 2001).

7. Kenneth N. Waltz, *Man, the State, and War: A Theoretical Analysis* (New York: Columbia University Press, 1959), 198; and Joseph Grieco, *Cooperation among Nations* (Ithaca, N.Y.: Cornell University Press, 1990).

8. Robert Powell, "Absolute and Relative Gains in International Relations Theory," *American Political Science Review* 85, no. 4 (1991): 1303–20.

9. Robert O. Keohane and Joseph S. Nye, *Power and Interdependence: World Politics in Transition* (Boston: Little, Brown, 1977).

10. Critical theory derives from the Frankfurt School; see Max Horkheimer, *Critical Theory: Selected Essays* (New York: Continuum, 1982). It was rearticulated in IR theory initially by Robert W. Cox, "Social Forces, States and World Orders: Beyond International Relations Theory," *Millennium: Journal of International Studies* 10, no. 2 (1981): 126–55.

11. Martha Finnemore and Kathryn Sikkink, "International Norm Dynamics and Political Change," *International Organization* 52, no. 4 (1998): 887–917.

12. Max Weber, *Economy and Society: An Outline of Interpretive Sociology* (Berkeley: University of California Press, 1978), 212–301.

13. Michael Barnett and Martha Finnemore, *Rules for the World: International Organizations in Global Politics* (Ithaca, N.Y.: Cornell University Press, 2004), 16–44.

14. Ibid., 39.

15. Michael Barnett, *Empire of Humanity: A History of Humanitarianism* (Ithaca, N.Y.: Cornell University Press, 2011).

16. Karl Marx lumps "humanitarians" together with other "hole-and-corner reformers" as impediments to the prospect of revolution in Karl Marx and Frederick Engels, *The Communist Manifesto* (London: Verso, 2012), 70.

17. Thomas Haskell, "Capitalism and the Origins of the Humanitarian Sensibility, Part 1," *American Historical Review* 90, no. 2 (1985): 339–61; and "Capitalism and the Origins of the Humanitarian Sensibility, Part 2," *American Historical Review* 90, no. 3 (1985): 547–66.

18. Slavoj Žižek, "Against Human Rights," *New Left Review* 34 (July–August 2005): 115–31.

19. Naomi Klein, *The Shock Doctrine: The Rise of Disaster Capitalism* (New York: Metropolitan, 2007).

20. J. Ann Tickner, *Gender in International Relations: Feminist Perspectives on Achieving Global Security* (New York: Columbia University Press, 1992), 27–66; Cynthia Enloe, *Maneuvers: The International Politics of Militarizing Women's Lives* (Berkeley: University of California Press, 2000).

21. Jean Bethke Elshtain, *Women and War* (Chicago: University of Chicago Press, 1987). Also see Carol Cohn, "Women and Wars: Towards a Conceptual Framework," in *Women & Wars*, ed. Carol Cohn (Cambridge: Polity, 2012): 1–35, especially 4–5.

22. Helen M. Kinsella, "Securing the Civilian: Sex and Gender in the Laws of War," in *Power and Global Governance*, ed. Michael Barnett and Raymond Duvall (Cambridge: Cambridge University Press, 2004), 249–72.

23. Dyan Mazurana and Daniel Maxwell, *Sweden's Feminist Foreign Policy: Implications for Humanitarian Response* (Boston: World Peace Foundation and Feinstein International Center, 2016); and Dyan Mazurana and Keith Proctor, "Gender and Humanitarian Action," in *Handbook on Humanitarian Action*, ed. Roger MacGinty and Jenny H. Peterson (New York: Routledge, 2014), 49–61.

24. Jennifer Hyndman and Malathi de Alwis, "Towards a Feminist Analysis of Humanitarianism and Development in Sri Lanka," *Women's Studies Quarterly* 31, no. 3/4 (2003): 212–26, quote on 212.

25. R. Charli Carpenter, "'Women and Children First': Gender Norms and Humanitarian Evacuation in the Balkans 1991-5," *International Organization* 57, no. 3 (2003): 661–94.

26. Anne Orford, "Muscular Humanitarianism: Reading the Narratives of the New Interventionism," *European Journal of International Law* 10, no. 4 (1999): 679–711.

27. Michel Foucault, *The Chomsky-Foucault Debate on Human Nature* (New York: New Press, 2005), 41.

28. Carl Schmitt, *The Concept of The Political: Expanded Edition* (Chicago: University of Chicago Press, 2008).

29. Michel Foucault, *The History of Sexuality, Volume I: An Introduction* (1978), part 5, "Right of Death and Power over Life," 138. Judith Butler similarly locates this power of aid agencies as a type of sovereignty in *Precarious Lives* (New York: Verso, 2004), 56.

30. Julien Reid, "The Biopoliticization of Humanitarianism: From Saving Bare Life to Securing the Biohuman in Post-Interventionary Societies," *Journal of Intervention and Statebuilding* 4, no. 4 (2010): 391–411.

31. Barbara Harrell-Bond, "Can Humanitarian Work with Refugees Be Humane?" *Human Rights Quarterly* 24, no. 1 (2002): 51–85.

32. Michael N. Barnett, "International Paternalism and Humanitarian Governance," *Global Constitutionalism* 1, no. 3 (2012): 485–521.

33. Ilana Feldman and Miriam Ticktin note the tension between seeing aid recipients as both an "object of care and source of anxiety" in their chapter "Government and Humanity," in *In the Name of Humanity: The Government of Threat and Care*, ed. Ilana Feldman and Miriam Ticktin (Durham, N.C.: Duke University Press, 2011), 1–27.

34. R. D. Laing, *The Divided Self* (Harmondsworth, UK: Penguin, 1969), 39.

35. Anthony Giddens, *The Consequences of Modernity* (Palo Alto, Calif.: Stanford University Press, 1990), 92.

36. Bruno Latour, *Science in Action: How to Follow Scientists and Engineers Through Society* (Cambridge, Mass.: Harvard University Press, 1987).

37. Edward W. Said, *Orientalism* (New York: Vintage, 1979).

38. Giorgio Agamben, *Homo Sacer: Sovereign Power and Bare Life* (Stanford, Calif.: Stanford University Press, 1998), 145.

39. Didier Fassin, "Humanitarianism as a Politics of Life," *Public Culture* 19, no. 3 (2007): 499–520.

40. Quincy Wright, *A Study of War* (Chicago: University of Chicago Press, 1983), 17.

41. F. H. Colson, ed., *Cicero: Pro Milone* (52 BCE; London: Bristol Classical Press, 1991).

42. Thucydides, "Sixteenth Year of War: The Melian Debate," in *The Peloponnesian War* (London: Cassell, 1962), book V, chapter 7, 360.

43. Michael Walzer, *Just and Unjust Wars: A Moral Argument with Historical Illustrations*, 3rd ed. (New York: Basic, 2000), 3–33.

44. Afghanistan Islamic Emirate, *Rules and Regulations for Mujahidin*, http://www-tc.pbs.org/wgbh/pages/frontline/obamaswar/etc/mullahomar.pdf.

45. Theodor Meron, *War Crimes Law Comes of Age* (Oxford: Oxford University Press, 1998), 1–66; 122–30.

46. Shakespeare, *Henry V* (London: Signet, 1998).

47. Hugo Grotius, *De Jure Belli ac Pacis Libri Tres*, trans. F. W. Kelsey (Washington, D.C.: Carnegie Council, 1925).

48. Brian Orend, "Justice after War," *Ethics & International Affairs* 16, no. 1 (2002): 43–56; Mark J. Allman and Tobias Winright, *After the Smoke Clears: The Just War Tradition and Post War Justice* (Maryknoll, N.Y.: Orbis, 2010); Carsten Stahn, Jennifer S. Easterday, and Jens Iverson, eds., *Jus Post Bellum: Mapping the Normative Foundations* (Oxford: Oxford University Press, 2014).

Chapter 2: Humanitarian Genesis and Gravity

1. Emmerich de Vattel, *Le Droit des Gens (The Law of Nations)*, II: 1, 5.

2. Jean Jacques Rousseau, *The Social Contract* (1762; London: Penguin, 1968), 57.

3. Katherine Davies, *Continuity, Change and Contest: Meanings of "Humanitarian" from the "Religion of Humanity" to the Kosovo War*, Humanitarian Policy Group (hereafter HPG) Working Paper, August 2012.

4. For example, 1792 saw publication of William Carey's *Enquiry into the Obligation of Christian to Use Means for the Conversion of the Heathens*.

5. Hannah Arendt, *On Revolution* (London and New York: Penguin, 1990), 66.

6. Davies, *Continuity, Change and Contest*.

7. Henry S. Salt, *Humanitarianism: Its General Principles and Progress* (London: Humanitarian League, 1906).

8. Michael Barnett, *Empire of Humanity: A History of Humanitarianism* (Ithaca, N.Y.: Cornell University Press, 2011), 57–75.

9. Max Weber, "Politics as Vocation," in *Max Weber's Complete Writings on Academic and Political Vocations*, ed. John Dreimanis; trans. Gordon C. Wells (New York: Algora, 2008), 155–208.

10. Francis Lieber, *Instructions for the Government of Armies of the United States in the Field, General Order No. 100*, April 24, 1863.

11. Helmuth von Moltke, "Letter to Professor Bluntschli, December 11, 1880," *Letters to The Times upon War and Neutrality* (London, 1909), 24–29.

12. St. Petersburg Declaration (1868); First Hague Peace Conference (1899); Hague Convention (1904); Geneva Convention (1906); Second Hague Peace Conference (1907); 1907 Hague Convention Relative to the Opening of Hostilities (1907); 1907 Hague Convention (IV) Respecting the Laws and Customs of War on Land (1907); London Declaration (1909).

13. Caroline Moorehead, *Dunant's Dream: War, Switzerland, and the History of the Red Cross* (New York: Carroll & Graf, 1998).

14. Henry Dunant, *A Memory of Solferino* (Geneva: ICRC, 1986), 17.

15. John F. Hutchinson, *Champions of Charity: War and the Rise of the Red Cross* (Boulder, Colo.: Westview Press, 1997), 128, 255; and Lynn McDonald, ed., *Florence Nightingale on Wars and the War Office: Collected Works of Florence Nightingale*, vol. 15 (Waterloo, Ontario: Wilfrid Laurier University Press, 2011), 583–84, 730.

16. Angela Bennet, *The Geneva Convention: The Hidden Origins of the Red Cross* (Gloucestershire, UK: Sutton, 2005), quote on 28.

17. David P. Forsythe, *The Humanitarians: The International Committee of the Red Cross* (Cambridge: Cambridge University Press, 2005), 13–50.

18. Jean Pictet, *The Fundamental Principles of the Red Cross* (Geneva: ICRC, 1979).

19. Estimates vary, but baseline data come from William L. Hosch, ed., *World War I: People, Politics, and Power* (New York: Britannica Educational Publishing, 2010), 217–19; Peter Gatrell, "World Wars and Population Displacement in Europe in the 20th Century," *Contemporary European History* 16, no. 4 (2007): 418.

20. Manus I. Midlarsky, "The Armenians," in *The Killing Trap: Genocide in the Twentieth Century* (New York: Cambridge University Press, 2005), 212–19.

21. Norman M. Naimark, *Stalin's Genocides* (Princeton, N.J.: Princeton University Press, 2010), 70–79; and Lizzie Collingham, *The Taste of War: World War II and the Battle for Food* (New York: Penguin, 2012).

22. Geneva Protocol on Gas and Bacteriological Warfare (1925); General Treaty for Renunciation of War as an Instrument of National Policy (1928); Geneva Conventions (1929); London Treaty (1930); and London Procès-verbal (1936).

23. Estimates come from William L. Hosch, ed., *World War II: People, Politics, and Power* (New York: Britannica Educational Publishing, 2010), 246–47; Gatrell, "World Wars and Population Displacement," 419.

24. William Shawcross, *The Quality of Mercy: Cambodia, Holocaust, and Modern Conscience* (New York: Simon and Schuster, 1984), 48; and Barnett, *Empire of Humanity*, 136.

25. Dan Plesch and Thomas G. Weiss, eds., *Wartime Origins and the Future United Nations* (London: Routledge, 2015).

26. An exception is Jessica Reinisch, "'We Shall Rebuild a Powerful Nation': UNRRA, Internationalism and National Reconstruction in Poland," *Journal of Contemporary History* 43, no. 3 (2008): 371–404; "Internationalism in Relief: The Birth (and Death) of UNRRA," *Past and Present*, supplement 6 (2013): 258–89; and "'Auntie UNRRA' at the Crossroads," *Past and Present*, supplement 8 (2013): 70–97.

27. Robert H. Jackson, Opening Statement, Nuremberg Trials, November 21, 1945.

28. Thomas G. Weiss and Kurt Campbell, "Military Humanitarianism," *Survival* 33, no. 5 (1991): 451–65.

29. See Thomas G. Weiss, David P. Forsythe, Roger A. Coate, and Kelly-Kate Pease, *United Nations and Changing World Politics*, 8th ed. (Boulder, Colo.: Westview, 2017), chapter 3.

30. Michael Barnett and Martha Finnemore, *Rules for the World: International Organizations in Global Politics* (Ithaca, N.Y.: Cornell University Press, 2004), 73–120.

31. Jean S. Pictet, "The New Geneva Conventions for the Protection of War Victims," *American Journal of International Law* 45, no. 3 (1951): 462–75.

32. Barnett, *Empire of Humanity*, 144–46.

33. Claire Magone, Michael Neuman, and Frabrice Weissman, eds., *Humanitarian Negotiations Revealed: The MSF Experience* (New York: Columbia University Press, 2011).

34. Peter Redfield, "Doctors, Borders, and Life in Crisis," *Cultural Anthropology* 20, no. 3 (2005): 328–61.

35. Paul Berman, *Power and the Idealists* (Brooklyn: Soft Skull, 2005), 232.

36. Rony Brauman and Joelle Tanguy, *The Médecins Sans Frontières Experience* (Paris: MSF, 1998), 1–13.

37. Alex de Waal, *Famine Crimes: Politics & the Disaster Relief Industry in Africa* (Oxford: James Currey, 1997), 26–48.

38. Barnett, *Empire of Humanity*, 157.

39. Christophe Gillioz, "On ICRC: Engagement with Non-State Armed Groups: Recent Developments," *Humanitarian Policy and Conflict Research*, April 2, 2012.

40. Peter Redfield, "Humanitarianism," in *A Companion to Moral Anthropology*, ed. Didier Fassin (West Sussex, UK: Wiley, 2012), 455–56.

Chapter 3: New Wars and New Humanitarianisms in the 1990s

1. Frédéric Maurice, "Humanitarian Ambition," *International Review of the Red Cross* 289 (July–August 1992): 365.

2. Mats Berdal and David M. Malone, eds., *Greed and Grievance: Economic Agendas in Civil Wars* (Boulder, Colo.: Lynne Rienner, 2000); Mary Kaldor, *New and Old Wars: Organized Violence in a Global Era*, 3rd ed. (Cambridge: Polity, 2012).

3. Adam Roberts, "Lives and Statistics: Are 90% of War Victims Civilians?" *Survival* 52, no. 3 (2010): 115–36.

4. Peter J. Hoffman and Thomas G. Weiss, *Sword & Salve: Confronting New Wars and Humanitarian Crises* (Lanham, Md.: Rowman & Littlefield, 2006), 81–118.

5. Thomas G. Weiss, *Military-Civilian Interactions: Humanitarian Crises and the Responsibility to Protect*, 2nd ed. (Boulder, Colo.: Rowman & Littlefield, 2005), 39–53.

6. The Report to the Secretary-General on Humanitarian Needs in Kuwait and Iraq in the Immediate Post-Crisis Environment by a Mission to the Area, UNSCOR, S/22366 (1991), p. 5, noted the impact of this bombing on Iraq "relegated to pre-industrial age."

7. *Report of the Secretary-General on the Work of the Organization*, A/46/1, 1991.

8. Abbas Alnasrawi, "Iraq: Economic Sanctions and Consequences, 1990–2000," *Third World Quarterly* 22, no. 2 (2001): 205–18; David Cortright and George A. Lopez, "The Iraq Quagmire," in *Sanctions and the Search for Security: Challenges to UN Action* (Boulder, Colo.: Lynne Rienner, 2002), 21–46.

9. Jeffrey A. Meyer and Cark G. Califano, *Good Intentions Corrupted: The Oil-for-Food Scandal and the Threat to the U.N.* (New York: Public Affairs, 2006).

10. Thomas G. Weiss, David Cortright, George A. Lopez, and Larry Minear, eds., *Political Gain and Civilian Pain: Humanitarian Impacts of Economic Sanctions* (Lanham, Md.: Rowman & Littlefield, 1997).

11. Ken Menkhaus, "Stabilisation and Humanitarian Access in a Collapsed State: The Somali Case," *Disasters* 34, no. 3 (2010): 322.

12. Alex de Waal, *Famine Crimes: Politics & the Disaster Relief Industry in Africa* (Oxford: James Currey, 1997), 159–78.

13. Weiss, *Military-Civilian Interactions*, 55–70.

14. James Orbinski, *An Imperfect Offering: Humanitarian Action for the Twenty-First Century* (New York: Walker & Company, 2009), 77.

15. Mohamed Sahnoun, "Mixed Intervention in Somalia and the Great Lakes: Culture, Neutrality, and the Military," in *Hard Choices: Moral Dilemmas in Humanitarian Intervention*, ed. Jonathan Moore (Boulder, Colo.: Rowman & Littlefield, 1999), 87–98.

16. Menkhaus, "Stabilisation and Humanitarian Access."

17. OCHA, *Humanitarian Needs Overview: Somalia* (November 2016).

18. Some estimates place this as high as 95 percent: *Report of the Secretary-General Pursuant to Security Council Resolution 1846 (2008)*, November 13, 2009, para. 74.

19. Edith R. Sanders, "The Hamitic Hypothesis; Its Origin and Functions in Time Perspective," *Journal of African History* 10, no. 4 (1969): 521–32.

20. Peter Uvin, *Aiding Violence: The Development Enterprise in Rwanda* (West Hartford, Conn.: Kumarian, 1998).

21. J. H. Bradol and J. Mamou, "La commémoration amnésique des humanitaires," *Humanitaire* 10 (2004): 12–28, quote on 14.

22. Weiss, *Military-Civilian Interactions*, 95–111; Michael Barnett, "The United Nations Security Council, Indifference and Genocide in Rwanda," *Cultural Anthropology* 12, no. 4 (1997): 551–78.

23. Jean-François Alesandrini, Director of Communication Department, MSF France, May 1994, in MSF Speaks Out, *Genocide of Rwandan Tutsi 1994* (Paris: MSF, April 2014), 36.

24. Quote cited in Fiona Terry, *Condemned to Repeat? The Paradox of Humanitarian Action* (Ithaca, N.Y.: Cornell University Press, 2002), 197.

25. This figure is calculated by adding the most recent budgetary data to an estimate of the total through 2013. Daniel McLaughlin, *International Criminal Tribunals: A Visual Overview* (New York: Leitner Center for International Law and Justice, 2015), 27.

26. Peter Uvin and Charles Mironko, "Western and Local Approaches to Justice in Rwanda," *Global Governance* 9, no. 2 (2003): 219–31.

27. UN Security Council, *Final Report of the Panel of Experts on the Illegal Exploitation of Natural Resources and Other Forms of Wealth of the Democratic Republic of the Congo*, S/2003/1027, October 23, 2003.

28. Taylor B. Seybolt, Jay D. Aronson, and Baruch Fischhoff, eds., *Counting Civilian Casualties: An Introduction to Recording and Estimating Nonmilitary Deaths in Conflict* (Oxford: Oxford University Press, 2013).

29. UNICEF, *Humanitarian Action for Children*, 2016.

30. Weiss, *Military-Civilian Interactions*, 71–93.

31. Peter Andreas, *Blue Helmets and Black Markets: The Business of Survival in the Siege of Sarajevo* (Ithaca, N.Y.: Cornell University Press, 2008), xi.

32. Sadako Ogata, *The Turbulent Decade: Confronting the Refugee Crises of the 1990s* (New York: Norton, 2005), 83.

33. Larry Minear et al., "Humanitarian Action in the Former Yugoslavia: The U.N.'s Role, 1991–1993," Watson Institute Occasional Paper Series #18 (1994), 83–103.

34. Ogata, *Turbulent Decade*, 55.

35. Weiss, *Military-Civilian Interactions*, 129–54.

36. Adam Roberts, "NATO's Humanitarian War over Kosovo," *Survival* 41, no. 3 (1999): 102–23; and David Rieff, "Kosovo's Humanitarian Circus," *World Policy Journal* 17, no. 3 (2000): 25–32.

37. Independent International Commission on Kosovo, *The Kosovo Report: Conflict, International Response, Lessons Learned* (Oxford: Oxford University Press, 2000).

38. Kofi A. Annan, "Secretary-General's Speech to the 54th Session of the General Assembly," September 20, 1999.

39. NATO press conference with NATO Secretary-General Javier Solana and British Prime Minister Tony Blair, April 20, 1999.

40. This estimate adds the 2014–2015 budget to through 2013 from McLaughlin, *International Criminal Tribunals*, 7.

41. Thomas G. Weiss, "Ethical Quandaries in War Zones, When Mass Atrocity Prevention Fails," *Global Society* 7, no. 2 (2016): 1–12.

42. David Rieff, "Humanitarianism in Crisis," *Foreign Affairs* 81, no. 6 (2002): 111–21.

43. David P. Forsythe, *The Humanitarians: The International Committee of the Red Cross* (Cambridge: Cambridge University Press, 2005); Michael Barnett, *Empire of Humanity: A History of Humanitarianism* (Ithaca, N.Y.: Cornell University Press, 2011); and Michael J. Barnett and Janice Stein, eds., *Sacred Aid: Faith and Humanitarianism* (Oxford: Oxford University Press, 2012).

44. Steven Pinker, *The Better Angels of Our Nature: Why Violence Has Declined* (New York: Viking, 2011).

45. Michael Barnett and Thomas G. Weiss, *Humanitarianism Contested: Where Angels Fear to Tread* (London: Routledge, 2011).

46. International Committee of the Red Cross, "Principles and Response in International Humanitarian Assistance (C. The Use of Armed Escorts)," presented at the 26th International Conference of the Red Cross and Red Crescent, September 15, 1995.

47. Christine Bourloyannis, "The Security Council of the United Nations and the Implementation of International Humanitarian Law," *Denver Journal of International Law and Policy* 20, no. 3 (1993): 43.

48. Mark Cutts, "The Humanitarian Operation in Bosnia and Herzegovina, 1992–1995: Dilemmas in Negotiating Humanitarian Access," in *New Issues in Refugee Research—Working Paper No. 8* (Geneva: UNHCR, 1999), 14–16.

49. *Report of the Panel on UN Peace Operations* (2000) assessed shortcomings of previous peacekeeping operations and made recommendations regarding resources and more credible and achievable mandates.

50. Nicholas J. Wheeler, *Saving Strangers: Humanitarian Intervention in International Society* (Oxford: Oxford University Press, 2000), 282.

51. Roger Cohen, "U.N. General Opposes More Bosnia Force," *New York Times,* September 22, 1994.

52. Antonio Donini et al., *Humanitarian Agenda 2015: Final Report, The State Humanitarian Enterprise* (Somerville, Mass.: Feinstein Center, 2008), 4.

53. Weiss, *Military-Civilian Interactions;* and Michael Barnett and Thomas G. Weiss, eds., *Humanitarianism in Question: Politics, Power, Ethics* (Ithaca, N.Y.: Cornell University Press, 2008).

54. Cutts, "The Humanitarian Operation in Bosnia and Herzegovina, 1992–1995," 7; and Astri Suhrke, Michael Barutciski, Rick Garlock, and Peta Sandison, *The Kosovo Refugee Crisis: An Independent Evaluation of UNHCR's Emergency Preparedness and Response* (Geneva: UNHCR, February 2000), 65.

55. David Shearer, "Aiding or Abetting? Humanitarian Aid and Its Economic Role in Civil War," in *Greed and Grievance,* ed. Berdal and Malone, 189–204.

56. Mary B. Anderson, *Do No Harm: How Aid Can Support Peace—Or War* (Boulder, Colo.: Lynne Rienner, 1999).

57. Kofi Annan, Nobel lecture, Oslo, December 10, 2001.

58. Kouchner, quoted in Rieff, "Kosovo's Humanitarian Circus," 30.

59. Toby Porter, "The Partiality of Humanitarian Assistance—Kosovo in Comparative Perspective," *Journal of Humanitarian Assistance* (June 17, 2000).

60. Orbinski, *An Imperfect Offering,* 173.

61. Joelle Tanguy and Fiona Terry, "Humanitarian Responsibility and Committed Action," *Ethics & International Affairs* 13, no. 1 (1999): 29–34.

62. Barnett, *Empire of Humanity,* 197.

63. Thomas G. Weiss, "Principles, Politics, and Humanitarian Action," *Ethics & International Affairs* 13, no. 1 (1999): 1–22.

Chapter 4: Humanitarianism and Security

1. Alex J. Bellamy, "Military Intervention," in *The Oxford Handbook of Genocide Studies,* ed. Donald Bloxham and A. Dirk Moses (Oxford: Oxford University Press, 2010), 597–616.

2. Sean D. Murphy, *Humanitarian Intervention: The United Nations in an Evolving World Order* (Philadelphia: University of Pennsylvania Press, 1996), 41.

3. Nicholas J. Wheeler, *Saving Strangers: Humanitarian Intervention in International Society* (New York: Oxford University Press, 2000), 55–138.

4. Mario Bettati, *Le droit d'ingérence: mutation de l'ordre international* (Paris: Odile Jacob, 1996); see also Mario Bettati and Bernard Kouchner, *Le devoir d'ingérence* (Paris: Denoël, 1987).

5. Boutros Boutros-Ghali, *An Agenda for Peace: Preventive Diplomacy, Peacemaking and Peacekeeping* (New York: UN, 1992), 4.

6. UNDP, *Human Development Report 1994* (New York: Oxford University Press, 1994), 3.

7. Kofi A. Annan, *The Question of Intervention* (New York: UN Department of Public Information, 1999).

8. Francis M. Deng, "Frontiers of Sovereignty," *Leiden Journal of International Law* 8, no. 2 (1995): 249–86; and "Reconciling Sovereignty with Responsibility: A Basis for International Humanitarian Action," in *Africa in World Politics: Post–Cold War Challenges*, ed. John W. Harbeson and Donald Rothschild (Boulder, Colo.: Westview, 1995), 295–310; Roberta Cohen and Francis M. Deng, *Masses in Flight: The Global Crisis of Internal Displacement* (Washington, D.C.: Brookings Institution, 1998); and Roberta Cohen and Francis M. Deng, "Sovereignty as Responsibility: Building Block for R2P," in *The Oxford Handbook of the Responsibility to Protect*, ed. Alex J. Bellamy and Tim Dunne (Oxford: Oxford University Press, 2016), 74–93. For more details, see Thomas G. Weiss and David A. Korn, *Internal Displacement: Conceptualization and its Consequences* (London: Routledge, 2006).

9. ICISS, *The Responsibility to Protect: The Report of the International Commission on Intervention and State Sovereignty* (Ottawa: International Development Research Centre, 2001). The commission's story is found in Thomas G. Weiss, *Humanitarian Intervention*, 3rd ed. (Cambridge: Polity, 2012), 123–60; and "The Responsibility to Protect (R2P) and Modern Diplomacy," in *The Oxford Handbook of Modern Diplomacy*, ed. Andrew Cooper, Jorge Heine, and Ramesh Thakur (Oxford: Oxford University Press, 2013), 763–78.

10. Alex Bellamy, *Responsibility to Protect: The Global Effort to End Mass Atrocities* (Cambridge: Polity, 2009); James Pattison, *Humanitarian Intervention and the Responsibility to Protect: Who Should Intervene?* (Oxford: Oxford University Press, 2010); Anne Orford, *International Authority and the Responsibility to Protect* (Cambridge: Cambridge University Press, 2011); and Aidan Hehir, *The Responsibility to Protect: Rhetoric, Reality and the Future of Humanitarian Intervention* (Houndmills, UK: Palgrave Macmillan, 2012).

11. For interpretations by commissioners, see Gareth Evans, *The Responsibility to Protect: Ending Mass Atrocity Crimes Once and For All* (Washington, D.C.: Brookings Institution, 2008); and Ramesh Thakur, *The United Nations, Peace and Security: From Collective Security to the Responsibility to Protect*, 2nd ed. (Cambridge: Cambridge University Press, 2017).

12. Gareth Evans, "Commission Diplomacy," in *The Oxford Handbook of Modern Diplomacy*, ed. Cooper, Heine, and Thakur, 289.

13. ICISS, *The Responsibility to Protect*, para. 2.

14. Grant Marlier and Neta C. Crawford, "Incomplete and Imperfect Institutionalisation of Empathy and Altruism in the 'Responsibility to Protect' Doctrine," *Global Responsibility to Protect* 5, no. 4 (2013): 397–422.

15. Anne-Marie Slaughter, "A Day to Celebrate, but Hard Work Ahead," *Foreign Policy*, March 18, 2011, available at http://foreignpolicy.com/2011/03/19/does-the-world-belong-in-libyas-war-2.

16. Adam Roberts, "Humanitarian War: Military Intervention and Human Rights," *International Affairs* 69 (1993): 429–49; David Rieff, *A Bed for the Night: Humanitarianism in Crisis* (New York: Simon & Schuster, 2002); and Gary Bass, *Freedom's Battle: The Origins of Humanitarian Intervention* (New York: Random House, 2008).

17. David Rieff, "R2P, R.I.P.," *New York Times*, November 7, 2011, is contradicted by Thomas G. Weiss, "Military Humanitarianism: Syria Hasn't Killed It," *Washington Quarterly* 37, no. 1 (2014): 7–20.

18. See Michael Walzer, *Just and Unjust Wars: A Moral Argument with Historical Illustrations*, 3rd ed. (New York: Basic, 2000), including a revised discussion on humanitarian intervention, 101–8; J. Bryan Hehir, "The Just-War Ethic Revisited," in *Ideas and Ideals: Essays on Politics in Honor of Stanley Hoffmann*, ed. Linda B. Miller and Michael Joseph Smith (Boulder, Colo.: Westview, 1993),144–61; and J. Bryan Hehir, "Intervention: From Theories to Cases," *Ethics & International Affairs* 9, no. 1 (1995): 1–13.

19. Chantal de Jonge Oudraat, *Intervention in Internal Conflicts: Legal and Political Conundrums* (Washington, D.C.: Carnegie Endowment for International Peace, 2000).

20. Thomas G. Weiss was present.

21. Peter J. Hoffman and Thomas G. Weiss, *Sword & Salve: Confronting New Wars and Humanitarian Crises* (Boulder, Colo.: Rowman & Littlefield, 2006), xx.

22. Alex J. Bellamy and Paul D. Williams, "The New Politics of Protection? Cote d'Ivoire, Libya and the Responsibility to Protect," *International Affairs* 87, no. 4 (2011): 825–50.

23. *A More Secure World: Our Shared Responsibility* (New York: United Nations, 2004), para. 203.

24. Kofi A. Annan, *In Larger Freedom: Towards Development, Security and Human Rights for All* (New York: United Nations, 2005).

25. Thomas G. Weiss and Barbara Crossette, "The United Nations: The Post-Summit Outlook," in *Great Decisions 2006* (New York: Foreign Policy Association, 2006), 9–20. The other two areas of agreement were the creation of the Human Rights Council and of the Peacebuilding Commission.

26. *Case Concerning the Application of the Convention on the Prevention and Punishment of the Crime of Genocide (Bosnia and Herzegovina v. Serbia and Montenegro)*, Judgment of February 27, 2007, para. 430.

27. Weiss and Crossette, "The United Nations," 9–20. See also Alexander J. Bellamy, "What Will Become of the Responsibility to Protect?" *Ethics & International Affairs* 20, no. 2 (2006): 143–69.

28. Martha Finnemore and Kathryn Sikkink, "International Norm Dynamics and Political Change," *International Organization* 52, no. 4 (1998): 887–917; Thomas Risse, Stephen Ropp, and Kathryn Sikkink, *The Power of Human Rights: International Norms and Domestic Change* (Cambridge: Cambridge University Press, 1999); Margaret Keck and Kathryn Sikkink, *Activists beyond Borders: Advocacy Networks in International Politics* (Ithaca, N.Y.: Cornell University Press, 1998).

29. Ramesh Thakur and Thomas G. Weiss, "R2P: From Idea to Norm—and Action?" *Global Responsibility to Protect* 1, no. 1 (2009): 22.

30. SG/SM/13838, September 23, 2011.

31. Mónica Serrano and Thomas G. Weiss, eds., *The International Politics of Human Rights: Rallying to the R2P Cause?* London: Routledge, 2014); and Rama Mani and Thomas G. Weiss, eds., *The Responsibility to Protect: Cultural Perspectives in the Global South* (London: Routledge, 2011).

32. Thakur and Weiss, "R2P: From Idea to Norm—and Action?" 39.

33. "Recent U.N. Actions Show Policy Shift, Analysts Say," *New York Times*, April 5, 2011.

34. Martin Gilbert, "The Terrible 20th Century," *The Globe and Mail*, January 31, 2007.

35. Greenberg Research, Inc., *The People on War Report: ICRC Worldwide Consultation on the Rules of War* (Geneva: International Committee of the Red Cross, October 1999).

36. Edward C. Luck, "The United Nations and the Responsibility to Protect," *Policy Analysis Brief* (Muscatine, Iowa: Stanley Foundation, 2008), 8.

37. Ban Ki-moon, "On Responsible Sovereignty: International Cooperation for a Changed World," address of the Secretary-General, Berlin, July 15, 2008, UN document SG/SM/11701.

38. "An Idea whose Time Has Come—and Gone?" *The Economist*, July 23, 2009.

39. "Statement by the President of the General Assembly, Miguel d'Escoto Brockmann, at the Opening of the 97th Session of the General Assembly," July 23, 2009.

40. For accounts of the debates and of previous statistics about resolutions, see Global Centre for the Responsibility to Protect, available at http://globalr2p.org.

41. Worldwide Independent Network of Market Research/Gallup International, *People on War—2016 Survey* (Washington, D.C.: WIN/Gallup International Association, 2016), 15.

42. Mohammed Ayoob, "Third World Perspectives on Humanitarian Intervention and International Administration," *Global Governance* 10, no. 1 (2004): 99–118.

43. Noam Chomsky, *The New Military Humanism: Lessons from Kosovo* (Monroe, Maine: Common Courage Press, 1999), 11.

44. Ramesh Thakur, "Global Norms and International Humanitarian Law: An Asian Perspective," *International Review of the Red Cross* 83, no. 841 (2001): 31.

45. Ramesh Thakur, "R2P after Libya and Syria: Engaging Emerging Powers," *Washington Quarterly* 36, no. 2 (2013): 66.

46. Mahmood Mamdani, "Responsibility to Protect or Right to Punish?" *Journal of Intervention and Statebuilding* 4, no. 1 (2010): 53. His full critique is *Saviors and Survivors: Darfur, Politics, and the War on Terror* (New York: Pantheon, 2009).

47. See Serrano and Weiss, eds., *The International Politics of Human Rights*; and Mani and Weiss, eds., *The Responsibility to Protect*.

48. Gareth Evans, "The Limits of Sovereignty: The Case of Mass Atrocity Crimes," *Prism* 5, no. 3 (2015): 3.

49. Alex J. Bellamy and Tim Dunne, eds., *The Oxford Handbook of the Responsibility to Protect* (Oxford: Oxford University Press, 2016).

50. Evans, *The Responsibility to Protect*, 28.

51. Edward C. Luck, "The Responsibility to Protect: The First Decade," *Global Responsibility to Protect* 3, no. 4 (2011): 387.

52. Bass, *Freedom's Battle*, 382.

53. Ramesh Thakur, "The Responsibility to Protect at 15," *International Affairs* 92, no. 2 (2016): 415–34, at 434.

Chapter 5: Humanitarianism Adjudicated

1. Carsten Stahn, Jennifer S. Easterday, and Jens Iverson, eds., *Jus Post Bellum: Mapping the Normative Foundations* (Oxford: Oxford University Press, 2014).

2. Martin Burke and Thomas G. Weiss, "The Security Council and Ad Hoc Tribunals: Law and Politics, Peace and Justice," in *Security Council Resolutions and Global Legal Regimes*, ed. Trudy Fraser and Vesselin Popovksi (London: Routledge, 2014), 241–65.

3. Cherif Bassiouni, "International Criminal Justice in Historical Perspective: The Tension between States' Interests and the Pursuit of International Justice," in *The Oxford Companion to International Criminal Justice*, ed. Antonio Cassese (Oxford: Oxford University Press, 2009), 132.

4. Theodor Meron, "Reflections on the Prosecution of War Crimes by International Tribunals," *American Journal of International Law* 100, no. 3 (2006): 551–79.

5. October 26, 1916 speech, quoted by Jan Willem Schulte Nordholt, *Woodrow Wilson: A Life for World Peace*, trans. Herbert H. Rowen (Berkeley: University of California Press, 1991), 360.

6. Ayse Zarakol, "Ontological (In)security and State Denial of Historical Crimes: Turkey and Japan," *International Relations* 24, no. 1 (2010): 3–23.

7. Quoted by Kirsten Sellars, *"Crimes against Peace" and International Law* (Cambridge: Cambridge University Press, 2013), 132.

8. Telford Taylor, *The Anatomy of the Nuremberg Trials: A Personal Memoir* (Boston: Little, Brown, 1992), 641, supra note 3. See also Dan Plesch, *Human Rights after Hitler: The Lost History of Prosecuting Axis War Crimes* (Washington, D.C.: Georgetown University Press, 2017).

9. Richard Rhodes, *Dark Sun: The Making of the Hydrogen Bomb* (New York: Simon & Schuster, 1995), 21.

10. David Cortright and George A. Lopez, *The Sanctions Decade: Assessing UN Strategies in the 1990s* (Boulder, Colo.: Lynne Rienner, 2000); and Thomas J. Biersteker, Sue E. Eckert, and Marcos Tourinho, eds., *Targeted Sanctions: The Impacts and Effectiveness of United Nations Actions* (Cambridge: Cambridge University Press, 2016).

11. International Law Commission, *The Charter and Judgment of the Nürnberg Tribunal: History and Analysis*, UN document A/CN.4/5, 1949.

12. International Law Commission, *Historical Survey of the Question of International Criminal Jurisdiction*, UN document A/CN.4/7/Rev.1, 1951.

13. *Revised Draft Statute for an International Criminal Court*, UN document A/2645, 1954.

14. International Law Commission, *Ninth Report on the Draft Code of Crimes against the Peace and Security of Mankind*, UN document A/CN.4/435 and Add.1 & Corr.1, 1991.

15. International Law Commission, *Draft Statute for an International Criminal Court* in *Yearbook of the International Law Commission*, 1994, vol. II (part two).

16. Richard J. Goldstone and Adam M. Smith, *International Judicial Institutions*, 2nd ed. (London: Routledge, 2015).

17. *Interim Report of the Commission of Experts Established Pursuant to Security Council Resolution 780*, UN document S/25274, February 10, 1993, para. 72.

18. *Report of the Secretary-General Pursuant to Paragraph 2 of Security Council Resolution 808 (1993)*, UN document S/25704, May 3, 1993. Statute of the International Criminal Tribunal for the Prosecution of Persons Responsible for Serious Violations of International Humanitarian Law Committed in the Former Yugoslavia Since 1991, annex to UN doc. S/25704, 36–48.

19. UN document S/PRST/1994/21, April 30, 1994.

20. A letter from the president of the council, UN document S/1994/546, 6 May 1994. The response is found in *The Report of the Secretary-General on the Situation in Rwanda*, UN document S/1994/565, May 13, 1994.

21. *Report of the Commission on Human Rights on Its Third Special Session*, UN document E/1994/24/Add.2, May 25, 1994.

22. *Preliminary Report of the Independent Commission of Experts Established in Accordance with S.C. Res. 935*, UN document S/1994/1125, October 4, 1994.

23. Ruti J. Teitel, *Transitional Justice* (Oxford: Oxford University Press, 2000); and Priscilla Hayner, *Unspeakable Truths: Transitional Justice and the Challenge of Truth Commissions* (London: Routledge, 2002).

24. Goldstone and Smith, *International Judicial Institutions*, 124–29.

25. Henry Kissinger, "The Pitfalls of Universal Jurisdiction," *Foreign Affairs* 80, no. 4 (2001): 86–96; Kenneth Roth, "The Case for Universal Jurisdiction," *Foreign Affairs* 80, no. 5 (2001): 150–54.

26. John R. Bolton, "The United States and the International Criminal Court," remarks to the Federalist Society, Washington, D.C., November 14, 2002.

27. Andrea Birdsall, "The 'Monster That We Need to Slay'? Global Governance, the United States, and the International Criminal Court," *Global Governance* 16, no. 4 (2010): 462.

28. Kathryn Sikkink, *The Justice Cascade: How Human Rights Prosecutions are Changing World Politics* (New York: Norton, 2011); Carsten Stahn, ed., *The Law and Practice of the International Criminal Court* (Oxford: Oxford University Press, 2015).

29. Hyeran Jo and Beth A. Simmons, "Can the International Criminal Court Deter Atrocity?" (unpublished manuscript, 2014), 1–53.

30. Danilo Zolo, *Victors' Justice: From Nuremberg to Baghdad* (New York: Verso, 2009), xii.

31. Steven C. Roach, "Courting the Rule of Law? The International Criminal Court and Global Terrorism," *Global Governance* 14, no. 1 (2008): 13–19.

Chapter 6: Humanitarianism in the Post-9/11 World

1. Speech to 27th Communist Party of the Soviet Union Congress, February 1986.

2. Fiona Terry, *Condemned to Repeat? The Paradox of Humanitarian Action* (Ithaca, N.Y.: Cornell University Press, 2002), 55–82.

3. UNDP, *Human Development Report 2000* (New York: Oxford University Press), 267.

4. Thomas G. Weiss, *Military-Civilian Interactions: Humanitarian Crises and the Responsibility to Protect* (Lanham, Md.: Rowman & Littlefield, 2005), 155–89.

5. UNDP, *Human Development Report 1991* (New York: Oxford University Press, 1991), 16.

6. *Report to the Secretary-General on Humanitarian Needs in Kuwait and Iraq in the Immediate Post-Crisis Environment by a Mission to the Area Led by Mr. Martii Ahtisaari, Under-Secretary-General for Administration and Management*, March 20, 1991, 5.

7. Gil Loescher, "An Idea Lost in the Rubble," *New York Times*, August 20, 2004.

8. Cameron Thibos, "35 years of Forced Displacement in Iraq: Contexualising the ISIS Threat, Unpacking the Movements," *Migration Policy Center Brief* (October 2014): 1–14.

9. UNDP, *Human Development Report 2011* (New York: Oxford University Press, 2011), 126.

10. Security Council statement, February 22, 2011, UN document SC/10180-AFR/2120.

11. UN document S/PV.6491, February 26, 2011.

12. Libyan Foreign Minister Musa Kousa, letter to Security Council, March 17, 2011.

13. On March 17, Gaddafi warned rebels in Benghazi, "We are coming tonight. . . . We will find you in your closets. . . . We will have no mercy and no pity." Quoted in Maria Golovnina and Patrick Worsnip, "U.N. Okays Military Action on Libya," *Reuters*, March 17, 2011.

14. Jon Western and Joshua S. Goldstein, "Humanitarian Intervention Comes of Age: Lessons from Somalia to Libya," *Foreign Affairs* 90, no. 6 (2011): 48–59; Thomas G. Weiss, "RtoP alive and well after Libya," *Ethics & International Affairs* 25, no. 3 (2011): 287–92.

15. S/PV.6498, March 17, 2011.

16. Bruno Rodríguez, Minister for Foreign Affairs of Cuba, 66th Session of General Assembly, September 26, 2011.

17. Dag Hennriksen and Ann Karin Larsen, eds., *The Political Rationale and International Consequences of the War in Libya* (Oxford: Oxford University Press, 2016).

18. Bob Woodward, *Plan of Attack* (New York: Simon & Schuster, 2004), 150.

19. "South Africa Says NATO Abusing UN Resolution on Libya," *Reuters*, June 14, 2011.

20. "Letter Dated 9 November 2011 from the Permanent Representative of Brazil to the United Nations Addressed to the Secretary-General," UN document A/66/551-S/2011/701, 1.

21. Tim Dunne and Katherine Gelber, "Arguing Matters: The Responsibility to Protect and the Case of Libya," *Global Responsibility to Protect* 6, no. 3 (2014): 326–49.

22. Alan Kuperman, "Lessons from Libya: How Not to Intervene," Policy Brief, Belfer Center for Science and International Affairs, John F. Kennedy School of Government, Harvard University, Cambridge, Mass., September 2013.

23. Madeleine K. Albright and S. Richard Williamson, *The United States and R2P: From Words to Action* (Washington, D.C.: US Institute of Peace, 2013), 16 and 10. For a contrary view, see Alan J. Kuperman, "A Model Humanitarian Intervention? Reassessing NATO's Libya Campaign," *International Security* 38, no. 1 (2013): 105–36.

24. Assessment Capacities Project, *Global Emergency Overview* (October 2015), 15.

25. See data collected by Syrian Centre for Policy Research, Syrian Observatory for Human Rights; OCHA, "Syrian Arab Republic," http://www.unocha.org/syria.

26. Statement in Explanation of Vote by Vitaly Churkin, Permanent Representative of the Russian Federation to the UN, on the Draft Resolution on the Situation in Syria, New York, October 4, 2011.

27. David Rieff, "Save Us from the Liberal Hawks: Syria's a Tragedy. But It's Not our Problem," *Foreign Policy*, February 13, 2012.

28. Craig Whiteside, "A Case for Terrorism as Genocide in an Era of Weakened States," *Dynamics of Asymmetric Conflict* 8, no. 3 (2015): 232–50.

29. Iraq Security and Humanitarian Monitor, "Monitoring the Crisis," December 16–22, 2016.

30. Edward C. Luck, "The Responsibility to Protect: Growing Pains or Early Promise?" *Ethics & International Affairs* 24, no. 4 (2010): 361.

31. Kofi Annan, "My Departing Advice on How to Save Syria," *Financial Times*, August 2, 2012.

32. Taylor B. Seybolt, Jay D. Aronson, and Baruch Fischhoff, eds., *Counting Civilian Casualties: An Introduction to Recording and Estimating Nonmilitary Deaths in Conflict* (Oxford: Oxford University Press, 2013).

33. Somini Sengupta, "Governments Abuses 'Far Outweigh' Syrian Rebels', Rights Chief Says," *New York Times*, April 9, 2014.

34. Alex J. Bellamy and Paul D. Williams, "The New Politics of Protection? Cote d'Ivoire, Libya, and the Responsibility to Protect," *International Affairs* 87, no. 4 (2011): 825–50.

35. Aidan Hehir, "The Permanence of Inconsistency: Libya, the Security Council, and the Responsibility to Protect," *International Security* 38, no. 1 (2013): 137–59.

36. Antonio Donini, *The Golden Fleece: Manipulation and Independence in Humanitarian Action* (Sterling, Va.: Kumarian, 2012), 67–88.

37. Ashley Jackson and Antonio Giustozzi, *Talking to the Other Side: Humanitarian Engagement with the Taliban in Afghanistan*, HPG Working Paper, December 2012, iii.

38. Quoted by Róisín Shannon, "Playing with Principles in an Era of Securitized Aid: Negotiating Humanitarian Space in Post-9/11 Afghanistan," *Progress in Development Studies* 9, no. 1 (2009): 22.

39. Jackson and Giustozzi, *Talking to the Other Side*, 2.

40. Quoted by Mark Mazzetti, Eric Schmitt, and Erin Banco, "No Quick Impact in U.S. Arms Plan for Syria Rebels," *New York Times*, July 14, 2013.

41. Lori Fisler Damrosch, "The Inevitability of Selective Response? Principles to Guide Urgent International Action," in *Kosovo and the Challenge of Humanitarian Intervention: Selective Indignation, Collective Action, and International Citizenship*, ed. Albrecht Schnabel and Ramesh Thakur (Tokyo: United Nations University Press, 2000), 405–19.

42. Hardeep Singh Puri is concerned about simplistic and wrong assumptions in *Perilous Interventions: The Security Council and the Politics of Chaos* (Delhi: HarperCollins, 2016).

43. Independent International Commission on Kosovo, *Kosovo Report: Conflict, International Response, Lessons Learned* (Oxford: Oxford University Press, 2000). Contrast is Christopher Greenwood, *Humanitarian Intervention: Law and Policy* (Oxford: Oxford University Press, 2001), and Michael Byers and Simon Chesterman, "Changing Rules about Rules? Unilateral Humanitarian Intervention and the Future of International Law," in *Humanitarian Intervention: Ethical, Legal and Political Dilemmas*, ed. J. F. Holzgrefe and Robert O. Keohane (Cambridge: Cambridge University Press, 2003), 177–203.

44. Michael Walzer, "On Humanitarianism," *Foreign Affairs* 90, no. 4 (2011): 77.

45. Mónica Serrano and Thomas G. Weiss, eds., *The International Politics of Human Rights: Rallying to the R2P Cause?* (London: Routledge, 2014).

46. Justin Morris, "Libya and Syria: R2P and the Spectre of the Swinging Pendulum," *International Affairs* 89, no. 5 (2013): 1265–83.

47. Ramesh Thakur, "R2P after Libya and Syria: Engaging Emerging Powers," *Washington Quarterly* 36, no. 2 (2013): 61.

48. "Memorandum from Alberto R. Gonzales, Counsel to George W. Bush, President, on Decision Re Application of the Geneva Convention on Prisoners of War to the Conflict with Al Qaeda and the Taliban," January 25, 2002.

49. Claudia Aradau, "Law Transformed: Guantanamo and the 'Other' Exception," *Third World Quarterly* 28, no. 3 (2007): 489–501.

50. Antonio M. Taguba, *Article 15-6 Investigation of the 800th Military Police Brigade* (May 2004).

51. Nicolas de Torrente, "Humanitarian Action under Attack: Reflections on the Iraq War," and Kenneth Anderson, "Humanitarian Inviolability in Crisis: The Meaning of Impartiality and Neutrality for U.N. and NGO Agencies Following the 2003–2004 Afghanistan and Iraq Conflicts," *Harvard Human Rights Journal* 17, no. 1 (2004): 1–30 and 41–74. See also *A Short Guide to Humanitarian Futures,* draft discussion paper by Kings College London, Feinstein International Center, and Humanitarian Policy Group, available at www.planningfromthefuture.org.

52. Christophe Fournier, "Our Purpose Is to Limit the Devastations of War," Speech at conference in Rheindahlen, Germany, organized by NATO's Allied Rapid Reaction Corps, December 7–8, 2009.

53. David Rieff, *A Bed for the Night: Humanitarianism in Crisis* (New York: Simon & Schuster, 2002).

54. Ashley Jackson, *Negotiating Perceptions: Al-Shabaab and Taliban Views of Aid Agencies*, HPG Policy Brief 61, August 2014.

55. Jasmine Mousaa, *Ancient Origins, Modern Actors: Defining Arabic Meanings of Humanitarianism*, HPG Working Paper, November 2014.

Chapter 7: Humanitarianism Forgotten and Forsaken

1. Andrew Natsios, *Sudan, South Sudan, and Darfur: What Everyone Needs to Know* (Oxford: Oxford University Press, 2012), 1.

2. Larry Minear et al., *Humanitarianism under Siege: A Critical Review of Operation Lifeline Sudan* (Trenton, N.J.: Red Sea Press, 1991).

3. Scott Straus, "Darfur and the Genocide Debate," *Foreign Affairs* 84, no. 1 (2005): 123–33.

4. OCHA, *Humanitarian Bulletin: Sudan* 52 (December 2016).

5. Michael Boyce and Mark Yarnell, "South Sudan: A Nation Uprooted," *Refugees International Field Report*, March 12, 2015, 1–15; Natsios, *Sudan, South Sudan, and Darfur.*

6. Lydia Tanner and Leben Moro, "Missed Out: The Role of Local Actors in the Humanitarian Response in the South Sudan Conflict," CAFODI and Trócaire in Partnership, Christian Aid, Oxfam GB and Tearfund, April 2016; Mark Canavera

et al., "'And Then They Left': Challenges to Child Protection Systems Strengthening in South Sudan," *Children & Society* 30, no. 5 (2016): 356–68.

7. OCHA, *Humanitarian Bulletin: South Sudan* 20 (December 2016).

8. Olara Otunnu, "The Secret Genocide," *Foreign Policy* 155 (July/August 2006): 44–46.

9. The Resolve, *The State of the LRA in 2016* (March 2016).

10. Maria Eriksson Baez and Maria Stern, "Why Do Soldiers Rape? Masculinity, Violence and Sexuality in the Armed Forces in the Congo (DRC)," *International Studies Quarterly* 53, no. 2 (2008): 495–518; Victoria Canning, "Who's Human? Developing Sociological Understandings of the Rights of Women Raped in Conflict," *International Journal of Human Rights* 14, no. 6 (2010): 849–64.

11. International Federation of the Red Cross and Red Crescent Society, *World Disasters Report 2007* (Bloomfield, Conn.: Kumarian, 2007), 121.

12. Donna Pankhurst, "Sexual Violence in War," in *Gender Matters in Global Politics: A Feminist Introduction to International Politic*, ed. Laura J. Shepherd (New York: Routledge, 2010), 148–60; Kerry F. Crawford, "From Spoils to Weapons: Framing Wartime Sexual Violence," *Gender and Development* 21, no. 3 (2013): 505–17.

13. R. Charli Carpenter, "Recognizing Gender-Based Violence against Civilian Men and Boys in Conflict Situations," *Security Dialogue* 37, no. 1 (2006): 83–103; Sarah Solangon and Preet Patel, "Sexual Violence against Men in Countries Affected by Armed Conflict," *Conflict, Security & Development* 12, no. 4 (2012): 417–42.

14. Elisabeth Jean Wood, "Variation in War Time Sexual Violence," *Politics & Society* 34, no. 3 (2006): 307–41.

15. Joshua Kaiser and John Hagan, "Gendered Genocide: The Socially Destructive Process of Genocidal Rape, Killing, and Displacement in Darfur," *Law & Society Review* 49, no. 1 (2015): 69–107.

16. Robert Jenkins and Anne-Marie Goetz, "Addressing Sexual Violence in Internationally Mediated Peace Negotiations," *International Peacekeeping* 17, no. 2 (2010): 261–77.

17. Zeid Ra'ad al-Hussein, *A Comprehensive Strategy to Eliminate Future Sexual Exploitation and Abuse in United Nations Peacekeeping Operations*, UN document A/59/710, March 24, 2005.

18. UNDT/GVA/2015/126; http://www.un.org/en/oaj/files/undt/orders/gva-2015-099.pdf.

19. Obi Anyadike, "Top UN Whistleblower Resigns, Citing Impunity and Lack of Accountability," IRIN, June 7, 2016, http://www.irinnews.org/analysis/2016/06/07/exclusive-top-un-whistleblower-resigns-citing-impunity-and-lack-accountability.

20. William Schabas, Carsten Stahn, Dan Plesch, Shanti Sattler, and Joseph Powderly, eds., "The United Nations War Crimes Commission: The Origins of International Criminal Justice," *Criminal Law Forum* 25, nos. 1 & 2 (2014).

21. Chantal de Jonge Oudraat, "UNSCR 1325—Conundrums and Opportunities," *International Interactions* 39, no. 4 (2013): 612–19.

22. Department of Peacekeeping Operations and the Department of Field Support, *Ten-year Impact Study on Implementation of UN Security Council Resolution 1325 (2000) on Women, Peace and Security in Peacekeeping* (New York: United Nations, 2010).

23. Laura Shepherd, "Power and Authority in the Production of the United Nations Security Council Resolution 1325," *International Studies Quarterly* 52, no. 2 (2008): 383–404.

24. Quoted in *Foreign Policy* (November/December 2015): 49.

25. UN Women, *Preventing Conflict, Transforming Justice, Securing the Peace: A Global Study on the Implementation of Security Council Resolution 1325* (New York: UN, 2015), 14.

26. Melissa Labonte and Gaynel Curry, "Women, Peace, and Security: Are We There Yet?" *Global Governance* 22, no. 3 (2016): 311–19, quote at 315.

27. Karin Landgren, "The Lost Agenda: Gender Parity in Senior UN Appointments," *Global Peace Operations Review*, December 14, 2015, available at http://peaceoperationsreview.org/commentary/the-lost-agenda-gender-parity-in-senior-un-appointments.

28. Global Humanitarian Assistance, *Global Humanitarian Assistance: Report 2015* (Bristol, UK: Development Initiatives, 2016), 26–27.

29. *Global Humanitarian Assistance (GHA) 2016*, 38.

30. http://dgecho-partners-helpdesk.eu/financing_decisions/dgecho_strategy/fca.

31. *GHA 2016*, 58.

32. For example, see Nira Yuval-Davis, "Intersectionality and Feminist Politics," *European Journal of Women's Studies* 13, no. 3 (2006): 193–209.

33. Miriam Ticktin, "The Gendered Human of Humanitarianism: Medicalising and Politicising Sexual Violence," *Gender & History* 23, no. 2 (2011): 250–65.

34. Mahmood Mamdani, *Saviors and Survivors: Darfur, Politics, and the War on Terror* (New York: Doubleday, 2009), 48–71.

35. Alan J. Kuperman, "Mitigating the Moral Hazard of Humanitarian Intervention: Lessons from Economics," *Global Governance* 14, no. 2 (2008): 219–40; and "Obama's Libya Debacle," *Foreign Affairs* 94, no. 2 (2015): 66–77.

36. Nicholas J. Wheeler, *Saving Strangers: Humanitarian Intervention in International Society* (Oxford: Oxford University Press, 2000).

Chapter 8: Humanitarian Limbo

1. Peter Gatrell, "World Wars and Population Displacement in Europe in the 20th Century," *Contemporary European History* 16, no. 4 (2007): 418–19.

2. Ibid., 419.

3. Rony Brauman, "Refugee Camps, Population Transfer and NGOs," in *Hard Choices: Moral Dilemmas in Humanitarian Intervention*, ed. Jonathan Moore (Boulder, Colo.: Rowman & Littlefield, 1999), 177–93.

4. Roberta Cohen and Francis M. Deng, *Masses in Flight: The Global Crisis of Internal Displacement* (Washington, D.C.: Brookings, 1998), 3. See also Roberta Cohen and Francis M. Deng, eds., *The Forsaken People: Case Studies of the Internally Displaced* (Washington, D.C.: Brookings, 1998); Francis M. Deng, *Protecting the Dispossessed: A Challenge for the International Community* (Washington, D.C.: Brookings, 1993).

5. Broader notions would encompass millions more uprooted by natural disasters and development according to Erin D. Mooney, "The Concept of Internal

Displacement and the Case for IDPs as a Category of Concern," *Refugee Survey Quarterly* 24, no. 3 (2005): 9–26.

6. UNHCR, *The State of the World's Refugees 2006: Human Displacement in the New Millennium* (New York: Oxford University Press, 2006), 108.

7. UNHCR, *Global Trends: Forced Displacement in 2015* (Geneva: UNHCR, 2016), 20.

8. Robin Davies, "Humanitarian Assistance: Negative Spin-Offs for the Host Country," in *War, Money and Survival*, ed. International Committee of the Red Cross (Geneva: ICRC, 2000), 82–87.

9. David Keen, "Incentives and Disincentives for Violence," in *Greed and Grievance: Economic Agendas in Civil Wars*, ed. Mats Berdal and David Malone (Boulder, Colo.: Lynne Rienner, 2000), 27, emphasis in original.

10. Myron Weiner, "Security, Stability, and International Migration," *International Security* 17, no. 3 (1992–1993): 91–126; and Jef Huysmans, *The Politics of Insecurity: Fear, Migration and Asylum in the EU* (New York: Routledge, 2006), 45–62.

11. Jorge Fernandes, "Ebola Takes to the Road: Mobilizing Viruses in Defense of the Nation-State," in *Sovereign Lives: Power in Global Politics*, ed. Jenny Edkins, Véronique Pin-Fat, and Michael J. Shapiro (New York: Routledge, 2004), 189–210; and Ayse Ceyhan and Anastassia Tsoukala, "The Securitization of Migration in Western Societies: Ambivalent Discourses and Policies," *Alternatives* 27, no. 1 (Supplement, 2002): 21–39.

12. High-Level Panel on Humanitarian Financing, *Too Important to Fail—Addressing the Humanitarian Financing Gap* (New York: UN, 2016), http://www .regeringen.se/contentassets/7c58cbe54ef9435db005aca302e8cd25/high-level -panel-on-humanitarian-financing-report-to-the-secretary-general.

13. Barbara Harrell-Bond, "Can Humanitarian Work with Refugees Be Humane?" *Human Rights Quarterly* 24, no. 1 (2002): 51–85.

14. Victor Turner, "Betwixt and Between: The Liminal Period in Rites of Passage," in *The Forest of Symbols* (Ithaca, N.Y.: Cornell University Press, 1967).

15. Hannah Arendt, *The Origins of Totalitarianism* (New York: Meridian Books, 1958), 280–81.

16. Sadako Ogata, "World Order, Internal Conflict, and Refugees," Address at the John F. Kennedy School of Government, Harvard University, Cambridge, Mass., October 28, 1996.

17. EXCOM, Standing Committee Follow-Up to ECOSOC Resolution 1995/56, *UNHCR Activities in Relation to Prevention,* EC/46/SC/CRP.33, May 28, 1996.

18. Michael J. Barnett, *Empire of Humanity: A History of Humanitarianism* (Ithaca, N.Y.: Cornell University Press, 2011), 207.

19. Jacob Stevens, "Prisons of the Stateless," *New Left Review* 46 (November–December 2006): 52–67.

20. Gil Loescher, Alexander Betts, and James Milner, *The United Nations High Commissioner for Refugees*, 3rd ed. (London: Routledge, forthcoming 2018).

21. Anne Stevenson and Rebecca Sutton, "There's No Place Like a Refugee Camp? Urban Planning and Participation in the Camp Context," *Refuge* 28, no. 1 (2011): 137–48.

22. See also Laura Hammond, "The Power of Holding Humanitarianism Hostage and the Myth of Protective Principles," Peter Redfield, "Sacrifice, Triage, and

Global Humanitarianism," and Jennifer C. Rubenstein, "The Distributive Commitments of International NGOs," in *Humanitarianism in Question: Politics, Power, Ethics*, ed. Michael Barnett and Thomas G. Weiss (Ithaca, N.Y.: Cornell University Press, 2008), 172–234.

23. Suzan Ilcan and Kim Rygiel, "'Resiliency Humanitarianism': Responsibilizing Refugees through Humanitarian Emergency Governance in the Camp," *International Political Sociology* 9, no. 4 (2015): 333–51.

24. Nick Micinski and Thomas G. Weiss, "International Organization for Migration and the UN System: A Missed Opportunity," September 2016, *FUNDS Briefing No. 42*, http://www.futureun.org/en/Publications-Surveys/Article?newsid=95&teaserId=1.

25. Brauman, "Refugee Camps, Population Transfer and NGOs," 177–93.

26. Ibid.

27. Aristide R. Zolberg, Astri Suhrke, and Sergio Aguayo, *Escape from Violence: Conflict and the Refugee Crisis in the Developing World* (New York: Oxford University Press, 1989), 275–78.

28. Stephen John Stedman and Fred Tanner, eds., *Refugee Manipulation: War, Politics, and the Abuse of Human Suffering* (Washington, D.C.: Brookings, 2003).

29. Mark Duffield, "Global Civil War: The Non-Insured, International Containment and Post-Interventionary Society," *Journal of Refugee Studies* 21, no. 2 (2008): 145–65.

30. Michel Agier, "Humanity as an Identity and Its Political Effects (A Note on Camps and Humanitarian Government)," *Humanity: An International Journal of Human Rights, Humanitarianism, and Development* 1, no. 1 (2010): 29–45.

31. Didier Fassin, *Humanitarian Reason: A Moral History of the Present* (Berkeley: University of California Press, 2011), 133–57.

32. Giorgio Agamben, *Homo Sacer: Sovereign Power and Bare Life* (Stanford, Calif.: Stanford University Press, 2004).

33. Katarzyna Grabska, "Constructing 'Modern Gendered Civilised' Women and Men: Gender-mainstreaming in Refugee Camps," *Gender & Development* 19, no. 1 (2011): 81–93.

34. MSF, *Where Is Everyone? Responding to Emergencies in the Most Difficult Places* (London: MSF, 2014), 16.

35. UNHCR, *UNHCR Policy on Refugee Protection and Solutions in Urban Areas* (Geneva: UNHCR, 2009), para. 27.

36. UNHCR, *Global Trends: Forced Displacement in 2015*, 2.

37. Michel Agier, *Managing the Undesirables: Refugee Camps and Humanitarian Government* (Cambridge: Polity, 2011), 12.

38. William Walters, "Foucault and Frontiers: Notes on the Birth of the Humanitarian Border," in *Governmentality: Current Issues and Future Challenges*, ed. Ulrich Bröckling, Susanne Krasmann, and Thomas Lemke (New York: Routledge, 2011), 138–64.

39. Katja Lindskov Jacobsen, "Experimentation in Humanitarian Locations: UNHCR and Biometric Registration of Afghan Refugees," *Security Dialogue* 46, no. 2 (2015): 144–64.

40. Jennifer Hyndman, *Managing Displacement: Refugees and the Politics of Humanitarianism* (Minneapolis: University of Minnesota Press, 2000), 2.

41. Arendt, *Origins of Totalitarianism*, 267–304.

42. Giorgio Agamben, *Homo Sacer: Sovereign Power and Bare Life* (Stanford, Calif.: Stanford University Press, 1995).

43. Alexander Betts, Louise Bloom, Josiah Kaplan, and Naohiko Omata, *Refugee Economies: Forced Displacement and Development* (New York: Oxford University Press, 2016).

44. Agier, *Managing the Undesirables*, 4.

Chapter 9: The Humanitarian-Industrial Complex

1. Thomas G. Weiss, *Humanitarian Business* (Cambridge: Polity, 2016).

2. Thomas Haskell, "Capitalism and the Origins of the Humanitarian Sensibility, Part 1," *American Historical Review* 90, no. 2 (1985): 339–61; and "Capitalism and the Origins of the Humanitarian Sensibility, Part 2," *American Historical Review* 90, no. 3 (1985): 547–66.

3. Michael Ignatieff, "The Stories We Tell: Television and Humanitarian Aid," in *Hard Choices: Moral Dilemmas in Humanitarian Intervention*, ed. Jonathan Moore (Boulder, Colo.: Rowman & Littlefield, 1999), 287–302.

4. Worldwide Independent Network of Market Research/Gallup International, *People on War — 2016 Survey* (Washington, D.C.: WIN/Gallup International Association, 2016), 12–13.

5. Martin Bell, "The Journalism of Attachment," in *Media Ethics*, ed. Matthew Kieran (London: Routledge, 1998), 16.

6. Birgitta Höijer, "The Discourse of Global Compassion: The Audience and Media Reporting of Human Suffering," *Media, Culture & Society* 26, no. 4 (2004): 513–31.

7. Ignatieff, "The Stories We Tell," 288.

8. Susan Sontag, *Regarding the Pain of Others* (New York: Farrar, Straus and Giroux, 2003), 23.

9. Dennis Kennedy, "Selling the Distant Other: Humanitarianism and Imagery—Ethical Dilemmas of Humanitarian Action," *Journal of Humanitarian Assistance* (February 2009): 12.

10. James Dawes, *That the World May Know: Bearing Witness to Atrocity* (Cambridge, Mass.: Harvard University Press, 2007), 22.

11. Quoted in Kennedy, "Selling the Distant Other," 9.

12. Andrew F. Cooper, *Diplomatic Afterlives* (Cambridge: Polity, 2015).

13. Emily Bent, "*Girl Rising* and the Problematic Other," in *Feminist Theory and Pop Culture*, ed. Adrienne Trier-Bieniek (Rotterdam: Sense Publishers, 2015), 89–101.

14. Ilan Kapoor, *Celebrity Humanitarianism: The Ideology of Global Charity* (New York: Routledge, 2013), 12–46.

15. Hugo Slim, "Marketing Humanitarian Space: Argument and Method in Humanitarian Persuasion," in *Essays in Humanitarian Action* (Oxford: Oxford Institute for Ethics, Law, and Armed Conflict, University of Oxford, 2012), 3.

16. Andrea Binder and Jan Martin Witte, *Business Engagement in Humanitarian Relief: Key Trends and Policy Implications*, HPG Background Paper (London: ODI, 2007); and Monika Krause, *The Good Project: Humanitarian Relief and the Fragmentation of Reason* (Chicago: University of Chicago Press, 2014).

17. Weiss, *Humanitarian Business*, 96–142. See also "Ethical Quandaries in War Zones, When Mass Atrocity Prevention Fails," *Global Society* 7, no. 2 (2016): 1–12.

18. Slim, "Marketing Humanitarian Space."

19. *Global Humanitarian Assistance Report 2014* (Somerset, UK: Development Initiatives, 2014), hereafter GHA, 4 and 21, http://www.globalhumanitarianassis tance.org/wp-content/uploads/2014/09/GHA-Report-2014-interactive.pdf (hereafter *GHA 2014*), 4–5.

20. High-Level Panel on Humanitarian Financing, *Too Important to Fail— Addressing the Humanitarian Financing Gap* (New York: UN, 2016), http://www .regeringen.se/contentassets/7c58cbe54ef9435db005aca302e8cd25/high-level -panel-on-humanitarian-financing-report-to-the-secretary-general.

21. *GHA 2016* (Somerset, UK: Development Initiatives, 2016), 5, http://www .globalhumanitarianassistance.org/report/gha2016.

22. Franz Baumann, "United Nations Management—An Oxymoron?" *Global Governance* 22, no. 4 (2016): 451–72.

23. Linda Polman, *The Crisis Caravan: What's Wrong with Humanitarian Aid?* (New York: Henry Holt, 2010).

24. *GHA 2013* (Somerset, UK: Development Initiatives, 2013), 6, http:// www.globalhumanitarianassistance.org/wp-content/uploads/2013/07/GHA -Report-20131.pdf, 20 and 30, and *GHA 2014*, 4–5 and 15.

25. *GHA 2014*, 4–7 and 34.

26. Abby Stoddard, Adele Harmer, and Katherine Haver, *Providing Aid in Insecure Environments: Trends in Policy and Operations*, HPG Report 23 (London: Overseas Development Institute, 2006).

27. Peter Walker and Catherine Russ, *Professionalizing the Humanitarian Sector: A Scoping Study*, Report Commissioned by the Enhancing Learning and Research for Humanitarian Assistance, April 2010, 11–12.

28. Alexander Cooley and James Ron, "The NGO Scramble: Organizational Insecurity and the Political Economy of Transnational Action," *International Security* 27, no. 1 (2002): 13 and 6.

29. Rony Brauman, *My Sweet La Mancha* (Geneva: MSF, 2005).

30. Alex de Waal, *Famine Crimes: Politics & the Disaster Relief Industry in Africa* (Oxford: James Currey, 1997), 66.

31. Neil Wright, "UNHCR and International Humanitarian Cooperation in the Former Yugoslavia," *Refugee Survey Quarterly* 18, no. 3 (1999): 50–54.

32. Sarah Collinson and Samir Elhawary, *Humanitarian Space: A Review of Trends and Issues*, HPG Report 32 (London: Overseas Development Institute, 2012), 21–22.

33. Stephen Hopgood, "Saying 'No' to Wal-Mart? Money and Morality in Professional Humanitarianism," in *Humanitarianism in Question: Politics, Power, Ethics*, ed. Michael Barnett and Thomas G. Weiss (Ithaca, N.Y.: Cornell University Press, 2008), 98–123.

34. Stephen John Stedman, Donald Rothchild, and Elizabeth M. Cousens, eds., *Ending Civil Wars: The Implementation of Peace Agreements* (Boulder, Colo.: Lynne Rienner, 2002).

35. Polman, *The Crisis Caravan*, 96–99.

36. Graciana del Castillo, *Rebuilding War-Torn States: The Challenge of Post-Conflict Economic Reconstruction* (Oxford: Oxford University Press, 2009).

37. Sphere Project, *Humanitarian Charter and Minimum Standards in Disaster Responses* (Geneva: IFRC, 1998).

38. Charles-Antoine Hofmann, Les Roberts, Jeremy Shoham, and Paul Harvey, *Measuring the Impact of Humanitarian Aid: A Review of Current Practice*, HPG Report 17 (London: Overseas Development Institute, 2004).

39. Relevant international laws and agreements include Hague V (Articles 4 and 6, 1907); Geneva III (Article 4, 1949); Additional Protocol to Geneva I (Article 47, 1977); Organization of African Unity Convention for the Elimination of Mercenarism (1977); and the United Nations Convention against the Recruitment, Use, Financing, and Training of Mercenaries (1989).

40. Abby Stoddard, Adele Harmer, and Victoria DiDomenico, *The Use of Private Security Providers and Services in Humanitarian Operations*, HPG report 27 (London: Overseas Development Institute, 2008), 1.

41. Tony Vaux, Chris Seiple, Greg Nakano, and Koenraad Van Brabant, *Humanitarian Action and Private Security Companies: Opening the Debate* (London: International Alert, 2002), 10.

42. Kofi Annan, "Intervention," Ditchley Foundation Lecture XXXV, June 26, 1998, http://www.ditchley.co.uk/page/173/lecture-xxxv.htm.

43. Michael Bryans, Bruce D. Jones, and Janice Gross Stein, *Mean Times: Humanitarian Action in Complex Political Emergencies—Stark Choices, Cruel Dilemmas*, Report of the NGOs in Complex Emergencies Project (Toronto: Center for International Studies, University of Toronto, January 1999).

44. Aid Worker Security Database (accessed January 1, 2017), https://aidworkersecurity.org/incidents.

45. Stoddard, Harmer, and DiDomenico, *Use of Private Security Providers*, 2.

46. Koenraad Van Brabant, "Humanitarian Action and Private Security Companies," *Humanitarian Exchange* 20 (March 2002): 25.

47. P. W. Singer, "Humanitarian Principles, Private Military Agents: Some Implications of the Privatised Military Industry for the Humanitarian Community," in *Resetting the Rules of Engagement: Trends and Issues in Military–Humanitarian Community*, ed. Victoria Wheeler and Adele Harmer, HPG Report 21 (London: Overseas Development Institute, 2006), 78; Abby Stoddard, Adele Harmer and Victoria DiDomenico, *Providing Aid in Insecure Environments: Trends in Violence against Aid Workers and the Operational Response*, HPG Briefing Paper 34 (London: Overseas Development Institute, 2009).

48. Charles Rogers and Brian Sytsma, *World Vision Security Manual: Safety Awareness for Aid Workers* (Geneva: World Vision, 1999), 2.

49. Michaël Neuman and Fabrice Weissman, "Humanitarian Security in the Age of Risk Management," in *Saving Lives and Staying Alive: The Professionalization of Humanitarian Security*, ed. Michaël Neuman and Fabrice Weissman (London: Hurst, 2014).

50. Fiona Terry, *Condemned to Repeat? The Paradox of Humanitarian Action* (Ithaca, N.Y.: Cornell University Press, 2002), 234–35.

51. Nick Downie, "Humanitarian Action in Insecure Contexts," in *Co-operation with Private Security and Military Companies*, MSF Dialogue 7 (2008): 7.

52. David Rieff, "Charity on the Rampage: The Business of Foreign Aid," *Foreign Affairs* (January/February 1997): 132–38.

53. Kennedy, "Selling the Distant Other."

54. Naomi Klein, *The Shock Doctrine: The Rise of Disaster Capitalism* (New York: Metropolitan, 2007).

Chapter 10: Humanitarianism Unbound

1. Alex de Waal and Alan Whiteside, "'New Variant Famine': AIDS and Food Crisis in Southern Africa," *The Lancet* 362 (2003): 1234–37.
2. David Quammen, *Spillover: Animal Infection and the Next Human Pandemic* (New York: Norton, 2012).
3. Wendy Orent, *Plague: The Mysterious Past and Terrifying Future of the World's Most Dangerous Disease* (New York: Free Press, 2012).
4. Mark Wheelis, "Biological Warfare at the 1346 Siege of Caffa," *Emerging Infectious Disease* 8, no. 9 (2002): 971–75.
5. Kelley Lee, *The World Health Organization (WHO)* (New York: Routledge, 2009).
6. UNAIDS, *Fact Sheet November 2016*, December 2016.
7. WHO, *Ebola Situation Report 40*, March 2016.
8. Tracy Kidder, *Mountains Beyond Mountains: The Quest of Dr. Paul Farmer, A Man Who Would Cure the World* (New York: Random House, 2003), chapter 26.
9. Sara Davies, "Securitizing Infectious Disease," *International Affairs* 84, no. 2 (2008): 295–313.
10. Sara E. Davies and Jeremy R. Youde, eds., *The Politics of Surveillance and Responses to Disease Outbreaks: The New Frontier for States and Non-State Actors* (New York: Routledge, 2016).
11. Jean-Hervé Bradol, "Caring for Health," in *Humanitarian Negotiations Revealed: The MSF Experience*, ed. Claire Magone, Michael Neuman, and Fabrice Weissman (New York: Columbia University Press, 2011), 199–218.
12. Rony Brauman and Claudine Vidal, "Natural Disasters: 'Do Something!'" in ibid., 219–36.
13. Norwegian Refugee Council and the Internal Displacement Monitoring Centre (IDMC), *Global Estimates 2015: People Displaced by Disasters* (Geneva: NRC, 2015).
14. OCHA, *World Humanitarian Data and Trends 2015* (New York: UN, 2015), 16–18, 64.
15. John Telford and John Cosgrove, "The International Humanitarian System and the 2004 Indian Ocean Earthquake and Tsunamis," *Disasters* 31, no. 1 (2007): 1–28.
16. John Hannigan, *Disasters without Borders* (Cambridge: Polity, 2012), 130–45.
17. International Commission on Intervention and State Sovereignty, *The Responsibility to Protect* (Ottawa: International Development Research Centre, 2001), 33.
18. Lloyd Axworthy and Allan Rock, "A Memorandum to the New UN Secretary-General," *Global Responsibility to Protect* 9, no. 1 (2017): 5–14.
19. Robyn Eckersley, "Ecological Intervention: Prospects and Limits," *Ethics & International Affairs* 21, no. 3 (2007): 293–316.
20. James Morrissey, "Rethinking the 'Debate on Environmental Refugees': From 'Maximalists and Minimalists' to 'Proponents and Critics,'" *Journal of Political Ecology* 19 (2012): 36–49.
21. Frank Biermann and Ingrid Boas, "Preparing for a Warmer World: Towards a Global Governance System to Protect Climate Refugees," *Global Environmental Politics* 10, no. 1 (2010): 60–88.

22. Norman Myers, "Environmental Refugees: An Emergent Security Issue," 13th Economic Forum (Prague: May 23–27, 2005), http://www.osce.org/eea/14851.

23. IPCC, *Climate Change Impacts, Adaptation and Vulnerability*, Contribution of Working Group II to the Fourth Assessment Report of the IPCC (Cambridge: Cambridge University Press, 2007), 299.

24. Norwegian Refugee Council and IDMC, *Global Estimates 2015*, 9.

25. Biermann and Boas, "Preparing for a Warmer World," 63–65; Koko Warner, Charles Ehrhart, Alex de Sherbinin, Susana Adamo, and Tricia Chai-Onn, *In Search of Shelter: Mapping the Effects of Climate Change on Human Migration and Displacement* (CARE International, CIESIN Columbia University, UNHCR, UNU-EHS, World Bank, May 2009), 2; Koko Warner, Tamer Afifi, Walter Kälin, Scott Leckie, Beth Ferris, Susan F. Martin, and David Wrathall, *Changing Climate, Moving People: Framing Migration, Displacement and Planned Relocation*, UNU-EHS Publication Series, Policy Brief 8 (June 2013), 10.

26. Carol Farbotko, "Wishful Sinking: Disappearing Islands, Climate Refugees and Cosmopolitan Experimentation," *Asia Pacific Viewpoint* 51, no. 1 (2010): 47–60.

27. Lloyd Axworthy, "Resetting the Narrative on Peace and Security: R2P in the Next Ten Years," in *The Oxford Handbook on the Responsibility to Protect*, ed. Alex J. Bellamy and Tim Dunne (Oxford: Oxford University Press, 2016), 968–83.

Chapter 11: The Study and Practice of Humanitarianism

1. James D. Fearon, "The Rise of Emergency Relief Aid," in *Humanitarianism in Question: Politics, Power, Ethics*, ed. Michael Barnett and Thomas G. Weiss (Ithaca, N.Y.: Cornell University Press, 2008), 49–72.

2. Development Initiatives, *Global Humanitarian Assistance 2016*, 6, http://www.globalhumanitarianassistance.org/report/gha2016/ (hereafter *GHA 2016*).

3. Partnership and Resource Mobilization Branch, United Nations Office for the Coordination of Humanitarian Affairs, *Global Humanitarian Overview 2016* (2016), 4. PRMB, OCHA, *Global Humanitarian Overview 2016: June Status Report* and *Funding Update* (October 2016).

4. MSF, *Where Is Everyone? Responding to Emergencies in the Most Difficult Places* (London: MSF, 2014), 9.

5. *GHA 2016*, 7.

6. Ibid., 57.

7. Ibid., 67–68.

8. Antonio Donini, "The Far Side: The Meta Functions of Humanitarianism in a Globalised World," *Disasters* 34, no. S2 (2010): 220–37.

9. International Committee of the Red Cross, "Principles and Response in International Humanitarian Assistance (C. The Use of Armed Escorts)," presented at the 26th International Conference of the Red Cross and Red Crescent, September 15, 1995. On December 8, 2005, Additional Protocol III to the Geneva Conventions supplemented the red cross and red crescent with the red crystal to denote a symbol "devoid of any political, religious or other connotation."

10. Sarah Collinson and Samir Elhawary, "Humanitarian Space: A Review of Trends and Issues," HPG Report 32 (April 2012), 3.

11. Michaël Neuman and Fabrice Weissman, "Humanitarian Security in the Age of Risk Management," in *Saving Lives and Staying Alive: The Professionalization of Humanitarian Security*, ed. Michaël Neuman and Fabrice Weissman (London: Hurst, 2014).

12. Antonio Donini and Daniel Maxwell, "From Face-to-Face to Face-to-Screen: Remote Management, Effectiveness and Accountability of Humanitarian Action in Insecure Environments," *International Review of the Red Cross* 95, no. 890 (2014): 383–413.

13. Didier Fassin, "Hierarchies of Humanity," in *Humanitarian Reason: A Moral History of the Present* (Berkeley: University of California Press, 2011), 223–42.

14. Tony Vaux, *The Selfish Altruist: Relief Work in Famine in War* (London: Earthscan, 2001), 1–16, 201–12.

15. Nicolas de Torrente, "The Relevance and Effectiveness of Humanitarian Aid: Reflections about the Relationship between Providers and Recipients," *Social Research* 80, no. 2 (2013): 607–34; Fassin, "Hierarchies of Humanity."

16. Mark Duffield, "Challenging Environments: Danger, Resilience and the Aid Industry," *Security Dialogue* 43, no. 5 (2012): 475–92 and "Risk-Management and the Fortified Aid Compound: Everyday Life in Post-Interventionary Society," *Journal of Intervention and Statebuilding* 4, no. 4 (2010): 453–74; Larissa Fast, *Aid in Danger: The Perils and Promise of Humanitarianism* (Philadelphia: University of Pennsylvania Press, 2014); and Silke Roth, "Aid Work as Edgework-Voluntary Risk-Taking and Security in Humanitarian Assistance, Development and Human Rights Work," *Journal of Risk Research* 18, no. 2 (2015): 139–55.

17. A fuller discussion is Peter J. Hoffman and Thomas G. Weiss, "Humanitarianism and Practitioners: Why Social Science Matters," in *Humanitarianism in Question: Politics, Power, Ethics*, ed. Michael Barnett and Thomas G. Weiss (Ithaca, N.Y.: Cornell University Press, 2008), 264–85.

18. Thomas G. Weiss and Peter J. Hoffman, "The Fog of Humanitarianism: Collective Action Problems and Learning-Challenged Organizations," *Journal of Intervention and State-Building* 1, no. 1 (2007): 47–65.

19. Alexander Betts and Louise Bloom, *Humanitarian Innovation: The State of the Art*, OCHA Policy and Study Series 9 (November 2014).

20. https://data.humdata.org.

21. *GHA 2016*, 82.

22. http://www.ecbproject.org/.

23. Ralph Waldo Emerson, "The American Scholar," delivered to the Phi Beta Kappa Society, Cambridge, August 31, 1837, in *The Collected Works of Ralph Waldo Emerson*, vol. 1, *Nature, Addresses, and Lectures* (Cambridge, Mass.: Harvard University Press, 1971), 56.

24. Sadako Ogata, *The Turbulent Decade: Confronting the Refugee Crises of the 1990s* (New York: Norton, 2005), 25.

25. This framing first appeared in Peter J. Hoffman, "Humanitarianism in Treatment: Analyzing the World Humanitarian Summit," *Future United Nations Development System Briefing* no. 41 (August 2016), 1–4.

Index

ABA. *See* American Relief Administration

accountability, 88; of agencies, 265–66; data collection and, 266, 268, 269–70; ECB and, 270; "Humanitarians Anonymous" and, 272; policy review mechanisms and, 269

Active Leaning Network for Accountability and Performance in the Humanitarian Action (ALNAP), 269

Afghanistan, *133*; aid worker victimization in, 136, *137*; casualties in, 135; Cold War and, 132; displacement and, 134, 135; humanitarian dynamics in, 136–37; Taliban in, 134; US expenditures on conflict in, 136; US forces in, 135–36

African Union: AMIS of, 171; AMISOM of, 70–71; on R2P, 156; UNAMID and, 172–73

African Union Mission in Somalia (AMISOM), 70–71

African Union Mission in Sudan (AMIS), 171

aftermath of war (*jus post bellum*), 114

Agamben, Giorgio, 27

agencies, 3; accountability of, 265–66; autonomy of, 267; funding and, 257, 258; in Global South, 264–65; local and national, 258; public health systems and, 246; self interest and, 264

An Agenda for Peace (Boutros-Ghali), 99

Agier, Michel, 201, 206, 208

Agincourt, battle of (1415), 32

Aidid, Mohamed Farah, 67, 69

aid worker victimization, 160, *261*; in Afghanistan, 136, *137*; bunkerization and localization and, 261–62; Daesh and, 155; in Darfur, 173; emblems and logos and, 260; funding and, 260–61; ICRC and, 87; increase in, 226; in Iraq, 141, *143*; in Libya, *148*, 149; new modalities of aid delivery and, 261; in Pakistan, *138*; perceptions of, 213; PSCs and, 226; in South Sudan, 176; in Syria, 155, *156*; UN Security Council resolution 2286 on, 260

Akayesu, Jean-Paul, 76

Aleppo, xviii

About the Authors

Peter J. Hoffman is assistant professor of International Affairs and Julien J. Studley Faculty Fellow in the Graduate Program in International Affairs at The New School, and Research Fellow at the Ralph Bunche Institute for International Studies, The Graduate Center of The City University of New York. His work spans the fields of international organization, strategic and security studies, international relations theory, and comparative historical sociology. Peter's central focus is on the dynamics of war and global responses, concentrating primarily on the international humanitarian system. Other major areas of his work encompass the United Nations, the private military and security sector, human rights, US foreign policy, and global commodity chains. His scholarship has appeared in academic journals and books, including *Sword & Salve: Confronting New Wars and Humanitarian Crises* (2006). He has been a consultant for a variety of nongovernmental organizations, conducting research and writing reports for the Future of the United Nations Development System, the Open Society, the Fund for Peace, the National Committee on American Foreign Policy, the Stanley Foundation, Friedrich Ebert Stiftung, and the Humanitarianism & War Project. He was also a member of the research team of the International Commission for Intervention and State Sovereignty.

Thomas G. Weiss is Presidential Professor of Political Science at The CUNY Graduate Center and Director Emeritus (2001–2014) of the Ralph Bunche Institute for International Studies. He was named 2016 Andrew Carnegie Fellow. Past president of the International Studies

Association (2009–2010) and recipient of its "IO Distinguished Scholar Award 2016," he also directed the United Nations Intellectual History Project (1999–2010) and was research professor at SOAS, University of London (2012–2015), chair of the Academic Council on the UN System (2006–2009), editor of *Global Governance*, research director of the International Commission on Intervention and State Sovereignty, research professor at Brown University's Watson Institute for International Studies, executive director of the Academic Council on the UN System and of the International Peace Academy, a member of the UN secretariat, and a consultant to public and private agencies. He has written extensively (over fifty books and 250 articles and book chapters) about multilateral approaches to international peace and security, humanitarian action, and sustainable development. Recent authored volumes include *The United Nations and Changing World Politics* (2017); *Humanitarianism Intervention: Ideas in Action* (2016); *What's Wrong with the United Nations and How to Fix It* (2016); *Governing the World? Addressing "Problems without Passports"* (2014); *Global Governance: Why? What? Whither?* (2013); *Humanitarian Business* (2013); *Thinking about Global Governance: Why People and Ideas Matter* (2011); *Humanitarianism Contested: Where Angels Fear to Tread* (2011); *Global Governance and the UN: An Unfinished Journey* (2010); and *UN Ideas That Changed the World* (2009).